新世纪高等学校教材 | 英语语言文学系列教材

U0854635

商务联络陪同口译教程

SHANGWULIANLUOPEITONG KOUYIJIAOCHENG

主　编　梁志刚　李汝成　祝丽丽
副主编　李　夏　刘静茹　陈昕晨
编　者　邓佳玉　曹祺镇　靖艳群　阚丽君

北京师范大学出版集团
BEIJING NORMAL UNIVERSITY PUBLISHING GROUP
北京师范大学出版社

图书在版编目（CIP）数据

商务联络陪同口译教程/梁志刚，李汝成，祝丽丽主编．—北京：北京师范大学出版社，2023.1

新世纪高等学校教材 英语语言文学系列教材

ISBN 978-7-303-28478-8

Ⅰ.①商… Ⅱ.①梁… ②李… ③祝… Ⅲ.①商务—英语—口译—高等学校—教材 Ⅳ.①F7

中国版本图书馆 CIP 数据核字（2022）第 242505 号

教材意见反馈 gaozhifk@bnupg.com 010-58805079
营销中心电话 010-58807651
北师大出版社高等教育分社微信公众号 新外大街拾玖号

SHANGWU LIANLUO PEITONG KOUYI JIAOCHENG
出版发行：北京师范大学出版社 www.bnupg.com
北京市西城区新街口外大街 12-3 号
邮政编码：100088
印　　刷：北京溢漾印刷有限公司
经　　销：全国新华书店
开　　本：787 mm×1092 mm 1/16
印　　张：24
字　　数：624 千字
版　　次：2023 年 1 月第 1 版
印　　次：2023 年 1 月第 1 次印刷
定　　价：59.00 元

策划编辑：翟　墨　周劲含　　责任编辑：冯　倩　王贺萌
美术编辑：李向昕　　装帧设计：李向昕
责任校对：段立超　王志远　　责任印制：马　洁

CONTENTS

Unit 1

迎送宾客 Meeting and Seeing-off

中国改革开放的大门不会关闭，只会越开越大。

China's door of opening-up will not be closed and will open up even wider.

久久不见久久见，久久见过还想见。

It has been a long time since we last met, and I hope it would be a long time before we have to depart.

改革开放只有进行时，没有完成时。

Reform and opening-up is always ongoing and will never end.

课文 A

SECTION Ⅰ: Dialogue A 机场接人 Meeting Someone at the Airport

Interpret the following dialogue from Chinese into English and vice versa.

A：您是从美国来的贝克先生吗？

B：Yes, I am James Baker. And you must be Peter Liang.

A：是的，我是梁彼得。您叫我彼得好了。贝克先生，我一直在此恭候您的到来。

B：Thank you for coming to meet me. Just call me Jim. First name is friendlier than last name.

A：好的，吉姆。欢迎您来青岛，旅途可好？

B：Not too bad. But we were later than expected. Our plane delayed taking-off as we ran into a tornado at Dallas. We were held up for several hours at the airport, waiting for the storm to clear up. But on the whole, we had good flying weather.

A：嗯，您安然无恙到达了，经过这么久的旅行肯定很累了，我们直接开车去宾馆吧。

B：Yes，I am a bit tired. But I'll be all right by tomorrow.

A：但愿如此，我们明天晚上为您安排了一个宴会。

B：You're very kind，indeed. I'm expecting to come.

A：好的，王总要我向您问好，遗憾的是他不能亲自来接您。他正在开董事会会议，但是他今晚要为您接风。

B：It doesn't matter at all. I'm expecting meeting him sooner at the dinner party.

A：祝您在青岛过得愉快。有什么需要帮忙的，请跟我说。我去推行李车，您到行李台那里等我。

B：Thank you so much.

(Waiting…)

A：行李都齐了，我们的车在外面等。我来帮您推行李车。

B：Thanks，Peter. I'll take my carry-ons.

相关词汇

常用机场英语

departure　出港；离开

arrival　到达

international airport　国际机场

domestic airport　国内机场

Terminal 1　第一航站楼

check-in　登机手续办理

boarding pass (card)　登机牌

airport terminal　机场候机楼

luggage claim/baggage claim　行李领取处

international departure　国际航班出港

international passenger　国际航班旅客

domestic departure　国内航班出站

transfers　中转

stop-over　转机

jet lag　时差

transit　过境

customs declaration　海关申报

customs declaration form　海关申报表

goods to declare　报关物品

nothing to declare　不需报关

V. I. P. room　贵宾室

customs　海关

departure gate　登机口

departure lounge　候机室

FLT No. (flight number)　航班号

scheduled time (SCHED)　预计时间

car hire　租车处

public phone/telephone　公用电话

departure time 起飞时间
delay 延误
boarding 登机
duty-free shop 免税店
post office 邮局
money exchange/currency exchange 货币兑换处
tour arrangement 旅行安排
luggage locker 行李暂存箱
luggage tag 行李牌
welcome banquet 接风
carry-on 随身行李
Jiaozhou Bay Express 胶州湾大道
flyover 立交桥
undersea tunnel 海底隧道
sea-crossing bridge 跨海大桥
high-speed train 高铁
High Speed Electric Multiple Unit 高速动车组
bonded area 保税区
supply chain resources 供应链区
lager 淡啤酒
stout 烈性黑啤酒

Dialogue B 前往宾馆 On the Way to the Hotel

Interpret the following dialogue from Chinese into English and vice versa.

A: 吉姆，这么长的飞行有没有感到时差？

B: A kind of, though it is not that obvious.

A: 谢谢你的耐心和理解。

B: Mr. Liang, the traffic in Qingdao is pretty good. But we were told the roads in China were quite crowded and traffic jams could occur anywhere.

A: 是的，不过那是以前的事了。自从青岛环湾大道、海底隧道、跨海大桥、地铁和其他许多通向胶东国际机场的立交桥竣工以来，交通状况得到了极大改善。

B: I've never expected that Qingdao is such a big metropolitan city. What's that on the right, I mean those structures with cable cars over them?

A: 是的，青岛是个大城市。你说的那个是2014年在青岛举行的世园会所在地，现在对游客开放，已经成为一个旅游景点，每天有许多世界各地的游客前来参观。青岛还是2008年北京奥运会帆船比赛项目的举办地。同时青岛也是亚太经合组织的会展中心。每年这个时候很多国际会议和国际贸易博览会都在这里举行。

B: Really? Qingdao is extremely international.

A: 是的，青岛是著名的旅游景点，也是避暑胜地，因此它一年四季都吸引了大量游客。

B：It's great. I am going to extend my length of stay so that I can have more opportunities to see Qingdao.

A：这是个英明决定。在你来访期间，我们既能探讨生意，你还可以游览一下青岛，这是一石二鸟的好事。

B：Oh, Mr. Liang, don't we get to the downtown area?

A：是的，这是一条通往市中心的主要大道——东海路，20 分钟我们就能到达你住的宾馆了。

B：Wow, you have beautiful beaches. It's a beautiful and modern city.

A：谢谢你对我们城市的夸奖。我们谈完生意后，我想先领你好好逛逛我们的青岛栈桥、青岛啤酒博物馆和中车四方厂。四方厂现在是制造高铁的公司，曾是火车机车和火车的制造厂。

B：Sure. Business first, sight-seeing second. I bet I'm expecting to see the places you mentioned sooner.

A：前面就是你住的宾馆，海景花园。

B：Great! It's a nice hotel.

A：是的，这是岛城最好的五星级宾馆，很漂亮。你的房间面对大海，景色迷人。

B：OK. I will proceed with my check-in at the reception first.

A：不要急，我们吃午饭前你休息一下，40 分钟怎么样？

B：No problem. 40 minutes is good. I will be down in the lobby at 11：50.

A：再见！

B：See you later.

SECTION Ⅱ：Warm-ups for Interpretation

➢ **Tongue twister.**

Peter Piper picked a peck of pickled peppers.

A peck of pickled peppers Peter Piper picked.

If Peter Piper picked a peck of pickled peppers,

Where's the peck of pickled peppers Peter Piper picked?

彼特·派柏夹起一小撮腌制辣椒。

这是彼特·派柏夹起的那一小撮腌制辣椒。

如果彼特·派柏夹起了一小撮腌制辣椒，

那么彼特·派柏夹起的那些腌制辣椒在哪儿?
She sells seashells by the seashore.
The shells she sells are surely seashells.
So if she sells sea shells on the seashore,
I'm sure she sells seashore shells.
她在海岸上卖贝壳。
她卖的贝壳是真贝壳,
所以如果她在海岸上卖的是海里的贝壳,
那我相信她卖的是岸上的真贝壳。

➢ **Interpret the following proverbs from English into Chinese.**

1. Actions speak louder than words.
2. Suit the action to the word.
3. Sweet are the uses of adversity.
4. Water afar does not quench a fire at home.
5. Beauty is only skin-deep.

➢ **Interpret the following sentences from English into Chinese.**

1. I would like to avail myself of this opportunity to extend my warm welcome to you all.
2. Permit me first of all, to thank our host, for your extraordinary arrangements and hospitality.
3. It gives me such a great pleasure to meet you and your family here in Shanghai and I am very glad that you will be working with us for the next three months.
4. Our general director will host a reception banquet in your honor at 7:00 tonight, and we would like you and your family to come.
5. It would be both an honor and a pleasure to have your presence.

➢ **Interpret the following paragraphs from English into Chinese and vice versa.**

1. Ministers and other distinguished delegates, first of all, let me welcome you to Sydney. While brief, I hope that your time in Sydney will be highly productive. I also hope you take the opportunity while you are here to enjoy a small taste of what

Australia's major city has to offer.

2. 我愿借此机会，谨代表我所有的同事，对你们的热情迎接和款待表示感谢。在中国度过的这五天令人感到愉快，难以忘怀。我特别要向我们的中国合作者致敬，他们的真诚合作与支持使这项协议得以签署。敬请各位与我一起举杯，为我们两家公司的永久友谊和合作干杯。

SECTION Ⅲ: Speech

Interpret the following speech from English into Chinese.

Ladies and gentlemen,

Taking this opportunity, I am ready to tell a story of China's high-speed railway.

Thanks to the size of its population and the speed of its development, China has occupied an important chapter in a storybook of modern human civilization. The China Story is as grand and monumental as it is twisty and complicated.

In the China Story, the high-speed railway is an important character because it is closely related to ordinary Chinese people's lives and the national economy.

I've closely observed the daily matters at CRRC Qingdao Sifang Co., Ltd., one of China's chief makers of high-speed trains, I've taken note of the fate and lives of different people connected to the company, I've talked to influential experts in China's high-speed railway industry, I've learnt about the high-speed railway from the perspective of foreigners travelling in China, and I've seen the varied Chinese landscape through the windows of high-speed trains...

In the 20th Century, against the backdrop of China's economic development is the pressure on the transport system caused by the movement of migrant workers and the business people, and every year it culminates in the great diaspora during the Spring Festival.

In this vast and thickly-populated country, to promote public transport rather than private automobiles is the priority of a wise government.

But even public transport must come in bigger sizes, considering the volume of the population. And they'd better be fast, because they must travel long distances. And thus came the age of the high-speed railway.

The high-speed railway is making the vast country smaller and helping the nation travel with greater efficiency, bringing benefits to passengers.

Self-guided tours have become the favorite of many tourists who expect speed, punctuality and comfort from their means of transportation. In the advent of the high-speed railway system, foreign tourists on self-guided tours find it easier to enjoy their trips.

We have a friend named Tom who compares China's high-speed trains to white tubes sliding quickly on the steel tracks. A tourist who has been to China once posted a video on Twitter, showing a coin standing steadily on the windowsill of a moving high-speed train for nine minutes.

Inside the carriage it is steady and quiet, the seats are bigger than those on a plane, and the gap is wide enough to stretch one's legs, there is even room for a walk in the public area on both ends of the carriage. But above all, Tom stressed the punctuality and the competitive price: "It is even cheaper than long distance buses."

The high-speed trains have become a symbol of China, and as the tour guides would say, you've not really visited China if you haven't taken the high-speed train.

The official term for the high-speed trains running in China is High Speed Electric Multiple Unit. So far, there are more than 3,600 high speed EMUs in the world, 2,000 of which are in China and of them 900 are manufactured by Sifang. That means if you take a high-speed train in this country, there is fifty-percent possibility that you are sitting in an EMU produced by this company. So I have to say that it's a worthy visit to Qingdao at Sifang G-train manufacturer and we hereby are very much appreciated for the municipal Foreign Affairs Office to have arranged for us this great visit.

SECTION Ⅳ: Speech

Interpret the following speech from Chinese into English.

女士们，先生们：

我来给大家介绍一下崂山。

崂山位于青岛东北方向 30 千米，主峰"崂顶"高 1133 米，它拔海而立，山海相连，流传着数不尽的动人传说。山上遍布奇石怪洞，清泉流瀑。

崂山自古被称为"神仙窟宅"，山上奇花异草，可去百病，使人长生不老。昔日秦始皇(259 BC—210 BC)、汉武帝(156 BC—87 BC)登临此山寻仙草。公元 8 世纪，唐明皇也曾派两位高官进山采仙药。公元 10 世纪后，崂山上的道观越来越多，但大部分道观后来被毁。

太清宫

太清宫又名下宫，位于崂山东南麓，临海而建。始建于宋朝年间(960—1279)，但现在的太清宫是明万历年间(1573—1620)建造的。

上清宫

上清宫又名上宫，建于1297—1307年，此后又有几次扩建。上清宫位于崂山东南麓、太清宫之上。前院有古银杏树，树龄几百年。上清宫以南有龙潭瀑，瀑布直下20米。

九水流经崂山北部，曲折蜿蜒，长约12千米。此地瀑布、怪石、石碑众多，犹如世外桃源。

参考译文

SECTION Ⅰ: Dialogue A

A: Excuse me. Are you Mr. Baker from America?

B: 是的，我是詹姆斯·贝克。你肯定是梁彼得了。

A: Yes, my name is Peter Liang. You may call me Peter. I have been expecting you.

B: 谢谢你来接我。叫我吉姆好了，叫名字更显亲切。

A: Great. Welcome to Qingdao, Jim. How was your journey (flight)?

B: 还可以。不过飞机晚点了。我们在达拉斯遇上了龙卷风，因此在达拉斯机场耽搁了几个小时，直到天气变好，飞机才起飞。总的来说，一路飞行天气不错。

A: Well, you are here safe and sound. You must be very tired after such a long flight. We'll drive you straight to your hotel.

B: 是有点累，不过明天就好了。

A: I hope so. We'll hold a dinner party for you tomorrow evening.

B: 你们想得真周到，我很期待前往。

A: Good. One thing I remember, Mr. Wang, our general manager, asks me to say hi to you but he is unable to come to meet you himself. You know, he is now having a board meeting. But he is to hold a welcome banquet for you tonight.

B: 没关系的。期待很快见到王总。

A: Hopefully you'll have a pleasant stay in Qingdao. If there's anything we can do for you, please let me know. Let me get a baggage cart and meet you over there at the baggage claim.

B：非常感谢！

（等待中……）

A：OK. All your baggages are here. Our transport is waiting outside. Let me help you with your suitcases.

B：谢谢你彼得！我来拿我的随身行李。

Dialogue B

A：Jim，are you feeling any jet lag after such a long flight?

B：有一点点，尽管不明显。

A：Thank you for your patience and understanding.

B：梁先生，青岛的交通很畅通呀！我们曾听说，中国的道路非常拥挤，随时随地都会堵车。

A：They used to be. That was in the past. The traffic conditions have been greatly improved after the completion of the Jiaozhou Bay Express，the construction of the undersea tunnel，the erection of the sea-crossing bridge，the operation of the metro system and many other flyovers leading to and from the New Jiaodong International Airport.

B：没想到青岛是这样大的一个城市。右边那些建筑是什么？我说的是上面有缆车的那些结构？

A：Yes，it is. Oh，that's the World Horticulture Exposition 2014，Qingdao. It was being held here. Now it has become a tourist spot attracting many visitors from all around the world. Qingdao，you know，sponsored Olympic Regatta in 2008 too，together with Beijing. And it is a famous convention center for APEC. Every year many international conferences and business fairs are held here，esp. at this time of the year.

B：哇，这样吗？青岛非常国际化。

A：Yes. Qingdao is also a popular tourist spot. Meanwhile it is a summer resort，too. It attracts a lot of tourists all the year round.

B：太棒了，我要延长我的访问时间，这样可以有更多机会了解青岛。

A：That's a great decision. During your stay in Qingdao，we can talk about our business and you can also tour the city. It's like the saying that one stone kills two birds.

B：梁先生，我们是不是到市中心啦？

A：You are right. This is Donghai Road, the main road leading to the town. We will get to your hotel in a score of minutes.

B：哇！你们的海滩很漂亮。青岛是座漂亮的现代化城市！

A：Thank you for your nice comments on our city. I will show you around the city after our business negotiation is done. I think the first place I will show you around is to visit the Qingdao Pier, the Qingdao Brewery Museum and CRRC Qingdao Sifang Co., Ltd., a high-speed trains manufacturer, formerly a locomotive and railway trains plant.

B：当然了，生意第一，观光第二。不过我也期盼着早早看到青岛栈桥，青岛啤酒博物馆和中车四方厂。

A：Your hotel "Sea View Garden" is in sight.

B：棒极啦！这个宾馆很好啊！

A：Yes, this is the best five-star hotel in Qingdao. It's lovely. Your room is facing the ocean. You can see the beautiful sea view.

B：好的，我先在服务台办理一下入住手续。

A：Take your time. Is it good for you to relax a bit before we go for the lunch? How about 40 minutes?

B：没问题，40分钟够了，11：50我下来到大厅等你们。

A：See you.

B：一会儿见。

SECTION Ⅱ：Warm-ups for Interpretation

➤ **Interpret the following proverbs from Chinese into English.**

1. 行胜于言。
2. 要言行一致。
3. 苦尽甘来。
4. 远水不救近火。
5. 人不可貌相。

➢ **Interpret the following sentences from Chinese into English.**

1. 我愿借此机会向各位来宾表示热烈的欢迎。
2. 首先，请允许我感谢东道主的精心安排和热情款待。
3. 能在上海接待您和您的家人我深感荣幸。能在今后的三个月里与您共事，我也非常高兴。
4. 今晚七点公司总经理将设宴为您洗尘，请您携家人光临。
5. 您能光临，我们感到非常荣幸。

➢ **Interpret the following paragraphs from Chinese into English and vice versa.**

1. 部长们，尊贵的代表们，首先，欢迎大家光临悉尼。尽管时间短暂，我希望你们在悉尼的造访富有成效。我也希望大家有机会感受一下澳大利亚这个大城市展示的风采。
2. I wish to take this opportunity to thank you on behalf of all my colleagues for your warm reception and hospitality. The past five days in China have been truly pleasant and enjoyable and most memorable. I particularly want to pay tribute to our Chinese partners for their sincere cooperation and support in concluding these agreements. May I ask all of you present here to join me in raising your glasses, to the lasting friendship and cooperation between our two companies.

SECTION Ⅲ: Speech

女士们，先生们：

借此机会我要讲一个有关中国高铁的故事。因为人口众多且发展迅速，中国在现代人类文明长卷中写下了重要的一章。它波澜壮阔，也丰富，也复杂。

在中国故事里，高铁是一个重要内容，因为它与普通人的生活密切相连，与国家经济紧密相关。

在中国高铁列车的重要制造者之一——中车青岛四方机车车辆股份有限公司，我观察了那里的日常时光，记录了与该公司相联系的不同人物的命运和生活，与中国高铁的主要专家交谈，了解行走在中国的外籍人士眼中的高铁，并通过不同高铁列车的窗口观赏了中国各种不同的地貌……

20 世纪，在中国经济发展的大背景下，农民工出行和商贸旅行带来的交通压力，在春运返乡潮期间逐年增加。

在这个地域辽阔却人口稠密的国家，发展公共交通而非汽车类的私人交通，是政府的明智首选。而即便是公共交通工具，考虑到人口总量，也应该是大交通工具；因距离远，最好是快捷的交通工具——于是，高铁时代应运而来。

高铁正将幅员辽阔的中国变小，高铁正让这个国家的人们更快地流动起来……而高铁的乘客们也获益良多。

旅行者都希望交通工具快速、准时、舒适。现在，自由行已成为许多旅行者的最爱。随着高铁时代的到来，外国游客会更享受在中国的自由行。

有一位叫汤姆的朋友觉得中国高铁像是一个个白色的管道在钢轨上快速滑行。有位来过中国的游客在推特上发了一个视频：在飞驰的高铁上，一枚硬币稳稳地立在高铁列车的窗台上 9 分钟不倒。

在车厢里人们感到平稳安静，高铁上的座椅比飞机上的还大，座位的前后空间足以伸开腿，还可以在车厢两端的公共空间散步……但最主要的是，汤姆强调了高铁准时，还有价格优势，“它甚至比长途汽车还便宜!”汤姆说。

高铁已成为中国的一大标志。借用导游的话，到中国没有坐高铁就不算是中国游。

中国高铁列车的标准名称叫“高速动车组”。全世界现有高速动车组 3600 多组，中国拥有 2000 组，其中有 900 组是四方股份制造的。也就是说，在中国坐高铁，有近 1/2 的概率坐的是这家企业制造的动车组。因此非常感谢青岛市外事办安排我们参观中车青岛四方高铁制造厂，我们受益匪浅，真是不虚此行。

SECTION Ⅳ: Speech

Ladies and gentlemen,

Let me spend some time to let you know something about Mount Lao.

Mount Lao, around which countless legends have been woven, lies 30km(19mi) northeast of Qingdao and falls steeply away towards the coast. Its tallest peak, Laoding (in Chinese meaning “the top of Mount Lao”), reaches a height of 1,133m(3,720ft). The mountain, rich in mineral water springs, displays bizarre rock formations, waterfalls and caves.

Many years ago it was revered as the “Home of Eternal Life”, where magic herbs grew which could cure all known diseases and make man immortal. It was in order to search for these wondrous plants that the Emperor Qin Shi Huang (259 BC-210 BC) and the Emperor Wu of Han Dynasty (156 BC-87 BC) climbed this mountain. In the 8th Century the Tang Emperor Xuanzong of Tang Dynasty sent two high officials to find and collect the magical herbs. After the 10th Century more and more Taoist monasteries sprung up here, but most of them were destroyed in later years.

Taoist Temple of Supreme Purity (Lower Temple)

The Taoist Temple of Supreme Purity (Taiqing Gong), or Lower Temple (Xia Gong), stands near the coast at the southeastern foot of Mount Lao. It dates originally from the Song period (960-1279), but the present buildings were built during the reign of the Emperor Wanli (1573-1620).

Temple of Great Purity

The Temple of Great Purity (Shangqing Gong), or Upper Temple (Shang Gong), built between 1297 and 1307 but later extended several times-lies up above the Temple of Supreme Purity, on the southeastern slope of Mount Lao. In front of the temple stand some ginkgo trees which are several hundred years old. South of the Temple of Great Purity the Longtan Waterfall plunges down from a height of 20m(66ft).

The Jiushui River, some 12km(7.5mi) long, snakes its way through the northern part of Mount Lao. Waterfalls, rock formations and monuments combine to make this region quite idyllic.

课文 B

SECTION Ⅰ: Dialogue 机场送人 Seeing Someone off at the Airport

Interpret the following dialogue from English into Chinese and vice versa.

A: It's very kind of you to come and see me off. I really had a delightful stay in Qingdao.

B: 时间过得真快，你在青岛待了五天了。记得我去机场接你的情景，仿佛是在昨天，而现在你却要走了。

A: Yeah, it's been a wonderful experience for me. I met you, your colleagues, visited the factories, and we signed a contract. Thank you for showing me around your beautiful city. My visit is very fruitful and rewarding.

B: 我们对我们双方的协同合作也非常满意。尽管你的行程很短，但颇具成效。明年的青岛贸易会，我们期待你的到来。

A：I hope so. I sincerely invite you to meet in New York at our headquarters some day before next spring.

B：谢谢你的邀请，我们将定一个合适的时间，并告知你。让我们保持联系。不知现在中国给你的印象如何？

A：Well, it's definitely different from what I had before I came. I think I have a much better understanding of China and Chinese culture now.

B：我很高兴你在中国过得愉快。

A：The more I know about China, the more I want to learn. There are still many places I would like to visit and many things I would like to see.

B：好的，我期待能有机会再次作为东道主接待你。

A：I really appreciated your escorting me along the way. You are very kind and thoughtful, that makes my trip so fruitful.

B：我很乐意帮助你。好了，该说再见了。

A：Thank you very much for everything you've done for me. It was really an unforgettable experience. Let's keep in touch.

B：当然，期待你的下一次中国之行。

A：I will certainly come again.

B：再见，一路平安。

SECTION Ⅱ: Warm-ups for Interpretation

➢ **Tongue twister.**

A flea and a fly flew up in a flue. Said the flea, "Let us fly!" Said the fly, "Let us flee!" So they flew through a flaw in a flue.

一只跳蚤和一只苍蝇飞进烟道里。跳蚤说："让我们飞吧！"苍蝇说："让我们逃跑吧！"就这样，它们飞越了烟道里的一条裂纹。

➢ **Interpret the following proverbs from Chinese into English.**

1. 有朋自远方来，不亦乐乎？
2. 海内存知己，天涯若比邻。

3. 但愿人长久，千里共婵娟。
4. 沉默是金。
5. 远亲不如近邻。

➢ **Interpret the following sentences from Chinese into English.**

1. 对东道主的隆重接待和无限盛情的款待，我再次表示感谢。
2. 对诸位的来访，我本人表示诚挚的欢迎，并衷心祝愿你们的访问有所收获。
3. 请允许我向远道而来的贵宾表示热烈的欢迎和亲切的问候。
4. 长途旅行后您应该好好休息一下。我们在晚上的招待宴会上见。
5. 这些良好的印象将永远珍藏在我们的美好记忆中。

➢ **Interpret the following paragraphs from Chinese into English and vice versa.**

1. I feel honored to come here on my first visit to your beautiful city. On behalf of all the members of my mission, I would like to take this opportunity to express our sincere thanks to our host for their earnest invitation and gracious hospitality we have received since we set foot on this charming land. I would like to extend in person our official invitation to the mayor of Shanghai. We would like His Honor to visit our city at his earliest convenience, so as to give us an opportunity to return the warm reception and hospitality we enjoy here.
2. 我代表我们代表团的全体成员，十分感谢贵公司的盛情邀请和款待。虽然我们在贵国仅待了五天时间，但是我们的访问十分成功。我们在这段时间会见了老朋友，结识了新朋友，参观了许多工厂和高科技企业。你们取得的新成就给我们留下了深刻印象。我们与中国有着悠久的友好交往历史，我们彼此之间不再陌生，我们是真诚的朋友和重要的贸易伙伴。

SECTION Ⅲ: Speech

Interpret the following speech from Chinese into English.

Speech A

女士们，先生们：

三天前，我们欢聚在这个会堂，举行宴会热烈欢迎吉姆·贝克先生。今天，在贝克先生参观访问了青岛的许多地方之后，我们怀着真诚和喜悦，再次相聚，与他话别。

明天他就要回国了。贝克先生的访问虽然短暂，但富有成效。青岛相关媒体对他的行程作了详细的报道，引起了社会关注。

在这短短几天内，他会见了市有关领导，参观了高新区和开发区出口加工区、保税区和供应链区并与各商界人士进行了广泛的交谈。

在向贝克先生告别之际，我们真诚地希望贝克先生再次来青岛考察并投资以扩大我们之间的合作。

同时，我们想借此机会请求他转达我们对美国人民的深厚友谊，请他转达我们对他家人的亲切问候。

在我结束讲话之际，我请各位与我一起举杯，祝贝克先生身体健康，祝贝克先生回国一路平安。

Speech B

青岛概述

青岛，简称“青”，位于中国东部沿海山东省东部，是一个特大城市、副省级城市、山东省经济中心、中国沿海重要中心城市、海滨度假旅游城市、国际港口城市、中国现代海洋产业发展的重要试验区、东北亚国际航运枢纽、海上运动基地、“一带一路”新欧亚大陆桥经济走廊的主要枢纽，及海洋合作战略的支点。

青岛位于山东半岛东南沿海，胶东半岛东部，中日韩自由贸易区的前缘地带。它地处黄海之滨，与朝鲜半岛隔海相望，东北与烟台相邻，西与潍坊相接，西南与日照相连。总面积11282平方千米，辖7个区及3个县级市。2017年，常住人口总数为929.05万人，地区生产总值110.3728亿元。

青岛是2008年北京奥运会和第十三届残奥会帆船比赛的主办城市，被誉为中国帆船之都、亚洲最佳航海城、世界啤酒之城、联合国“电影城”，也是中国首批沿海开放城市之一、国家文明城市、中国最幸福的城市之一。青岛还赢得了欧式城市“东方瑞士”和“中国品牌之都”的美誉。

青岛是国际海洋科学研究和教育中心，有山东大学(青岛校区)、中国海洋大学、中国石油大学等26所大学。清华大学、北京大学等29所大学也被相继引入青岛。青岛有多样化的异域风格建筑，因此被称为“世界建筑博览会”。八大关的建筑群被授予“中国最美城区”称号。

SECTION Ⅳ: Speech

Interpret the following speech from English into Chinese.

Speech A

Ladies and Gentlemen,

First of all, allow me to thank you all for your kind invitation to attend this party. I am greatly pleased to have a chance once more to visit your city and meet with so many of its great people.

This tour has been full of interesting things and everything here impressed me a great deal. I have visited factories, schools and cultural institutions. I have talked and made friends with many workers, government officials, managers, engineers, teachers and students.

We talked about work, investment, business, study and life together and I have learned a lot during my short stay here. All this has given me a better understanding of your country, your people and your opening-up policy.

It gives me great pleasure to express once again to our host my deep appreciation for the boundless and generous hospitality I enjoy here.

I feel reluctant to part from each other at this moment. I regret, Mr. President, that I couldn't accept your invitation to visit your Beijing headquarters right now, but it will happen at a different time.

I wish the friendly Chinese people prosperity and happiness. May the friendship between our peoples be further developed and consolidated. Good bye, dear friends!

Speech B

"Ganbei!" We cheers over the meal that my colleague and friend, Ning, has ordered for us to try. He's originally from Qingdao, and so has a far better knowledge than me of the local dishes and what will go best with the locally brewed beer, Tsingtao.

Tsingtao is the much loved beer of Qingdao and indeed the country. In fact, it was the first beer I ever tried when I landed in China for the first time three years ago, and is up there as one of the country's most famous. It seems fitting to be enjoying a glass or two right over the road from the brewery the way it's meant to be had—out of a small, almost shot—sized glass with fresh seafood and barbequed meat.

We try a variety of dishes—my personal favorite a scallop dish with soy and salad. The food, compared to other dishes in China, is not overly spicy and lets the seafood speak for itself. The clean taste of Tsingtao really goes hand in hand with the fresh taste of the food.

Among the beautiful coastal bays and bright lights of Qingdao's skyline, the local culture of Qingdao is here on Beer Street, as you watch people pass through for dinner and drinks that last until late into the night. The smell of the sea, the cool air and the sense of relaxation you feel here is contagious. There isn't a bar culture here in Qingdao, instead people meet their friends at a restaurant just like this, a round table on the street, and drink beer and enjoy hours of company and conversation.

In a world that constantly feels like it's speeding up, life slows down a little round these tables.

Before sampling the delicious spread in front of me, I got to taste test the fresh beer across the road at the original brewery. Tsingtao brewery was originally opened by the Germans way back in 1903 and you can still see the architecture that stands out compared to the surrounding Chinese-style buildings. The name "Tsingtao" comes from the original Latin spelling of the city's name before the modern phonetic alphabet, pin-yin, was developed. Tsingtao's brewing methods have stayed pretty similar since then, apart from upgrading machinery to keep up with the sheer demand required today.

The ingredient list has only changed slightly since it was first developed. Of course, China grows a lot of rice, and it's found its way into the ingredient list alongside hops and grains to make the beer I've been drinking all day. The beer takes around 40 days to go from grain to bottle and the city is the only place you can get a taste of the "fresh beer", which has a shelf life of only 24 hours. It's less filtered, and has a stronger, full bodied taste that goes with the higher alcohol content. During my visit, I was lucky enough to catch up with Dong Fang, the Curator of Tsingtao Brewery Museum, over a German styled lunch, and, of course, a few glasses of Tsingtao, to discuss how the brewery has developed since it opened over 100 years ago.

"When they first built the brewery, Germans began a high-quality industry. Then, Chinese people infused our brilliant traditional culture into it, using management skills and local advantages to develop the beer into a global brand," he said. Dong explained that due to benefits of the Belt and Road Initiative, Tsingtao is now exported to over 100 countries. When asked about the upcoming Shanghai Cooperation Organization Summit to be held in Qingdao this June, he added "to SCO-associated countries, our exports have increased rapidly as well, with an average year-on-year increase of over 70%."

The expansion of the Tsingtao brewery across the whole country and indeed world is something that people from the city are incredibly proud of. As I cheer a group of dinner goers back on Beer Street, they tell me about a bar that I need to check out before my time in Qingdao is up. By this stage, I've been drinking since 10 am and am starting to feel a little dizzy, but there's no way I can pass up on the opportunity when I hear the bar serve one of Tsingtao's new stout!

Walking into the local community bar and restaurant, we order some more local dishes including sea cucumber, octopus and to my delight, more clams, along with a "one by one plus" which includes all the beer that Tsingtao produce at the moment—lager, fresh beer, IPA and the much anticipated stout. The array of beer shows that Tsingtao, although already successful, has not become complacent. China's interest in different beers has been growing steadily for the past few years, and Tsingtao has produced an IPA and stout to compete with an international market and appeal to a wider audience. The stout has a coffee and chocolate tinge that I really enjoy, less heavy than a UK stout but still rich in flavor and somewhat easier to drink in one go.

Qingdao is gearing up for the 18th Shanghai Cooperation Organization Summit this June, and the city is already getting ready. Renovations are obvious, and the beautiful skyline has been upgraded to rival light shows all over the world.

But, for me, it's here on Beer Street with Qingdao locals that you truly feel a part of the city and community, and can enjoy the simple things in life like some great food and a glass of beer with friends.

参考译文

SECTION Ⅰ: Dialogue

A：谢谢你来送我。我在青岛过得很愉快。

B：How time flies! You've been in Qingdao for 5 days. It seems as if it were only yesterday when I picked you up at the airport. And now you are leaving.

A：是啊，对我来说，这是一段美好的经历。在青岛认识了你、你的同事，还参观了工厂，最终签订了合同。谢谢你带我游览了漂亮的城市。我这趟出差可谓收获满满！

B：We are also pleased with our joint collaboration. Your visit is short but it bears fruits. We look forward to seeing you soon at Qingdao Commodity Fair next spring in Qingdao.

A：我也希望如此。我衷心邀请你们明年春天到纽约我们的总部来访问。

B：Thank you for your kind invitation. We will fix a proper time for our visit and let you know. Let's keep in touch. What's your impression of China now, Jim?

A：嗯，跟我来之前的印象截然不同。我想现在对中国和中国文化，我有了更好的了解。

B：I am glad you have enjoyed your stay in China.

A：对中国知道得越多，就越想了解她。还有很多地方我想去走一走，还有很多东西我想去看一看。

B：Well, I am looking forward to hosting you here again.

A：非常感谢你一路的陪同。你们的周到照顾使我这次旅行收获很大。

B：The pleasure is mine. It's time for us to say goodbye, Jim.

A：非常感谢你为我所做的一切。这真是一次难忘的经历。让我们保持联系。

B：Sure, and I'll look forward to your next visit to China.

A：我一定会来的。

B：Goodbye. And Bon voyage!

SECTION Ⅱ: Warm-ups for Interpretation

➢ **Interpret the following proverbs from English into Chinese.**

1. It is such a delight that I have friends visiting from afar! /Isn't it a delight that con-

genial minds come to seek you from afar?

2. A bosom friend afar brings a distant land near.
3. I wish you a long life and the joy of sharing the silvery moonlight even with a thousand miles' distance between us.
4. Silence is gold.
5. A relative far off is less help than a neighbor close by.

➢ **Interpret the following sentences from English into Chinese.**

1. It gives me great pleasure to express once again to our host my deep appreciation for the grand reception and boundless and generous hospitality we enjoy here.
2. I want to extend my personal earnest welcome to all of you and sincerely hope that your visit here will be rewarding.
3. Allow me to express my warm welcome and gracious greetings to our distinguished guests coming from afar.
4. I'm sure you need a good rest after such a long flight. See you again at the reception banquet tonight.
5. These fine impressions will remain forever in our most cherished memories.

➢ **Interpret the following paragraphs from Chinese into English and vice versa.**

1. 这是我首次访问你们这座美丽的城市，我为此深感荣幸。我愿借此机会，代表我们团队全体成员，对东道主的诚挚邀请，对一踏上这块充满魅力的土地便受到的友好款待，向东道主表示真诚的感谢。我想亲自向上海市市长发出我们的正式邀请，希望市长您在方便的时候尽早访问我市，以便我们能有机会回报您的热情款待。
2. On behalf of all the members of my delegation, I would like to thank your company for the gracious invitation and hospitality. Although we have stayed in China for only five days, our visit is one of a great success. During our stay, we've met old friends, made new friends, and visited many factories and high-tech enterprises. The new progress that you have achieved impressed us deeply. We have a long friendly relationship with China. We are no longer strangers to each other, but cordial friends and important trading partners.

SECTION Ⅲ: Speech

Speech A

Ladies and Gentlemen,

It was just three days ago that we, with great joy, gathered here in this hall to give Mr. Baker a warm welcome party. Today, it is with our cordiality and joy that we are here again to give a farewell party to Mr. Baker when he has concluded a tour of many places of Qingdao.

He will leave for home tomorrow. Mr. Baker's visit was short but very fruitful. His trip was widely reported by some local media, which caught attention of the public.

During his short stay in Qingdao, he met with the leaders of the municipal government, visited Qingdao New Hi-Tech Park and the Export Processing Zones in Qingdao Development Zone, inspected the bonded area and our supply chain resources. He also held talks with prominent individuals of various commercial circles.

In bidding him farewell, we sincerely hope Mr. Baker will plan his next trip to Qingdao for new investment, inspect our business fruits and expand our collaboration.

We would like to take this opportunity to ask him to convey our profound friendship to American people and our best regards and respects to his family.

In closing, I would like you to join me a toast, to Mr. Baker's good health and pleasant journey home.

Speech B

Qingdao

Qingdao, "Qing" for short, is a city in eastern Shandong Province on the east coast of China. It is a megacity, a sub-provincial city, the economic center of Shandong Province, a coastal important central city of China, a coastal city for resort and tourism, an international port city, an important pilot zone for development of modern marine industry of China, an international shipping hub of Northeast Asia, a marine sports base, a main hub in the economic corridor of New Eurasian Land Bridge of "the Belt and Road" and a pivot of marine cooperation strategy.

Qingdao is located on the southeast coast of Shandong Peninsula, in the east of Jiaodong Peninsula and in the frontal zone of China-Japan-South Korea free trade area. It borders on Yellow Sea, facing Korean Peninsula across the sea, adjacent to Yantai in the northeast, connected to Weifang in the west and neighboring Rizhao in the southwest. It has a total area of 11,282 km^2, administering 7 districts and managing 3 county-level cities. In 2017, its total number of permanent residents was 9,290,500 and its total regional GDP was RMB 1,103,728,000,000 *yuan*.

Qingdao is the host city of sailing races of 2008 Beijing Olympic Games and of the 13th Paralympic Games, known as the Sailing City of China, the Best Sailing City of Asia, the World Beer City, the "Cinema City" of the United Nations, one of the first coastal open-up cities of China, the National Civilized City, one of the Happiest Cities of China. It also won the reputations of the European-style city as "the Oriental Switzerland" and "the City of Brands of China".

Qingdao is an international marine scientific research and education center where reside 26 universities such as Shandong University (Qingdao Campus), Ocean University of China, China University of Petroleum. Another 29 universities such as Tsinghua University and Peking University have been introduced into Qingdao. There are diversified exotic-style architectures in Qingdao, so it is called "the Universal Exposition of Architectures". The architectural complex in Eight Great Passes was awarded the title—"the Most Beautiful Urban Area of China".

SECTION Ⅳ: Speech

Speech A

女士们，先生们：

首先，感谢你们盛情邀请我出席今天的宴会。很高兴有机会再次访问这座城市，会见这么多各界人才。

这次旅行所见所闻非常有趣，给我留下了非常深刻的印象。我参观了工厂、学校和文化机构，与工人、政府官员、经理、工程师、教师和学生进行了交谈，并结下了深厚友谊。

我们讨论了工作、投资、商贸、学习和生活。在短暂的访问期间我学到了很多东西，这使我对贵国和贵国人民以及开放政策有了更好的了解。

在此我受到了隆重热情的接待和无限盛情的款待，再次向我们的东道主表示深深的谢意。

临别的时刻，我满怀留恋。总裁先生，很遗憾这一次我不能应您的邀请访问北京的分部，以后有机会我一定去。

祝友好的中国人民繁荣幸福。祝我们两国人民之间的友好关系进一步发展和巩固。再见了，亲爱的朋友们!

Speech B

“干杯!”饭桌上的酒菜是宁帮我们订购的。宁既是我的同事，也是我的朋友。宁来自青岛，因此比我更了解当地菜肴，以及吃什么与当地酿造的啤酒——青岛啤酒最搭配。

青岛啤酒是青岛乃至全国颇受欢迎的啤酒。事实上，这是三年前我第一次到中国时尝过的第一款啤酒，也是中国最著名的啤酒之一。在啤酒厂的马路对面，喝上一两杯似乎是再合适不过的事情了。喝啤酒应该用一个小小的、烈酒杯大小的玻璃杯，并佐以新鲜的海鲜和烤肉。

我们品尝了各种菜肴——我个人最喜欢的是扇贝配大豆和沙拉。与其他菜相比，这道菜不会过于辛辣，从而使海鲜的鲜味得以充分体现。青岛啤酒的清醇味道确实与海鲜的鲜味相得益彰。

在美丽的滨海海湾和高楼大厦的璀璨灯光中，青岛的当地文化在啤酒街上得以充分体现。人们来来往往，吃晚餐、喝饮料，一直持续到深夜。大海的味道，凉爽的空气和身心的放松感无不深深地感染着人。青岛没有酒吧文化，相反，人们就在这样的餐馆里与朋友相聚，围坐在街边的圆桌旁，喝着啤酒，聚会、聊天。

在一个让人感觉节奏越来越快的世界里，围坐在桌旁会让生活节奏放慢一点。

在品尝面前的各种美味之前，我要先试喝一下马路对面青岛啤酒原厂的鲜啤。1903年，德国人最早开办青岛啤酒厂，与周围的中式建筑相比，至今仍能看出厂房建筑显得非常突出。“Tsingtao”这个名字是在现代拼音字母形成之前，使用原拉丁语拼写而成。从那时起，除升级机器以满足当今的大量需求外，青岛啤酒一直保持着与最初非常相似的酿造方法。

成分表自首次研发以来，仅略有变化。当然，中国种植了很多大米，它与啤酒花和谷物一起被列入了成分表，制成了我一整天都在喝的啤酒。啤酒从谷物酿造到装瓶大约需要40天，而青岛是唯一可以品尝到“鲜啤”的地方。鲜啤的保质期只有24小时。它过滤较少，味道更浓郁醇厚，酒精含量也较高。在参观期间，我有幸与青岛啤酒博物馆馆长董方一起享用了德式午餐，当然还喝了几杯青岛啤酒，并一起讨论了青岛啤酒厂自100多年前创办以来的发展情况。

“当德国人首次创建啤酒厂时，他们就是以一个高质量产业为开端的。然后，中国人将我们辉煌的传统文化注入其中，利用管理方法和当地优势将青岛啤酒发展成为一个全球品牌”，他说。董馆长解释说，受益于“一带一路”倡议，青岛啤酒现在出口到100多个国家。当被问及即将于今年6月在青岛举行的上海合作组织峰会时，他补充说：“我们对上海合作组织的相关国家的出口也已大幅增长，平均同比增长超过70%。”

青岛啤酒厂在全国乃至全世界的发展让青岛人感到无比自豪。我在啤酒街和一群吃晚餐的人一起喝酒时，他们告诉我一家酒吧，得在离开青岛前去看看。从上午10点开始就一直在喝酒，喝到现在，我开始感到有点头晕。但当我听到酒吧供应一种新的青岛啤酒——烈性黑啤酒时，我可不能错过这个品尝机会！

走进当地社区的酒吧餐厅，我们又点了一些当地菜肴，包括海参、章鱼，令我高兴的是，还点了更多的蛤蜊，以及“啤酒六联杯”——其中包括青岛啤酒目前生产的所有啤酒——淡啤酒、鲜啤、IPA和备受期待的烈性黑啤酒。琳琅满目的啤酒表明虽然青岛啤酒已经很成功，但它并没有骄傲自满。在过去的几年里，中国对不同啤酒的兴趣一直在稳步增长，而青岛啤酒已经生产出了IPA和烈性黑啤酒与国际市场竞争，并吸引了更广泛的受众。烈性黑啤酒有一种我非常喜欢的咖啡和巧克力色调，它没有英国黑啤酒那么烈，但仍然味道浓郁，而且更容易一口气喝完。

青岛正在为今年6月举行的第十八届上海合作组织峰会做准备，并且即将准备就绪。翻新是显而易见的，高楼大厦形成的美丽的天际线已可以与世界各地的灯光秀相媲美。

然而，对我来说，在啤酒街上与青岛当地人一起，才能真的感受到与这座城市和社区融为一体，才能和朋友一起享受生活中的简单事物，如一些美味的食物和一杯啤酒。

Unit 2 海关手续 Customs Formalities

"亲望亲好，邻望邻好。"中国坚持与邻为善、以邻为伴，坚持睦邻、安邻、富邻，践行亲、诚、惠、容理念，努力使自身发展更好惠及亚洲国家。中国将同各国一道，加快推进丝绸之路经济带和21世纪海上丝绸之路建设，尽早启动亚洲基础设施投资银行，更加深入参与区域合作进程，推动亚洲发展和安全相互促进、相得益彰。

"Neighbors wish each other well, just like family members do to each other." China always pursues friendship and partnership with its neighbors, and seeks to bring amity, security and common prosperity to its neighborhood. It practices the principles of amity, sincerity, mutual benefit and inclusiveness and works hard to make its development bring more benefits to countries in Asia. China will work with other countries to speed up the development of an economic belt along the Silk Road and a 21st Century maritime silk road, and hopes that the Asian infrastructure investment bank could be launched at an early date. China will get more deeply involved in the regional cooperation process, and play its due part to ensure that development and security in Asia facilitate each other and are mutually reinforcing.

课文 A

SECTION Ⅰ: Dialogue 通过海关 At the Customs

Interpret the following dialogue from Chinese into English and vice versa.

A：下午好。欢迎您来到中国。请出示您的护照和海关申报表。

B：Yes. Here they are. I have only a few small gifts. I don't think I have anything to declare.

A：您带了多少现金？

B：500 dollars.

A：请把这个包打开。这个小盒子里面装的是什么？

B：It's medicine for my stenocardia. These are my personal belongings. And these are gifts for friends.

A：我可以看看您提到的礼物吗？

B：Yes. There are two bottles of Chivas Regal and two bottles of Rémy Martin (VOSP).

A：您有这些酒的收据吗？

B：Yes, I do. Here it is.

A：每个旅客只允许免税带两瓶酒。按规定另外两瓶酒必须交税。

B：OK.

A：任何植物、谷物、水果、肉类，包括动物都不允许携带入境。如果有的话，你要到那边柜台的关员那里处理。您的这些名包和香水都需要纳税。

B：How much should I pay?

A：我们会给您计算。

相关词汇

常用海关英语

customs officer　海关关员

customs formalities　通关法定手续

declare　(通关)申报

oral(written) declaration　口头(书面)报关

customs inspection　海关检查

inspect　检查

confiscate　没收

Passed Inspection　验讫

assessment　评估

customs area　海关检查区

violation　违反

duties/customs duties/tariff/import duty　关税

levy duty　课税；征税

restricted article　限制物品

personal belongings　(个人)随身物品

prohibited article　违禁品

dutiable goods　(需)征税物品

duty-free/tax-exempt　免税的

tariff rates　关税率

quarantine/health control 检疫

vaccination certificate/certificate of vaccination 预防接种证明书

stenocardia 心绞痛

animal and plant inspection 动(植)物检疫检查

Chinese herbal medicine 中草药

narcotics 麻醉毒品

SECTION Ⅱ: Warm-ups for Interpretation

➢ **Tongue twister.**

Can you can a can as a canner can can a can?

你能够像罐头工人一样装罐头吗?

How many cookies could a good cook cook if a good cook could cook cookies? A good cook could cook as much cookies as a good cook who could cook cookies.

如果一个好厨师能做小甜饼，那么他能做多少小甜饼呢? 一个好厨师能做出和其他好厨师一样多的小甜饼。

➢ **Interpret the following proverbs from English into Chinese.**

1. Well begun is half done.
2. A bird in the hand is worth two in the bush.
3. By scratching and biting cat and dog come together.
4. We all have our blind spots.
5. Pay on the spot and borrow a lot; pay slow and you'll get no dough.

➢ **Interpret the following sentences from English into Chinese.**

1. May I see your passport, your customs and health declaration forms, please?
2. Put your carry-ons on the belt, please.
3. May I have a customs declaration form, please?
4. What's the maximum amount of wine you're allowed to take through customs duty-free?
5. Please fill out this certificate of Entrustment, so that when your baggage arrives, we can go through the customs formalities for you.

➢ **Interpret the following paragraphs from English into Chinese and vice versa.**

1. When you return to Canada, you have to declare all of the goods you acquired while outside Canada, such as purchases, gifts, prizes or awards that you are bringing with you or are having shipped to you. Include goods that are still in your possession that you bought at a Canadian or foreign duty-free shop. As well, make sure you declare any repairs or alterations you made to your vehicle, vessel or aircraft while you were out of the country.
2. 中华人民共和国海关是国家的进出关境(以下简称进出境)监督管理机关。海关依照本法和其他有关法律、行政法规,监管进出境的运输工具、货物、行李物品、邮递物品和其他物品(以下简称进出境运输工具、货物、物品),征收关税和其他税费,查缉走私,并编制海关统计和办理其他海关业务。

SECTION Ⅲ: Speech

Interpret the following speech from English into Chinese.

Customs Declaration Explanations

1. Print your last (family) name. Print your first (given) name. Print the first letter of your middle name.

2. Print your date of birth in the appropriate day/month/year boxes.

3. Print the number of family members traveling with you (do not include yourself).

4. Print your current street address in the United States. If you are staying at a hotel, include the hotel's name and street address. Print the city and the state in the appropriate boxes.

5. Print the name of the country that issued your passport.

6. Print your passport number.

7. Print the name of the country where you currently live.

8. Print the name of the country or countries that you visited on your trip prior to arriving to the United States.

9. If traveling by airline, print the airline's name and flight number. If traveling by vessel (ship), print the vessel's name.

10. Mark an X in the Yes or No box. Are you traveling on a business (work-related) trip?

11. Mark an X in the Yes or No box. Are you bringing with you:

a. Fruits, plants, food, or insects?

b. Meats, animals, or animal/wildlife products?

c. Disease agents, cell cultures, or snails?

d. Soil or have you visited a farm/ranch/pasture outside the United States?

12. Mark an X in the Yes or No box. Have you or any family members traveling with you been in close proximity of (such as touching or handling) livestock outside the United States?

13. Mark an X in the Yes or No box. Are you or any family members traveling with you bringing $10,000 or more in U. S. dollars or foreign equivalent in any form into the United States?

Read definition of monetary instruments on the reverse side of the form. Examples: coins, cash, personal or cashier's check, traveler's checks, money orders, stocks, bonds. If yes, you must complete the Customs Form 4790.

14. Mark an X in the Yes or No box. Are you or any family members traveling with you bringing commercial merchandise into the United States? Examples: all articles intended to be sold or left in the United States, samples used for soliciting orders, or goods that are not considered personal effects.

15. If you are a U. S. resident, print the total value of all goods (including commercial merchandise) you or any family members traveling with you have purchased or acquired abroad (including gifts for someone else, but not items mailed to the United States) and are bringing into the United States.

Note: U. S. residents are normally entitled to a duty-free exemption of $800 on items accompanying them.

If you are a visitor (non-U. S. Resident), print the total value of all goods (including commercial merchandise) you or any family members traveling with you are bringing into the United States and will remain in the United States.

Note: Visitors (non-U. S. Residents) are normally entitled to an exemption of $100.

Declare all articles on this form. For gifts, please indicate the retail value. Use the reverse side of this form if additional space is needed to list the items you will declare.

The U. S. Customs and Border Protection officer will determine duty. Duty will be assessed at the current rate on the first $1,000 above the exemption.

- Read the notice on the reverse side of the form.
- Sign the form and print the date.
- Keep the complete form with you and hand it to the CBP officer when you approach the U. S. Customs and Border Protection area.

Controlled substances, obscene articles, and toxic substances are generally prohibited entry.

Thank you, and Welcome to the United States.

SECTION Ⅳ: Speech

Interpret the following speech from Chinese into English.

赴中国须办理中国签证，护照有效期不少于6个月。根据访问的目的，签发不同类型的签证。

申请旅游签证只需提供个人基本信息。申请商务签证需持有中国商业伙伴的邀请函。

中国签证可通过中国大使馆、领事馆或者中国旅行社申请。

自入境之日起，旅游签证的有效期通常为30天，如需延长，可向当地公安局申请。

前往未对外开放的城市旅游，须持有旅游通行证。旅游通行证可向当地公安局出入境办公室申请。参观西藏需要另外的签证。

抵达中国以后，在海关外国游客须填写《旅客行李申报单》，并接受海关人员检查。外国游客不得为他人将物品带出中国。

参考译文

SECTION Ⅰ: Dialogue

A: Good afternoon. Welcome to China. May I see your passport, customs declaration form.

B: 好的，给您。我只带了几件小礼物。没有什么需要申报的东西。

A: How much cash are you carrying with you?

B: 500美元。

A：Would you please open this bag? What's in this small box?

B：这是治心绞痛的药。这些是我的私人物品，那些是给我朋友带的礼物。

A：May I see the gifts you mentioned?

B：可以。两瓶芝华士和两瓶人头马。

A：Do you have a receipt for the liquor?

B：有的，在这儿。

A：According to the regulations, you can only take two bottles for duty free. So you must pay tax for the other two.

B：好的。

A：Any plants, cereals, fruits and meat including animals are not permitted to bring in. If you have any with you, you have to speak to the officers at that counter. You have to pay tax on these luxurious bags and perfumes.

B：我该交多少税？

A：We will figure it out for you.

SECTION Ⅱ: Warm-ups for Interpretation

➢ **Interpret the following proverbs from Chinese into English.**

1. 良好的开端是成功的一半。
2. 多得不如现得。
3. 不打不相识。
4. 金无足金，人无完人。
5. 好借好还，再借不难。

➢ **Interpret the following sentences from Chinese into English.**

1. 请您出示护照、海关申报表和体检表，好吗？
2. 请您把随身携带的行李放在传送带上。
3. 请给我一份海关申报表，好吗？
4. 海关允许携带酒品的最高免税额是多少？
5. 请您填写一张委托书，这样行李抵达后，我们可以代您接受海关检查。

➢ **Interpret the following paragraphs from Chinese into English and vice versa.**

1. 当您返回加拿大时，您须申报在加国之外获得的所有物品，包括您现在随身携带的、或托送给您的东西，如购买的物品、礼品、获得的奖品等。您在加拿大或国外的免税店所购买的、现在归您所有的任何物品也须申报。同时，请申报您在国外对您的汽车、船或飞机进行过的所有修理或变动。
2. The Customs of the People's Republic of China is a State organ responsible for supervision and control over all arrivals in and departures from the customs territory (hereinafter referred to as the territory in short). It shall, in accordance with this law and other related laws and administrative regulations, exercise control over the means of transport, goods, travelers' luggage, postal items and other articles entering or leaving the territory (hereinafter referred to as inward and outward means of transport, goods and articles in short), collect customs duties and other taxes and fees, prevent and suppress smuggling, prepare customs statistics and handle other customs operations.

SECTION Ⅲ: Speech

海关申报须知：

1. 用印刷体(大写字母)书写您的姓名。
2. 用印刷体(大写字母)书写您的出生日期(日/月/年)。
3. 用印刷体(大写字母)书写随行的家庭成员人数(除您以外)。
4. 用印刷体(大写字母)书写当前您在美国的街道地址。如果住在旅馆，请写下旅馆的名字和地址。在对应的方框内正确填入所在的州、市。
5. 用印刷体(大写字母)书写护照签发国名称。
6. 用印刷体(大写字母)书写您的护照号码。
7. 用印刷体(大写字母)书写您当前的居住国名称。
8. 用印刷体(大写字母)书写您本次旅行抵美前曾去过的国家。
9. 如果您本次是乘飞机旅行，用印刷体(大写字母)书写航空公司名称和航班号。如乘船旅行，用印刷体(大写字母)书写船只名称。
10. 您本次是公务旅行吗？如“是”，请在“Yes”对应的方框内画√；如“否”，请在“No”对应的方框内画×。

11. 您是否携有以下物品？如“是”，请在“Yes”对应的方框内画√；如“否”，请在“No”对应的方框内画×。

a. 水果、植物、食品，或昆虫？（ ）

b. 肉类、动物，或动物/野生动物制品？（ ）

c. 致病原、细胞培养物，或蜗牛？（ ）

d. 土壤，或在抵美前曾去过其他国家或地区的农场/牧场/草场？（ ）

12. 您或随行的家人在美国以外曾近距离接触（触摸或搬运）家畜？如“是”，请在“Yes”对应的方框内画√；如“否”，请在“No”对应的方框内画×。

13. 您或随行的任何一名家庭成员所携带的货币或任何形式的金融票据是否超过10000美元或与其等值的外币？如“是”，请在“Yes”对应的方框内画√；如“否”，请在“No”对应的方框内画×。

参看表格背面对金融票据的定义。如硬币、现金、个人或银行支票、旅行支票、汇票、股票、债券等。

如“是”，您必须填写“海关申报表4790”。

14. 您或随行的家人是否携带商品入境？例如，所有打算留在美国或在美国出售的商品，用于征集订单的样品，或不属于个人使用的物品。

15. 如果您是美国居民，请用印刷体（大写字母）书写您或随行的家人在国外购买或获得，并要携带入境的所有物品（包括所有商品、为他人带的礼物，但不包括邮递到美国的物品）。

注意：美国居民通常可携带800美元的免税物品。

如果您只是到访美国（非美国居民），请用印刷体（大写字母）书写您或随行的家人携带入境并将留在美国的所有物品（包括商品）的总价值。

注意：到访者（非美国居民）通常可携带100美元的免税物品。

请填写本表申报所有物品。如果是礼物，请注明零售价。如果指定位置空间不够，无法列出所有需要申报的物品，请参考本表背面的说明。

美国海关和边境保卫局的工作人员将计算关税。第一次超出免税额度之外的1000美元将按当前税率征收关税。

- 请参看本表背面，了解需要注意的内容。
- 签上您的名字和日期（日期用大写字母书写）。
- 拿好申报表，在通关时交给美国海关和边境保卫局人员。

管制物品、淫秽物品和有毒物品禁止入境。

谢谢。美国欢迎您。

SECTION Ⅳ: Speech

Traveling to China requires a visa stamped on a full passport with validity of not less than 6 months upon entry to China. Various types of visas are issued depending on the purpose of your visit.

Tourist visa applications require only basic personal information. Business visa applications require the presentation of an invitation to visit from a business counterpart in China.

Chinese visas can be applied through Chinese embassies/consulates or Chinese travel agencies.

A tourist visa is usually valid for 30 days from the day of entry, and it might be extended through applications to the local public security bureau.

A travel permit is needed for a foreigner who wishes to visit any of the non-open cities. Travel permits can be applied to the entry and exit office of the local public security bureau. A separate visa is required for visiting Tibet.

Upon arrival in China, a foreign tourist must fill in a Passenger's Luggage Declaration at the customs and accept customs officers' check. Foreign tourists are not allowed to take objects out of China for other people.

课文 B

SECTION Ⅰ: Dialogue 通过海关 At the Customs

Interpret the following dialogue from English into Chinese and vice versa.

A: May I see your passport, please?

B: 当然，给您。这是入境申请表。

A: What's the purpose of your visit?

B: 我来这里履行公务，确切地说是参加2022中国国际大数据产业博览会。

A: The validity of your visa is for three months. How long will you be staying?

B: 10天。

A: And do you plan to travel during your stay?

B：是的，我要去青岛、成都、重庆、上海和厦门，去拜访这些地方的朋友。

A：Is this all your baggage here?

B：是的，这全是我的。两只箱子和一件随身行李。

A：Would you mind opening your carry-on for me?

B：好的。这是照相机、手提电脑、平板电脑、衣服和一些书籍。

A：Anything else?

B：是的。我还带了两瓶威士忌。

A：Alright，sir. Thank you for your time. Enjoy your trip.

B：谢谢。

SECTION Ⅱ：Warm-ups for Interpretation

➢ **Tongue twister.**

Peter poked a poker at the piper，so the piper poked pepper at Peter.

彼得用拨火棍戳了风笛手，所以风笛手将胡椒粉撒向了彼得。

I wish to wish the wish you wish to wish，but if you wish the wish the witch wishes，I won't wish the wish you wish to wish.

我希望梦想着你梦想中的梦想，但是如果你梦想着女巫的梦想，我就不想梦想着你梦想中的梦想。

➢ **Interpret the following proverbs from Chinese into English.**

1. 以其人之道，还治其人之身。
2. 读万卷书，行万里路。
3. 趁热打铁。
4. 强将手下无弱兵。
5. 说是一回事，而做又是另外一回事。

➢ **Interpret the following sentences from Chinese into English.**

1. 我们的行李已经通过了安全检查。
2. 请将这张申报卡交给出口处的官员。
3. 如果您在洛杉矶转机，您需要在那通过海关检查。

4. 如果你携带的东西超出免税范围或属于禁带的物品，你就得走红色通道并向海关官员申报物品。
5. 有时海关的复杂手续会造成拖拉现象。

➤ **Interpret the following paragraphs from Chinese into English and vice versa.**

1. 进出口货物应当接受海关查验。当海关查验货物时，进口货物的收货人、出口货物的发货人应当到场，并负责搬移货物、开拆和重封货物的包装。
2. You must be of legal age in the province of importation. While you are permitted to import alcoholic beverages in excess of the amounts listed above, we remind all travelers that they will be responsible for paying duty and taxes on the additional alcoholic beverages they are importing.

SECTION Ⅲ: Speech

Interpret the following speech from Chinese into English.

美国或加拿大公民赴中国大陆从事经贸活动或旅游，须提前申请，并获得中国签证。如果仅赴香港特别行政区或澳门特别行政区旅行且停留不超过 30 天，可免签证。

然而，如果旅行范围在香港特别行政区或澳门特别行政区以外，哪怕仅逗留几个小时，也必须持有中国签证。事实上，大多数国家的游客前往中国大陆都需要签证。

一次入境签证通常自签发日起三个月内有效，可允许你在中国大陆最多停留 30 天。持这种签证，可在中国旅游或者进行一般的商务活动。大多数人只需申请一次入境签证。

启程前一个月是办理签证的最佳时间。签证通常自签发日起 90 天内有效，一次入境签证允许 30 天停留时间，即自入境日算起的 30 天。

我们推荐使用可追索的快递服务来寄送您的护照和重要文件，如联邦快递、UPS(联合包裹服务公司)、安邦快递、中外运敦豪或者邮政快递及挂号信。建议不要使用平信。

SECTION Ⅳ: Speech

Interpret the following speech from English into Chinese.

Chinese border crossings are generally very easy. Visitors entering China must fill out customs declaration form upon arrival. A departure copy will be stapled in your passport and must be presented when you exit China.

Reasonable amounts of money (currently up to US $5,000), alcohol and cigarettes, cameras, and laptops or iPads can be brought into China. Certain valuable items, such as amateur video and camera equipment, computers and gold must be declared on the form.

The limit of Renminbi for inbound and outbound passengers is 6,000 *yuan*. Inbound and outbound passengers with more than 6,000 *yuan* will not be allowed to enter or leave the territory.

If inbound passengers with cultural relics want to carry the relics out of the territory, they should make a clear declaration to the customs. Passengers may carry out the relics bought in China with the appraisal by the Chinese administrative department for cultural relics.

Tourists may bring small-format digital video camcorders. However, they must be declared upon entry, and the tapes produced in China may not be intended for commercial use. Professional video or audio recording equipment requires special authorization.

Any arms, ammunition, narcotics, porno, or printed or video material detrimental to China's politics, economy, culture, or ethics are extremely prohibited entry.

参考译文

SECTION Ⅰ: Dialogue

A：我可以看一下您的护照吗？

B：Sure, here you are. And this is the declaration form.

A：请问您此行的目的是什么？

B：I'm here on a business trip. Actually, I'm attending the 2022 China International Big Data Industry Expo.

A：您的签证期限是三个月，您打算待多长时间？

B：For ten days.

A：这期间您会去旅行吗？

B：Yes, I want to spend a couple of days to travel to Qingdao, Chengdu, Chongqing, Shanghai and Xiamen. I will visit some friends in these places.

A：您所有的行李都在这儿吗？

B：Yes，this is all mine，two suitcases and one carry-on.

A：请您把这个随身行李箱打开，好吗？

B：Sure. There is a camera，a laptop，an iPad，some clothes and some books.

A：还有别的东西吗？

B：Yes，I have two bottles of whiskey.

A：可以了，先生。谢谢您，耽搁您了。祝您旅途愉快。

B：Thank you.

SECTION Ⅱ: Warm-ups for Interpretation

➢ **Interpret the following proverbs from English into Chinese.**

1. An eye for an eye，and a tooth for a tooth.
2. Read ten thousand books，travel ten thousand miles.
3. Strike while the iron is hot. /Make hay while the sun is hot.
4. There are no poor soldiers under a good general.
5. Saying is one thing and doing is another.

➢ **Interpret the following sentences from English into Chinese.**

1. Our baggage has cleared customs.
2. Please give this declaration card to that officer at the exit.
3. You must go through customs inspection if you transfer in Los Angeles.
4. If you have more than the duty-free allowance or prohibited goods，you should go through the red channel and declare them to a customs officer.
5. Sometimes cumbersome procedures at customs offices create delays.

➢ **Interpret the following paragraphs from English into Chinese and vice versa.**

1. All import and export goods shall be subject to customs examination. While goods are being examined by the customs，the consignee for import goods or consignor for export goods shall be present and responsible for moving the goods，opening and re-storing the package.

2. 您必须达到法定年龄才允许带酒精饮品入境。如果您所携带的酒精饮品超过上面所列出的规定量，我们提醒所有入境者，请您履行相关责任，为超出规定的部分支付税费。

SECTION Ⅲ: Speech

Americans or Canadians traveling to Mainland China, whether for business or pleasure, require a visa, which should be obtained in advance. You are exempt from this requirement if you travel and stay only in Hong Kong SAR or Macao SAR for less than 30 days.

However, if you travel beyond Hong Kong SAR or Macao SAR, even for a few hours, you will need a China visa. As a matter of fact, visas are required for visitors from most foreign countries to Mainland China.

Single-entry visas are usually valid for 3 months after the issuing date, and will permit you to stay in Mainland China for a maximum of 30 days. This visa will allow you to travel as a tourist or attend business activities. Most people need only to apply for a single-entry.

The best time to apply for your visa is one month before your departure. The visa is normally good for entry within 90 days of issuance. Single-entry visa is usually valid for a 30-day visit, which means the visa is only good for 30 days after your entry date.

We highly recommend you use a traceable courier service to send your passport and valuable documents, such as FedEx, UPS, Airborne, DHL or United States Express, registered or certified mail. Regular mails are not recommended.

SECTION Ⅳ: Speech

中国过关手续通常比较简单。进入中国的旅客，在抵达时必须填写《海关申报表》。离境联会被订在你的护照上，在离开中国时提交。

适当数额的现金(目前规定为不超过 5000 美元)、烟酒、相机、笔记本电脑和平板电脑可以带入中国。某些贵重物品，如非专业录像和摄影设备、计算机和黄金必须在申报表上注明。

出入境旅客可携带的人民币限额为 6000 元。携带超过 6000 元现金的旅客将被禁止入境或离境。

携带文物的入境旅客如需将文物再带离中国，须在海关申报表上明确注明。旅客如需将在中国购买的文物携带出境，须持有中国文物管理部门的估价鉴定。

旅客在向海关申报以后，可携带小型便携式数码摄像机入境，但必须保证在中国录制的相带不作商业用途。专业的录像和录音设备必须经过特别授权。

任何武器、弹药、毒品、色情产品，或者是“对中国政治、经济、文化和道德有害的”印刷品和音像制品等一律严禁携带入境。

Unit 3 宾馆入住 Check-in at a Hotel

与君远相知，不道云海深。

True friendship brings people close however far apart they may be.

面向未来，我们将同各方继续高质量共建“一带一路”。

Going forward, we will continue to work with other parties in high-quality The Belt and Road cooperation.

同舟共济扬帆起，乘风破浪万里航。

By setting sail together, we could ride the wind, break the waves, and brave the journey of ten thousand miles.

课文 A

SECTION Ⅰ: Dialogue 在服务台 At the Reception Desk

Interpret the following dialogue from Chinese into English and vice versa.

A：晚上好，欢迎光临海景花园大酒店。我能为您效劳吗？

B：Yes, I'd like to check in, please.

A：好的，请问您的姓名？

B：Yes, it's Jim Baker.

A：先生，您有没有预约？

B：Yes, I booked a double-bed room with breakfast last week.

A：请稍等，我查一下预约纪录。(一分钟后)先生，这是您的预订：一间法式套房，从今天到 15 号。

B：Yes，exactly.

A：我能看下您的护照吗？谢谢，先生。请您填一下入住登记表，然后在这里签名，好吗？

B：I'll take care of it.（Filling out the form）Here you are.

A：谢谢。您准备如何付款呢？支付宝还是信用卡？

B：Could I use my card？Or I'd try to scan the QR code to make my payment.

A：当然可以，扫码支付更快更方便。您的房间号是 1009，海景房。这是您的钥匙。门童会带您上去的。

B：Thank you. By the way，I've just arrived after a long flight，I am really tired. Do you have 24-hour massage service？

A：有的。我们提供 24 小时按摩服务，需要时随时打电话给服务台，或直接到一楼娱乐中心隔壁的按摩室。晚安，先生。祝您过得愉快。

B：Thank you.

相关词汇

常用酒店英语

double room　双人房
single room　单人间
twin room　标准间
deluxe suite　豪华套房
presidential suite　总统套房
room charge　房价
special rate　优惠价
service charge　服务费
departure date　离店日期
sundry fee　杂费
exchange rate　兑换率
off-season　淡季
peak-season　旺季
IDD　国际直拨
DDD　国内直拨
cocktail　鸡尾酒
liquor　烈酒
champagne　香槟
brandy　白兰地
vodka　伏特加
Rémy Martin　人头马
Chivas Ragal　芝华士威士忌
Jack Daniels　杰克·丹尼
Johnnie Walker 尊尼获加
Martell　马爹利
Bacardi　百加得
Martini　马提尼
rum　朗姆酒

dry-clean　干洗
indemnity　赔偿
iron　熨烫
laundry　洗衣
endorsement　在(支票等)背面签名，背书

Alipay	支付宝	mobile payment	移动支付
credit card	信用卡	QR code payment	二维码支付
Apple Pay	苹果支付	online payment	线上支付
WeChat pay	微信支付	card payment	银行卡支付

SECTION Ⅱ: Warm-ups for Interpretation

➢ **Tongue twister.**

Picky people pick Peter Pan Peanut-Butter,
this the peanut-butter picky people pick.
挑剔的人选购彼得·潘牌的花生酱，
这就是那些挑剔的人所挑选的花生酱。
Spring is showery, flowery, bowery.
Summer is hoppy, croppy, poppy.
Autumn is wheezy, sneezy, freezy.
Winter is slippy, drippy, nippy.
春天雷雨阵阵，百花吐艳，树荫宜人。
夏天欢快跳跃，庄稼喜人，爆竹声声。
秋天空气凉爽，喷嚏连连，神轻气爽。
冬天滴水成冰，雨雪茫茫，地冷天寒。

➢ **Interpret the following proverbs from Chinese into English.**

1. 欲速则不达。
2. 习惯成自然。
3. 与人方便，自己方便。
4. 谁笑到最后，谁笑得最美。
5. 水滴石穿。

➢ **Interpret the following sentences from Chinese into English.**

1. 请您填写一下这张登记表，好吗？
2. 行李员会为您提行李，并为您领路。
3. 我应该明天离店，但我想延长两至三天离店。
4. 如您在下午 6 点以后退房将收全天房费。
5. 早餐送餐服务是从早上 7 点至上午 10 点。如果您想在房间用早餐，请打电话叫送餐服务。

➢ **Interpret the following paragraphs from Chinese into English and vice versa.**

1. 宾馆提供各种便利服务项目，包括出租车联系、机票和火车票预订、外汇兑换、国际电话直拨、因特网使用等；宾馆接受主要信用卡，提供衣服洗烫、美容美发、桑拿沐浴、按摩推拿等服务。
2. The Shangri-La Hotels and Resorts is a hotel chain based in Hong Kong. It is the largest Asian-based deluxe hotel group in the region. The group started in 1971 with its first and flagship hotel in Singapore, and now has 55 deluxe hotels and resorts located in key Asian, Australian and Middle Eastern cities with hotel room inventory of over 27,000. The hotel group also has a sister brand called Traders Hotel, established in 1989 to cater mostly to business travelers.

SECTION Ⅲ: Speech

Interpret the following speech from Chinese into English.

早上好，贝克先生。祝您生日快乐！我们是从您的登记卡上得知您的生日的。这是我们宾馆经理送给您的蛋糕和鲜花，还有他的贺信。祝您健康长寿。

这里有些蜡烛供您挑选。

请大家注意，我要和大家说几句话，谢谢。我谨代表我们总经理借此机会向吉姆·贝克先生及在座的各位贵宾表达诚挚的谢意并和各位话别。

感谢各位的光临。希望贝克先生和各位贵宾能喜欢我们的饭店和服务。并希望你们在未来的季节里带着亲朋好友很快重游青岛。

祝愿大家接下来旅途愉快。注意不要遗忘了您的物品。欢迎您带走我们的友谊，留下您的微笑。感谢您的光临。希望能再次为您服务。旅途愉快！

SECTION Ⅳ: Speech

Interpret the following speech from English into Chinese.

Ladies and Gentlemen,

Good morning! It's a cold spell (寒流) today, but our heartfelt warmth to welcome our friends from Chicago is melting the ice and the snow.

On behalf of all our staff of Sea View Garden Hotel, I would like to extend the warmest welcome to you. We hope that all our guests will make our hotel their "home away from home" and feel happy and comfortable during your stay.

Our hotel has an access to public transport both within the city center and has a good connection to outside of Qingdao. It is just a few steps away from the metro station which links up to most of Qingdao's commercial and business centers. Donghai Road in front of the hotel is a beautiful broad way leading you to Qingdao International Airport, Qingdao Train Station, downtown commercial areas and most of the sight-seeing spots.

We would be pleased to offer our guests all kinds of services to make their stay enjoyable. We have many facilities to meet the needs of our guests, such as a business center, a recreation center, a health club, massage rooms, a bowling room, rooms for pingpong and mahjong.

There are four restaurants serving both Chinese and Western foods, a cafeteria, coffee bars and a souvenir shop. Every hotel room boasts the usual collection of five-star facilities including a private bath, air-conditioning, hair dryer, an electric iron, a safe, Satellite TV, WiFi, an IDD telephone, and a minibar.

To welcome our friends from Chicago, here is a small souvenir for every one of you. Allow me present it to you as a token of our friendship. I hope you'll enjoy your stay with us.

参考译文

SECTION Ⅰ: Dialogue

A: Good evening. Welcome to Sea View Garden Hotel. May I help you, sir?

B：我要登记住宿。

A：Certainly，sir. May I have your name，please?

B：我叫吉姆·贝克。

A：Do you have a reservation with us，sir?

B：是的，我上周预订了一个大床双人房，可提供早餐。

A：Just a moment，please. Mr. Baker，I will check the reservation record. (After one moment) Yes，sir，you have reserved a French suite from today to 15th.

B：是的。

A：Could I see your passport. Please? Thank you，sir，and would you please fill in the registration form and sign here?

B：好的。(填完表)给你。

A：Thank you. How are you going to pay，with Alipay or with credit card?

B：我可以用我的银行卡付款吗？或让我尝试一下扫码支付吧。

A：Certainly. Scan to pay is more convenient and faster. Your room number is 1009，a sea view suite. Here is the key. The bellboy will show you up.

B：谢谢。顺便问下，我刚坐了很长时间的飞机，现在很累。你们有全天 24 小时的按摩服务吗？

A：Yes，massage service is available 24 hours a day. You may call the receptionist any time or go straight to the massage room next to our Recreation Center on the first floor. Have a nice evening，sir. And enjoy your stay.

B：谢谢。

SECTION Ⅱ: Warm-ups for Interpretation

➢ **Interpret the following proverbs from English into Chinese.**

1. Haste makes waste.
2. Habit is second nature.
3. He who helps others helps himself.
4. He who laughs last laughs longest.
5. Constant dripping wears away the stone.

➢ **Interpret the following sentences from English into Chinese .**

1. Would you please complete this registration form?
2. The porter will take your luggage and show you the way.
3. I'm due to check out tomorrow, but I'd like to extend my stay by two or three days.
4. Full-day room rate will be added if you check out after 6 pm.
5. Breakfast is served in your room from 7 am till 10 am. If you wish to have breakfast in your room, ask for Room Service on the phone.

➢ **Interpret the following paragraphs from English into Chinese and vice versa.**

1. The hotel provides comprehensive convenience services, such as taxi arrangement, airline and train ticket booking, foreign currency exchange, international direct dial telephone (IDD), internet service, payment by all major credit cards, laundry service, a beauty parlor and a sauna bath on the premises, as well as a health service with medical massage.
2. 香格里拉酒店是一家总部位于香港的连锁酒店，它是亚洲最大的豪华酒店集团。从1971年新加坡第一间香格里拉旗舰酒店开始，香格里拉酒店今日已在亚洲、澳洲和中东地区的主要城市建有55间豪华酒店，共可接待27000多名客人。1989年，香格里拉酒店集团成立商贸饭店，主要为商务旅客提供服务。

SECTION Ⅲ: Speech

Good morning, Mr. Baker. Happy birthday to you! We knew your birthday from your registration form. Our hotel manager presents the birthday cake and the flowers to you on this occasion. Here is his congratulation card. We all wish you healthy and many returns of the day.

Here are some tiny candles for you to choose.

May I have your attention, please? On behalf of our general manger, I'd like to take this opportunity to express our heartfelt thanks to Mr. Baker and you all for choosing our hotel and bid good-bye to all our distinguished guests.

I appreciate your favor of our hotel and thank you very much for your coming. I wish that you like our hotel and enjoy our service. I also wish you come back to our city sooner with more friends or relatives in the coming seasons.

I wish you a pleasant trip to your next destination. Be sure not to forget any personal belongings. Take our friendship with you and leave your smile to us. Thank you again for coming. We look forward to seeing you soon in our hotel. Bon voyage.

SECTION Ⅳ: Speech

女士们、先生们：

早上好。受寒潮影响，天气很冷，但我们仍满怀热情欢迎来自芝加哥的客人。

我谨代表海景花园大酒店的全体员工向你们致以热烈的欢迎。希望我们的酒店能够使顾客出门在外也能有家的感觉，在此过得舒适、开心。

我们酒店出入交通便捷，不论是在本地还是去外地。地铁站仅仅几步之遥，通达全市各个商务中心。酒店紧邻宽阔的东海路，景色迷人，可直达青岛国际机场、青岛火车站、各个商务中心及众多的景点。

我们给客人提供了多种多样的服务使他们住得称心。我们拥有完备的设施，满足客人的各种需要，如商务中心、娱乐中心、健身俱乐部、按摩室、保龄球馆、乒乓球室、麻将室等。

我们有四家餐厅分别供应中餐和西餐，还有一家自助餐厅、几间咖啡厅和一个纪念品商店。客房中都配有齐全的五星级酒店设备，包括单独浴室、空调、电吹风、电熨斗、保险柜、国际卫星电视、无线网络、国际直拨电话和房内小酒吧。

我给每一位都准备了一份小小的纪念品，欢迎你们从芝加哥来到青岛。以此作为我们酒店与各位友谊的象征。希望你们在此住得愉快。

课文 B

SECTION Ⅰ: Dialogue 打电话给接待员 On the Phone with the Receptionist

Interpret the following dialogue from English into Chinese and vice versa.

A：Is that room service?

B：是的。请问您有什么需要？

A：I'd like to order a Continental Breakfast.

B：请说一下您的姓名和房间号码。

A：This is Jim Baker in room 1009.

B：好的，我们稍后送上来。您还需要其他服务吗？

A：Yes，could you send someone up for my laundry，please?

B：当然，我帮您接通洗衣部。他们会派人来拿衣服。

A：How long will it take to get them done?

B：通常是要两天的时间。不过您是要快洗服务还是当日取？

A：What is the difference in price?

B：快洗我们要多收 50%的费用，但是只需要 5 个小时。

A：And for same-day service，will I get the laundry back this evening?

B：是的，先生。晚上六点之前都会送到。

A：I'll have same-day service then.

B：好的，先生。

A：And just one more thing—how do I arrange for a wake-up service?

B：请稍等。我帮你转到总机处。

A：All right. But my Chinese is naught. I don't think I could understand the operator.

B：我能帮您什么吗？

A：I would like to have the wake-up call service for tomorrow morning. I will catch up the early plane at 6 am.

B：先生，你想几点被叫醒？我转告接线员好啦。

A：At 4∶30 am，please.

B：好的，先生。我们会明早四点半打电话叫醒您的。祝您愉快。

A：Thanks a lot.

SECTION Ⅱ：Warm-ups for Interpretation

➢ **Tongue twister.**

There is no need to light a night light on a light night like tonight. For a bright night light is just like a slight night.

像今夜这样明亮的夜晚，就不需要点一盏夜灯，因为明亮的夜灯也会变得微弱。

Mary Mac's mother's making Mary Mac marry me.

My mother's making me marry Mary Mac.
Will I always be so Merry when Mary's taking care of me?
Will I always be so merry when I marry Mary Mac?
玛丽·马克的母亲让玛丽·马克嫁给我。
我妈敦促我娶了玛丽·马克。
如果玛丽总是呵护我，我会总是一个开心果吗？
我娶了玛丽·马克后我能一直开心吗？

➢ **Interpret the following proverbs from English into Chinese.**

1. The game isn't worth the candle.
2. Look before you leap.
3. He can't see the forest for the tree.
4. He who keeps company with a wolf will learn to howl.
5. If you don't enter a tiger's den, you can't get his cubs.

➢ **Interpret the following sentences from English into Chinese.**

1. You can get your laundry back earlier, but there is an extra charge for quick service.
2. Could you send someone to pick up my laundry, please?
3. Your final bill has not reached our department yet, sir. Would you please wait a moment while I chase it down?
4. Please leave your key at the service desk when you leave.
5. Our check-out time is 12 noon. But you used the room until 6 pm. I'm afraid that for late check-outs we charge an extra 50% of the room rate.

➢ **Interpret the following paragraphs from English into Chinese and vice versa.**

1. Yes, it's expensive and not always good (or good for you), but when you're tired from a long day of meetings, the last thing you want to do is drive around town looking for something to eat. At the very least, you'll want the hotel to have some sort of mini-mart where you can pick up water, soda, and small bites to tide you over.
2. 无论是商务会议、观光旅游还是度假休闲，您都可以享受到饭店的综合娱乐设施，健身中心(国际标准恒温游泳池、健身房、跳操房、动感单车、瑜伽)、SPA、茶艺居、棋牌室、美容美发、豪华 KTV 俱乐部，还有与饭店相连的购物中心。高雅的购物环境，琳琅满目的商品，让您尽享休闲之旅。

SECTION Ⅲ: Speech

Interpret the following speech from Chinese into English.

首先我代表本店全体员工，欢迎大家来到青岛。

请允许我对本店的服务做些介绍。本宾馆为一流宾馆，是各国重要人士、政府官员以及商务人士的首选。

这里有400多间国际标准客房，宽敞通风。还有三间中式餐厅、一间豪华西式餐厅、大小宴会厅、酒吧、24小时咖啡厅及室内饮品店。

除此之外，还有美容沙龙、理发店、温泉洗浴、纪念品店等。每一楼层都有服务台供应香烟、青岛啤酒、喜力啤酒、朝日啤酒、百威啤酒以及可口可乐、雪碧、百事可乐、七喜、纯果乐、胡椒博士等各种饮料。

我在这里要提醒您，一天以上住房，12时以前离店，免收当日房费；12至18时离店，收当日房费50%；18时以后离店，照收当日房费。长期住房每半个月结算一次。

如果你们有任何需要，请告诉我们。希望大家在这里住得愉快。

SECTION Ⅳ: Speech

Interpret the following speech from English into Chinese.

Dear Guests,

You are welcome to our hotel. Your advice, suggestions and criticisms are always appreciated. I'd like to give you some information about our services in order to make your stay pleasant and comfortable.

In the lobby on the first floor, you will find our central service desk or Reception Desk, which deals with services, such as check-ins and check-outs, tickets booking for air and D-train and car rentals, calling taxi, and that kind of thing. There are umbrellas, rain boots and wind coats to lend.

The dining rooms are on the second floor. However, coffee room is on the first floor, where in addition to coffee, you may have famous wines and liquor, drinks and snacks.

The hotel also has a special food restaurant to the east of the compound where famous local dishes are prepared by top chefs. For banquet, reception, cocktail party, or birthday cake reservations, please contact the service desk of the dining hall.

To the south of the lobby, there is a store where foods, liquors, cigarettes are for sale. Next to it there is a painting shop where arts and crafts, paintings and scripts by noted artists could be bought. You may exchange money on the foreign exchange desk located in the lobby. In case of need, you may place an international call in the lobby, too.

The barber shop is on the third floor to the north. Please pay the charge at the service desk for a hair cut. Please put your laundry into a laundry bag in the room and hang it to door-knob near the corridor so that the floor service desk will collect it before 8:00 in the morning.

Thank you. Have a pleasant stay in our hotel.

参考译文

SECTION Ⅰ: Dialogue

A: 是客房服务吗?

B: Yes. What can I do for you?

A: 请送一份欧式早餐。

B: May I know your name and room number?

A: 吉姆·贝克,1009 房间。

B: OK, we'll bring it up right away. Anything else I can do for you?

A: 请问你们能派人来拿要洗的衣服吗?

B: Certainly, I'll put you through to the laundry service. They'll come and pick up your laundry.

A: 要多久可以洗好?

B: Usually it takes about two days to have the laundry done. But would you like express laundry service or same-day laundry service?

A: 价格有什么不同吗?

B: We charge 50% more for express laundry, but it only takes 5 hours.

A：如果当日取，今天晚上能取回衣服吗？

B：Yes，sir. All deliveries will be made before 6 pm.

A：那就当日取吧。

B：OK，sir.

A：还有一件事。我怎么安排电话叫醒服务呢？

B：One second，please. I am going to put you through to the operator.

A：好的。不过我不讲汉语，我担心我听不懂话务员说什么。

B：What can I do for you then?

A：我想明天早晨要叫醒服务。我要赶早上 6 点的飞机。

B：At what time do you want us to call you up，sir? I can inform the operator.

A：早晨四点半。

B：Alright，sir. The operator will call you up at 4：30 tomorrow morning. Have a nice day.

A：好，多谢您。

SECTION Ⅱ：Warm-ups for Interpretation

➢ **Interpret the following proverbs from Chinese into English.**

1. 得不偿失。
2. 三思而后行。
3. 只见树木，不见森林。
4. 近朱者赤，近墨者黑。
5. 不入虎穴，焉得虎子。

➢ **Interpret the following sentences from Chinese into English.**

1. 衣服可以早些送回，但您要付额外的加急费。
2. 您能派人来取一下我送洗的衣服吗？
3. 先生，您最后的账单还未送到，请您稍等一下，我将它调来。
4. 当您离开房间时，请将房间钥匙放在服务台。
5. 我们宾馆每天结账时间是中午 12 点，可是您下午 6 点才退房，对中午 12 点以后结账的客人我们需要额外收取 50％的房费。

➢ **Interpret the following paragraphs from Chinese into English and vice versa.**

1. 是的，客房服务很贵，并且不一定总是好的，但是在你开了一天冗长的会议后感到疲惫不堪时，你最不愿做的事情就是开着车到镇上找吃饭的地方。至少，你会希望酒店有小型超市让你可以买一些水、饮料、食品来填饱肚子。
2. No matter for business conferences, sightseeing, tourism or taking a holiday, here you can always enjoy the comprehensive entertainment equipment, including the Fitness Center (consisting of a gym, bikes, yoga, aerobics room and a swimming pool at internationally standardized temperature), the SPA, a tea house, a chess room, a hair salon and a luxury KTV club. The adjacent shopping center will also offer you elegant shopping environment and numerous items that maximize your fun in the journey.

SECTION Ⅲ: Speech

First, on behalf of the staff of our hotel, I would like to extend our warm welcome to you. Welcome to Qingdao.

Let me tell you something about our hotel services. Ours is a first-class hotel and it's the ideal hotel favored by many VIPs, governmental officials and business people from all over the globe.

There are over 400 standard rooms, all spacious and well-ventilated. It comprises three Chinese restaurants, a deluxe Western-style restaurant, large and small banquet halls, a bar, a 24-hour cafe and an indoor drinks patio.

A beauty salon, a barber shop, a SPA, a souvenir shop and etc are also available. There is a service desk on each floor where cigarettes, beer like Tsingtao, Heineken, Asahi and Budweiser. Coke, Sprite, Pepsi cola, 7Up, Tropicana, Doctor Pepper and all other types of beverages are also available.

There is one more thing I want to highlight you. If you leave before 12 : 00 in the morning, the charge of the room will be free on the day of your departure. If you leave after 12 : 00 but before 18 : 00, an extra half day's charge will be added to your bill. If you leave after 18 : 00, a full day's charge will be paid. For the long-term resident accounts are settled every fortnight.

If you have anything that we can do for you, please let us know. We wish you a very pleasant stay here.

SECTION Ⅳ: Speech

亲爱的宾客：

欢迎您下榻我们宾馆。我们随时欢迎您的建议、意见和批评，这对我们来说很重要。为使您在此住得舒适、愉快，特向您介绍我们宾馆的服务项目。

总服务台设在一楼大厅内，办理客房入住、离店结账、预定飞机票或动车车票、租车、叫出租汽车等各种代办服务项目。本宾馆还出租雨伞、雨鞋、大衣等物品。

餐厅设在二楼。咖啡厅设在一楼，供应咖啡、各类名酒、饮料和点心。餐厅还设有特别风味餐厅，位于中院东面，有名厨烹制各种地方名菜。如需预定宴会、招待会、酒会、生日蛋糕等，可直接与餐厅服务台联系。

大厅南面的商店出售各种食品、烟酒。商店旁有字画馆，专售各种工艺品和名人字画。外币兑换台、长途电话台都设在一楼大厅内。

理发店设在三楼北翼。请在服务台处付费。此外，需要换洗的衣服请放在洗衣袋里，并挂在门外的把手上，楼层服务台将在上午 8 时以前把衣服收走。

祝您生活愉快！谢谢！

Unit 4 交通 Transport

亲戚越走越近，朋友越走越亲。

Relatives and friends become closer with increasing visits to each other.

一花独放不是春，百花齐放春满园。

A single flower does not make a spring, but one hundred flowers in full blossom bring spring to a beautiful garden.

课文 A

SECTION Ⅰ: Dialogue　问路 Asking for Directions

Interpret the following dialogue from English into Chinese and vice versa.

A: Excuse me, which metro shall I take to get to the Pier?

B: 你可以先乘二号线，到五四广场换乘三号线。

A: Can you tell me when the next train goes to the May Fourth Square?

B: 大约两分钟后。

A: How long will it take to get there?

B: 大概五分钟。

A: Where is the entrance?

B: 从那边的闸机口进站，然后乘扶梯下去。你要先去售票处买票。2 元一张。

A: How can I tell for sure the train goes to the May Fourth Square?

B: 你可以依据"五四广场"的标识确认。

A：When I get there，how can I change to Line 3？

B：站内有明确的标识，你可以按箭头所指方向换乘。

A：Do I need another ticket to enter？

B：不用，票价中已经包括了。

A：I see. I really appreciate your kind help.

B：不用谢，欢迎你来中国。如果有什么问题你尽管询问周围的人。这座城市每个人都很友好。祝你在青岛一切顺利。

相关词汇

常用交通英语词汇

guide post 路标

milestone 里程碑

traffic lights 交通信号灯

carriageway 车道

single carriageway 单向车道

dual carriageway 双向车道

zebra crossing 斑马线

artery road 交通干线

auxiliary lane 辅助车道

designated bicycle lane/bike lane 自行车道

bus lane 公交车道

traffic jam 交通拥挤

double-deck bus 双层公共汽车

coach/bus 大客车

taxi/cab 出租汽车

trolleybus 无轨电车

tramcar/streetcar 电车；有轨电车

sky train/mono-train 轻轨列车

maglev（magnetically levitated train） 磁悬浮列车

D-train 动车

G-train 高铁

underground railway/subway/metro 地铁

railway/railroad 铁路

express train 特快列车

fast train 快车

booking office/ticket office 售票处

terminal/terminus 终点站

ferry 轮渡

tunnel 隧道

（passenger）liner 客轮

（ocean）liner 远洋班轮

yacht 游船

cabin 客舱

airliner 班机

economy class 普通舱，经济舱

first class 头等舱

flyover 立交桥

cable bridge 缆桥，索桥

SECTION Ⅱ: Warm-ups for Interpretation

➢ **Tongue twister.**

There was a fisherman named Fisher,
who fished for some fish in a fissure.
Till a fish with a grin,
pulled the fisherman in.
Now they're fishing the fissure for Fisher.
有个渔夫叫费希尔。
某天他在海沟里垂钓，
鱼儿朝着他咧着嘴笑，
反把他拉进了海里的裂缝。
现在人们忙着把费希尔拉出海里的裂纹。

➢ **Interpret the following proverbs from English into Chinese.**

1. Danger is next neighbor to security.
2. He robs Peter to pay Paul.
3. Diamonds cut diamonds.
4. Blood is thicker than water.
5. Easy come, easy go.

➢ **Interpret the following sentences from English into Chinese.**

1. I'd like to reserve an Economy Class seat to San Francisco on your Flight 903. Are there any seats available for tomorrow?
2. That's three hundred and fifty dollars altogether, sir. The flight number and boarding gate are indicated on your tickets.
3. It is said that the public transportation of American cities is not very desirable, is it?
4. When driving on expressways, the driver must control his or her speed within the range of the posted maximum and minimum speed limit.
5. Greyhound is the largest long distance coach company, which offers the monthly pass.

➤ **Interpret the following paragraphs from English into Chinese and vice versa.**

1. In the United States, riding bicycles has become increasingly popular. In the past, bicycles were sold to parents for their children. Now those same parents are buying bicycles for each other, as well as for their children. Young executives ride bikes to work to stay out traffic jams. Young mothers are finding a way to do their shopping without competing for a parking place at the shopping center. College and high school students find biking an economical alternative to cars and buses. And even grandma and grandpa enjoy bicycling to picnics and barbecues.
2. 正在建设之中的浦东国际机场位于长江入海口南岸的濒海地带，占地约 32 平方千米。浦东国际机场的最大设计容量是年旅客客运量 8000 万人次，货运量 500 万吨。机场全部建成后，绿化覆盖率将达到 50%以上。

SECTION Ⅲ: Speech

Interpret the following speech from Chinese into English.

女士们、先生们：

请允许我借此机会就青岛市近年来交通设施发展情况向大家简单做些介绍。

近年来，青岛的市政基础设施建设使游客们惊叹不已。跨越黄岛的世界级跨海大桥、海底隧道、地铁、城轨、环弯大道、市内高架道路、立交桥、通往全国各地的高速公路以及通往全国的动车和高铁等都为青岛增添了光彩。

高架交通网和颇有运载能力的地铁线路极大缓解了城市交通的拥挤状况。

例如，地铁二号线与地铁一号线交会于汇泉广场下，穿越海底，将繁华的市中心和西海岸经济开发区连接在一起，成为青岛黄岛之间最重要的交通轨道线，大大缓解了两岸间的交通压力。

城轨、地铁、跨海大桥以及海底隧道的成功运行标志着现代化的地下交通层、地面交通层和高架道路等三层立体交通网已颇具规模。

我们相信，青岛市的交通设施一定会越来越完善、便利，人们的生活一定会芝麻开花节节高。

SECTION Ⅳ: Speech

Interpret the following speech from English into Chinese.

Distinguished Chinese friends,

I'm really amazed at the speed of the development in your city, especially your infrastructure development. Many projects, traffic projects in particular, have been completed to help improve the quality of people's life.

For instance, the cross-sea bridge, the subsea tunnel and the construction of metros service as a great link of the east coast and the west coast of Qingdao, which facilitates the foreign investment. The newly-built bridges and the subsea tunnel spanning the Huiquan Bay carry more than 50 percent of the sea-crossing transport. I'm fully aware of the operation of these modern transportation facilities, marking the great establishment of a modern, tri-level transportation network of underground, ground level and elevated highway and roadway systems.

What impressed me most is the G-train from Qingdao to Beijing. It is certain that this is the first-class commercial rail line of its quickest type in the world. The D-train connecting Qingdao to Beijing, traveling at the top speed of 430 kilometers per hour costs only 2 hour and half to be there. That's extremely amazing! D-trains commuting to every corner of China are very much impressive, with a combination of the integrity of luxuries, great speed and comfort.

Qingdao is planning its one-hour urban transit system which connects Qingdao to the surrounding cities within one hour to establish a special economic zone. Different from maglev train in Shanghai, the urban transit links Qingdao with its satellite cities in the vicinity of Qingdao and other cities in Shandong Province such as Jiaozhou, Jimo, Laixi, Pingdu and other cities such as Yantai, Weihai, Longkou, Weifang, etc. You may get to any of these cities within one hour.

The recent opening of Qingdao Jiaodong International Airport is of the 4F-level international airport, the highest class of airport capable of handling a variety of large aircraft. The new airport makes Qingdao a comprehensive international transportation hub and a gateway for China's higher-level opening-up. The new gigantic airport will strengthen the role of Qingdao as a gateway to Japan and Korea. It will open four new routes linking

South Korea and five new routes linking Japan in the coming five years, and add more flights to existing destinations in the two countries such as Seoul, Busan, Jeju, Tokyo, Osaka and Sapporo. It is expected to annually handle nearly 3 million passengers to and from South Korea, and 1.7 million to and from Japan. Qingdao Jiaodong International Airport is one of the first batch of demonstration projects of the safe, green, smart and humanistic airport. The novel 4F-class airport can take off and land the largest types of civil aviation aircraft, such as Airbus 380 and Boeing 747, has made a qualitative leap in operation grade, service quality and comprehensive transportation system, showing its late-mover advantages.

The new airport serves as an international transfer hub, transferring flights from Southeast Asia to Japan and South Korea; from Southeast Asia to Europe and the United States; from central and western China to Japan and South Korea; from central and western China to Europe, the US and Australia and etc.

All the above-mentioned infrastructure development projects completed brings a speed revolution to the ground transportation in Qingdao. The smooth traffic has promoted the city's prosperity as well as the development of its local economy. The rapid development of Qingdao announces to the world that Qingdao has a bright prospect in the years to come.

参考译文

SECTION Ⅰ: Dialogue

A：你好，请问如果我要去栈桥，应该乘几号线？

B：You can first take Metro Line 2 to the May Fourth Square and then switch to Metro Line 3.

A：你能告诉我下一班开往五四广场方向的地铁什么时候来吗？

B：In about two minutes.

A：到那里需要多长时间呢？

B：About five minutes.

A：进站口在哪儿？

B：You can enter from the turnstile gate there, and then take the escalator down. But you need to buy the ticket first. Mind you, it will cost 2 *yuan*.

A：我怎样才能确定哪列车是开往五四广场方向的？

B：Just watch the sign indicating "May Fourth Square".

A：我到那里后怎么换乘 3 号线？

B：There are clear signs. You can find it by looking at the arrow signs pointing to the right direction.

A：我需要再买票吗？

B：No need. The ticket you bought has already covered all.

A：知道了，真心感谢你的帮助。

B：Pleasure is mine. Welcome to China! If you have other questions there, don't hesitate to ask anyone nearby. Everyone in this city is friendly. I wish you a good stay in Qingdao.

SECTION Ⅱ：Warm-ups for Interpretation

➢ **Interpret the following proverbs from Chinese into English.**

1. 安危是毗邻。
2. 拆东墙补西墙。
3. 棋逢对手，将遇良才。
4. 血浓于水。
5. 来得容易，去得快。

➢ **Interpret the following sentences from Chinese into English.**

1. 我要预订到旧金山的 903 航班，明天的经济舱有空位吗？
2. 总共要 350 美元，先生，班机号码和登机门可以从你的机票上查看。
3. 听说美国城市的公共交通不尽如人意，有没有这回事？
4. 当在高速公路开车时，司机必须将行车速度控制在标牌规定的最高限速和最低限速之间。
5. "灰狗"汽车公司是美国最大的长途汽车公司，有月票出售。

➤ **Interpret the following paragraphs from Chinese into English and vice versa.**

1. 在美国，骑自行车已变得越来越流行。过去，自行车是父母买给孩子的。今天，同样是这些父母，除了给孩子买以外，还给自己买自行车。年轻的管理者骑自行车上班以避免交通堵塞。年轻的母亲找到一条购物捷径，使她们不用在购物中心争停车位。大、中学生把自行车当作汽车和公交车的廉价代步工具。连祖母和祖父也高高兴兴地骑着自行车去野餐和烧烤。
2. Pudong International Airport, now under construction, is located on the south bank of the Yangtze (Changjiang) estuary, covering an area of 32 square kilometers. The maximum design capacity of the airport is 80 million passengers and 5 million tons of freight annually. After the completion of the whole airport project, green space will account for over 50% of the area.

SECTION Ⅲ: Speech

Ladies and Gentlemen,

Please allow me to introduce to you the recent development of transportation facilities in Qingdao.

In recent years, Qingdao shocked visitors in infrastructure projects. World-class sea-crossing bridges, undersea tunnels, metro lines, monorails, inner-city elevated express, elevated highways to other cities, flyovers and urban transit trains, etc., all bring more glory to Qingdao.

Major highway links and a massive subway system have greatly helped to ease traffic jams in the city.

For instance, Metro Line 2, which intersects with Metro Line 1 at the Huiquan Square and crosses the under-sea tunnel, links up the prosperous downtown area in Qingdao and Huangdao, new area of its west coast. It is considered the most important traffic artery which will greatly relieve the traffic congestion across the two banks.

The operation of monorails, metro lines, the sea-crossing bridges, and the under-sea tunnel marked the great establishment of a modern, tri-level transportation network of underground, ground level and elevated highway and roadway systems.

We firmly believe that Qingdao's transportation system will continue to develop, making people's lives more convenient and their living standards are getting better and better.

SECTION Ⅳ: Speech

尊敬的中国朋友们：

青岛的发展，尤其是基础设施的发展，让我极为惊叹。为了提高人们的生活质量，贵城市完成了许多工程项目，尤其是交通工程。

例如，连接青岛黄岛这两个东海岸和西海岸的跨海大桥、海底隧道以及地铁的建造为外商投资和运营提供了便利。新建的跨越汇泉湾的跨海大桥和海底隧道承担着50%的跨海运输任务。我注意到以上这些现代化交通设施的运营标志着地下、地面、高架结合的交通体系现已形成。

给我印象最深的莫过于青岛开往北京的高铁。可以说它是世界上一流的商用高速列车。连接青岛北京的高铁最高时速430千米，不到三个小时便可到达北京，真是棒极啦！我对通往中国各地的动车也是印象深刻，这些动车集速度惊人、建设豪华、舒适性极强等优点为一体。

青岛正规划建设城市轨道系统，把周边的城市全部衔接起来，打造一小时经济圈。不同于上海的磁悬浮列车，这些轨道铁路系统把山东省，尤其是青岛周边的卫星城市如胶州、即墨、莱西、平度以及烟台、威海、龙口、潍坊等地连接起来，一小时内都能到达目的地。

最近启用的4F级的青岛胶东国际机场是能够处理各种大型飞机的最高级别机场。它使青岛成为综合性国际交通枢纽和更高水平开放的门户枢纽，起到了加强青岛作为通往日本和韩国的门户枢纽作用。胶东国际机场将在未来五年内开通四条连接韩国的新航线和五条连接日本的新航线，并增加更多飞往首尔、釜山、济州、东京、大阪和札幌等两国现有目的地的航班。预计每年将处理往返韩国的近300万乘客，以及往返日本的170万乘客。

新机场作为国际中转枢纽，可以中转从东南亚到日本和韩国；从东南亚到欧美，从中国中西部到日本和韩国以及从中国中西部到欧洲、美国和澳大利亚等国家的航班。

以上提到的这些基础设施开发项目给青岛的地面交通带来了一场速度革命。顺畅便捷的交通不仅促进了城市的繁荣，也推动了城市的发展。青岛的飞速发展向世界宣告青岛的未来充满光明和希望。

课文 B

SECTION Ⅰ: Dialogue 租车 Rent a Car

Interpret the following dialogue from English into Chinese and vice versa.

A：Do you have any car rentals here in Qingdao? I'd like to rent a car tomorrow for a couple of days.

B：可以。没问题。

A：How about the fees?

B：哪种车？

A：Any small American compact. Two-door is preferable.

B：每天大概要 300 元，大约为 50 美元，不限里程；汽油费用一般由顾客负担。取车时帮你灌满油箱，还车时你也得加满油。

A：Is there a weekly rate?

B：也许会有。这取决于不同的租赁公司。

A：Then I can pick up the car?

B：还需要有驾驶执照。

A：I have an international driver's license.

B：那应该可以，另外需要交些保证金。你也可以选择是否要买保险。

A：I see. Are there any other formalities?

B：我突然想起来，也许要你的护照。

A：Thanks a lot.

B：不用谢。

SECTION Ⅱ: Warm-ups for Interpretation

➢ **Tongue twister.**

How much wood would a woodchuck chuck,
If a woodchuck could chuck wood?

He would chuck, he would, as much as he could,
And chuck as much wood as a woodchuck would,
If a woodchuck could chuck wood.
如果土拨鼠能伐木的话，
土拨鼠能伐多少木头？
如果土拨鼠可以伐木头，
它能伐多少就伐多少吧。

➢ **Interpret the following proverbs from Chinese into English.**

1. 公事公办。
2. 人人都有缺点。
3. 我们有天壤之别。
4. 岁月不等人。
5. 一个巴掌拍不响。

➢ **Interpret the following sentences from Chinese into English.**

1. 我很遗憾，你必须至少提前 14 天预定机票，才能减 30％的票价。
2. 这个国家没有统一的飞机票价，各家航空公司常常通过竞相降价吸引更多的旅客。
3. 事实上，较为方便的做法是按电话簿中黄页部分所列的出租车公司的号码打电话叫车，让他们派车上门来接你。
4. 据说美国是一个由汽车驱动的国家，美国实际上是一个生活在轮子上的民族。
5. 一些相距不远的大城市之间，也有穿梭于两地之间的航班。

➢ **Interpret the following paragraphs from Chinese into English and vice versa.**

1. 昨天上午 10 点在高速公路上，一辆卡车翻了车。卡车上的电子产品散落在路上。司机受了伤，被送进医院。事故使交通大大拥挤，用了两小时才清理好路面。据后续报道司机两条腿都断了。
2. There are about 3.4 billion rides on New York City subways and buses every year. That is about one-third of all mass transit trips in the United States. New York's mass transit system operates 24 hours a day, seven days a week. Many people believe public transit is less costly than car use and is good for the environment. New York City is planning several major expansions of its public transportation system.

One project is a new ＄4.7 billion subway line.

SECTION Ⅲ: Speech

Interpret the following speech from Chinese into English.

女士们、先生们：

下面，我向大家介绍一下青岛胶州湾跨海大桥。青岛胶州湾跨海大桥（又叫青岛海湾大桥）位于中国山东省青岛市，为跨越胶州湾、衔接青兰高速公路的一座公路跨海大桥，全长41.58千米，是世界上已建成的最长的跨海大桥，比前任“冠军”杭州湾跨海大桥长了5.58千米。工程总投资100多亿元，连接青岛、黄岛、红岛“三极”，后期计划增建胶州联络线。

大桥主桥设双向8车道，连接线东起青岛东部城区海尔路，越过胶州湾，西至黄岛红石崖，主桥中部建设互通立交桥与红岛相连，青岛、黄岛和红岛由此实现“品”形连接。大桥的海上钻孔灌注桩数量为5127根，居世界第一。大桥的红岛立交桥是中国首座海上互通立交桥。

此前，青岛东西海岸被胶州湾天然隔断，轮渡常因大风和大雾停航；陆路需绕行高速公路，行车需1.5小时且经常拥堵。此大桥建成通车后，将使东西两岸路程缩短约30千米。胶州湾隧道则使两地互通只需10分钟左右。

大桥于2007年5月动工，总投资148亿元，由山东高速集团投资、建设、经营、管理。建设大桥共动用了万余名工人，使用了45万吨钢铁和230万立方米的混凝土。2010年12月22日实现主线合龙贯通，2011年6月30日建成通车，同时中国最长的海底隧道——全长9.47千米的青岛胶州湾隧道也于当日建成通车。由此，青岛至黄岛陆路距离缩短了近30千米，车程缩短至10余分钟。

总之，我想说，这里交通相当便利。青岛无疑是投资和旅行的理想之地。

SECTION Ⅳ: Speech

Interpret the following speech from English into Chinese.

Dear friends,

Now let me spend a bit time to introduce to you Qingdao Jiaozhou Bay Tunnel.

Qingdao Jiaozhou Bay Tunnel is an undersea road tunnel located in Shandong Province in eastern China. It crosses underneath Jiaozhou Bay, connecting Huangdao to the south with the city of Qingdao in the north at the narrow entrance to the bay. It starts at Tuandao Road in the north and ends between Beizhuang village and Houchawan village on Xuejia Island in the south.

Construction began on December 27, 2006 and was completed five years later when it opened on June 30, 2011, two months after the scheduled opening date. It opened the same day as the nearby Jiaozhou Bay Cross-sea Bridge, considered at the time the world's longest open water bridge by Guinness World Records. The bridge and tunnel were planned together as the Jiaozhou Bay Connection Project.

The length of the tunnel road is 7.8 km. The tunnel travels underground for 5.55 km with a subsea portion of 3.95 km. There are two tubes of 3-lanes each for a total of 6-lanes. It is the milestone of Qingdao's urban construction, marking the rapid development of its transportation and its national economy.

Please enjoy the magnificent structure of the Qingdao Jiaozhou Bay Tunnel.

参考译文

SECTION Ⅰ: Dialogue

A：你们青岛有汽车租赁公司吗？明天我想租辆车用。

B：Sure. No problem.

A：费用情况如何呢？

B：What kind of car do you want to rent?

A：任何小型的美国车，最好是双门的。

B：It charges 300 *yuan* per day, about \$50. There's no limited mileage. Generally, the customer buys the gas. You pick up the car with the full gas and the customer fills the gas full when returning it.

A：有没有周价优惠？

B：I'm not quite certain. It depends on different car-rental companies.

A：然后我就可以取车了吗？

B：You need to produce your driving license.

A：我有国际驾照。

B：That will do. You may need to pay a deposit. You can also choose whether to purchase a kind of insurance.

A：我知道了。还需要其他手续吗？

B：It just comes to me that maybe need your passport.

A：非常感谢。

B：You're welcome.

SECTION Ⅱ: Warm-ups for Interpretation

➢ **Interpret the following proverbs from English into Chinese.**

1. Business is business.
2. He is lifeless that is faultless.
3. We are as different as night and day.
4. Time and tide wait for no man.
5. It takes two to tango.

➢ **Interpret the following sentences from English into Chinese.**

1. I'm sorry, you must book your flight at least 14 days in advance to get a 30% discount.
2. Airfare in this country is not regulated, and airlines often make special offers in order to attract customers.
3. It's actually easier to call a taxi company listed in the Yellow Pages of a telephone directory and ask them to send a cab to pick you up at your doorstep.
4. It is said that the United States is a country driven by automobiles, and Americans are actually a people living on wheels.
5. There are also shuttle and commuter flights between some major cities that are close to each other.

➢ **Interpret the following paragraphs from English into Chinese and vice versa.**

1. Yesterday at 10 o'clock in the morning on the Highway, a lorry overturned. The

electronic goods in the lorry spilled onto the road. The driver was injured and was taken to hospital. The accident caused a big traffic jam and it was two hours before the road was finally cleared. It was later reported that the driver had broken both legs.

2. 每年大约有 34 亿人乘坐纽约的地铁和巴士，大约占美国所有使用公共交通出行人数的三分之一。纽约的公共交通每周运行 7 天，每天运行 24 小时。很多人认为公共交通比汽车使用成本更低，并且有益于环境保护。纽约正在筹划几个项目来对其公共交通系统进行扩张。其中一个项目是修建一条新的地铁线路，该项目耗资 47 亿美元。

SECTION Ⅲ: Speech

Ladies and Gentlemen,

Now, I would like to introduce to you the Jiaozhou Bay Cross-sea Bridge. Jiaozhou Bay Cross-sea Bridge (also called the Qingdao Haiwan Bridge) in Qingdao spans Jiaozhou Bay and links the Qingdao-Lanzhou highway. It has been officially named the world's longest bridge across water, measuring 41.58 km (26.4 mile) long, 5.58 km (3.5 mile) longer than the previous record holder Hangzhou Bay Bridge. The bridge costs more than 10 billion *yuan* ($1.5 billion) to build and it links Qingdao, Huangdao Island and Hongdao Island. The Jiaozhou linking-up roads have also been completed.

The bridge starting from Haier Road in the downtown of Qingdao in the east, transects Jiaozhou Bay and ends at Red Cliff town of Huangdao Island in the west. The main span of the bridge has an 8-lane dual carriageway. A branch to Hongdao Island is connected by a semi-directional "T" interchange to the middle part of the main span. Qingdao, Huangdao Island and Hongdao Island are linked by the bridge in the shape of Chinese character "品" or letter "T". It is supported by 5,127 concrete pillars, the most solid and strongest in the world. And Hongdao Interchange is China's first interchange across the sea.

Before the completion of the bridge, Qingdao east coast and west coast were separated by Jiaozhou Bay. Ferry services were often disrupted by thick fog or gales. Travelling on land had to make a detour to the highway with one and a half hours driving and constant traffic jams. Now the Jiaozhou Bay Cross-sea Bridge will cut the travel distance by

30km. Furthermore, the Qingdao Jiaozhou Bay Tunnel will reduce the travel time between Qingdao east coast and west coast to only about 10 minutes.

The construction started in May, 2007, with a total investment of 14.8 billion *yuan* ($2.4 billion). It was invested, constructed, operated and supervised by the Shandong Expressway Group. It employed at least 10,000 people to build and nearly 450,000 tons of steel was used in its construction along with 2.3 million cubic meters of concrete. Its main span was completed on December 22, 2010 and it opened on June 30, 2011 for traffic. It opened the same day as China's longest undersea tunnel, the 9.47 km long Qingdao Jiaozhou Bay Tunnel. And since then, travel distance is cut by 30 km and driving from Qingdao to Huangdao Island only takes about 10mins.

All in all, I would like to say that a wide range of transport options are accessible here and Qingdao is undoubtedly an ideal destination for investors and tourists.

SECTION Ⅳ: Speech

亲爱的朋友们：

下面，我简短地向大家介绍一下“青岛胶州湾隧道”。

“青岛胶州湾隧道”位于中国东部的山东省，是一条公路海底隧道，从海底穿越胶州湾，北起团岛路，南止于薛家岛的北庄村和后岔湾村之间，使黄岛和青岛在胶州湾狭窄的入口处南北相接。

隧道于2006年12月27日动工，历时5年，于2011年6月30日建成通车。同时，作为当时世界上最长的跨海大桥而被载入“吉尼斯世界纪录”的“青岛胶州湾跨海大桥”也于当日建成通车。“青岛胶州湾隧道”和“青岛胶州湾跨海大桥”都是“胶州湾连接线工程”的计划项目。

隧道分为两条主隧道、双向6车道。线路全长7.8千米，其中地下隧道部分长5.55千米，穿越海底段长3.95千米。“青岛胶州湾隧道”是青岛城市建设的里程碑，大大加快了青岛的交通和经济发展。

下面就请大家一起欣赏雄伟壮观的“青岛胶州湾隧道”。

Unit 5 宴会招待 At the Banquet

制止餐饮浪费是一项长期任务，要坚持不懈抓下去。

Curbing food waste is a long-term task that requires unremitting efforts.

浪费之风务必狠刹！

Food waste must be stopped.

要加强立法，强化监管，采取有效措施，建立长效机制，坚决制止餐饮浪费行为。

We need to take effective measures and establish long-term mechanisms to curb the wasting of food by strengthening legislation and supervision.

课文 A

SECTION Ⅰ: Dialogue 宴请宾客 At the Banquet

Interpret the following dialogue from Chinese into English and vice versa.

A：女士们，先生们，请随便坐。我们今晚准备了中国式的酒菜，希望各位喜欢。

B：That sounds delicious.

A：我想大家都彼此熟悉，就不必再做介绍了。

B：It's wonderful to meet so many friends here.

A：这是中国式的凉菜，请大家随便用。

B：Please don't worry about us. We won't miss anything delicious.

A：请尝一下这个烤鸡，这是我们当地的特产。我们叫它香酥鸡。

B：Yeah. Its skin is crisp and its meat is very tender. It's good.

A： 中国式的烹调丰富多彩。

B： That makes it perfectly wonderful in appearance，smell and taste.

A： 请多吃点鱼。

B： The dinner was so delicious.

A： 各位能够赏光到此，我感到非常荣幸。让我们举杯敬祝贝克先生和夫人健康。

B： Thank you very much. I also propose a toast for our friendship between America and China and our joint collaboration.

A： 各位干杯！

B： Cheers！

相关词汇

常用餐饮英语

dim sum 点心
wonton 馄饨
moo goo gai 蘑菇炖鸡
kungpao chicken 宫保鸡丁
beef chow mein 牛肉炒面
lobster 龙虾
prawn 对虾
shrimp 小虾
mantis shrimp 虾虎
clam 蛤蜊
scallop 扇贝
oyster 牡蛎
octopus 章鱼
abalone 鲍鱼
sea cucumber 海参
crab 螃蟹
jellyfish 海蜇
inkfish 墨鱼
catfish 鲶鱼
belt fish 带鱼
croaker 黄花鱼
skate 鳐鱼
halibut 比目鱼
carp 鲤鱼
codfish 鳕鱼
salmon 三文鱼
mackerel 鲅鱼
sweet and sour pork/fish/shrimp 糖醋里脊/鱼/虾
kimchi 韩国泡菜
sashimi 生鱼片
wasabi 芥末酱
sushi 寿司
teppanyaki 铁板烧
steaming 清蒸
deep frying 油炸

braising 红烧
stewing 炖
smoking 熏
stir-fried pork shreds with chili sauce 鱼香肉丝
egg roll 春卷
hotpot 火锅
spaghetti 意大利面
macaroni 空心面
vermicelli 米线；粉条
tofu 豆腐
kebab 烤肉串
kebab squid 烤鱿鱼
pork slices in brown sauce 回锅肉
fried pork chop 炸猪排
roast Beijing duck 北京烤鸭
stir-fried mixed vegetables/chop suey 什锦炒蔬
hot and spicy soup 酸辣汤
staple food 主食
steamed bread 馒头
steamed rice 米饭
egg fried rice 蛋炒饭
cold noodle 冷面
fried glutinous vermicelli 炒米粉
noodles with fried brown sauce 炸酱面
pot-sticker 锅贴
steamed twisted roll 花卷
doggybag 打包
leftover 剩菜

SECTION Ⅱ: Warm-ups for Interpretation

➢ **Tongue twister.**

A silly sheep weep and sleep.

一只傻羊哭着睡着了。

Of all the felt I ever felt, I never felt a piece of felt which felt as fine as that felt felt, when first I felt that felt hat's felt.

在我所触摸过的毡子中，我从未触摸过一块如此舒适的毡子，直至我摸过这顶毡帽。

➢ **Interpret the following proverbs from English into Chinese.**

1. A thousand toasts are not enough among bosom friends.
2. A new broom sweeps clean.
3. Never too old to learn.
4. Seeing is believing.
5. One for all, all for one.

➢ **Interpret the following sentences from English into Chinese.**

1. I'd like to thank you for your presence at the party, and wish everyone good health and the very best of luck in everything in days to come.
2. I hope this party will give us an opportunity to get to know each other better in a less formal way and to increase personal friendships.
3. The party was perfectly organized and I enjoyed every minute of it. And I am very grateful for this nice arrangement.
4. Maotai is China's best-known liquor, it is delicious and yet doesn't go to the head.
5. Dim Sum, wonton, moo goo gai, kungpao chicken, beef chow mein and egg roll are very popular in the States.

➢ **Interpret the following paragraphs from English into Chinese and vice versa.**

1. These visits are clear signals of the highly productive relationship which Wales and China have developed. Judging by the crowd that have gathered here tonight, I am very confident that the relationship will continue to grow. Thank you for taking the time to include a visit to Wales in your busy and demanding program. We are honored by your presence here this evening and would ask you to take back with you the warmest good wishes from the people of Wales and the United Kingdom. May I now propose a toast.
2. 我谨代表所有的美国客人向你们表示感谢，感谢你们无与伦比的盛情款待。我既要感谢那些准备了这次盛大晚宴的人，还要感谢那些带来绝好音乐的演奏家。我在国外从来没有听过美国音乐被演奏得如此之美妙。

SECTION Ⅲ: Speech

Interpret the following speech from Chinese into English.

女士们、先生们：

首先，请允许我向全体来宾表示热烈欢迎。

中美两国的贸易关系，比任何时期都好。我们这次展览会，正是在这个时候举行的，我们两国之间的贸易往来，已有大幅度的增加。

在 2014 年，我们热情地接待了许多来自美国的重要贸易代表。另一方面，我国商务人士也不断到贵国访问。

此次展览会的目的是加强这些方面的交流。它将为中国人民——特别是各个政府部门、国营企业、贸易公司、专家和科学工作者展现美国工业的整体成就。

我非常珍视中美两国在贸易合作中发展建立起来的友谊和信心。我确信，这次展览会将进一步加强我们两国的关系，并对扩大两国间的互利贸易做出贡献。

今天，我们在这举办宴会，款待各位朋友，旨在创造契机增进中美双方商务人士之间的了解和交流。让我们举杯，祝愿本次展会圆满成功！干杯！

SECTION Ⅳ: Speech

Interpret the following speech from English into Chinese.

Good evening, ladies and gentlemen,

First of all, I would like to thank all of the guests present here for your coming. Now I am honored to declare the beginning of the celebration ceremony of the Canadian-Chinese Trade Fair.

Let me briefly sum up the trade fair. The fair has lasted for a week. It has achieved great success. More than 80 contracts have been signed with about 60 representative companies from China. The total value will be over 9 billion USD.

Some are still making their best efforts to look for the possibilities of establishing joint ventures. Everything went on in a friendly and lively atmosphere. We greatly thank all the guests for your successful cooperation.

As we know, China is one of the developing countries. Great changes have taken place in the country with the opening-up of the government. The investment environment has improved greatly. More and more overseas enterprises have taken the opportunity to enter into joint ventures with yours. We will also try every way possible to cooperate with you.

Ladies and gentlemen, you have my best wishes for your still greater achievements in your career and excellent cooperation between us. Welcome to Canada again.

Now, let's celebrate the great success of this fair and may the friendship between our two countries last forever! Cheers!

参考译文

SECTION Ⅰ: Dialogue

A: Please be seated, ladies and gentlemen, and make yourselves comfortable. We have prepared a Chinese meal for you this evening. I hope you will all like it.

B: 一听就好吃。

A: I think you have been very familiar to each other, so there is no need for me to make any introduction.

B: 在此见到这么多朋友，真是好极了。

A: Here are some Chinese appetizers. Please help yourselves and choose what you like.

B: 请别客气。好吃的东西我们不会错过的。

A: Why don't you try this local toast chicken? It's a specialty here. We call it *xiangsu chicken*.

B: 好的。它的皮脆而肉嫩。很好吃。

A: Chinese cooking has a charming variety.

B: 色、香、味都非常好。

A: Please help yourselves to some more fish.

B: 今天饭菜很好吃。

A: It's a great honor to have you all here. Let us drink to the health of Mr. and Mrs. Baker.

B: 十分感谢各位。我也提议为我们中美友谊和我们的合作干杯!

A: Everybody! Cheers!

B: 干杯!

SECTION Ⅱ: Warm-ups for Interpretation

➢ **Interpret the following proverbs from Chinese into English.**

1. 酒逢知己千杯少。
2. 新官上任三把火。

3. 学无止境；活到老学到老。
4. 眼见为实。
5. 我为人人，人人为我。

➢ **Interpret the following sentences from Chinese into English.**

1. 感谢各位嘉宾的光临，并祝各位在未来的日子里身体健康、万事如意。
2. 希望在这次晚会上，我们可以无所拘束地了解彼此，增进相互之间的友谊。
3. 晚会组织得完美无缺，令人尽兴尽致。对这次美好的安排，我感激不尽。
4. 茅台是我国最负盛名的烈酒，上口不上脑。
5. 茶点、馄饨、小鸡炖蘑菇、宫保鸡丁、牛肉炒面和春卷在美国都很受欢迎。

➢ **Interpret the following paragraphs from Chinese into English and vice versa.**

1. 这些访问清楚地显示，威尔士和中国之间已经发展出很有成果的关系。根据今晚在场的人数来看，我很有信心，这一关系将继续发展下去。感谢你们从紧张的日程中抽出时间访问威尔士。今晚有你们在场，我们感到很荣幸。我请你们把威尔士人民以及全英国人民的热情问候带回中国。请允许我祝酒。
2. On behalf of all your American guests, I wish to thank you for the incomparable hospitality. I particularly want to pay tribute, not only to those who prepared the magnificent dinner, but also to those who have provided the splendid music. Never have I heard American music played better in a foreign land.

SECTION Ⅲ: Speech

Ladies and Gentlemen,

First, please allow me to extend warm welcome to all of the distinguished guests.

The trade relations between the United States and China have never been better. The exhibition was staged at this time. There has already been a steep increase in the level of our commercial exchanges.

In 2014, we were pleased to welcome many important business delegates from America, while many Chinese businessmen also went to your country.

The aim of the Exhibition is to build and strengthen these exchanges. It brings to the Chinese people and in particular to the ministries, state enterprises, trade corporations, specialists and scientists a comprehensive display of American industrial achievements.

I greatly value the friendship and confidence that were established and developed in Sino-US trade cooperation. I'm certain the Exhibition will strengthen our relationship and help further trade expansion to the benefit of both our countries.

Today, we hold the banquet here to entertain our dear friends. Our aim is to create an opportunity for the businessmen of the two sides to improve mutual understanding and exchanges. Let me propose a toast, and wish the exhibition a complete success! Cheers!

SECTION Ⅳ: Speech

晚上好，女士们、先生们：

感谢各位今晚大驾光临。现在，我荣幸地宣布，国际贸易展览会的庆祝仪式正式开始。

首先，请允许我对展会情况做个总结。这次展会持续一周，获得了极大的成功。我国企业与贵国的 60 多家代表公司签定了 80 多份合同。总额达 90 亿美元之多。

一些公司仍在努力寻求建立合资企业的可能性。本次展览会在友好活跃的氛围中展开。我们衷心感谢各位与会嘉宾的精诚合作。

众所周知，中国是发展中国家之一。在政府的开放政策下，国家发生了翻天覆地的变化，投资环境大大改善。越来越多的海外企业愿意借机和你们建立合资企业。我们会尝试用各种方式与你们合作。

女士们、先生们，我最衷心地祝福你们，希望你们在工作上取得更大的成就，希望我们之间可以进行卓越的合作。欢迎再来加拿大。

现在，让我们庆祝本次展会的圆满结束，并祝我们两国友谊长存。干杯！

课文 B

SECTION Ⅰ: Dialogue 在宴会上 At the Banquet

Interpret the following dialogue from English into Chinese and vice versa.

A：What's the dish? They look so cute.

B：这是小笼包，是正宗的上海小吃。蘸着香醋吃，别有风味。

A: Let me have a try. Would you please pass me the vinegar?

B: 给你。

A: Thank you. We have a good appetite. The cooking is excellent.

B: 谢谢。请再多吃点宫保鸡丁。

A: Yes, I will. This is my favorite. Actually I love both Kungpao chicken and sweet and sour pork. They are very popular in the States.

B: 再来点广东点心怎么样?

A: I've had enough. Thank you so much.

B: 你爱吃真是太好了!

A: Oh, Peter, I'm afraid it's rather late. We have to go back to hotel to do some packing for tomorrow's flight. Thank you for your hospitality.

B: 好的，要不要再吃点主食?

A: Oh, no more. We are fine. Thanks for the nice dinner. Everything is fine.

B: 没什么。我很高兴你喜欢今天的饭菜。

A: Because Chinese cuisine is the best.

B: 谢谢。祝你在青岛一切顺利。

A: Thank you. Good evening.

B: 再见。

SECTION Ⅱ: Warm-ups for Interpretation

➢ **Tongue twister.**

A pleasant peasant keeps a pleasant pheasant and both the peasant and the pheasant are having a pleasant time together.

一位和气的农民养了一只伶俐的野鸡，并且这位和气的农民和这只伶俐的野鸡在一起度过了一段美好的时光。

➢ **Interpret the following proverbs from Chinese into English.**

1. 男孩子就是男孩子。
2. 条条大道通罗马。
3. 熟能生巧。

4. 祸不单行，福无双至。
5. 有其父必有其子。

➢ **Interpret the following sentences from Chinese into English.**

1. 让我们在成功合作的第二个年头结束之际，共同举杯，祝贺这喜庆的时刻。
2. 回顾过去，展望未来，我认为一个新的伙伴关系必须建立在相互尊重和平等互利的基础上。
3. 今晚在座的各位嘉宾都证明了我们两家公司关系的活力，我们合作之广泛给人以深刻的印象。
4. 请允许我邀请各位与我一起举杯，为我们两市的友谊与合作干杯！
5. 龙虾、对虾、蛤蜊、扇贝、牡蛎、章鱼、鲍鱼、螃蟹、海螺、海参是青岛附近最受欢迎的海产品。其实水母、墨鱼、鲅鱼、带鱼、黄花鱼、鳐鱼、比目鱼也是当地的特产。

➢ **Interpret the following paragraphs from Chinese into English and vice versa.**

1. 山东菜的特色是：清香、鲜嫩、味纯；江苏菜选料严格，制作精细，讲究造型，酥烂可口；四川菜以麻辣、味厚著称，调味品众多；湖南菜口味重酸辣、鲜香、软嫩；广东菜用料广泛，菜的特点多以清淡、生脆、爽口、偏甜为主。
2. It is my privilege and great pleasure to host this banquet in honor of Vice President and Mrs. Williams and other distinguished guests. I would like to avail myself of this opportunity to extend my warm welcome to you all. A remark in *The Analects of Confucius* can best express what I feel now, "It is such a delight to have friends coming from afar!"

SECTION Ⅲ: Speech

Interpret the following speech from Chinese into English.

晚上好！借着今晚的海风，我们相聚在海景花园。我谨代表青岛市人民政府和人民，对各位的光临表示热烈欢迎。

我愿借此机会，向你们，向所有关心和支持青岛发展的朋友们，表示诚挚的谢意和良好的祝愿！

中国加入世贸组织，标志着对外开放进入一个崭新的阶段，我们正在更大范围内、更广领域和更高层次上参与国际竞争。

青岛，作为山东省的龙头，已经率先感受到前所未有的发展机遇和严峻挑战。

青岛人民正聚精会神地全面建设小康社会，加快实现现代化，这将为所有朋友创造更多的发展机会和空间。

让我们举杯，为这次国际咨询会议的圆满成功，为我们的真诚合作，为在座各位的事业辉煌、身体健康、家庭幸福，干杯！

SECTION Ⅳ: Speech

Interpret the following speech from English into Chinese.

Dear Chinese friends, my colleagues and I are so glad to gather with you here. Thank you for your invitation and hospitality.

The consultants and guests here consist of high-level leaders of the international companies, the famous economists, the accomplished experts and scholars. I'm so glad to share my opinions with you. And I deeply felt the sincere cooperation spirit and pragmatic attitude.

We should give a full play of our cooperation spirit and collective wisdom, which will not only benefit the planning and promoting of the development of Qingdao, but also be conducive to our mutual cooperation and development in all the fields.

I was looking forward to this consultant meeting for long, to provide my suggestions as regard to Qingdao's development. We gather here for the same objective: to strengthen the cooperation and exchanges, and to enlarge the development scope.

It is known to all that in the environment of economic globalization, we have to seize the novel opportunities, meet new challenges, and spare no efforts to create a new phase of economic cooperation, and hence to achieve the advantages of economic compensation, mutual benefits, long-term cooperation and mutual development.

I hope today's discussion will promote the economic and social development of Qingdao, and create opportunities for international business development. Qingdao's economy, full of vigor and bright prospect, is striding forward with the driving stance. Let us hold hands together, work for the modernization of Qingdao and our mutual prosperity! Cheers!

参考译文

SECTION Ⅰ: Dialogue

A：这道是什么点心？看上去好可爱。

B：This is *xiaolongbao*, an indigenous Shanghai dish. It tastes better when it is dipped in vinegar.

A：让我尝尝，麻烦您能不能把醋递给我？

B：OK.

A：谢谢。今晚胃口很好。这儿的厨艺真不错。

B：Thank you. Please eat some more kungpao chicken.

A：好的，这是我的最爱。实际上，宫保鸡丁和糖醋里脊是我最喜欢吃的，这两道菜在美国很火。

B：How about some more dim sum?

A：我已经吃了很多了，谢谢。

B：I'm so glad that you like it.

A：噢，彼得，恐怕太晚了。我们现在要赶回宾馆收拾一下行李，明天还得赶航班。谢谢你的盛情款待。

B：OK. But would you like some staple food?

A：不吃了，我们吃饱了。所有的菜都很好吃。谢谢您安排的丰盛晚餐。

B：You're welcome. I'm glad that you like the dishes.

A：因为中国的烹饪水平世界最好。

B：Thank you. Wish you all of the best in Qingdao!

A：谢谢，晚安。

B：Goodbye.

SECTION Ⅱ: Warm-ups for Interpretation

➢ **Interpret the following proverbs from English into Chinese.**

1. Boys will be boys.

2. All roads lead to Rome. /There are many roads to success.
3. Practice makes perfect.
4. When it rains, it (always) pours.
5. Like father, like son. Like mother, like daughter.

➢ **Interpret the following sentences from English into Chinese.**

1. I would like to toast with you to this happy moment at the close of the second year of our wonderful cooperation.
2. When we look back on the past experiences and into the future, I believe that a new partnership should be constructed on the basis of mutual respect, equality and mutual benefit.
3. All the guests here tonight prove the vitality of the relations of our two companies. The range of those relations is impressive.
4. May I ask you to join me in a toast to the friendship and cooperation between our two cities.
5. Lobsters, prawns, clams, scallops, oysters, octopus, abalones, crabs, conch, sea cucumbers are the most favorite sea food in the vicinity of Qingdao. Actually, jelly fish, inkfish, mackerel, belt fish, croakers, skates, halibut are also the local specialties.

➢ **Interpret the following paragraphs from English into Chinese and vice versa.**

1. The dishes of Shandong cuisine feature delicate fragrance, freshness and pure flavor; Jiangsu cuisine is particular with materials and meticulous makings; Sichuan cuisine is well-known for its spicy, hot dishes with a wide range of flavorings; Hunan dishes are characterized by hot and soft taste; Cantonese cuisine emphasizes varieties of materials, and light, crisp and sweet taste.
2. 我为能在此设宴招待威廉姆斯副总统和夫人以及其他贵宾而深感荣幸和愉快。我愿借此机会向各位来宾表示热烈的欢迎。我此时的心情可以用孔子在《论语》中的一句话来表达:“有朋自远方来,不亦乐乎。”

SECTION Ⅲ: Speech

Good evening. With the cool ocean breeze, tonight we're gathering here at the Sea

View Garden. On behalf of Qingdao Municipal Government and its people, I would like to extend a warm welcome to you.

I would also like to take this opportunity, extend my heartfelt gratitude and good wishes to you and those who have been caring and supporting the development of Qingdao.

China's accession to the WTO symbolized a new stage of the opening-up effort. We are taking part in the international competitions on a larger scale, in a wider field, and at a higher level.

Qingdao, as the leader of Shandong Province, has already been aware of the unprecedented developing opportunities and challenges.

People in Qingdao are concentrating on building up a well-off society in an all-around way and accelerating the pace of realizing the modernization program, which will bring more opportunities for all of our friends.

Let us propose a toast, to the complete success of this international consultation seminar, to your sincere cooperation, to the success of your career, to your health and happy family! Cheers!

SECTION Ⅳ: Speech

亲爱的中国朋友们，我和我的同事们在这里与各位欢聚一堂，我们感到非常高兴。感谢你们的盛情邀请和款待。

本次与会的顾问和嘉宾，有跨国公司的高级领导，有国际知名的经济专家，有造诣精深的专家学者。很高兴与各位共事，我深切地感受到了各位真诚合作的精神和积极务实的态度。

我们要充分发挥合作精神和集体智慧，这不仅有利于谋划和推动青岛的发展，而且有利于共同推进彼此在各个领域的合作和发展。

为了给青岛的发展献计献策，我一直期待本次咨询会议的到来。今天我们欢聚在这里，为的是一个共同的目标：加强合作与交流，扩大发展规模。

在经济全球化的大背景下，我们必须紧紧抓住新机遇，迎接新挑战，不遗余力地开创经济合作的新局面，实现优势互补、互惠互利、长期合作和共同发展。

希望我们这次研讨能为青岛的经济和社会发展增添活力，也为外商事业的发展创造机会。充满蓬勃生机和广阔前景的青岛经济，继续以强劲的姿态向新的高度跨越。让我们携手共进，为青岛的现代化和我们的共同繁荣努力！干杯！

Unit 6 商贸之余 Beyond Business

事实再次表明，在全球性危机的惊涛骇浪里，各国不是乘坐在 190 多条小船上，而是乘坐在一条命运与共的大船上。小船经不起风浪，巨舰才能顶住惊涛骇浪。

Facts have shown once again that amidst the raging torrents of a global crisis, countries are not riding separately in some 190 small boats, but are rather all in a giant ship on which our shared destiny hinges. Small boats may not survive a storm, but a giant ship is strong enough to brave a storm.

课文 A

SECTION Ⅰ: Dialogue 定做服装 To Order Custom Clothing

Interpret the following dialogue from English into Chinese and vice versa.

A: I'm very fond of your Chinese traditional garments, and I'd like to buy a Tang uniform.

B: 你身材高大，很难找到一件合身的成衣，我想你还是定做一件吧。

A: But where can I find a tailor to make it?

B: 我们的裁缝部可以给你定做。不过你需要先选一块料子。

A: What fabrics have you got? I want something warm but not too heavy.

B: 这块料子就符合你的要求，且质地好，耐穿又不走样。

A: Do you have something a little lighter? This seems too dark for spring wear.

B: 这块如何？这种料子不起皱，不用熨烫。

A: This is beautiful. I think I will pick this. How many feet do I need for myself?

B：先让我给你量一下尺寸。请脱下外衣。

A：I prefer it a bit looser，you know，just comfortably loose，especially round the collar.

B：让我看看，这料子三英尺宽，五英尺半就够了。

A：What's the charge for the material and the tailoring?

B：包括衬料在内，总共要 1270 元。请先支付 1000 元，剩余的钱可以取衣服时再付。

A：OK. Could you possibly have it finished earlier for me? You know I'm going back to my country in four days.

B：我给你赶一下，你明天下午来取吧。

A：Many thanks.

相关词汇

常用服装及汽车类英语

ready-made clothes/ready-to-wear clothes 成衣

dress coat/tails 燕尾服；礼服

windcoat 风衣

scarf 围巾

pyjamas 睡衣

blouse 紧身女衫

kimono 和服

jeans 牛仔裤

underwear/underclothes 内衣裤

suit 西装

sports wear 运动服

vest 背心

cape 披肩

hanbok 韩服

pullover 套头衫

cheongsam 旗袍

leather jacket 皮上衣

sedan car 轿车

convertible 敞篷车

station wagon 商务车

compact car 小轿车

limousine 高级轿车

lorry/truck 卡车

van 面包车

fire engine 消防车

ambulance 救护车

sports car 跑车

jeep 吉普车

SUV (Sports Utility Vehicle) 运动型多功能汽车

pickup 小卡车

SECTION Ⅱ: Warm-ups for Interpretation

➢ **Tongue twister.**

Give papa a cup of proper coffee in a copper coffee cup.
给爸爸一杯用铜制咖啡杯盛着的正统咖啡。
He thrusts his fists against the posts and still insists he sees the ghosts.
他用拳头猛推柱子，而且声称见鬼了。

➢ **Interpret the following proverbs from Chinese into English.**

1. 情人眼里出西施。
2. 不闻凶讯便是吉。
3. 光阴似箭。
4. 百艺不如一艺精。
5. 诚实总是上策。

➢ **Interpret the following sentences from Chinese into English.**

1. 股市一开盘，道琼斯工业平均指数就暴跌了184点(即16%)，标准普尔指数下跌了30点(即2.5%)，纳斯达克指数也跌了82点(即3.2%)。
2. 我国有世界上最发达的租车业，你若打算在我国开车旅行，完全可以通过你自己国家的旅行社办理租车预定事宜。
3. 如果你是外国人，又没有某州的驾驶执照，可你想开车，那你最好携带一张国际驾驶执照。
4. 有着1800年历史的“苏绣”，中外驰名，其中双面绣因其所绣图案两面可看，备受青睐。
5. 对那些宁愿露宿户外而不愿睡在旅馆里的人来说，城市可不是他们的乐园，因为大多数城市没有邻近的野营地。

➢ **Interpret the following paragraphs from Chinese into English and vice versa.**

1. 请看周围，你一定注意到了，这里满街都是游人。他们到这里为了一个目的，就是目睹即将揭幕的盛大的爱丁堡国际音乐与戏剧节。自1947年以来，该音乐戏剧节每年举行一次，吸引了一些世界上最伟大的艺术家。你可以听音乐，欣赏戏剧，或者观赏这座城市的美景。爱丁堡音乐戏剧节已成为世界上的盛大节日之一。

2. If you're traveling abroad on business, your most difficult problem is not the language barriers or the jet lag, but the lunch. Every country has different customs and you can't afford to get it wrong. Down in the south of Europe, lunch breaks last a long time. In Italy, for example, they can last three hours. Some lunches are lighter than others. If you're in Scandinavia, a business lunch is sometimes just a plate of sandwiches. And don't be surprised if your hosts refuse alcohol and drink milk instead. Not all places are so health-conscious. The Americans are always complaining about smoking and drinking. But in Russia people do both during the lunch.

SECTION Ⅲ: Speech

Interpret the following speech from Chinese into English.

欢迎您入住海景花园大酒店。我们全部房间都有电话分机，您可以在房间里打长途电话，电话费会记在您的账上。当然您也可以使用自己的手机。

每个房间的门上都有猫眼和保险链，以确保您的安全。朝南的房间可以望见大海的壮观景色。酒店为顾客提供洗衣服务，包括干洗服务。如果您有要洗的衣服，就放在房内的洗衣袋里，并挂在门外把手上。

每个房间都配有免费使用的保险箱。如果您有信件需要邮寄，可以把信件放在门厅的问讯处，那里的服务员会代您寄走。

同时，问讯处免费向入住者提供介绍这个城市的小册子。酒店电话接线员可以根据您要求的时间，提供叫醒服务。

在晚间，酒店有各种各样的娱乐活动。我们酒店还有供商务会议使用的场所和设备，每个楼面都有供开会使用的贵宾室。

如果您有任何需要，请与总服务台联系，我们将竭诚为您服务。希望您有舒适如归的感觉，并祝您愉快。

SECTION Ⅳ: Speech

Interpret the following speech from English into Chinese.

The cheongsam is a body-hugging one-piece Chinese dress for women, also known in

Mandarin Chinese as qipao, and Mandarin gown in English. The stylish and often tight-fitting cheongsam or qipao (chipao) that is best known today was created in the 1920s in Shanghai and made fashionable by socialites (社会名流) and upper-class women.

The original qipao was wide and loose. It covered most of the woman's body, revealing only the head, hands, and the tips of the toes. The baggy nature of the clothing also served to conceal the figure of the wearer regardless of age.

The modern version, which is now recognized popularly in China as the "standard" qipao, was first developed in Shanghai in the 1920s, partly under the influence of Beijing styles. People eagerly sought a more modernized style of dress and transformed the old qipao to suit their tastes. Slender and form fitting with a high cut, it had great differences from the traditional qipao. It was high-class courtesans and celebrities in the city that would make these redesigned tight-fitting qipao popular at that time.

Since 1930s, cheongsam was popularized from young female students to all women in China regardless of their ages and social status. More and more female workers and celebrities put on cheongsam. The style of cheongsam also varied due to western costume's influence. It changed from a wide and loose style to a more form fitting and revealing cut. The length of cheongsam was also reduced from ankle reaching to above the knee. Besides, the design of cheongsam got various inventions like ruffled collar, bell-like sleeves and black lace frothing. Starting from that, the priority of cheongsam moved from a political expression to aesthetic and ornamental emphasis.

参考译文

SECTION Ⅰ: Dialogue

A: 我很喜欢你们中国的传统服装，我想买一套唐装。

B: You are big and tall. I don't think it easy to find any ready-made one that fits you. I suggest you order one to your size.

A: 那我去哪儿定做呢？

B: Our tailor department can do it for you. But you have to choose a suitable fabric first.

A: 你们都有什么料子？我想要颜色不太深的暖色布料。

B：This material is what you like. It is of good quality，durable，and does not shrink.

A：有没有颜色稍浅一点的？春天穿这个颜色好像太深了。

B：How about this one? It is wrinkle-free and free of ironing.

A：很漂亮。就是它了。像我这样需要买几英尺呢？

B：Let me measure your size first. Will you please take off your jacket?

A：我喜欢做得宽松一些，就是穿起来合身又舒服，特别是在衣领周围。

B：Just a minute. This fabric is 3 feet in width. I think 5 and a half feet is good enough.

A：料子和做工共需要多少钱？

B：The total charge is 1,270 *yuan*，including lining. You may first leave 1,000 *yuan* for deposit and pay the remaining when you fetch it.

A：好的。可以快些做吗？我四天后就要回国了。

B：I'll rush it up for you. You may come for it tomorrow afternoon.

A：多谢你了。

SECTION Ⅱ：Warm-ups for Interpretation

➤ **Interpret the following proverbs from English into Chinese.**

1. Love is blind.
2. No news is good news.
3. Time flies.
4. Jack of all trades，master of none.
5. Honesty is the best policy.

➤ **Interpret the following sentences from English into Chinese.**

1. At the open，the Dow Jones industrial average was down 184 points，or 1.6%；the S & P 500 lost 30 points，or 2.5%；and the Nasdaq Composite dropped 82 points，or 3.2%.
2. My country has the most developed car rental industry in the world，so you may very well want to reserve a car through your travel agent in your own country if you intend to drive while traveling in my country.
3. When you drive in the U. S.，it's a good idea to have an international driver's license if you are a foreigner and don't have a state license.

4. With a tradition dating back 1,800 years, Suzhou embroidery enjoys its fame across the world, among which those products with two-sided patterns are the most popular among buyers.
5. People who prefer camping to staying in hotels will have a hard time in the cities, because most of these cities don't have camp-grounds nearby.

➢ **Interpret the following paragraphs from English into Chinese and vice versa.**

1. Now please look around, and you must have noticed it already. The streets are full of tourists and they are here for a good reason of seeing Edinburgh's great international festival of music and drama, which is about to begin. This festival has been held every year since 1947 and it attracts some of the world's greatest artists. You can listen to music and see any kind of plays, or just enjoy the beauty of the city itself. The Edinburgh Festival has become one of the great festivals of the world.
2. 如果你因公出差，最让你感到困难的问题不是语言障碍或飞行时差综合征，而是午餐问题。每个国家都有不同的习俗，你可马虎不得。在欧洲南部，午餐休息时间很长。如在意大利，可能会长达三小时。有些地方的午餐分量比较小。如果你到斯堪的纳维亚，工作午餐就是一份三明治。如果你的主人拒绝饮酒而只喝牛奶，千万别大惊小怪。不是所有地方都有这样的健康意识。美国人总抱怨午餐时有人抽烟喝酒，但俄罗斯人在午餐时又抽烟又喝酒。

SECTION Ⅲ: Speech

Welcome to Sea View Garden Hotel. All our rooms are equipped with extensions. You can make long distance calls in your room. We'll put the charge on your bill. Of course, you may use your own cell phone.

A sighting glass and a security chain have been fixed on your door to ensure your personal security. Rooms facing south will show you a beautiful ocean view. The hotel offers laundry, including dry cleaning service. If you have any laundry, just leave it in the laundry bags and place them on the door handle.

Every room has a safe for your personal valuables, free of charge. If you have mails to post, you can drop them off at the lobby's information desk. The clerks there will take care of them.

Meanwhile, the information desk also provides you with free brochures of the city tours. The hotel telephone operator will wake you up if you ask for the service.

The hotel provides various kinds of recreation activities in the evening. We also offer venues and facilities for business meetings and conventions. There are hospitality suites for meetings on every floor.

If you need anything that we can do for you, please contact our information desk. We'll do everything we can to make your stay comfortable. We wish you a happy stay in our hotel.

SECTION Ⅳ: Speech

"旗袍"是一种由单片衣料制成的紧身长裙，英文叫"cheongsam"或"Mandarin gown"，是中国女性的服装。现在人们普遍熟悉的旗袍，是一种现代风格的束身礼服，产生于20世纪20年代的上海，社会名流和贵妇人使其流行开来。

最初的旗袍很宽松，它几乎将女性的全身都遮盖起来，只有头、手和脚趾露在外面。同时，这种宽松的特性也可以使不同年龄的女性的体形特征毫不外露。

现代风格的旗袍是在20世纪20年代的上海首先出现并逐渐兴起的，这种风格在一定程度上受到北京旗袍款式的影响，并被普遍认为是"标准"旗袍。人们热衷于寻找一种更具现代风格的裙装，于是将旧式旗袍进行改进以符合不同人的喜好。新式旗袍更加纤长、贴身且开叉较高，与传统的旗袍差异很大。上海上流社会的交际名媛、各界名流普遍穿着这种紧身的新式旗袍，在当时非常流行。

自20世纪30年代起，旗袍深受青年女学生，乃至各年龄段、各社会阶层中国女性的喜爱。越来越多的女性工作者、社会名流等都穿旗袍。旗袍的样式也受西方服饰的影响而有所变化。由宽松变得更贴身，对身体的遮盖也有所减少。旗袍的裙长也由脚踝处上升到膝盖以上。此外，旗袍的设计也更加多变新颖，如荷叶领、钟形袖和黑色蕾丝装饰等。自此，旗袍逐渐淡出政治场合，增加了审美和装饰色彩。

课文 B

SECTION Ⅰ: Dialogue　租车 Rent a Car

Interpret the following dialogue from Chinese into English and vice versa.

A：下午好，先生，有什么能为您效劳的吗？

B：Yes，I'd like to rent a car，starting from tomorrow.

A：您要租用几天呢？

B：About 5 days. What kinds of vehicles do you have?

A：我们有各种轿车、面包车和敞篷车。不过如果你们一行有 5～6 人，租用一辆商务车好一些。

B：You are right. It brings a lot of convenience to rent such a van. Could you tell me what the rate is?

A：嗯，要付 5000 元押金，另外每天 300 元，每千米加 16 元。

B：Good，I'll have one.

A：您要买保险吗？每天另收 12 元，全保。

B：Yes，I'd like to buy one. By the way，do you have drop-off service at your chain shop anywhere?

A：您可以把车还在机场，我们在那儿有自己的连锁店。我得看看你的护照或驾驶证和信用卡。

B：Here you are. Should I pay for the deposit now?

A：是的，现在就要支付。请填一下这份表格，然后在这儿签字。明天上午 6 点以后的任何时间你都可以来这里取车。

B：Who shall I call if anything goes wrong?

A：您可以致电我们的客户服务中心。电话号码在合同上。请保存合同的原件，把副本还给我。

B：Thank you for your help.

SECTION Ⅱ：Warm-ups for Interpretation

➢ **Tongue twister.**

Any noise annoys an oyster，but a noisy noise annoys an oyster more!

任何噪声都会惹恼一只牡蛎，可是吵闹的噪声会惹得牡蛎更火大。

I thought a thought. But the thought I thought wasn't the thought I thought I thought.

我思考了一个问题。可是，我所思考的问题并不是我认为自己正在思考的问题。

➢ **Interpret the following proverbs from English into Chinese.**

1. When the pear is ripe, it falls.
2. Out of sight, out of mind.
3. Sorrow is the bitter pill in every cup of mirth.
4. Bad news travels fast.
5. Rome was not built in a day.

➢ **Interpret the following sentences from English into Chinese.**

1. This means there are "thousands of flights canceled, with 150 to 200 people a flight", said Michael, speculating that "probably tens of thousands of people" are affected by the Covid-19 pandemic.
2. Japanese costumes are kimonos, but the Koreans likes to wear hanbok while Chinese are proud of our cheongsam, a body-hugging one-piece Chinese dress for women.
3. The two largest American car rental companies, Hertz and Avis, have offices all over the U. S. , with counters at most airports and in many international cities.
4. In order to rent a car, you have to have a major credit card, such as MasterCard, Visa, or American Express. Without a credit card you may have to pay a very high deposit on the car.
5. The way we Chinese handle our chopsticks is quite artistic and varies from person to person like one's signature.

➢ **Interpret the following paragraphs from English into Chinese and vice versa.**

1. Broadway is the street where you will find New York's best-known theaters. But away from the bright lights and elegant clothes of Broadway are many smaller theaters. Their plays are called "off-Broadway" and are often more unusual than the Broadway shows. As well as many theaters, New York has a famous opera house. This is the Metropolitan, where international stars sing from September until April. Carnegie Hall is the city's more popular concert hall. But night life in New York offers more than classical music and theaters. There are hundreds of nightclubs where people dine and dance.
2. 野营，作为一种更为自由的度假方式，已成为越来越多年轻人钟爱的户外活动。事实上，现代化的营地所具有的设施可以满足野营者的基本需求。最使年轻人动心的不是低廉的花费和自由度，而是贴近自然的野外生活。野营使我们的城市生活方式发生了真正的变化。在一年中珍贵的几天里，我们采纳了一种新的生活方式，这才是真正意义上的娱乐和享受。

SECTION Ⅲ: Speech

Interpret the following speech from Chinese into English.

在中国的饮食文化中，筷子有着举足轻重的地位。中文"筷子"的第一个汉字"筷"是由表示读音的"快"，和表示意义的"竹"组合成的形声字。

使用筷子的时候，通常下面要用拇指、无名指和中指固定。上面像拿铅笔一样，用拇指尖、食指尖和中指尖控制。在使用的时候，只动上面的筷子，将食物夹住。在中餐餐桌上，当不用筷子的时候，要将筷子放在盘子的右侧或下面。据说，使用筷子可以增强记忆，使手指更灵巧。

筷子的使用也具有诸多文化内涵。在使用时要注意一下禁忌。例如，使用筷子时，不要将食指伸出，这被认为是在指责别人。在用餐时，不要将筷子垂直插入食物中，因为中国人在祭祀祖先时才这样做。此外，在中国文化中，用嘴嘬筷子是一种缺少家教、不礼貌的行为。用筷子敲击碗盘也是一种不礼貌的行为，因为乞丐在乞讨的时候为了引起行人注意才这样做。如果筷子长短不齐地放在桌子上，则暗示此人出行时会错过轮船、飞机或火车。如果筷子落地则是一种不祥之兆。

SECTION Ⅳ: Speech

Interpret the following speech from English into Chinese.

Advances in technology have made it more convenient for people to travel around. Travelers' checks save people much trouble of carrying large amounts of cash with them. It can be said that it's a very good way to carry big sums of money.

You can cash travelers' checks in any local bank, hotel or motel, and in most restaurants. When you do shopping, you can purchase items with the most shops as well.

Compared with cash, travelers' checks are far safer as they must be signed before they can be cashed. When you sign the bottom line of the check, you should make sure the person cashing your check watches you sign and date it.

If you lose your checks or someone steals them, call the bank from which you bought them immediately and report the numbers. Therefore, in the first place, be sure to write down your check numbers on a piece of sheet and keep it separate from your checks.

For lost checks, the bank will give you a cash refund or replace the checks. By doing so, even if they are stolen or accidentally lost, your money is still there.

Checks come in various denominations at your choice, but there is a one percent service fee which you must pay the bank when purchasing travelers' checks.

参考译文

SECTION Ⅰ: Dialogue

A: Good afternoon, sir, May I help you?

B: 明天我想租一辆车。

A: For how many days?

B: 大概5天吧。你们都有什么车?

A: We've got varieties of cars, vans and convertibles. However, if you have five or six people in your package, I suggest you rent a station wagon.

B: 你说得对。租一辆商务车出行会方便许多。请问租金是多少?

A: Well, there's a 5000 *yuan* deposit. And then it's 300 *yuan* per day plus 16 *yuan* per kilometer.

B: 好,我租一辆吧。

A: Would you like to buy insurance? It is 12 *yuan* per day for all risks.

B: 是的,我要买一份保险。顺便问一下,你们在别处有连锁店可以交车吗?

A: You can drop the car off at the airport. We do have our own chain shop there. I'll need your passport or driving license and credit card.

B: 好。我现在就要付押金吗?

A: Yes, you are supposed to. Please fill out this form, then sign here. You can come to pick up the car any time after 6:00 a.m. tomorrow morning.

B：如果有什么问题，我和谁联系呢？

A：You can call our customer service. The telephone number is printed on the contract. Please keep the original contract and give the carbon copy back to me.

B：谢谢你。

SECTION Ⅱ：Warm-ups for Interpretation

➢ **Interpret the following proverbs from English into Chinese.**

1. 瓜熟蒂落。
2. 眼不见，心不烦。
3. 乐极生悲。
4. 好事不出门，恶事传千里。
5. 罗马不是一天建成的；冰冻三尺，非一日之寒。

➢ **Interpret the following sentences from English into Chinese.**

1. 也就是说“数千次航班都取消了，乘坐每次航班的旅客有150～200人”，迈克尔说。他推测“很可能数万人”都受到了新冠肺炎疫情的影响。
2. 日本的民族服饰是和服，韩国人则喜欢穿韩服，而让中国人引以为豪的是旗袍。旗袍是中国妇女穿的一种紧身长裙。
3. 美国最大的两家租车公司Hertz和Avis在全美都有公司办事处，在大部分机场和许多国际都市也设有租车站。
4. 租车时你必须拥有一张大公司的信用卡，如“万事达”卡、“维萨”卡，或者“美国运通”卡。你若没有信用卡，也许就得支付一笔高额押金了。
5. 我们中国人使用筷子的方法很有艺术性，各人有各人的方法，就好像签名一样，不尽一致。

➢ **Interpret the following paragraphs from English into Chinese and vice versa.**

1. 在百老汇，你可以找到纽约最著名的剧院。但在远离百老汇那耀眼的灯光和人们高雅的衣着外，有许多小剧院。他们的剧目被称为“非百老汇剧”，通常比百老汇的剧目更具特色。纽约还有一座著名的歌剧院——大都会歌剧院，从9月一直持续到第二年4月，这里有世界级歌星的演出。卡内基音乐厅是城中更受青睐的音乐厅。纽约的夜生活不仅是经典音乐和剧院，还有成百上千的夜总会，人们在那里用餐、跳舞。

2. Camping as a cheaper and freer way of spending a holiday has become the great pursuit of outdoor activity among an increasing number of young people. As a matter of fact, modern camping sites are well-equipped with facilities which will meet the basic needs of campers. What attracts young people most is not the low cost and freedom, but the closeness to nature when living in the wilderness. Camping provides us with a real change from our urban way of life. For a few precious days in the year, we adopt a new way of life which is the essence of real recreation and enjoyment.

SECTION Ⅲ: Speech

Chopsticks play an important role in Chinese food culture. The Chinese term for chopsticks is *kuaizi* (筷子). The first character (筷)is a semantic-phonetic compound with a phonetic part meaning "quick" (快), and a semantic part meaning "bamboo"(竹).

To use chopsticks, the lower chopstick is stationary, and rests at the base of the thumb, and between the ring finger and middle finger. The second chopstick is held like a pencil, using the tips of the thumb, index finger, and middle finger, and it is moved while eating, to pull food into the grasp of the chopsticks. Chopsticks, when not in use, are placed either to the right or below one's plate in a Chinese table setting. It is believed that the use of chopsticks improves the power of memory and increases finger dexterity.

The use of chopsticks also indicate other cultural meanings. There are some taboos associated with its use. While using chopsticks, it is advised not to stretch out the index finger as it is considered a kind of accusation to others. And the chopsticks should not be inserted vertically into the food because the Chinese do this at the time of burning incense to sacrifice the dead. Also, in Chinese culture, sucking of chopsticks is considered as an impolite behavior and lack of family education. It is poor etiquette to tap chopsticks on the edge of one's bow, as beggars make this sort of noise to attract attention. A set of uneven length of chopsticks on a table suggests that the person will surely miss the boat, plane or train, which he/she is going to board. It is also a sign of bad luck if one drops a chopstick.

SECTION Ⅳ: Speech

科学技术的发展使人们的出行越来越方便了。旅行支票更是为人们省去了携带大量现金的麻烦，可以说，这是随身携带巨款的一个非常方便的办法。

旅行支票可以在任何一家当地银行、旅馆或汽车旅馆兑现，也可以在大多数餐馆兑现。当你在逛街购物时，也可以在大多数商店里用旅行支票支付。

比起现金，旅行支票安全得多，因为在兑现时必须签字。字要签在支票底下的那条线上，注意要当着承兑人的面签字并写上日期。

如果旅行支票丢失或被窃，你要马上打电话把号码告知卖给你支票的银行。因此，一定要把你的支票号码写在一张纸上，这张纸不要和支票放在一起。

对于丢失的那些支票，银行可以退给你现金或者给你补发支票。这样一来，即使支票被偷或者不慎丢失，你也不会有金钱损失。

旅行支票有多种票面可供选择，但购买旅行支票时，要向银行支付支票总额百分之一的服务费。

Unit 7 会议接待 Conference Reception

经济全球化是时代潮流。大江奔腾向海，总会遇到逆流，但任何逆流都阻挡不了大江东去。动力助其前行，阻力促其强大。尽管出现了很多逆流、险滩，但经济全球化方向从未改变、也不会改变。世界各国要坚持真正的多边主义，坚持拆墙而不筑墙、开放而不隔绝、融合而不脱钩，推动构建开放型世界经济。

Economic globalization is the trend of the times. Though countercurrents are sure to exist in a river, none could stop it from flowing to the sea. Driving forces bolster the river's momentum, and resistance may yet enhance its flow. Despite the countercurrents and dangerous shoals along the way, economic globalization has never and will not veer off course. Countries around the world should uphold true multilateralism. We should remove barriers, not erect walls. We should open up, not close off. We should seek integration, not decoupling. This is the way to build an open world economy.

课文 A

SECTION Ⅰ: Dialogue 商定招待会细节 Discussing the Details of Reception

Interpret the following dialogue from English into Chinese and vice versa.

A: Mr. Liang, our conference will begin tomorrow and our participants have arrived. We would like to use your hospitality suite from 7 o'clock to 9 o'clock this evening. Now let's be seated and discuss a few details.

B：没问题。先说一下你们的菜单怎么样？

A：As for the menu，we prefer the routine main course and chef's recommendation for the banquet.

B：宴会要采取哪一种服务方式呢？法式服务还是中式服务？

A：French service. But we may favor Chinese service tomorrow for the farewell banquet.

B：实际上我们这两种服务都有。你可以自己选择。因为你们的宾客差不多有 200 人，我推荐人工倒酒。

A：I think so. It will make the atmosphere of the banquet livelier. What is the minimum you charge for each person?

B：每人 500 元，不包括名牌饮品。

A：How do you charge call brands?

B：有两种收费方式。通常我们按瓶收费。如果你喜欢的话，也可以按饮用的杯量收费。

A：I prefer the latter. Anyway，is there any extra service charge?

B：有的，比如说，我们要收开瓶费。

A：I see. Now let's talk about the table decoration. Would it be good to put the flags of every participating country on it?

B：这是个好主意。如果放些花，再放点轻音乐的话就更妙了。

A：Great idea! Anyway，thank you for your time and suggestion，Mr. Liang.

B：不客气，先生。如果还有疑问的话，请及时与我联系。我随时为您服务。

相关词汇

常用餐饮类英语

buffet　自助餐；冷餐
appetizer　开胃菜
chef's special　主厨特菜
entree　正菜
main course　主菜
specialty　招牌菜
dessert　甜品
snack　点心；小吃

cold dish　冷盘
sake　日本米酒
Chinese Mao Tai　茅台
martini　马提尼酒
champagne　香槟
premium brand　高档品牌
call brands　点叫品牌
corkage　开瓶费

Sprite　雪碧
Pepsi Cola　百事可乐
Coca Cola　可口可乐
Fanta　芬达
7 Up　七喜
Dr. Pepper　胡椒博士
Tropicana　纯果乐
iced tea　冰茶
cappuccino　卡布其诺
to lay the table/to set the table　摆桌子
tablecloth　桌布
napkin/serviette　餐巾

SECTION Ⅱ: Warm-ups for Interpretation

➢ **Tongue twister.**

I wish you were a fish in my dish.
我巴不得你是我盘中餐碟中鱼。
Knife and fork, bottle and cork, that is the way you spell New York.
刀和叉，瓶和塞，纽约就是这么拼写的。

➢ **Interpret the following proverbs from English into Chinese.**

1. East or west, home is the best.
2. There is no royal road to learning.
3. After a storm comes a calm.
4. Art is long, but life is short.
5. Two heads are better than one.

➢ **Interpret the following sentences from English into Chinese.**

1. Kiwi fruits, coconuts, pineapples, pitaya, papaya, and radish have been very popular among the vegetarians.
2. A standard banquet will consist of four to eight prepared cold dishes, eight hot dishes served one at a time, two to four whole-size showpiece dishes (such as a whole fish, a whole suckling pig or a whole chicken), in addition to soups, we have staple food as steamed rice, jiaozi and Chinese pastries. The dinner finishes up with fruits.
3. One should never take a sip of any beverage at the table until the mouth is empty and has been wiped with the napkin.

4. If one is serving himself from a buffet, he needs not take anything he does not like if there is a wide enough choice of food.
5. Every table, no matter how informal the dinner be, should be laid with care and attention to detail.

➢ **Interpret the following paragraphs from English into Chinese and vice versa.**

1. Conference and resort hotels are hotels which often contain full-sized luxury facilities with full-service accommodations and amenities. These hotels may attract both business conferences and vacationing tourists and offer more than a convenient place to stay. These hotels may be referred to as major conference center hotels, flagship hotels, destination hotels, and destination resorts.
2. 过去，在"非常正式的宴会"上，常常是所有的客人围着一张长长的 U 形桌而坐，桌上铺有白色锦缎台布。大家知道，这样一来，相互交谈就比较困难，而且餐厅也要很长。现在，人们开始用能坐八至十人的圆桌。至于餐桌中央的装饰品，女主人可以充分施展自己的想象力。漂亮的餐桌布置可以给餐桌上的食物添色增味，让客人感受到主人为此付出的心血。

SECTION Ⅲ: Speech

Interpret the following speech from Chinese into English.

我想向你简要介绍一下下周你们会议结束后举办告别宴会的一些细节。宴会的时间是 8 月 18 日晚上，地点在国际宴会厅，与会者为海外销售人员。由于你们行程紧张，宴会将为你们提供预先点菜和一些特色中式凉菜。

餐桌的摆设是一桌八个人。上面摆放绿色亚麻布和白色餐巾，每张餐桌上都会摆放花瓶。

我们也可以满足 VIP 的特殊点酒点菜要求。因为你们之中有一些素食主义者，我们也精挑细选了一些素食菜肴。

现在我们说一下费用。一次 150 人的宴会，最低收费标准是 30,000 元，不包括饮料，饮料是单独收费的。

因为是一场中等规模的宴会，客人有 150 位，我建议你们按饮用量付费。此外，不要忘了你们要预付总费用的 20%作为保证金。

以前你们提出过要在 5 月 20 日举办冷餐会。现在我告知你们冷餐会将在主餐厅举行，时间是中午 12 点到下午 2 点。

SECTION Ⅳ: Speech

Interpret the following speech from English into Chinese.

Our catering department will provide a variety of foods and beverages during this conference. We offer a complete range of services to meet your demands.

Due to our company regulations, leftover food and beverages are not allowed to be taken away from the facilities. Our department is responsible for disposing of them at the conclusion of the conferences.

Alcoholic beverages will not be served to minors or persons who are drunk at the banquet.

During the meetings, the speaker's podium will be provided with ice water. If the attendants require water service, there will be additional charges.

Our food and beverage sales staff provides high quality catering services within the facility. They are responsible for meeting your various demands including holding banquets, providing coffee and other beverages. We are ready to produce our health permits during the catering service.

In order to ensure all required foods and beverages timely served, you have to sign the Catering Sales Order and submit it to our department 14 days before the function date. Please call our catering department at (562)499-7565, if you have any questions.

参考译文

SECTION Ⅰ: Dialogue

A: 梁先生，我们的会议明天开始，与会者已到达。今晚 7～9 点我们要用一下迎宾厅。现在我们来讨论一些细节吧。

B: No problem. Let's talk about the menus first.

A：关于菜单，我们喜欢常规的主菜以及厨师的推荐菜肴。

B：How would you like the banquet to be served? French service or Chinese service?

A：法式服务。不过明天的告别宴会我们将选择中式服务。

B：In fact，we have both services. It is up to you. Since you have approximately 200 guests，I recommend free pour.

A：我同意，我想这样会让宴会的气氛更加活跃一点。你们对每个人的最少收费是多少？

B：500 *yuan* per person，not including the premium brands.

A：对指定品牌饮品你们怎么收费？

B：There are two ways of charging. Usually we charge by bottle，but we can also charge by cups if you like.

A：我喜欢第二种。还有额外的服务费吗？

B：Yes，for example，we collect corkage fees.

A：我明白了。现在我们来谈一下餐桌的装饰。把每一个与会国家的旗子放在上面，你觉得怎么样？

B：I think it's a good idea. By the way，it is even better to put some flowers on the table and play some light music.

A：这个主意太棒了！梁先生，谢谢你抽出时间和我们敲定细节并提供这么好的建议。

B：You are welcome，Sir！If you have any questions，please do not hesitate to contact me. I am at your service any minute.

SECTION Ⅱ：Warm-ups for Interpretation

➢ **Interpret the following proverbs from English into Chinese.**

1. 金窝银窝，不如自己的草窝。
2. 学无坦途。
3. 雨过天晴。
4. 人生有限，学海无涯。
5. 三个臭皮匠，赛过诸葛亮。

➢ **Interpret the following sentences from English into Chinese.**

1. 猕猴桃、椰子、菠萝、火龙果、木瓜和水萝卜一直以来深受素食主义者的喜爱。

2. 在中国，一桌标准宴席包括四至八个事先制作好的冷盘，八道现做的热炒，两道观赏性大菜(如全鱼、乳猪、全鸡等)，此外还有汤、米饭、饺子和油酥火烧。晚宴结束前还有一道水果。
3. 在喝饮料前，你必须等嘴里的食物都咽下去，并且用餐巾擦干净嘴。
4. 在吃自助餐时，如果有很多食物可供挑选，不必盛自己不喜欢的东西。
5. 无论宴会正式程度如何，桌上的东西都必须一丝不苟地摆好。

➢ **Interpret the following paragraphs from English into Chinese and vice versa.**

1. 会议度假型酒店通常配备全套豪华设施及全套住宿服务和便利服务。这类酒店既是举办商务会议的场所，又受度假旅行者的青睐。酒店不仅仅是一个方便的住宿之地。这类酒店通常是指大型会议中心酒店、旗舰酒店、度假酒店及度假村。
2. For a "truly formal dinner", we used to have all guests sit at one long U-shaped table covered with a white damask cloth. You know, this arrangement made conversation difficult and required a very lengthy dinning room. Now people begin to use round tables for eight or ten. And as for the centerpiece decoration on the table, the hostess' own imagination should come into full play. A pretty setting of the table for guests helps make the food better and taste better. It makes the guests feel that an effort has been made on their behalf.

SECTION Ⅲ: Speech

Now I'd like to brief you on the banquet to be held next week after your conference ends. It will be held on the evening of Aug. 18th in International Banquet Hall. It is a banquet only for overseas sales reps. Since you have a tight schedule, we are to offer à la carte with some special fixed Chinese appetizers.

As for the table setting, each table is seated by 8 people, covered with jade linen and white napkins, together with a flower vase.

We can also meet the VIP's special demands for special liquor or different foods. We also prepare a good selection of vegetarian dishes, since there are several vegetarians in your group.

Now let's turn to the charges. For a banquet of 150 persons, the minimal charge is RMB 30,000 *yuan*, not including drinks, which will be charged separately.

Since it is a medium banquet, with 150 guests, I suggest you pay by the drinks. And mind you, you'll have to pay a deposit of 20 percent of the total costs in advance.

By the way, you had asked for a buffet lunch on May 20th before. Now I'd like to inform you that the buffet will be served in the main dining hall from 12 p. m. to 2 p. m.

SECTION Ⅳ: Speech

我们餐饮部负责在会议期间专门提供食物和饮料。我们提供周到的服务以满足你的要求。

我们公司规定剩余的食物和饮料不允许带出会议场所。我们餐饮部负责在会议结束后处理剩余食品。

在宴会中，我们不提供酒精饮料给未成年人和已醉者。

在会议中，我们会为演讲人提供冰水。如果与会者需要喝水的话，将另外收费。

我们的食品和饮料销售员在会议场所内专门提供高质量的餐饮服务。他们负责满足你们的各种需求，包括举行宴会、提供咖啡和各种饮料。在餐饮服务期间，我们愿意随时提供健康证明。

为确保所有的食物和饮料能及时供应，请签署这份餐饮销售订单，并在用餐日期 14 天前交到我们餐饮部。如果有任何问题，请拨打(562) 499-756。

课文 B

SECTION Ⅰ: Dialogue 了解宾馆的会议服务 Consult Receptionist about Conference Services

Interpret the following dialogue from English into Chinese and vice versa.

A: Good morning, Madam. What can I do for you?

B: 早上好，我可以见一下销售经理吗?

A: I am really sorry, but he is out at the moment. Do you have an appointment with him? Mrs. Wang…?

B: 我没和他预约过。我想和他谈谈，了解一下在你们大酒店举办会议的情况。

A: Oh, I see, Mrs. Wang. I can give you some information that might be interesting to you.

B: 那很好。事实上，我已经访问过你们宾馆的网站了，上面说你们在举办会议方面有很多经验。

A: Yes, quite a lot. Let me show you the photos of past successful conferences we have ever held here.

B: 这是什么？这张图片是2002年在青岛举行的数学家大会吗？是在你们宾馆举办的？

A: Exactly! It was a very successful event. You must have heard a lot about it. Actually we are now engaged in holding another two global conferences in six months.

B: 真的吗？现在我对你们的宾馆信心倍增了。

A: Thank you, Madam. I have other things to show you. This is a pamphlet on the details about our hotel's convention department.

B: 我可以带回去研究研究。如果不麻烦的话，可以带我参观一下你们的会议中心吗？

A: My pleasure. Please come this way.

B: 谢谢。这是你们的会议中心？

A: Yes. It is newly-designed and has the latest rear screen projector. I will guide you through our convention department and see how efficient they are.

B: 谢谢，好极了。

SECTION Ⅱ: Warm-ups for Interpretation

➢ **Tongue twister.**

So she bought a bit of butter, better than her bitter butter,
and she baked it in her batter, and the batter was not bitter.
So it was better Betty Botter bought a bit of better butter.
所以她买了一些奶油，比她原来的苦涩黄油好多了。她把这些奶油放进她的面糊，烤出来的面糊不苦了。这是贝蒂波特用她买的这点奶油做出好点心的原因。
While we were walking, we were watching window washers wash Washington's windows with warm washing water.
然而在散步时，我们看到清洁窗户的人用温水清洗华盛顿的窗户。

➢ **Interpret the following proverbs from Chinese into English.**

1. 十年树木，百年树人。

2. 一不做，二不休。
3. 你敬我一尺，我敬你一丈。
4. 不管张三李四。
5. 瞎猫碰上了死耗子。

➢ **Interpret the following sentences from Chinese into English.**

1. 许多人讨厌大型鸡尾酒会，喜欢别人邀请他们“来家里坐一坐、喝一杯”，这样客人不太多，但每个人都可以坐着，很放松，很惬意。
2. 中国宴席桌上的酒通常为啤酒、黄酒和烈性白酒三种。人们往往以“干杯”的方式互相敬酒。
3. 准备 10 道分量适中的菜肴并不为过，即使献上 16 道菜，亦不足为奇。
4. 用餐时，臂肘不应放在桌面上，除非是一道菜用完而另一道菜还没有上来。
5. 餐桌是最能体现个人行为举止的场所之一。

➢ **Interpret the following paragraphs from Chinese into English and vice versa.**

1. 在正式公共宴会上，必须提前离开的客人应在演说之前或演说间隙悄悄离去，但不能在主宾演说时或奏国歌时走开。离开时，通常从最近的出口出去，在路上碰到别的客人，也只是朝他们点点头，不应停下来与之交谈或说“再见”。
2. There are two elements of the formal dinner that have not changed over the years. One is the use of a butler and waiters for serving, and the other is the necessity for a chef who can produce a fabulous meal of five courses—usually soup, fish, meat or fowl, salad and cheese, and dessert. At a formal dinner, we usually have white wine, red wine, and champagne served with the meal (sometimes sherry first, too). The way the food is served is extremely important at a formal dinner. The platters must all be garnished beautifully, so that the guests will admire each one as a work of art, not just the serving of a dish. For example, the butter might be rolled into balls or carved into flowers. The vegetables and desserts are served in imaginative ways.

SECTION Ⅲ: Speech

Interpret the following speech from Chinese into English.

Speech A

1965 年，弗雷德·德卢卡开始为实现自己当医生的梦想而努力奋斗。为了想办法支付学费，弗雷德的世交彼得·巴克建议他开一家潜水艇三明治快餐店。

彼得·巴克借给弗雷德1,000美元，两人成为合作伙伴。这一合作关系使世界快餐业的格局发生了改变。

1965年，第一家三明治店成立于美国康涅狄格州的布里奇波特。随后，他们定了一个目标：10年内开32家快餐店。弗雷德很快掌握了经商的基本知识，同时知道精心制作高质量产品、完美的服务、保持低运营成本及良好的商业选址也是非常重要的。这些早期的经验一直是全世界“赛百味”快餐店成功运营的基础。

到1974年，弗雷德和彼得在美国的康涅狄格州拥有并经营着十六家快餐店。意识到实现不了10年内开32家快餐店的目标后，他们开始开展特许经营，“赛百味”快餐店也进入了蓬勃发展期，其快速发展势头延续至今。

如今，“赛百味”是世界上最大的三明治连锁店，在全世界拥有37,000家分店，已成为适合全家人共享的营养快餐之首选。“赛百味”提供新鲜、美味及按顾客需求定制的三明治，怀着令每位顾客满意的服务热情，“赛百味”不断发展壮大。

Speech B

亚士兰公司是一家遵照规章制度办事的公司。我们深信应该：

以诚信一致的态度经营我们的业务，

爱护环境，

提供安全和不危害健康的工作环境，

客户至上，

不断改进我们的经营，

在工作中发扬团队精神相互合作，

根据事实做出决策，并且

积极参与所在地区的社区活动。

这些价值观反映在我们的《商业行为准则》中，可概括为三项简明扼要的指导原则：我们遵守法律，我们坚持高道德标准，我作为所在社区负责任的成员从事各项活动。遵守《准则》，并遵守所有的法律和规则，这是我们做生意的前提。遵守法律和规则并不仅是一项预期行为，它是一种强制性的要求。

我们的董事会和管理团队认为，您了解这些原则至关重要。因此，我们准备分发这本手册。本《商业行为准则》突出了您在从事商业活动中必须注意的亚士兰公司的一些政策和法律。我们并不期待您在读完这本手册后成为一名法律专家。事实上，这里包括的例子并不代表一项政策或法律本身所适用的每一种情况。

但是，我们的确期望您遵守本《准则》的规定和亚士兰公司的政策，对某些法律和规则有一般性的认识，并且能够辨认出敏感问题。最重要的是，我们期望您提出问题并寻求指导。请记住：最好的办法始终是先提出问题以避免日后出现麻烦。

如果您对您代表亚士兰公司从事活动时的指导法律有疑问，请与您的主管、法律部、或法律总顾问联系。了解并遵守《准则》是您的责任。如果您怀疑某项行动或行为不道德或违反任何亚士兰公司的政策、《准则》或法律，您应该把情况报告给您的主管、法律部或法律总顾问，或者拨打电话 1-800-ASHLAND(1-800-274-5263)。如果您在美国以外地区，请拨对方付费号码 1-606-329-5701。

兑现我们的价值观是我们的本质所在，也是亚士兰公司所向披靡(The Who in How Things Work. TM)的利器。我们期待您遵守这些原则。

SECTION Ⅳ: Speech

Interpret the following speech from English into Chinese.

Speech A

Gift giving varies according to different cultures. Today let's see business gift giving in the UK. Giving gifts is not a normal part of British business culture. Indeed, British business colleagues are quite likely to feel embarrassed to receive any gift at all. The only exception would be at the conclusion of a deal when it might be appropriate to give a unique commemorative item to mark the occasion.

Small gifts such as a pen or a book, again suitably inscribed, are suitable tokens of genuine gratitude, and flowers or wine or champagne suffice to thank junior colleagues for their services. Do not, however, appear patronizing or unduly forward, especially if the recipient is a woman.

Alternatively, it will often be appreciated if you invite your hosts, or others you wish to thank, out for a meal or to the theatre or opera.

It is always a good form to buy a round of drinks for your colleagues after work. This is also the most common way of celebrating someone's birthday.

Business gifts are never exchanged at Christmas but it may be appropriate to send a card, particularly as an expression of thanks to your business associates but also as a means of maintaining valuable contacts.

If you are invited to a British home, it is a standard practice to bring wine, flowers, or chocolates for your hosts. The usual European taboos apply when giving flowers: no red roses, white lilies or chrysanthemums.

Speech B

Gifts and Entertainment

Ashland desires to treat fairly and impartially to all persons and companies with whom it has business relationships, including its customers, distributors and suppliers. Giving or accepting gifts and entertainment can be construed as an attempt to improperly influence the relationship or allow the relationship to be improperly influenced. Generally, you should not provide or accept gifts of more than nominal value or entertainment of greater than usual or customary expense. Gifts of money, including gift certificates, are never permissible.

Your judgment should tell you when a gift is improper and should be refused to prevent embarrassment to everyone involved and to avoid what may be an unintentional violation of the law. However, business entertainment is an ambiguous area. Picking up the check (or letting someone else pay the tab) for a business lunch or dinner or a trip to a sporting event or the theater is usually permissible, but a clear business purpose should be involved. Employees will be reimbursed for reasonable business-related travel and entertainment expenses. The expenses must be necessary, legally incurred, and properly authorized, reported and approved.

参考译文

SECTION Ⅰ: Dialogue

A: 早上好，女士。我能为您做点什么？

B: Good morning. May I see the sales manager?

A: 对不起，他现在不在。您和他预约过吗？请问您贵姓？

B: I have no appointment with him, but I would like to talk to him about holding a conference in your hotel.

A: 我明白了，王女士。我可以提供一些你感兴趣的信息。

B: That'll be very good. In fact, I've visited your hotel's website, which says you have a lot of experience in sponsoring conferences.

A: 对的，我们在这方面有相当多的经验。我可以给你看一些照片，这是我们以前成功举办会议的资料。

B: What's this? Is it the International Congress of Mathematicians, Qingdao 2022? Was it held in your hotel?

A: 完全正确！这次会议十分成功，你一定有所耳闻吧。现在我们正在着手准备六个月后在这里举行的另外两场全球会议。

B: Really? Now I have more confidence in your hotel.

A: 谢谢你。我还有其他东西给你看。这本小册子是对我们会议部的介绍。

B: Oh, I can study it when I get back to my office. Can you show me around your convention center, if it isn't too much trouble to you?

A: 乐意之至。请这边走。

B: Thank you. Is this the convention center?

A: 是的，它是全新设计的，并有最先进的背投影仪。现在让我带你去看看我们的会议部并见一下我们高效的员工。

B: Thank you. That would be great.

SECTION Ⅱ: Warm-ups for Interpretation

➢ **Interpret the following proverbs from Chinese into English.**

1. It takes time to educate a person.
2. In for a penny, in for a pound.
3. You respect me and I will respect you more. /Give me an inch, you will take a mile.
4. Every Tom, Dick and Harry.
5. Every dog has his day. /Everyone has good days.

➢ **Interpret the following sentences from Chinese into English.**

1. Many people who hate large cocktail parties enjoy an invitation "to come by for a drink", with just a handful of guests, and everyone seated and relaxed.
2. Often beer, yellow rice wine and strong white liquor are served at a Chinese banquet. People at a table will usually "Gan Bei" when toasting each other.

3. Ten courses of dishes, not necessarily prepared in huge quantities, would not be considered excessive, and few people would blink at sixteen.
4. Elbows on the table are permissible between courses but not while one is eating.
5. Table manners are one of the most visible signals of the state of one's manners.

➢ **Interpret the following paragraphs from Chinese into English and vice versa.**

1. At formal public dinners guests who must leave early go quietly either before the speeches begin or between them, never while a guest of honor is speaking or while a national anthem is being played. Those who must leave, leave by the nearest exit without stopping to talk or bid farewell to guests encountered en route, except to bow briefly.
2. 正式宴会有两点多年来始终没有改变，一是司膳管理员和服务员，二是一位能烹饪五道精美菜肴的厨师：汤、鱼、肉或家禽、色拉与奶酪以及甜点。正式宴会上一般选择白葡萄酒、红葡萄酒和香槟(有时也有先喝雪利酒的)。正式宴会上，如何上菜极为重要。盘子必须装饰得好看，这样客人们会把它们当作艺术品欣赏，而不仅仅当作盛菜的盘子。黄油可以卷成球状或刻成花状，蔬菜和点心可做得别出心裁。

SECTION Ⅲ: Speech

Speech A

Back in 1965, Fred DeLuca set out to fulfill his dream of becoming a medical doctor. Searching for a way to help pay for his education, a family friend suggested he open a submarine sandwich shop.

With a loan of $1,000, the friend—Dr. Peter Buck—offered to become Fred's partner, and a business relationship was forged that would change the landscape of the fast-food industry.

The first store was opened in Bridgeport, Connecticut in August, 1965. Then, they set a goal of having 32 stores opened in 10 years. Fred soon learned the basics of running a business, as well as the importance of serving a well-made, high-quality product, providing excellent customer service, keeping operating costs low and finding great locations. These early lessons continue to serve as the foundation for successful SUBWAY restaurants around the world.

By 1974, the duo owned and operated 16 submarine sandwich shops throughout Connecticut. Realizing they would not reach their 32-store goal in time, they began franchising, launching the SUBWAY brand into a period of remarkable growth which continues to this day.

Today, the SUBWAY brand is the world's largest sandwich chain with more than 37,000 locations around the world. It has become the leading choice for people seeking quick, nutritious meals that the whole family can enjoy. With the passion for delighting customers by serving fresh, delicious, made-to-order sandwiches, SUBWAY continues to grow.

Speech B

Ashland is a principled company. We believe in:

conducting our businesses honestly and with integrity,
being good stewards of the environment,
providing safe and health-conscious work environments,
focusing on the customer,
continuously improving our operations,
working collaboratively as a team,
making decisions based on fact, and
being involved in the communities where we operate.

These values are expressed in our Code of Business Conduct, which sums up our guiding values in three simple statements: We obey the law. We adhere to high ethical standards. We act as responsible members of the communities where we operate. Compliance with the Code and therefore all laws and regulations forms the foundation of our business. Compliance is not simply expected; it is mandatory.

Our board and management team believe it is critically important for you to know these principles. That's why we have prepared and distributed this booklet. This Code of Business Conduct highlights some of Ashland's policies and laws you must be aware of in conducting your business activities. We don't expect you to become a legal expert as a result of reading this booklet. In fact, the examples included do not represent every instance where a policy or law applies.

However, we do expect you to comply with the Code and Ashland's policies, to be generally aware of certain laws and regulations and to recognize sensitive issues. Most importantly, we expect you to ask questions and seek advice. Remember: It is always better to ask questions first to avoid problems later.

If you have questions about the laws governing your activities on behalf of Ashland, talk to your supervisor, the Law Department or the General Counsel. It is your responsibility to be aware of and comply with the Code. If you suspect any activity or conduct to be unethical or in violation of any Ashland policy, this Code or the law, you should report the circumstances to your supervisor, the Law Department or the General Counsel or simply call 1-800-ASHLAND (1-800-274-5263). If you are outside the United States, call collect at 1-606-329-5701.

Living up to our values is part of who we are, part of what makes Ashland "The Who In How Things Work™". We are counting on you to comply with these principles.

SECTION Ⅳ: Speech

Speech A

不同的文化有不同的送礼方式，今天我们来看一下在英国的商务场合如何送礼。在英国的商业文化中，赠送礼物并不常见。实际上，如果英国人收到商务伙伴的礼物很可能会感到尴尬。但以下场合除外，如在一笔生意谈妥时，赠送一份独特的纪念品来纪念这一时刻。

钢笔或是书籍一类的小礼物——如果刻上或写上合适的文字，会是不错的表达真心感谢的礼物。鲜花或者葡萄酒/香槟足以用来对下级的帮助表示感谢。赠送礼物时不要让人感觉你高人一等，也不要过于热情，尤其对女性受礼者。

你也可以请招待过你的人或其他你想感谢的人去吃顿饭、看场电影或者听场歌剧，这些通常都是受人欢迎的做法。

下班之后，请你的同事们每人喝上一杯总是不错的做法。这也是为别人庆祝生日最常用的方式。

英国人从不在圣诞节互赠商务礼品，但是寄张卡片是合适的——尤其当你用这张卡片对你的商业伙伴表示感谢，并以此保持你们之间的重要交往时。

如果你被邀请去一个英国人家里做客，标准惯例是给主人带些酒、鲜花或巧克力。

送花时通常应遵循欧洲人的禁忌：不要送红玫瑰、白百合和菊花。

Speech B

礼品和招待

亚士兰公司希望公正地且不偏袒地对待与自己有业务往来的所有人和公司，其中包括亚士兰公司的顾客、分销商和供应商。给予或接受礼品和招待可以被解释成意图不正当地影响这种关系或使这种关系受到不正当的影响。总体而言，您不应该提供或接受高于小金额标准的礼品或大于正常或常例开支的招待。绝对不允许提供或接受现金礼品，包括礼品券。

您的判断力会告诉您什么时候一件礼品属于不正当礼品并且应该加以拒绝，以避免使相关的每个人难堪和可能于无意中违反法律。业务招待是一个模棱两可的领域。为工作午餐或晚餐或体育比赛或电影付账(或让别人付账)通常是允许的，但这应该涉及明确的业务目的。员工可以报销合理的出差和娱乐费用。这类费用必须是必要的、合法的，并且得到适当授权、上报和批准。

Unit 8 机器人技术支持 Technical Support by Robots

疫情发生以来，中国在防控、治疗等方面采取了严格措施，一直向社会公布有关信息，及时向世界卫生组织和有关国家和地区通报情况。中国愿与国际社会一道，有效应对疫情蔓延，维护全球卫生安全。

Since the outbreak of the coronavirus pandemic, China has taken strict measures in prevention, control and treatment, and has been releasing relevant information to the public and keeping the World Health Organization as well as relevant countries and regions informed in a timely manner. China is willing to work with the international community to effectively tackle the spread of the disease and maintain global health security.

课文 A

SECTION Ⅰ: Dialogue 高科技手术 High-tech Surgery

Interpret the following dialogue from English into Chinese and vice versa.

A: Hello, I hear that you have employed robots to help with your operation and ward service.

B: 是的。在与冠状病毒的斗争中，医生和护士冒着生命危险抢救患者，对严重的冠状病毒感染者，我们依靠医生进行对症治疗，同时采用智能机器人提供必要的技术支持。

A: Could you let me know the advantages of your medical service with the help of robots?

B：好的。对严重的冠状病毒感染者，我们靠医生进行对症治疗，甚至必要的器官支持，但简单而重复的任务，如药物输送和体温测量，对智能机器人来说非常简单。它最大的优势是从根本上避免必要的人与人之间的接触，并切断感染的可能性。

A：It's amazing. A friend told me the robot on display often performs operations with the guide of doctors.

B：确实如此。智能机器人成功从一位病人的肝部切除了一个恶性大肿瘤，手术在青岛举行，由另一头上海的著名外科医生遥控指导。你可以看一下这些图片。

A：Oh yes, the instruction says that the robot ALSONTECH has 3D vision positioning system which gives a pair of eyes and an AI brain to the robot, enabling the robot to see and perceive the things three dimensionally, and helping it position precisely the part that the patient needs to be examined or treated.

B：真是不可思议啊！智能机器人如此高大上，能为医生、护士和医务工作者做这么多事情。

A：Could you introduce to us more functions of this type of robot?

B：好的。这个高科技产品 ALSONTECH 机器人是很好的医疗助理。她是天生的好帮手，可以协助医生和护士完成简单而重复的差事，并能保护他们免受病毒侵害，还给他们一定的休息时间。她可以在病房之间来回穿梭，执行诸如体温测量、送药、送餐等任务。

A：All right. What else can an intelligent robot do in hospitals in addition to above performances?

B：机器人可以准确地向患者和医务人员送药物、送饭、送测试报告等。

A：Hum, she's very efficient. And she never feels exhausted after a day's work.

B：或许对一些人来说，采用机器人听上去可能不安全，但这是人类对完美精确度追求过程中跨出的一步。

A：Yeah, we are really amazed at the breakthrough made in the medical world.

B：完全赞同。我认为机器人做起事来精确度会更高。

A：Generally, with the help of robots, especially the AI robots, surgeons can also perform operations much better.

相关词汇

常用医学类、家电类英语词汇

coronavirus 新冠
ward 病房
malignant 恶性的
benign 良性的
tumor 肿瘤
physician 内科医生
pediatrician 儿科医生
obstetrician 产科医生
dentist 牙医
surgeon 外科医生
anesthetist 麻醉师
epidemic 流行病
fever 发热
arthritis 关节炎
rheumatic arthritis 风湿性关节炎
bronchitis 支气管炎
tracheitis 气管炎
diabetes 糖尿病
bird flu 禽流感
pneumonia 肺炎
hepatitis 肝炎
hepatitis B 乙型肝炎
heart stroke 心脏病突发
SARS 非典
liver 肝脏
gall bladder 胆囊
appendix 阑尾
appendicitis 阑尾炎
kidney 肾脏
air conditioner 空调
microwave oven 微波炉
dishwasher 洗碗机
electric iron 电熨斗
oven 烤箱
vacuum cleaner 吸尘器
fridge 电冰箱
toaster 烤面包机
washing machine 洗衣机
laptop 笔记本电脑
tablet PC 一体机
plasma 等离子电视
light pen 光笔
gadget 小电子产品

SECTION Ⅱ: Warm-ups for Interpretation

➢ **Tongue twister.**

On a lazy laser raiser lies a laser ray eraser.

一个懒惰的激光器上放了一个激光消除器。

As I was in Arkansas I saw a saw that could out saw any saw I ever saw saw. If you happen to be in Arkansas and see a saw that can out saw the saw I saw saw I'd like to see the saw you saw saw.

我在阿肯色州的时候，看到一把锯子，我曾经看到的锯子都锯不过这一把。要是你正好在阿肯色州，并见过一把这样的锯子，那么我想看你的锯子锯东西。

➢ **Interpret the following proverbs from Chinese into English.**

1. 患难见真情。
2. 得寸进尺。
3. 今日事，今日毕。
4. 偷鸡不着蚀把米。
5. 会叫的狗不咬人；会抓耗子的猫不叫。

➢ **Interpret the following sentences from Chinese into English.**

1. 心血管疾病、阿尔茨海默病(老年痴呆症)和糖尿病是对人类威胁最大的三种疾病。同时，肝炎、肺结核和恶性肿瘤也不可小觑。
2. 有些年轻的科学家一直以来致力于发明和设计核潜艇、航空母舰和两栖飞机等最尖端的海军装备。
3. 虽然医学方面取得的很多成果提高了老年人的生活质量，但是，另外一些成果却产生了相反的作用，即在延长生命的某个方面的同时强化了依赖性。
4. 神经科医师利用磁共振成像仪观察大脑的工作情况，人的思维和情感可以生动地跃然屏幕之上。
5. 天文学家装备了大得惊人和清晰无比的望远镜后，有史以来第一次记录到了太阳系外一颗行星反射出的光线。

➢ **Interpret the following paragraphs from Chinese into English and vice versa.**

1. 目前地球与无人驾驶探测器之间的通信不仅费用昂贵，而且信息专有、操作复杂。有了星际网后，我们可以简化所有程序，降低成本，更有效地使公众入网。
2. We currently have nearly 100 new medicines in various stages of development, and are working on dozens of new uses for our current medicines. Our targets include many of humanity's most feared illnesses, including cardiovascular disease, diabe-

tes, Alzheimer's, cancer, HIV/AIDS, depression and schizophrenia.

SECTION Ⅲ: Speech

Interpret the following speech from Chinese into English.

波音 787 梦幻客机是由波音公司研发的中型、双引擎广体机。

它的卓越性能基于一整套新技术和全新的设计。

波音 787 主体结构的 50% 由复合材料制成，包括机身和机翼。

波音 787 设计的核心是现代化的系统架构，与其他飞机相比结构更简约、功能更强大、效率也更高。例如，波音 787 上安装了飞机健康监测系统，使飞机能够进行自我监测，并将系统维护需求报告给地面计算机系统。

发动机技术的改进是飞机整体燃油效率提高的最重要因素。波音 787 安装了通用电气公司和劳斯莱斯公司的新发动机，标志着中型飞机市场在发动机技术上实现了近两代的飞跃。

787 的设计和制造流程进一步提高了效率。波音及其供应合作伙伴开发了新技术和新工艺，实现了效率的提升。例如，787 用一个整件桶状机身段取代了分段机身，也就是 1,500 张铝板和 4 万～5 万个紧固件。

SECTION Ⅳ: Speech

Interpret the following speech from English into Chinese.

When the nuclear magnetic moment associated with a nuclear spin is placed in an external magnetic field, the different spin states are given different magnetic potential energies. In the presence of the static magnetic field which produces a small amount of spin polarization, a radio frequency signal of the proper frequency can induce a transition between spin states. This "spin flip" places some of the spins in their higher energy state.

If the radio frequency signal is then switched off, the relaxation of the spins back to the lower state produces a measurable amount of RF signal at the resonant frequency associated with the spin flip. This process is called Nuclear Magnetic Resonance (NMR).

The application of nuclear magnetic resonance best known to the general public is magnetic resonance imaging for medical diagnosis and magnetic resonance microscopy in research settings; however, it is also widely used in chemical studies, notably in NMR spectroscopy. Biochemical information can also be obtained from living tissue with the technique known as in vivo magnetic resonance spectroscopy or chemical shift NMR Microscopy.

参考译文

SECTION Ⅰ: Dialogue

A: 你好！听说你们用机器人来帮助进行手术，并由机器人提供病房服务。

B: Yes. In the battle against the coronavirus, doctors and nurses are risking their lives to rescue the affected. So in this case, we employ smart robots to provide technical support.

A: 你能告诉我在医疗服务上使用机器人的优势是什么吗？

B: Sure. You know, for patients with severe coronavirus disease, they rely on doctors for symptomatic treatment and even necessary organ support, but for simple and repetitive tasks like medicine delivery and temperature taking, it's a piece of cake for our smart robots. And it will fundamentally avoid necessary person-to-person contact, and cut off the possibility of infection.

A: 太棒了！有朋友告诉我正在展示的机器人可以在医生的指令下做手术。

B: That is completely true. A big malignant tumor was removed smoothly from a patient's liver by this intelligent robot with the remote guidance of a very influential surgeon at the consoles in Shanghai. Please look at these pictures.

A: 噢，是的，说明书指出 ALSONTECH 机器人具有 3D 功能，可以为机器人提供一双眼睛和一个智能大脑，使机器人能够三维地观察和感知人体部位，并帮助它给患者精确定位和检查要治疗的部位。

B: It is unbelievable! The AI robots are so intelligent to perform so many things for doctors, nurses and medical workers.

A: 你还能介绍一下这款智能机器人的其他功能吗？

B: OK. This hi-tech ALSONTECH is our robotic medical assistant. She is born to help doctors and nurses with simple and repetitive errands in the hope of protecting them from the virus and giving them some time to rest. She can shuttle between wards, and perform tasks such as temperature taking, medicine delivering, meal delivering, etc.

A: 除此之外，机器人在医院还能做其他事情吗？

B: Oh, the robot can deliver medicines, test reports and food correctly to the patients and also medical personnels and bla, bla, bla.

A: 嗯，机器人的效率太高了，而且她工作一天也不会感到劳累！

B: Perhaps it sounds unsafe to some people. But it is a step of human's quest for perfect precision.

A: 是的。医学界中的进步真让我们惊叹不已。

B: I quite agree. I think the intelligent robots can perform things with much higher precision.

A: 总的来说，在机器人尤其是智能机器人的助力下，外科医生可以把手术做得更加精湛。

SECTION Ⅱ: Warm-ups for Interpretation

➢ **Interpret the following proverbs from Chinese into English.**

1. A friend in need is a friend indeed.
2. Give him an inch and he'll take a mile.
3. Never leave today's work till tomorrow.
4. Many go out for wool and come home shorn.
5. Barking dogs don't bite.

➢ **Interpret the following sentences from Chinese into English.**

1. Cardiovascular disorders, Alzheimer, diabetes are the most threatening diseases to human beings. Meanwhile, hepatitis, tuberculosis and malignant tumors should not be negligible.
2. Some young scientists have been dedicating to designing and inventing the most sophisticated navy equipment such as the nuclear submarine, aircraft carriers and amphibious landing craft.
3. While many medical advances have increased the quality of life for older people,

many have had the opposite effect by prolonging only one aspect of life and increasing dependency.

4. Neurologists use magnetic resonance imagers to watch the brain at work, thoughts and feelings vividly lighting up the screen.
5. Astronomers armed with telescopes of awesome size and clarity have for the first time recorded the reflected light of a planet outside our solar system.

➢ **Interpret the following paragraphs from Chinese into English and vice versa.**

1. Today's communications between earth and unmanned probes are expensive, proprietary, and complex. With Internet, we can simplify everything, cut costs and engage the public more effectively.
2. 目前，我们有将近 100 种新药品正在开发的不同阶段中。我们还开发了现有药品的新用途。我们的目标包括一些人类最恐惧的疾病，如心血管病、糖尿病、阿尔茨海默症、癌症、艾滋病、抑郁症和精神分裂症。

SECTION Ⅲ: Speech

The Boeing 787 "Dreamliner" is a mid-size, twin-engine, wide body jet developed by the Boeing company.

The key to the exceptional performance of the 787 Dreamliner is its suite of new technologies and its revolutionary design.

Composite materials make up 50 percent of the primary structure of the 787, including the fuselage and wing.

At the heart of the 787 design is a modern systems architecture that is simpler, more functional and more efficient than that of other airplanes. For example, onboard health-monitoring systems allow the airplane to self-monitor and report systems maintenance requirements to ground-based computer systems.

Advances in engine technology are the biggest contributor to overall fuel efficiency improvements on the Dreamliner. The 787 features new engines from General Electric and Rolls-Royce that represent nearly a two-generation jump in technology.

The design and build process of the 787 has added further efficiency gains. Boeing and its supplier partners developed new technologies and processes to enhance efficiency. For example, manufacturing the 787 fuselage as one-piece sections eliminated 1,500 aluminum sheets and 40,000 to 50,000 fasteners per section.

SECTION Ⅳ: Speech

当原子核自旋产生核磁矩时，将原子核置于外加磁场中，不同的自旋状态就会被赋予不同的核势能。静磁场会产生弱自旋极化作用，其固定频率发出的射频信号就能引起自旋核的自旋状态跃迁。这种"自旋跃迁"使一些自旋核跃迁到高能态。

如果再切断射频信号，那么高能态的核就可以返回到低能态，这种自旋弛豫的过程在发生自旋跃迁的共振频率下会产生可测量的射频信号。这一过程就是核磁共振。

核磁共振的应用最广为人知的是医学诊断使用的核磁共振成像以及各种研究中使用的核磁共振显微技术。在化学研究中，尤其是核磁共振光谱学的研究中也广泛应用到核磁共振技术。体内磁共振波谱技术和化学位移核磁共振显微镜还可以从有机体内获得各种生化信息。

课文 B

SECTION Ⅰ: Dialogue 在展位前 At an Exhibition Booth

Interpret the following dialogue from English into Chinese and vice versa.

A: Welcome to the exhibition! Please look at this Tablet PC.

B: 一体式电脑？这是什么呢？

A: Generally speaking, it is an electronic notebook.

B: 我怎么使用呢？

A: Oh, it is very simple. Please use this special pen and write on the pressure-sensitive screen.

B: 让我来试一下，但这不是我写的单词啊。

A: You should make your writing larger and clearer. Please watch my way to write the word.

B: 让我再来试一下。好，这次成功了！

A: Congratulations! You can also use this pen to highlight existing documents.

B：让我看看。确实用起来十分方便。顺便问一下，我可以改变笔的线宽和墨水的颜色吗？

A：Of course. Please choose your preferences in the setting menu.

B：真是一件奇妙的玩意！它还有其他功能吗？

A：You can regard it as a mini laptop，equipped with the normal functions of a PC. For example，you can send and receive e-mails if you have a network connection.

B：谢谢你的帮助。以后我可能会买一台。

A：You're welcome! Enjoy the exhibition!

B：谢谢。再见！

SECTION Ⅱ：Warm-ups for Interpretation

➢ **Tongue twister.**

Luke's duck likes lakes.
Luke Luck licks lakes.
Luke's duck licks lakes.
Duck takes licks in lakes Luke Luck likes.
Luke Luck takes licks in lakes duck likes.
卢克的鸭子喜欢湖。
幸运卢克拍打湖面。
卢克的鸭子拍打湖面。
鸭子在幸运卢克喜欢的湖上游泳。
幸运卢克在鸭子喜欢的湖里游泳。

➢ **Interpret the following proverbs from English into Chinese.**

1. Out of the frying pan into the fire.
2. Kill two birds with one stone.
3. There is no smoke without fire.
4. Better late than never.
5. When in Rome，do as the Romans do.

➢ **Interpret the following sentences from English into Chinese.**

1. The advancement of telecommunication technology has given us the ability to know and understand what is going on in any part of the world at any given time.
2. With rapid spread of the Internet and the relentless technological innovations generated through it, the information era is truly upon us, profoundly influencing and changing not only our lifestyle, but also the way we work, do business, think and communicate with others.
3. Meteorologists use computer models to more accurately predict the course of killer hurricanes.
4. Researchers have already built a transistor so small it can hide under a virus.
5. As speech-recognition algorithms improve, the spoken word would become the main interface to the network. This will be especially valuable with mobile device, because it overcomes the limitations of a fiddly keypad and a screen-tapping stylus.

➢ **Interpret the following paragraphs from English into Chinese and vice versa.**

1. In the 1990s the developments of music hardware continue, with the main purpose of transferring and recording the astonishingly clear digital sound of CD, without the "hiss" noise often affecting magnetic tape. The digital formats vary and include digital audio tape (DAT), digital compact cassette (DCC) and the minidisc (MD).
2. 用不了多久，分散的微处理器可能被编织在一起，组成一台台执行特定任务的计算机。不要把这类系统认作是个人电脑网络，它们的终端机很可能是一些手掌大小的手机，其智能程度远远超过当今最先进的台式计算机。

SECTION Ⅲ: Speech

Interpret the following speech from Chinese into English.

青岛国际会展中心占地 25 万平方米，5 万多平方米的室内展览面积共可设置 3,000 多个国际标准展位，同时拥有 5 万多平方米的室外展览面积。室内有一个可容纳 400 人的豪华会议厅，有 6 个可容纳 200 人的会议室及多个洽谈室和贵宾室，近万平方米的餐饮区可为来宾提供各种餐饮服务。

青岛国际会展中心实现了楼宇控制自动化、消防自动化和保安监控自动化及通信和网络信息管理自动化。会展中心与国内外展览机构建立了广泛的关系网，它还是IAEE世界展览机构的会员。

青岛国际会展中心以先进的硬件设施和优质的服务受到各界盛赞，成为举办各种大型展览和会议的理想场所。现已成功举办了“中国国际渔业博览会”“中国国际消费电子博览会”“APEC中小企业技术交流暨展览会”“全国新特药品交易会”“中国国际航海博览会”“全国五金商品交易会”“全国摩托车及配件交易会”“中国国际医药原料药中间体包装设备交易会”“中国针棉织品交易会”“全国汽车配件交易会”等大型展会。

SECTION Ⅳ: Speech

Interpret the following speech from English into Chinese.

The Qingdao Guest House, to the south of Signal Hill, was originally named the Governor's Official Residence, as it was the official residence of the German governor-general of Jiao'ao. In 1934, it was formally renamed Guest House, and became important as a retreat to receive the VIPs of military affairs and politics.

It was built in the popular Jugendstil or Art Nouveau style, with the adoption of a rough, granite exterior, steep roofs, thick walls and narrow windows reflecting the distinctive style of such German buildings.

The delicate shape, splendid ornaments, graceful lines and bold colors make the Governor's Mansion one of the best examples of German Imperial architecture anywhere in the world.

The majestic Guest House is more than 30 meters high, covering an area of over 4,000 square meters. The four-story Guest House has 15 rooms of various sizes and functions. The interior decoration is extremely luxurious and elegant. The paneling and elaborately embossed ceilings remain in excellent condition. Glittering jade stone is inlaid in the pendant lights, wall lamps and fireplaces.

Germany furniture, antiques, calligraphy and paintings from the Qing Dynasty (1644—1911) are also kept in their original locations. All the fireplaces and radiators are in different styles, and some of the original German products remain in good working order today.

Examples of this extraordinary structure, with extensive features of that period, are now rare in Germany. It is considered a valuable example of this architectural style. Many overseas architects have come to see and marvel at this masterpiece.

参考译文

SECTION Ⅰ: Dialogue

A：欢迎参观展会！请看一下这台一体式电脑。

B：Tablet PC? What is it?

A：简单地说，它是一台笔记本电脑。

B：How can I use it?

A：非常简单。请用这支特殊的笔在这块压力敏感的屏幕上书写。

B：Let me have a try… but it is not the word I expect.

A：你的笔迹应该更大、更清楚一些。请看我是怎么写的。

B：Let me give it another shot. Yes! It works this time!

A：祝贺你！你也可以用这支笔在现有文件上画重点或签署文件。

B：Let me see. I think it is pretty much easy to use. By the way, can I choose the pen's line width and ink color?

A：当然了。请在设置菜单里选择你喜欢的内容。

B：What a fancy gadget! Does it have any other functions?

A：你可以把它看作一台迷你手提电脑，它具有一般电脑的功能。比如，如果联网的话，还可以收发电子邮件等。

B：Thank you for your help. Maybe I will buy one in the future.

A：不客气！祝你参观愉快！

B：Thanks. Bye-bye!

SECTION Ⅱ: Warm-ups for Interpretation

➢ **Interpret the following proverbs from English into Chinese.**

1. 一波未平一波又起。

2. 一举两得。
3. 无风不起浪。
4. 晚做总比不做强。
5. 入乡随俗。

➢ **Interpret the following sentences from English into Chinese.**

1. 电信技术的进步使我们能够了解并理解世界上任何一个地方，在任何时间发生的事情。
2. 因特网迅速普及，以及因特网带来的势不可当的技术创新，使我们真正进入了信息时代，并深刻地影响和改变着我们的生活、工作、商务活动、思考和沟通方式。
3. 气象学家利用计算机模型更准确地预测致命飓风的路线。
4. 研究人员早已制造出一种小得可以隐藏在病毒下面的晶体管。
5. 随着语音识别法的改进，语音将变成网络的主要接口。这项技术在移动设备上尤其能够体现其价值，因为它克服了键盘和触控笔的限制。

➢ **Interpret the following paragraphs from English into Chinese and vice versa.**

1. 进入20世纪90年代后，音响行业还在继续发展，发展重点放在转录CD无比清晰的数码声音的技术上，这种技术不会产生使用磁带时通常会出现的"咝咝"的噪声。使用数码声音技术可以有各种不同的编排格式，其中包括数码音带(DAT)、数码微型盒式带(DCC)和数码微型光盘(MD)等格式。
2. Before long, discrete microprocessors will probably be knitted together into adhoc distributed computers. Don't think of these as PC networks. The terminals would just as likely be cell phones of palm-like devices, each one far smarter than today's heftiest desktops.

SECTION Ⅲ: Speech

Qingdao International Convention Center (QICC) covers an area of 250,000 m^2. The indoor exhibition area comprising 50,000 m^2 can hold 3000 standard exhibition booths. An outdoor exhibition area provides an additional 50,000 m^2. The indoor area includes a luxurious conference room which can cater up to 400 people, six meeting rooms each with a capacity of 200 people, and many negotiation and VIP rooms. The snack area of nearly

10,000 m^2 provides delicious food and beverage service.

QICC has completely automated building control system, fire control system, security surveillance system, communication system and network information system. It has established a broad network with both domestic and overseas exhibition agencies and is a member of the IAEM.

QICC has been widely praised for its advanced facilities and high-quality service. It is an ideal place for holding large-scale exhibitions and conventions. Many major international exhibitions have been held here including the "China Fisheries & Seafood Expo""China International Consumer Electronics Show""APEC Medium & Small Enterprises Technology Conference and Fair""New Drugs China""China International Marine Fair""National Hardware Fair""National Commodity Fair of Motorcycle and accessories""API China" "China Knitwear & Cotton Goods Fair" and "China Automobile Parts Purchase Fair" and so on.

SECTION Ⅳ: Speech

青岛迎宾馆坐落于信号山南麓，是当年德国胶澳总督的官邸，故最早称为"总督官邸"。1934年改称为"迎宾馆"，并成为招待军政要人的重要场所。

迎宾馆是一座"新艺术派"风格的建筑，外部采用粗糙的花岗岩石料装饰，尖形屋顶、墙壁较厚、窗户略窄，反映出此类德国建筑的独特风格。

其造型之典雅，装饰之豪华，轮廓线条之优美，色彩之瑰丽，是世界上最具德国皇家风格的建筑典范之一。

迎宾馆气势宏伟，高30多米，建筑面积4000多平方米。楼内共4层，有15个房间，各房间大小不同、功能各异。楼内装饰异常富丽堂皇。内墙装饰、精雕细刻的雕花天花板皆完好如新。吊灯、壁灯和壁炉内皆镶嵌着闪闪发光的宝石。

清朝年间(1644—1911)的德国家具、古董、字画都原封不动地保存在原位。房内所有的壁炉、暖气风格各异，部分当年的德国产品现在还可以正常使用。

现在，这种气派非凡、极具那个时代风格的建筑在德国已不多见了。众多国外建筑家慕名而来，他们都对这个完美的建筑艺术杰作赞叹不已。

Unit 9 工业展览会 Industrial Exhibition

和平发展、合作共赢才是人间正道。不同国家、不同文明要在彼此尊重中共同发展、在求同存异中合作共赢。

The right way forward for humanity is peaceful development and win-win cooperation. Different countries and civilizations may prosper together on the basis of respect for each other, and seek common ground and win-win outcomes by setting aside differences.

课文 A

SECTION Ⅰ: Dialogue 商定合同 Contract Negotiation

Interpret the following dialogue from Chinese into English and vice versa.

A：贝克先生，您对这些条款都满意吗？

B：Yes, Mr. Liang, we have checked our contract once again. Now we have finally come to a basic agreement.

A：太好了。谢谢您的合作。

B：But there are still some fundamental problems which need to be solved. Do you think we have to discuss them again?

A：好啊，我们现在就讨论一下。有些重要的条款的确需要写明白。

B：First of all, about the format of our contract, we always use copies prepared and printed by our own company. Will that be all right?

A：可以，合同中所有内容都得用中英两种文字说明。

B：Now，let's check the items in the contract. Let's start from the names of the commodity，specifications，quantity，unit prices，the total payment，logistics company and shipment.

A：嗯，非常好，但我必须在这里指出，货运必须在10月底之前完成。我们不能接受任何耽搁。

B：Of course not. But since our price is determined on the basis of C. I. F.，the insurance premium should be borne by your side.

A：那没问题。还有其他问题吗？

B：No more，we've discussed everything.

A：那太好了！

B：Mr. Liang，when will the contract be ready?

A：后天下午三点我们可以在此签约了。

B：Awesome. I will see you then.

A：到时候见。

相关词汇

常用商贸会展英语词汇

all risks　一切险
partnership　合伙企业
stockholder　股东
foreign-funded enterprise　外资企业
joint venture　合资企业
cooperative enterprise　合作企业
private enterprise　私营企业
world/international market price　国际市场价格
wholesale price　批发价
discount/allowance　折扣
retail price　零售价
total value　总值
bulk sale　整批销售
wholesale　批发
retail　零售
wholesaler　批发商
retailer　零售商
contract　合同
transaction　交易
commission　佣金
logistics　物流
purchase　购买
promotion　促销

commodity 商品
participate 参加
participant 参与者
trade fair 商品交易会
fair 商品展销会
exhibition 展览会
display 展出
bazaar (中东、印度等地的)集市
exposition 博览会
venue 举办场所
pavilion 展馆
booth 展位
showroom 展室
exhibition hall 展厅
display counter/shelf 展示柜/架
exhibit 展品
exhibitor 参展商
convention center 展览馆
buying group 采购团
quoted company 上市公司
ruling price 现行价格
consumer goods 日用品

SECTION Ⅱ: Warm-ups for Interpretation

➢ **Tongue twister.**

Betty and Bob brought back blue balloons from the big bazaar.
贝蒂和鲍勃从大自由市场买回了蓝色气球。
I know a boy named Tate,
who dined with his girl at eight eight.
I'm unable to state what Tate ate at eight eight,
or what Tate's tête à tête ate at eight eight.
我认识一个叫泰特的男孩，在八点八分和女友一起就餐。
我描述不出泰特八点八分吃的什么，或泰特在八点八分吃的什么。

➢ **Interpret the following proverbs from English into Chinese.**

1. Where there is a will, there's a way.
2. History repeats itself.
3. The grass is always greener on the other side (of the fence).
4. All work and no play makes Jack a dull boy.
5. Monkey see, monkey do.

➤ **Interpret the following sentences from English into Chinese.**

1. The company proposed a six-month contract at a 14% discount of the quoted price and is waiting for a positive react.
2. Let me run through this again: 2,000 units at a discount of 15%; the shipment for the first 500 units to be delivered in 20 days, by the 21st.
3. If you place your order in ten days, we can make the shipment in March.
4. Please feel free to contact me if you have any further queries on this or any other matter.
5. I'm glad we've arrived at an agreement on price. Shall we come to the payment terms now?

➤ **Interpret the following paragraphs from English into Chinese and vice versa.**

1. It is evident that a business deal can't be completed without caring for the quantity of the goods sold and bought. It is the quantity that counts for much. The business laws of certain countries stipulate that the quantity of the goods delivered should be identical to that called for in the contract. The buyer is entitled to reject the goods if the quantity delivered is less or more than agreed upon. Therefore, attention should be paid to the quantity terms when negotiating business.
2. 不同厂家的产品有时在设计、质量和做工上不具有可比性。你说的对，我们的新产品价格高很多。你知道，新产品的成本比较高。我们不可能以低于其价值的价格出售。另外，我们的产品质量上乘，售价理应较高。

SECTION Ⅲ: Speech

Interpret the following speech from Chinese into English.

很高兴今天晚上能来到这里，感谢你们所有人来参加这次盛大的新展览会开幕式。这是国际货币基金组织参观中心展览会的常规项目之一。在此，非常荣幸能够使美国史密森国家自然博物馆作为我们的共同赞助者。如果博物馆内没有这么多此类收藏品，我想今晚的展会会黯然失色。

在基金组织里，我们每个工作日都与钱打交道。当然，我们非常了解货币与主权的关系，但很少有时间思考这种关系的历史，这正是展览会如此吸引人的原因。由于现在要四处观看展览品，我希望您稍后抽时间思考货币与主权的关系，你将看出这两者的关系是多么根深蒂固。

SECTION Ⅳ: Speech

Interpret the following speech from English into Chinese.

The Dynamic Macao Business and Trade Fair opened on October 13 in the eastern coastal city of Qingdao, Shandong province.

The three-day event is being held at the Qingdao International Convention and Exhibition Center, where six special exhibition areas have been set up to promote the gourmet food, traditional crafts, innovative products, fashionable items, and unique culture of Macao and other Portuguese-speaking regions.

According to the organizing committee, this is the largest promotional event held by Macao in the Chinese mainland so far this year.

Around 300 representatives from the government of the Macao Special Administrative Region, the Permanent Secretariat of the Forum for Economic and Trade Cooperation between China and Portuguese-speaking Countries (Forum Macao), and guests from the industry, commerce, tourism and education sectors of Macau will attend the event.

Macao will also hold a series of economic and trade activities with a number of enterprises in Qingdao to facilitate investment and cooperation between the two sides.

参考译文

SECTION Ⅰ: Dialogue

A: Mr. Baker, are you satisfied with all the terms here?

B: 是的，梁先生，我们又检查了一遍合同。现在我们终于基本达成了一致。

A: Great, thank you for your collaboration.

B: 但是，还有一些根本问题亟待解决。您认为我们有必要再讨论一下这些问题吗？

A: It's a good idea. We can do it now. Some important items should be clearly clarified.

B：首先，就合同的格式而言，我们公司通常准备和打印合同副本。您看，这样行吗？

A：Yes. All the contents are written both in Chinese and English.

B：现在让我们检查一下合同中的条款，我们先从品名、规格、数量、单价、总额、物流公司、以及运输来看吧。

A：Yes, very good. But I want to point out here that shipment should be completed before the end of October. We cannot accept any delay.

B：那是当然。但是我们的价格是按到岸价定的，保险费应由贵方负担。

A：Certainly. Are there any other problems?

B：现在没有了，所有的问题都已经讨论过了。

A：Fantastic!

B：梁先生，合同什么时候能准备好？

A：We can sign it here at three o'clock sharp the day after tomorrow afternoon.

B：那真是太好了，到时候见。

A：See you then.

SECTION Ⅱ: Warm-ups for Interpretation

➢ **Interpret the following proverbs from English into Chinese.**

1. 功夫不负有心人。
2. 历史总在重演。
3. 东西总是人家的好。
4. 只会工作不会玩的人是没意思的人。
5. 东施效颦(机械模仿)。

➢ **Interpret the following sentences from English into Chinese.**

1. 那家公司提议签署一份折扣 14%、为期半年的合同，目前正在等待对方做出积极回应。
2. 我再重复一遍：订货量 2,000 件，折扣 15%；第一批 500 件 20 日内交货，也就是 21 日前运到。
3. 如果你们能在 10 天内下订单，我们可以在 3 月份装运。
4. 若您对此事或其他未及事宜有疑问，请随时跟我联系。

5. 很高兴我们就价格问题达成一致。现在我们该谈付款方式了吧?

➢ **Interpret the following paragraphs from English into Chinese and vice versa.**

1. 显然，不涉及购买商品的订货量，生意就不能成交。因此，订货量很重要。有些国家的商贸法规定，发货数量应该和合同上商议的数量一致，如果货物在数量上多出或者不足，买家有权拒绝接收。因此在经贸商谈中，一定要注意有关数量的条款。
2. Products of different companies are not always comparable in design, quality and workmanship. You are right when you say our new models are much more expensive. Their cost is higher, you know. We can't sell them under their true value. What's more, they should be sold for better prices for their top quality.

SECTION Ⅲ: Speech

I'm delighted to be here this evening, and I am glad that you could all join us to mark the opening of this splendid new exhibition. This is one of a regular series of exhibitions in the IMF Visitor Center, and on this occasion, we are very grateful to have the Smithsonian National Museum of American history as co-sponsor. Without access to this, one of the largest such collections in the world, I think the displays would have looked somewhat less enticing than they do!

In the Fund we deal with money every working day, of course, and are in one sense keenly aware of the relationship between money and sovereignty. But we rarely have time to reflect on the history of this relationship, which is why this exhibition is so fascinating. As you wander around the displays—and I hope you will take the time to do so later—you will see how deep-rooted the relationship is.

SECTION Ⅳ: Speech

活力澳门商贸展于10月13日在东部沿海城市山东省青岛市开幕。

为期三天的商展活动在青岛国际会展中心举行，设立了六个特别展览区，以推广澳门和其他葡语地区的美食、传统工艺品、创新产品、时尚物品和独特文化。

据组委会介绍，这是澳门今年迄今为止在中国大陆举办的规模最大的商贸宣传活动。

来自澳门特别行政区政府、中葡国家经贸合作论坛（中葡论坛）常设秘书处以及澳门工商旅游及教育界约300名代表将出席活动。

澳门还将与青岛多家企业举行一系列经贸活动，促进双方的投资合作。

课文 B

SECTION Ⅰ: Dialogue 商议合资事宜 Discuss Details on Running Joint Venture

Interpret the following dialogue from Chinese into English and vice versa.

A： 我是山东绮丽集团公司的总代理，很高兴见到你。

B： Nice meeting you. I've come here to discuss with you the issue of establishing a joint venture.

A： 合资意味着投资者可以享受优惠的税费待遇，我们对此也很感兴趣。

B： Let's talk about the details of the project. What are your terms and conditions on joint venture?

A： 我们希望能得到技术上的支持。如果有必要，最好安排一些技术研讨会和培训班。

B： Certainly. What are the regulations regarding the foreign party's share in registered capital?

A： 根据有关规定，外国投资者的注册资本投资比例不应少于25％。

B： I suppose we would be responsible for the machinery and other capital equipment.

A： 产品价格由你方定还是双方协定？

B： Oh, the price should be fixed in parallel to that at the international markets. It should be set by both sides to make a win-win.

A： 合资经营期限多长？

B： As it is a small venture, I propose 6 years to start with.

A： 作为合资伙伴，我方是否有权自行招聘或解雇人员？

B： Yes, both parties should have the right to hire or fire staff, except the members of the Board of Directors.

A： 我们将草拟一份合同，明天下午送给你。

B： OK. See you then.

SECTION Ⅱ: Warm-ups for Interpretation

➢ **Tongue twister.**

If you stick a stock of liquor in your locker,
it is slick to stick a lock upon your stock.
Or some joker who is slicker,
is going to trick you of your liquor,
if you fail to lock your liquor with a lock.
如果你在更衣柜里储藏了一些酒，
聪明的话你应该在储藏的酒柜上上把锁。
如果你没有用锁锁好你的酒，
或许一个狡猾的人就会和你开玩笑。
好骗走你柜子里的酒，

➢ **Interpret the following proverbs from Chinese into English.**

1. 说曹操，曹操到。
2. 一朝被蛇咬，十年怕井绳。
3. 谋事在人，成事在天。
4. 无风不起浪。
5. 家丑不可外扬。

➢ **Interpret the following sentences from Chinese into English.**

1. 请准备中英文合同各一份，两份同样有效。
2. 我们来讨论一下建立合资企业的事宜。您能告诉我您的设想吗？如您打算在合资企业中占多少投资份额？
3. 投资办合资企业时，通常由外方提供资金、机械、先进技术和管理方法，而中方则提供土地、劳工以及部分用于基础设施建设的资金。
4. 我们的合作期定为 10 年，只要双方愿意，期满后我们还可以续签合同。
5. 我建议成立董事会监管公司的运作，并以平等的伙伴关系分享权力，承担义务。

➢ **Interpret the following paragraphs from Chinese into English and vice versa.**

1. 我们的休闲服饰包括夹克、裤子、衬衫、套头衫和西服等。面料有两种：全棉以及尼龙和棉的混纺。有人喜欢穿全棉衣服，也有人喜欢混纺面料。全棉的比较柔软，但混纺的不易起褶、耐穿、不变形。我们的大部分服装都可以用温水进行机洗和甩干。

2. Well, I'm much impressed by your showroom. Most of the models are new to our customers in America, but I believe some have potential markets there. I've already seen some items we'd like to order, and I know you will give us a favorable discount for the first possible order, which of course cannot be a large one. I'll talk to my office about the size of the order and we have to study it a bit further. I'll probably let you know by the next Monday.

SECTION Ⅲ: Speech

Interpret the following speech from Chinese into English.

中国出口商品交易会，又称广交会，创办于1957年春季，每年春秋两季在广州举办，迄今已有五十余年的历史，是中国目前层次最高、规模最大、商品种类最全、到会客商最多、成交效果最好的贸易展会。

广交会在延续传统的基础上，发展成为一个综合、多功能的国际性盛会。

广交会由48个交易团组成，有数千家资信良好、实力雄厚的外贸公司、生产企业、科研院所、外资企业、合资企业和私营企业参展。

广交会的贸易谈判及促销方式灵活多样，除传统的看样成交外，还举办网上交易会。

广交会以出口贸易为主，也做进口生意，还可以开展多种形式的经济技术合作与交流，以及商检、保险、运输、广告、咨询等业务活动。

来自世界各地的客商云集广州，互通商情，增进贸易往来。

SECTION Ⅳ: Speech

Interpret the following speech from English into Chinese.

Councilor Mark Hackett, Lord Mayor of Manchester,

Sir Warren Smith, Lord Lieutenant of Greater Manchester,

Professor John Brooks, Vice Chancellor of Manchester Metropolitan University,

Consul-General Ni Jian,

Ladies and Gentlemen,

Thank you very much for joining us for the opening of "EXPO NOW", the photo exhibition of the Shanghai World Expo, in Manchester.

Since its opening 2 months ago, the Expo has proved to be a major attraction for Chinese and overseas visitors, receiving 18 million visitors in total, or 330 thousand per day on average. Enthusiastic visitors often have to queue for hours to get into the UK National Pavilion and other popular venues. Not surprisingly, football has become a new highlight in many venues. Someone came up with the smart idea of installing a wax figure of Wayne Rooney in the entrance of the UK Pavilion, which as you can imagine has made your pavilion even more popular.

The UK is the birthplace of the modern Expo and a star performer at the Shanghai Expo. The UK pavilion, nicknamed as Dandelion by Chinese internet users, symbolizes the modern creative vigor of Britain. The UK has also made full use of the Expo by organizing events and visits to promote cooperation in business, science, technology and culture between our two countries.

In hosting this photo exhibition, we would like to share with the British public the joy the Expo brings and also encourage the British public to learn more about Shanghai and China. The 100 photos on display here capture some of the memorable moments of the Expo and offer breath-taking views of the different pavilions. It also traces China's participation in the World Expo over the past century and shows a real Shanghai, both past and present.

I also wish to take this opportunity to thank ARUP for their strong support and to thank Bank of China (UK)and Communications Bank of China for sponsoring this event. My thanks also go to my colleague Consul-General Ni Jian and his staff for their hard work and to Manchester Metropolitan University for providing a wonderful venue and thoughtful services for the exhibition.

Finally, I wish Expo Now in Manchester a great success. Thank you.

参考译文

SECTION Ⅰ: Dialogue

A: I'm the sales rep of Shandong Cherry Group. Nice to meet you.

B: 我也很高兴见到你。我这次来是想和你们谈谈建立合资企业的问题。

A: Joint ventures investors are entitled to preferential taxation. We have interest in that, too.

B: 那我们现在就谈谈项目的具体事宜吧。贵方合资经营的条件是什么?

A: We hope to get your technical support. It's most necessary to hold some technical seminars and special training programs for us.

B: 那当然可以。在注册资本中，对国外合营者的投资比例有什么明文规定吗?

A: According to the regulations concerned, the foreign party's share should be no less than 25%.

B: 我想我们将负责机械设备和其他资本设备。

A: Do you fix the product price by yourself or bilaterally?

B: 哦，产品价格应根据国际市场价格，由双方共同协商确定，以使合作双方双赢。

A: What is the duration of the joint venture?

B: 这个企业规模不大，我建议先定为 6 年。

A: As one partner of the joint venture, do we have the right to recruit or layoff employees?

B: 是的，双方均有权招聘或解雇人员，董事会成员除外。

A: We'll draft the contract and bring it to you tomorrow afternoon.

B: 好，到时再见。

SECTION Ⅱ: Warm-ups for Interpretation

➢ **Interpret the following proverbs from Chinese into English.**

1. Talk of the devil and he's sure to appear.
2. Once bitten, twice shy.

3. Man proposes and God disposes.
4. Where there's smoke, there is fire.
5. It's dirty bird that fouls her own nest. /Don't wash the dirty linen in public.

➢ **Interpret the following sentences from Chinese into English.**

1. Please prepare both Chinese and English versions of the contract. Both should be equally valid.
2. Let's get down to the business of establishing a joint venture. May I have some idea of your plan? For instance, how much would your share of investment be in this venture?
3. When establishing a joint venture, the foreign partner usually brings into the enterprise capital funds, machinery, advanced technology and management, while the Chinese partner supplies land, labor, and a portion of the funds for the infrastructure.
4. Let's say we begin with a 10-year term of a renewable partnership; we can extend our contract for another term before it expires, if both parties intend to.
5. I suggest that we should set up a board of directors for the management of the company and share rights and obligations as equal partners.

➢ **Interpret the following paragraphs from Chinese into English and vice versa.**

1. Our casual ware includes jackets, pants, shirts, pullovers and suits. They are available in 100% cotton and blend of nylon and cotton. Some people prefer the cotton ones, but others like the blends. The cotton clothes are softer; the blend is wrinkle-resistant, durable, and keeps good shape. Most of them are machine washable in warm water and tumble dryable.
2. 你们的展室给我留下了很深的印象。尽管美国的客户对你们的大部分型号比较陌生，但我觉得其中一些产品会有潜在的市场。我已经看过一些打算下订单的产品，我也明白你们在价格方面会给我们的第一笔订单提供优惠。当然，第一笔订货量不会很大。我得和公司方面讨论一下订货量，再进一步研究研究，然后在下个星期一可能会告知你们讨论结果。

SECTION Ⅲ: Speech

Chinese Export Commodities Fair (CECF), also called the Canton Fair, is held twice a year in both spring and autumn since it was first held in the spring of 1957. It has a history of more than fifty years. CECF is China's largest trade fair of the highest level and the largest scale, of the most complete varieties of commodities and of the largest attendance and business outcome.

Preserving its traditions, the fair develops itself into a comprehensive and multi-functional event of international importance.

Forty-eight trading delegations take part in the fair. Comprised of thousands of China's best foreign trade corporations with good credibility and sound financial capabilities, the delegations include foreign trade companies, manufacturers, scientific research institutions, foreign enterprises, joint venture enterprises and private enterprises.

The fair features in flexible and diversified ways of business negotiation and business promotion. In addition to the traditional way of negotiating against samples, the fair also holds its online fair.

The commodity fair mainly deals with export business as well as import business. Apart from this, other types of business activities such as economic and technical cooperations and exchanges, commodity inspection, insurance, transportation, advertising, consultation, etc. also take place here.

Every year, business people from all over the world are gathering in Guangzhou, exchanging business information and pursuing business transactions.

SECTION Ⅳ: Speech

尊敬的曼彻斯特市长哈克特先生，

尊敬的大曼彻斯特地区女王代表史密斯爵士，

尊敬的曼彻斯特城市大学校长布鲁克斯先生，

尊敬的倪坚总领事，

女士们，先生们：

欢迎大家出席上海世博会图片英国巡回展“世博风”曼彻斯特站开幕活动。

上海世博会已开幕 2 个月，共接待 1,800 万人次海内外观众，平均每天接待游客 33

万人次。像英国馆这样的热门场馆，尽管需要排数小时的长队，观众仍然热情不减。适逢世界杯举行，各国展馆相应地增加了足球元素。英国参展方将球星鲁尼的蜡像放在了英国馆前，这无疑是个绝妙的主意，吸引了更多观众前往英国馆。

英国是世博会的发源地，此次在上海世博会也有着出色的表现。英国馆被中国网友昵称为“蒲公英”，生动展现了现代英国的形象。英国各界也积极抓住上海世博会的机遇，组织了各种活动，推动加强了双边经贸、科技和文化等各领域的合作。

为了让英国民众更好地感受上海世博会，更好地了解中国，了解上海，中国驻英国大使馆主办了此次世博会图片英国巡回展。展出的近100张图片，展示了许多颇具特色的场馆，记录了各国人民欢庆世博会的难忘瞬间，反映了中国参与世博会的百年历程，体现了新旧上海的发展变化。

我愿借此机会，感谢英国奥雅纳集团(ARUP)和上海联谊会的大力协助，感谢中国银行(英国)和中国交通银行为巡回展提供赞助。同时感谢倪坚总领事及总领馆人员的辛勤筹办，也非常感谢曼彻斯特城市大学为巡回展提供场地和各项周到服务。

最后，我预祝上海世博会图片英国巡回展在曼彻斯特的举办圆满成功！谢谢。

Unit 10 工业展览 At the Industrial Exhibition

中国将继续降低关税和交易成本，发展示范区以促进进口，并从世界各地购买更多高质量的商品和服务。

China will continue to lower tariffs and transaction costs, develop demonstration zones to promote imports, and purchase more high-quality goods and services from around the world.

中国将继续按照广泛协商、共同贡献和利益共享的原则推进"一带一路"合作。

China will continue to advance the Belt and Road cooperation following the principle of extensive consultation, joint contribution and shared benefits.

我们都必须把人类的共同利益放在第一位，而不是把自己的利益置于所有人的共同利益之上，我们必须共同努力"让全球市场的蛋糕变得更大"。

We must all put the common good of humanity first rather than place one's own interests above the common interests of all, and we must make joint efforts to "make the global market pie even bigger".

课文 A

SECTION Ⅰ: Dialogue 在展位前 At the Booth

Interpret the following dialogue from Chinese into English and vice versa.

A：欢迎参观我们的展位。

B：Oh, it's a gracious showroom.

A：这是我们工具的样品，各种型号的都有。

B：Mm… They look very gorgeous.

A：我们的工具质量又好又耐用，很受欧洲和美国市场的欢迎。

B：Actually，tools made in China are also very popular in our market.

A：那太好了！您今天想订些货吗？

B：The quality seems all right. But I have to consider their competitive price.

A：这很正常。可是，请看我们的工具，质量好、用途广、做工精细。

B：But your prices are a bit high.

A：诚实地讲，你看到的工具在其他市场上以这个价格很难买到。

B：I would place a big order if you're to include a reasonable discount.

A：我们保证工具的质量，至于折扣问题，我们可以给你打个 9 折。

B：Well，could you give me a lower price， say 20% off.

A：对不起，9 折已是我们的底价了。

B：I appreciate your frankness. Your offer is much beyond my knowledge. Still，I would like to make a trial order.

A：谢谢。相信你会对我们的产品质量很满意，并且还会订更多的货。

B：Hopefully，our initial cooperation will lead to more in the future.

相关词汇

常用工具及汽车类相关英语

wrench 扳手
screwdriver 螺丝刀
pliers 钳子
saw 锯
chisel 凿子
hammer 锤子
jackhammer 手提钻
jack 千斤顶
Audi 奥迪
BMW 宝马
Bentley 宾利
Buick 别克
Cadillac 凯迪拉克
Citroen 雪铁龙
Chevrolet 雪佛兰
Ferrari 法拉利
Fiat 菲亚特
Ford 福特
Honda 本田
Hyundai 现代
Jeep 吉普
Kia 起亚

Land Rover　路虎
Lexus　雷克萨斯
Lincoln　林肯
Mazda　马自达
Benz　奔驰
Nissan　尼桑
Peugeot　标致
Porsche　保时捷
Rolls-Royce　劳斯莱斯
Toyota　丰田
Volkswagen　大众
Volvo　沃尔沃

windscreen　挡风玻璃
windshield　雨刷
rear mirror　后视镜
bonnet/hood　发动机盖
boot/trunk　行李箱
bumper　保险杠
engine　引擎
diesel engine　柴油发动机
steering wheel　方向盘
sunroof　通风口
air bag　气囊
transmission　传动系统

SECTION Ⅱ: Warm-ups for Interpretation

➢ **Tongue twister.**

How many berries could a bare berry carry,
if a bare berry could carry berries?
Well they can't carry berries,
which could make you very wary,
but a bare berry carried is more scary!
如果一棵秃的浆果树能结浆果的话，
一棵光秃的浆果树能结多少粒浆果？
别说啦，它们不可能结果，
但是一棵不结果的秃树是多么难看。

➢ **Interpret the following proverbs from Chinese into English.**

1. 老马识途。
2. 同舟共济。
3. 酒后吐真言。
4. 健康胜于财富。

5. 一夜暴富。

➢ **Interpret the following sentences from Chinese into English.**

1. 你们的产品给我留下了深刻的印象，品种多样，具有独创性。相信这些产品在我们地区很有市场潜力。
2. 如果订货量大，我们就在折扣上给予优惠。
3. 如今，平板电脑、笔记本电脑、空调、手机等各种家用电器也走进了偏远地区的千家万户。
4. 我们产品的特点是耐用、稳定和轻便。
5. 我们空调的一大特色是噪声小。空调的运行声音很恼人，我们已经把这种声音降到了最低限度。

➢ **Interpret the following paragraphs from Chinese into English and vice versa.**

1. 你们能看出我们的产品和其他商家产品的不同吗？我们的产品要么是新开发产品，要么是改进型的。我们采用的是高科技材料，因此我们的产品耐用、轻便、舒适。另外，我们的产品很容易保养：可以机洗和烘干。这是我们的产品说明和价目表。请大家仔细看一看，然后再做决定。
2. If you wish, you can visit our showroom any time in February between 9 am to 5 pm. Our newly-developed and modified products are displayed there. The two-door frost-free refrigerator, our featured product which you are particularly interested in is among them. You can also see other similar products, which, I am sure, have ready markets in your area.

SECTION Ⅲ: Speech

Interpret the following speech from Chinese into English.

2019年青岛汽车工业展是迄今为止在中国举办的规模最大的车展，参展面积达到了12万平方米。

除此之外，各家汽车公司都为这次展览做了大量的准备工作。参展商想要的参展空间远远超过了展会场所所能提供的空间。

尽管参展空间有限，每位参展商仍把这次车展视为A级国际展。各位参展商对展位预定、展位设计、展品和供货商的选择、现场表演的安排等工作，做得都很到位。他们的努力使此次展览毫不亚于其他一流水平的国际展览。

各位汽车巨头都组织大批人员参加这次汽车展，他们借此强调品牌概念，把品牌意识和品牌观念带给中国观众。

使用清洁能源的高科技环保车也在此次展会上展出。这些汽车的展出把人与自然的和谐体现得淋漓尽致。它们的展出也十分切合举办这次车展的目的，那就是坚持科技发展的理念。

中国巨大的潜在市场已经吸引了许多高级汽车，宾利汽车和劳斯莱斯的参展是本次车展的又一个亮点。此外，许多世界知名品牌的最新车型也都首次亮相于2019年青岛汽车工业展。毫无疑问，一辆接一辆出现在本次展会上的新车肯定会吸引无数车迷的目光。

SECTION Ⅳ: Speech

Interpret the following speech from English into Chinese.

One of Haier's most valuable assets is its body of corporate business information. Failure to adequately protect this corporate information can lead to the loss of highly confidential data that may place Haier at a disadvantage in the marketplace.

As an employee, you are responsible and accountable for the integrity and protection of all business information in your possession (including your electronic mail and voice mail) and you must take steps to protect information that has been entrusted to you. For example, you must not inappropriately modify information or destroy, disfigure or disclose Haier information. Customer lists, property records and other business information—even if compiled from public sources—are the property of Haier and cannot be taken or used for personal benefit or to benefit a competitor or third party.

Documents containing sensitive data should be handled carefully during working hours and must be properly secured at the end of the business day. Particular attention must be paid to the security of computer systems. You must ensure the physical security of these systems as well as protect them from unauthorized access through the use of passwords. Passwords should never consist of family names or birth dates and must be set and maintained in compliance with established password formatting standards. If you see people that you do not recognize using computers in your area, immediately report this to your supervisor.

参考译文

SECTION Ⅰ: Dialogue

A：Welcome to our booth.

B：噢，你们的展厅很雅致。

A：Here are some samples of our tools in all sizes.

B：嗯，这些工具棒极了。

A：Our tools are well-known for their fine quality and durability. They are popular among the European and American markets.

B：的确，中国制造的工具在我们的市场上也很受欢迎。

A：That's great! Would you like to place an order today?

B：看上去质量很不错，但我也得考虑一下其竞争性价格。

A：That's quite natural. Look at our tools. They're of great quality, multi-function and fine workmanship.

B：但是你们的价格有点贵。

A：Honestly, tools at our stand are not available at other markets with this same price.

B：如果您能给我一些合理的折扣，我可能会大批订货。

A：We guarantee the quality of our tools. As for the discount, we may consider a 10% discount.

B：嗯，价格能不能再低一点？打个 8 折吧！

A：Sorry, 10% off is our bottom line.

B：我很欣赏你的直率。虽然您给我的价格超出我的预料，我仍愿意试定一批货。

A：Thank you. I firmly believe you will be pleased with our product quality. And I hope you will place a big order in future.

B：希望我们这次合作仅仅是个开始，今后将有更多合作机会。

SECTION Ⅱ: Warm-ups for Interpretation

➢ **Interpret the following proverbs from Chinese into English.**

1. Sense comes with age.
2. Those are in the same boat should row together.
3. The heart is seen in wine.
4. Wealth is nothing without health.
5. Make a fortune overnight.

➢ **Interpret the following sentences from Chinese into English.**

1. I am deeply impressed by the diversity and creativity of your products. I am sure they have market potential in my area.
2. If you place a large order, you will enjoy a profitable discount.
3. IPad, laptops, AC, cell phones and other types of home appliances have been widely used in remote regions nowadays.
4. Durability, stability, and light weight are typical of our products.
5. Low noise is characteristic of our air-conditioners. The offensive operating noise has been reduced to a minimum.

➢ **Interpret the following paragraphs from Chinese into English and vice versa.**

1. Do you see the differences between our products and others? Ours are either newly-developed or modified models. They are made of high-tech materials so that they are durable, light and comfortable. What's more, they are easy to care: machine washable and tumble dryable. Here are some of the brochures and price lists. You may have a good study of them before you make a decision.
2. 如果你们愿意，可以在 2 月份任何一天，上午 9 点至下午 5 点来我们展厅。展厅内展示了我们的新产品和改进型产品，其中包括你们特别感兴趣的特色产品双门无霜冰箱。另外，你们也会看到其他类似产品。相信这些产品在你们那也会有一定的市场潜力。

SECTION Ⅲ: Speech

Qingdao International Auto Show in 2019 is the largest auto exhibition ever held in China. The total exhibition space area reaches 120,000 square meters.

In addition, each auto company makes great efforts on the preparation and the expected exhibiting space from the exhibitors were far more than the venue could possibly offer.

Despite space limitations, each exhibitor still regards Auto Show Qingdao 2019 as an A-Class international show, as they did a good job for booth reservation, booth design, selection of exhibits and suppliers to the arrangement of on-site activities, which make their presentations equal to other top international exhibitions.

Coming to the show in a big group, each auto giant will highlight the concept of brands, thus bringing the brand awareness and brand conscious to Chinese visitors.

The new environmentally friendly car with high technology to use clean energy is also on display, which fully reflects a kind of harmony, which is symbolized by its scientific development concept.

China's huge market has a big potential and has attracted numerous high-class autos, and the presence of Bentley and Rolls-Royce at the Auto Show will be another attraction in the exhibition. Besides, many latest models of world-famous brand autos made their first appearance in Auto Show Qingdao 2019. These initially launched cars consecutively appearing at the show will surely attract the eyes of numerous auto fans.

SECTION Ⅳ: Speech

海尔公司最有价值的资产之一是其公司的商业信息。如果未能妥善保护公司的这些信息，则可能导致高度机密的数据丢失，从而可能使海尔公司在市场上处于劣势地位。

作为一名员工，您要对您掌握的所有商业信息(其中包括您的电子邮件和电话留言)的完整性负责，并且您必须采取措施保护委托给您的信息。例如，您不得不当地修改信息，或销毁、破坏、披露海尔公司的信息。顾客清单、财产记录和其他商业信息，即使从公开来源汇编的，也是海尔公司的财产，不能为个人利益，或者使竞争对手或第三方受益。

包含敏感数据的文件应在工作时间内认真处理，并且必须在工作日结束时加以妥善保管。必须特别注意计算机系统的安全性。您必须确保这些系统的物理安全，并防止有人使用密码对这些系统进行未经授权的访问。密码绝对不应该包含家族姓氏或出生日期，并且必须按照既定的密码生成标准加以设定和维护。如果您看到不认识的人在您的区域使用计算机，请立即把情况报告给您的主管。

课文 B

SECTION Ⅰ: Dialogue　在汽车展厅 At the Auto Exhibition Hall

Interpret the following dialogue from Chinese into English and vice versa.

A： 早上好！很乐意为您效劳。

B： Good morning. This is a great showroom. I'm looking for some two-door cars—something nice, but not too expensive. Would you recommend some practical types to me?

A： 当然可以。这些是我们新推出的和一些改进型的款式，大部分都是经济实用型的。操作系统有自动型和手动型两种。

B： What's the price difference?

A： 嗯，自动操作的当然要贵一些。你必须考虑服务费用。自动操作的汽车服务费用自然要比手动的高一点。

B： I see. Is that one over there one of your latest models? It looks great! Does it have a manual transmission?

A： 是的。它的后备箱空间很大，头顶空间也不小，还有一个带 AM/FM 立体收音机的 DVD 播放器。这个款式刚刚上市约半年时间，很受东南亚客户青睐，特别是在那里的大城市很受欢迎，因为那里不少人每天必须在家和工作单位之间通勤。

B： It sounds nice. What else does it have?

A： 其他的特点包括：活动式座椅、倾斜方向盘，还有气囊。

B： An air bag is especially useful. It protects the driver and passengers in an accident. Is it possible to get air conditioning?

A： 当然有的。没有空调的车现在已经过时了。另外，这款车还有着色玻璃、钢边轮胎、车垫和车顶通风口。

B： They're quite attractive. I'll own one if you grant me a favorable discount, say 20%.

A： 对不起。这种车手动型的每辆 7,000 美元，自动的 9,000 美元。说实话，我最多能给你打 9 折，因为这些都是新产品。

B：I see. What about the color? Are they available in blue, white, and yellow?

A：有蓝色、白色、还有红色，灰色和粉红色，但是目前没有黄色。因为我们的市场调查表明，黄色汽车在美国和欧洲市场销路不是很好。

B：But many people in Beijing do love yellow cars. There are differences between people with different cultural backgrounds. Anyway, I was greatly impressed by your products, and we'll study your catalog further and let you know our decision as early as possible.

A：谢谢！期待您的回音。

SECTION Ⅱ：Warm-ups for Interpretation

➢ **Tongue twister.**

A big black bug bit a big black bear, made the big black bear bleed blood.
大黑虫咬了大黑熊，使大黑熊流血！
Chicken in the car and the car can go, that is the way you spell Chicago.
装着鸡的轿车也能跑，芝加哥的拼写就是这么来的。

➢ **Interpret the following proverbs from English into Chinese.**

1. First come, first served.
2. Money talks.
3. A penny saved, a penny gained.
4. Waste not, want not.
5. Paradise lost, paradise gained.

➢ **Interpret the following sentences from English into Chinese.**

1. Our designers attach great importance to both comfort and beauty, and they always maintain a perfect balance between the two.
2. Discounts depend on the quality of the goods and the size of the order.
3. Our products are sold to the United States, France, Germany and some other European countries.
4. There is a ready market in China for top quality products at reasonable prices.

5. This model is available in gray and pink.

➢ **Interpret the following paragraphs from English into Chinese and vice versa.**

1. L50 的推出标志着新车家族系列推出的开始。这将给我们带来全套新车，3 门车、5 门车、连箱车、柴油车，小到 1.0 排量大到 2.0 排量的豪华车，应有尽有。敞篷车和四轮驱动车也已经进入设计的最后阶段。有了这个新车家族，我们就可以与任何美国厂家进行有力竞争，一比高低，而且可以进军欧洲市场。
2. Second, Rockwell Automation Power Systems. The business is organized into two groups, including Dodge mechanical power transmission products and Reliance Electric industrial motors and drives found in every industry and commercial application. Reliance Electric and Dodge products have been powering industrial plants since the early 1900s, controlling machine movement and speed in some of the most demanding manufacturing environments.

SECTION Ⅲ: Speech

Interpret the following speech from Chinese into English.

Speech A

女士们、先生们：

我向诸位汇报一下最近我对中国汽车市场现状所做的调查。基于轿车目前在中国的占有率仅为每 580 人一台，这个潜在的市场具有极大的诱惑力。今年中国已将关税从 23%降低到 17%。这为其加入世贸组织、进而敞开汽车市场大门创造了条件。

Speech B

欢迎光临 IBM 上海公司的正式开张典礼。各位对 IBM 的产品如此感兴趣，这对我们的业务来说是一个好兆头。你们将与我们一起度过 IBM 历史上的这一重要日子，我感到万分荣幸。IBM 作为世界电脑产品行业的领先者，希望同中国客户分享我们的成功。我们期待着同我们的客户和伙伴建立长期合作关系，这将有助于进一步巩固我们在世界电脑市场的领先地位。

SECTION Ⅳ: Speech

Interpret the following speech from English into Chinese.

For this session, I will talk about the rise of so-called green architecture, a term which first came to use in the 1990s. Green architecture origins come from the energy crisis of the 1970s, when architects began to question the wisdom of building enclosed glass-and-steel boxes that required massive heating and cooling systems.

Proponents argue that green architecture has many benefits. In the case of a large office, for example, the combination of green design techniques and clever technologies can not only reduce energy consumption and environmental impact, but also reduce running cost, create a more pleasant working environment, improve employees' health and productivity, reduce legal liability, and boost property values and rental returns.

A few forward-looking architects began to exploring designs that focused on the long-term environmental impact of maintaining buildings. This approach has since been formalized in a number of assessment and rating systems, such as the LEED (Leadership in Energy and Environmental Design) standards in the USA.

LEED standards are intended to produce "the world's greenest and best buildings" by giving developers a straightforward checklist of criteria by which the greenness of a building can be judged. Points are awarded in various categories, such as energy use, water efficiency and indoor environment quality.

A building that achieves a score of 39 points earns a "gold" rating; 52 points earns "platinum". A gold-rated building is estimated to have reduced its environmental impact by 50% compared with an equivalent conventional building, and a platinum-rated building by over 70%.

The highest profile green building currently on the drawing board is the Freedom Tower, which will be built on the site of the World Trade Center in New York. Like other green buildings, it will rely on natural light and ventilation, and energy-efficient lighting.

参考译文

SECTION Ⅰ: Dialogue

A： Good morning! May I help you?

B： 早上好！这个展室很漂亮啊。我想看看你们的两门汽车，质量好又不太贵的。你能给我推荐几种吗？

A： I'd love to. Here are our new or modified models. Most of them are economy models. They are available in two transmissions: the automatic and the manual.

B： 价格有什么不同？

A： Well, of course an automatic car costs more. You have to consider the service charges. Cars with automatic transmission are generally more expensive to service.

B： 我明白了。那边的那辆是不是你们的最新款式？看起来很不错！它是手动的吗？

A： You're right. It has plenty of trunk space, plenty of headroom, and a DVD player with an AM/FM stereo system. It has been on the market only for about six months, but it has become a great favorite with customers in Southeast Asian countries, especially in big cities there, as you know, many people have to commute from home to work every day.

B： 很好。这款车还有什么特点？

A： Well, it also features reclining seats, a tilt steering wheel, and an air bag.

B： 气囊特别有用，可以在发生车祸时保护司机和乘客。车里有空调吗？

A： Yes, of course. Cars without an air conditioning system are out of fashion now. And it also has tinted windows, steel-belted tires, floor-mats and sunroofs.

B： 这款车很吸引人。如果你能给我打 8 折的话，我就买一辆。

A： Sorry. This manual one costs $7,000 and the automatic is $9,000. Honestly, I can give you a 10% discount at most, you know, they are new products.

B： 我明白了。那颜色呢？有蓝色、白色和黄色的吗？

A： They're available in blue, white as well as in red, gray and pink. But we don't have yellow ones yet. Our market research shows that yellow cars do not sell well in American and European markets.

B：但北京有不少人喜欢黄色车。不同文化背景的人有不同的喜好。不过，你们的展室让我印象深刻。我们会进一步研究你们的产品目录，也会将我们的决定尽早通知你们。

A：Thank you. I look forward to your reply.

SECTION Ⅱ: Warm-ups for Interpretation

➢ **Interpret the following proverbs from English into Chinese.**

1. 以先后顺序为准。
2. 有钱能使鬼推磨。
3. 省一分是一分。
4. 细水长流；精打细算。
5. 失而复得。

➢ **Interpret the following sentences from English into Chinese.**

1. 我们的设计师既注重舒适，也注重美观，并且他们总能在这两者之间找到一个绝好的平衡点。
2. 折扣的大小取决于产品的质量和订货量的大小。
3. 我们的产品远销美国、法国、德国和其他欧洲国家。
4. 只要价格合理，高质量的产品在中国是有市场的。
5. 这种型号有灰色和粉红色两种颜色。

➢ **Interpret the following paragraphs from English into Chinese and vice versa.**

1. The launch of this L50 will mark the beginning of a series of launches, giving us a full range of new cars, 3-door, 5-door, estate, diesel, and from 1 liter all the way up to our luxury 2 liter saloon. A convertible and a 4-wheel drive are also in the final design stage. With this new family, we'll be able to compete robustly with any competitor in US, and will be able to take on the EU market, too.
2. 第二，罗克维尔自动动力系统。这方面的业务分成两组，一个是道齐公司的机械传动产品，另一个是瑞恩电气公司的工业马达和各种行业以及商业用途的驱动器。瑞恩电气公司和道齐公司自 20 世纪初期就开始为工厂提供动力，在一些最苛刻的制造业环境中控制机械的移动和速度。

SECTION Ⅲ: Speech

Speech A

Ladies and gentlemen,

I'd like to report on my recent investigation of the current situation of China's automobile market. Considering the fact that there is only one car for every 580 Chinese at present, the potential auto market is extremely attractive. China has cut its average tariff rate from 23% to 17% this year. It has created conditions for its entry into the World Trade Organization and in turn for the inevitable opening of its auto market to the outside world.

Speech B

Welcome to the official launch by IBM of Shanghai. It's a sign of good business that you show so much interest in IBM products. I regard it as a great honor that you'd be with us at this important occasion in IBM's history. As a world leader in computer products, IBM would like to share with Chinese customers our success. We are looking forward to a long-term relationship with clients and partners, which will help further strengthen our position in the world's computer market.

SECTION Ⅳ: Speech

在这一部分，我将谈谈绿色建筑的兴起。绿色建筑是20世纪90年代才开始使用的一个词汇，但它源于20世纪70年代的能源危机。当时，建筑师们开始质疑用玻璃和钢筋建造盒状的封闭式建筑是否明智，因为这样的建筑需要庞大的供热和制冷系统。

倡导者认为绿色建筑益处多多。比如，以一间大办公室为例，绿色设计方式和巧妙的技术结合不仅能减少能源消耗和对环境的负面影响，而且还能降低运营成本，创造一个更愉悦的工作环境，保障员工身体健康并提高生产效率，减少法律责任，并且提高资产价值和房租收入。

一批有远见的建筑师开始探索新的设计，着重从长期环境影响的角度考虑对建筑的维护。这种做法业已正规化，形成了若干评估和分级体系，诸如美国使用的LEED（能源及环境领导计划）标准。

LEED 标准旨在为开发商提供一系列评判建筑物环保程度的清晰标准，从而建造出“世界上最环保、最好的建筑物”。该评分取自不同方面，如能源利用、用水效率和室内环境质量。

评分为 39～51 的建筑可为“黄金”级，52 分以上为“白金”级。据估，与同类传统建筑相比，黄金级建筑对环境的负面影响减少了 50%，白金级建筑对环境的负面影响则减少了 70%多。

目前尚处在设计阶段的最令人瞩目的绿色建筑是自由大厦，自由大厦将建于原纽约世贸中心。像其他绿色建筑一样，该建筑会更多地利用自然光、通风以及高效节能的照明条件。

Unit 11 科技展览 At the Scientific and Technological Exposition

我们需要推广更简单、更环保、更低碳的生活方式，反对过度行为，培养绿色生活和健康生活的文化。

We need to promote a simpler, greener and more low-carbon lifestyle, oppose excessiveness and foster a culture of living green and living healthy.

创新是一个民族进步的灵魂，是一个国家兴旺发达的不竭动力。

Innovation is the soul of a nation's progress, the inexhaustible force enhancing a country's prosperity.

课文 A

SECTION Ⅰ: Dialogue 在展室中 In the Showroom

Interpret the following dialogue from English into Chinese and vice versa.

A: I've browsed your posters, and quite impressed by the variety of machines you manufacture.

B: 很高兴您对我们的产品感兴趣。请进来看看我们的展品吧。

A: Well, your exhibits are really rich in variety. Would you please make a brief introduction to me?

B: 好的，我们的机床按类型可划分为很多种，有空气压缩机，研磨机等。您想着重了解哪一方面呢？

A: Let me see. Well, what about the air compressors?

B：空气压缩机分为离心式空气压缩机、活塞式压缩机和旋转螺旋式压缩机等，主要用于工艺压缩系统。

A：Great. And what about your casting machines?

B：铸造机主要分为两种，一种是模铸机，一种是连铸机。

A：Wonderful. Can I make an inquiry?

B：当然，这是我们产品的价目单。

A：Well, your prices seem not so attractive to me.

B：当然这还不是我们的最终价格。

A：What's the maximum discount if I place a bulky order?

B：我们可以将所列的价格再减去5%。

A：OK, I'll let you know our decision when I get back to my office. I have your phone number and fax code on your catalogue.

B：好的，我们期待与您合作。

相关词汇

常用科技、机械类英语

punching machine　冲床

hydraulic machine　液压机

lathe　车床

welder　电焊机

grinder　研磨机

air compressor　空气压缩机

centrifugal compressor　离心式压缩机

piston compressor　活塞式压缩机

casting machine　铸造机

artificial intelligence　人工智能

conductor　导体

touch screen　触屏

computer-aided manufacturing (CAM)　计算机辅助制造

computer-aided design(CAD)　计算机辅助设计

computer crime　计算机犯罪

facsimile transmission machine　传真机

image scanner　图形扫描仪

voice/speech recognition　语音识别

fingerprint identification　指纹识别

bluetooth-ray disc　蓝牙光盘

mobile hard disk　移动硬盘

laser printer　激光打印机

semiconductor material　半导体材料

hire-purchase　分期付款购买

fluctuate in line with market conditions　随行就市

preference 优惠关税

tariff barrier 关税壁垒

inquiry 询盘

commission 佣金

customs duty/tariff 关税

SECTION Ⅱ: Warm-ups for Interpretation

➢ **Tongue twister.**

Dennis sees the fleece,
Dennis sees the fleas.
At least Dennis could sneeze.
And feed and freeze the fleas.
丹尼斯看到羊毛，丹尼斯看到跳蚤。至少丹尼斯会打喷嚏，还能喂饱和冻死跳蚤。
I scream, you scream, we all scream for ice-cream!
我叫喊，你叫喊，我们都喊着要冰激凌!

➢ **Interpret the following proverbs from English into Chinese.**

1. Cats hide their claws.
2. Bread is the staff of life.
3. A baker's wife may bite of a bun, a brewer's wife may bite of a tun.
4. A young idler, an old beggar.
5. Do not teach fish to swim.

➢ **Interpret the following sentences from English into Chinese.**

1. Your local market must have potential for these hot-selling electronic products.
2. In this information age, new computers come out every day, and the old ones are bound to be replaced.
3. I hope this quotation will prove acceptable to you.
4. This machine is in many ways superior to other models and you'll learn from our price list that our prices compare favorably with those of other producers.
5. Here are our brochures and relevant publicity materials which may help you make a good decision.

➢ **Interpret the following paragraphs from English into Chinese and vice versa.**

1. Our reputation for engineering excellence has created a sound base for our future business. The Holset turbocharger is an intrinsic part of the modern diesel engine, delivering efficient combustion and high levels of power density reliably. Wherever you are in the world we will provide you with a comprehensive range of replacement turbochargers and spare parts.
2. 惠普公司于 20 世纪 80 年代成为计算机的主要制造商，其产品种类多样，有台式电脑、笔记本电脑及功能强大的微型电脑。惠普公司还将电脑与其生产的电子设备、医疗设备、分析设备等连接起来，使这些设备运行更快速、功能更强大。

SECTION Ⅲ: Speech

Interpret the following speech from Chinese into English.

各位下午好，欢迎参观我们公司的展位。我们是一家 IT 公司，主要为客户提供网络维护、网络安全以及网络管理等方面的服务。

我们公司向来以管理科学、技术先进、能源消耗低、环境污染小，以及服务速度快为骄傲，并且我们仍在继续努力取得更大进步。

公司配备的设施有网络安全中心、网络运行中心、交互式多媒体实验室、个人电脑和计算机培训实验室以及 IT 网络基础设施等。

今后我们还会加强网络病毒防治功能，注重网络的安全与加密，提高网络运行速度，以更好地为客户服务。

我们公司时刻注重科技的创新与提高，众多优秀的员工以及他们创新的热情也推动了公司的飞速发展。

通过和其他展位公司的对比，您可以发现我们公司的优点。我们将为您提供热情周到的服务，期待与您的真诚合作。

SECTION Ⅳ: Speech

Interpret the following speech from English into Chinese.

Speech A

具有科技创新之都名称的上海将作为东道主举办 2022 年第九届上海国际青少年科技博览会(线上)暨“明日科技之星”邀请赛。

上海位于中国东海岸，是历史文化名城，也是中国的国际大都市，国土面积 6300 多平方公里，人口近 2500 万，以其繁荣的城市特色和丰富的人文资源在国内外广为人知。

近年来，上海一直站在改革创新的最前沿，致力于打造具有全球影响力的科技创新中心。在深化教育全面改革的过程中，城市以推动教育高质量发展面向世界和未来。科技创新教育注重激发学生的好奇心和想象力，点燃学生的科学兴趣，同时通过培养创新思维和实践能力，不断提高青少年的科学素质和创新能力，为青少年的个性化成长搭建支点。

在第九届上海国际青少年科技博览会(线上)暨“明日科技之星”邀请赛中，来自世界各地的师生围绕“科学·创新·梦想”主题，通过想象人类未来的生活和技术发展，分享他们的感受。

青年科技博览会将致力于打造一个科学技术无国界的互动平台，为来自世界各地的青年科技爱好者搭建一个探索、学习、合作和交流的舞台，并为科技教育工作者和管理者搭建一个交流和学习科普活动先进经验的桥梁。

Speech B

Let me spend a few minutes to talk about SAIC Motor. SAIC Motor Corporation Limited is the largest Chinese automaker enlisted in the Fortune 500 Global list.

The company has made to the elite list twelfth time in a row, reflecting on the company's ever-expanding business. The company is also considered as belonging to the “Big 4” Chinese top car brands owned by the government and has its headquarter in Shanghai, China but is operating worldwide. The company's main business includes vehicles, components, auto trade & services, and financing. SAIC Motor has been dominating the auto market in China since 2006 with its current domestic market share which stands at around 23%. The Company has a new SAIC plant coming up in Thailand and is involved in constructing the vehicle and auto-parts park in Indonesian. They have also negotiated for the acquisition of GM India factory. In the international operation, the Company has witnessed a higher sales volume in the overseas key regional markets where the sales of MG brand and Maxus light commercial vehicles both increased by 20% and 53% respectively. The company also operates through many joint ventures with renowned brands. Along with VW, SAIC has sold more than two million cars in China alone. SGMW maintained the first place in the sales market of vehicles in China and successfully broke into Top Four companies with the largest sales volume of passenger vehicles in the domestic market.

参考译文

SECTION Ⅰ: Dialogue

A: 我已经浏览过你们的海报，对你们生产的各种机器印象深刻。

B: I am glad you are interested in our products. Please come in and have a look at our exhibits.

A: 嗯，你们展品的种类确实很多，您愿意简单地向我介绍一下吗？

B: OK. Our machine tools have a variety of categories, such as air compressors, grinders, etc. And which type are you interested in?

A: 让我看看，空气压缩机怎么样？

B: Air compressors are divided into centrifugal compressors, piston compressors, and rotary screw compressors, etc. And they are mainly applied to technological air compressing system.

A: 很好，那么你们的铸造机怎么样？

B: Casting machines are classified into two main types. One is die casting machines, and the other is continuous casting machines.

A: 好极了！我可以向您询价吗？

B: Sure. Here is our catalogue and price list.

A: 嗯，你们的报价对我可没什么吸引力呀。

B: Of course, these are not our final offer.

A: 我的需求量很大，有没有折扣？

B： We can reduce the listed prices by 5% off.

A： 好的，回去后我会将我们的决定告诉你，我在产品说明书上能够找到你们的电话和传真。

B： All right. We look forward to cooperating with you.

SECTION Ⅱ: Warm-ups for Interpretation

➢ **Interpret the following proverbs from English into Chinese.**

1. 知人知面不知心。
2. 民以食为天。
3. 近水楼台先得月。
4. 少壮不努力，老大徒伤悲。
5. 不要班门弄斧。

➢ **Interpret the following sentences from English into Chinese.**

1. 这些热销的电子产品在你们本地一定会有不小的市场潜力。
2. 在这个信息时代，计算机日新月异，老的产品注定要被淘汰。
3. 我希望这个报价令你们满意。
4. 这个机器在很多方面优于其他型号，而且你也可以从我们的价目表上看出，我们的价格也比其他厂家的价格低。
5. 这是我们的说明书和有关宣传材料，也许有助于你做出一个明智的决定。

➢ **Interpret the following paragraphs from English into Chinese and vice versa.**

1. 我们在工程方面声誉卓著，为未来的业务打下了坚实的基础。霍尔塞特涡轮增压器是现代柴油发动机不可缺少的部分，它可以改善燃烧效益，提高功率密度，非常可靠。不管您身在何处，我们都能为您提供整套的涡轮增压器替换件和零配件。
2. HP becomes a major player in the computer industry in the 1980s with a full range of computers, from desktop machines to portables to powerful minicomputers. HP also links computers with its electronic instruments and medical and analytical products, making them faster and more powerful.

SECTION Ⅲ: Speech

Good afternoon, everyone. Welcome to our stand. We are an IT company that mainly provides our clients with services on network maintenance, network security, network administration, and so on.

We have always been proud of our scientific management, advanced technology, low resources consumption, little environmental pollution and quick services. And we are striking to make continuous progress.

Our company is equipped with facilities such as Network Security Centre, Network Operating Centre, Interactive and Multimedia Lab, PC and Computing Training Lab, and IT Network Infrastructure.

In the future, we will strengthen the network virus prevention, focus on the network safety and added security, and speed up the network operation, so as to better serve our clients.

Our company emphasizes the renovation and improvement of science and technology at all times. Numerous excellent employees and their innovative enthusiasm also accelerate our company's development.

Comparing with other companies participating in the exhibition, you may find advantages of our company. And with enthusiastic and thoughtful services, we look forward to further collaboration with you.

SECTION Ⅳ: Speech

Speech A

Shanghai, a city of Innovation in Science and Technology is hosting the 9th Shanghai International Youth Science and Technology Expo 2022 (Online) and "Science & Technology Stars of Tomorrow" Invitational Tournament.

Situated on the East coast of China, Shanghai is a famous city of history and culture and also an international metropolis in China, with a land area of over 6300 square kilometers and a population of close to 25 million, always well—known at home and abroad for its prosperous urban features and rich humanitarian resources.

In recent years, Shanghai has stood at the forefront of reform and innovation as it is committed to building a scientific and technological innovation center with global influence. In the process of deepening the comprehensive reform of education, the city faces the world and the future by promoting the high－quality development of education. Science and technology innovation education focuses on stimulating students' curiosity and imagination, as well as igniting students' scientific interest while continuously improving the scientific qualities and innovation abilities of the young through the cultivation of innovative thinking and practical abilities in using scientific and technological innovation to set up a fulcrum for the personalized growth of the young.

The 9th Shanghai International Youth Science and Technology Expo 2022 (Online) and "Science & Technology Stars of Tomorrow" Invitational Tournament will be held in this beautiful city. Students and teachers from all over the world will focus on the theme of "Science · Innovation · Dream" by imagining the future of human life and technological development, and share their thoughts.

The Youth SciTech Expo will be committed to creating an interactive platform for science and technology without borders, building a stage for young science and technology enthusiasts from all over the world for exploration, learning, cooperation and exchange in addition to building a bridge for science and technology educators and managers to exchange and learn from their advanced experience in popular science activities.

Speech B

再给我几分钟来介绍一下上汽集团。上汽集团有限公司是入选《财富》500强全球榜单的中国最大的汽车制造商。

该公司已连续十二次荣膺精英榜单，彰显了该公司在规模上的不断扩张。上汽集团总部位于中国上海，业务涵盖全球，是公认的国有“四大”中国顶级汽车品牌。该公司的主营业务包括车辆生产、零配件、汽车贸易、服务以及融资。2006年以来，上汽集团一直主导中国汽车市场，目前国内市场占有率约为23%。公司将在泰国新建工厂，并参与建设位于印度尼西亚的汽车和零部件产业园。上汽还就通用汽车的印度工厂收购事宜进行了磋商。在国际业务方面，MG名爵和Maxus轻型商用车在主要海外市场的销量分别增长了20%和53%。该公司还通过与知名品牌组建合资企业发展业务。上汽集团与大众合作，仅在中国就售出了200多万辆汽车。上汽通用的五菱保持着中国汽车销售冠军的位置，是国内乘用车市场销量四强之一。

课文 B

SECTION Ⅰ: Dialogue　展会邀请 An Invitation to the Exhibition

Interpret the following dialogue from English into Chinese and vice versa.

A：Hello, Nancy. Here is an invitation to the fifth China International Invention Exhibition.

B：哇，太好了！谢谢，凯文。什么时间，在哪儿开始呢？

A：It is being held at the Shanghai Exhibition Centre from last week to next Saturday.

B：我很高兴受到你们的邀请，可以介绍一下细节吗？我还想多了解一些情况。

A：Sure! Actually, till now 40 exhibitor delegations from 11 countries and regions have attended this exhibition and you know, the booth area is over 9,000 square meters.

B：我以前去过上海会展中心。它的确是一个开办会展的理想之地。看来这次又是一次盛事喽！

A：The exhibition was approved by the Ministry of Science and Technology and sponsored by the Chinese Association of Inventors.

B：开幕式呢？有什么特别之处吗？

A：Well, I think the most eye-catching one is the speech delivered by Mossa, chairman of the International Federation of Inventors' Associations (IFIA).

B：太遗憾了！我错过了！

A：Don't feel too bad. He will attend the closing ceremony to present the awards to the winners.

B：太棒了！奖项设置怎样？

A：Awards will be presented for about 800 inventions. Both the number of awards and the number of specialized awards exceed those of the previous exhibitions.

B：我明白了！

A：Besides, I want to tell you that, with the theme "Innovation, Exchange, Development", this exhibition including various events attracted about 14,000 visitors in just four days.

B：哦，我已经迫不及待了！

SECTION Ⅱ：Warm-ups for Interpretation

➢ **Tongue twister.**

Roberta ran rings around the Roman ruins.
罗伯特绕着罗马废墟遗迹跑步。
Dr. Johnson and Mr. Johnson,
After great consideration,
Came to the conclusion,
That the Indian nation,
Beyond the Indian Ocean,
Is back in education.
Because the chief occupation is cultivation.
约翰逊博士和约翰逊先生经过深思熟虑后得出了结论，
印度人应重返教育，因为他们主要的职业是教育。

➢ **Interpret the following proverbs from Chinese into English.**

1. 隔墙有耳。
2. 三十六计，走为上计。
3. 贪多必失。
4. 不入虎穴，焉得虎子。
5. 好聚好散。

➢ **Interpret the following sentences from Chinese into English.**

1. 我想给你们特别推荐一款新开发的数码照相机。
2. 我们在这一行有良好的声誉，而且我们和中国的批发商、连锁店和分销商都有很好的关系。
3. 我们的产品在质量上颇具竞争力，在本土和国际市场都享有很好的声誉。
4. 我们万能工具公司是全球电子生产专业公司，提供富有创新的线路板、半导体、后方组装技术和设备、集成系统解决方案和流程技术。我们服务电子行业所有的制造厂商。

5. 我们的产品保证质量。一旦发现假货，我们会退款的。

➢ **Interpret the following paragraphs from Chinese into English and vice versa.**

1. 我们的顾客大多数不是专业摄影师。因此，我对傻瓜相机特别感兴趣。这种相机具有自动上胶卷和倒胶卷、自动曝光、自动对焦等功能，还有内置闪光灯。照相时，只要对着人或者景物按一下按钮就行。傻瓜相机的另一个特点是比较轻，可以随身携带。有些数码相机更小，只有火柴盒那么大。
2. HP makes its entry into the printer market with the launch of inkjet printers and laser printers that connect to personal computers. HP's high-quality, inexpensive inkjet printers spell the end of dot-matrix printers. The HP Laser Jet printer line, which debuts in 1984, goes on to become the company's most successful single product line ever. The quality and reliability of HP's printers make HP a highly recognizable brand by both consumers and businesses.

SECTION Ⅲ: Speech

Interpret the following speech from Chinese into English.

各位来宾、女士们、先生们：

很高兴在这里向各位简要介绍一下北京数字博物馆研讨会的情况。

信息化社会的飞速发展为我们开拓了一个集信息、数字、网络、博物馆于一体的新领域——数字博物馆。本次研讨会的主题是“数字博物馆的建设与发展”。

本次研讨会的议题是数字博物馆的现状与发展，包括博物馆数字化、寓教于乐、知识产权保护，以及数字奥运博物馆的建设与管理。

我们的主要目的是吸取国内外数字博物馆建设的成功经验，给国内外数字博物馆方面的专家学者提供一个交流和学习的机会，加快北京数字博物馆建设的发展。

届时将有来自法国、意大利、日本、澳大利亚，以及来自中国北京、上海、广州等地的近100名国内外数字博物馆方面的专家和学者聚集在一起，共同研讨数字博物馆的建设与发展。

毫无疑问，未来数字博物馆在将会发挥很大的作用。

SECTION Ⅳ: Speech

Interpret the following speech from English into Chinese.

China develops techniques of electric vehicles. An industry vice-minister has said a European-style timeline to stop "sales of traditional fuel cars" will also be implemented in China. He predicted "turbulent times" as a result. He is right — there will be a scramble for scale.

The country's pollution problems mean it has every incentive to push electric propulsion. It also sees electrification as an opportunity for its domestic auto industry to catch up with established western carmakers.

China's problem with EV economics is the same as everyone else's. Bernstein estimates that a mid-size combustion vehicle costs ＄15k to produce compared with ＄24k for a comparable EV. The differential is down to the battery, which accounts for half of an EV's cost. A combustion engine is just 15 per cent of a traditional car.

Currently, state subsidies helped make EVs affordable for consumers while helping manufacturers with the higher build costs. But the subsidy system will overhaul to focus more on quotas and credits.

参考译文

SECTION Ⅰ: Dialogue

A：你好，南希。我们公司想邀请您参加"第五届中国国际发明展览会"。这是请柬。

B：Wow，cool！Thank you，Kevin. When and where will it open?

A：地点在上海会展中心，时间是从上周到下个周六。

B：I am delighted to accept the invitation and I would like to know more about it. Would you please introduce more?

A：当然！事实上，截至目前，共有来自 11 个国家和地区的 40 个展团参展，展区面积达 9,000 平方米。

B：I have been to the Shanghai Exhibition Center before. It is the ideal place for such exhibition. It seems like a big occasion again!

A：当然。本次会展由国家科技部批准，中国发明协会主办的。

B：How about the opening ceremony? Is there anything special?

A：我想最受瞩目的应当是发明者协会国际联合会主席穆萨先生的致辞了。

B：What a pity! I missed it!

A：别沮丧，他还将出席闭幕式，并会为获奖者颁奖。

B：Terrific! How about the award?

A：嗯，大约会评选出800余项获奖项目，获奖项目的数量以及专项奖的数量，都超过历届。

B：I got it!

A：除此之外，我还想告诉您，围绕"创新、交流、发展"这一主题，本次会展开展了丰富多彩的活动。短短4天时间吸引观众约1.4万人次。

B：Wow, I can't wait to see it!

SECTION Ⅱ: Warm-ups for Interpretation

➢ **Interpret the following proverbs from Chinese into English.**

1. Even woods have ears.
2. Go while the going is good.
3. Grasp all, lose all.
4. Go to the sea, if you would fish well.
5. Merry meet, merry part.

➢ **Interpret the following sentences from Chinese into English.**

1. I'd like to specially recommend a newly developed model of digital camera to you.
2. We are a well-established firm in this industry, and we enjoy good relations with wholesalers, chain stores and distributors in China.
3. Our products are competitive in quality and enjoy a very good reputation in both domestic and international markets.
4. Universal Instruments is a global electronics productivity specialist, providing innovative circuit, semiconductor, and back-end assembly technologies and equipment,

integrated system solutions, and process expertise to manufacturers in every sector of the electronics industry.

5. We have quality guarantee for our products. If you find they are bogus, we'll refund you.

➢ **Interpret the following paragraphs from Chinese into English and vice versa.**

1. We have most of customers who are not serious photographers. That's why I'm particularly interested in foolproof cameras. Their function includes automatic film loading and winding, automatic exposure, automatic focus, and built-in flash. All you have to do is to point and then press a button. Another feature is it is light and easy to carry. Some digital cameras are even smaller, about the size of a matchbox.
2. 惠普公司推出连在个人电脑上的喷墨打印机和激光打印机，从此进军打印机市场。惠普喷墨打印机质量好、价格低，淘汰了点阵打印机。惠普激光打印机系列产品于1984年开始推出，成为该公司一直以来最成功的单一系列产品。惠普打印机的质量和可靠性使该品牌在普通顾客和公司企业中辨识度很高。

SECTION Ⅲ: Speech

Distinguished guests, ladies and gentlemen,

It is my great pleasure to give you a brief introduction to this digital museum seminar in Beijing.

Along with the rapid development of information society, a new field, "digital museum", has been explored, which incorporates information, digital, Internet and museum. The theme of this seminar is the Digital Museum Construction and Development.

The topics of the seminar include the status quo and development of digital museum. That includes museum digitalization, making entertainment medium of education, intellectual property right protection as well as construction and management of the Digital Olympic Museum.

Our purpose is to learn from those successful experiences in exploiting and constructing digital museums arising both at home and abroad, to provide an opportunity for the communication and exchange of ideas among domestic and foreign experts in the field of digital museums and promote the rapid development of digital museums construction.

Attending the seminar are over about 100 experts and scholars in the field of digital museums from France, Italy, Japan, Australia, and China, including some experts from

Beijing, Shanghai, Guangzhou, etc. They will meet and discuss about the construction and development of digital museums.

There's no doubt that digital museums will play an important role in the future.

SECTION Ⅳ: Speech

中国发展电动汽车技术。工信部的一名副部长表示，中国也将实施欧洲那种停止“生产销售传统能源汽车”的时间表。他预测，这将给汽车产业带来“剧烈的”变革。他说得对——将会有一场竞相扩大规模的角逐。

中国的污染问题意味着它有强大动力推动电动推进技术。中国还把电气化视为国内汽车产业追赶西方汽车制造商的一个契机。

就电动车经济性而言，中国面临的问题与其他国家一样。伯恩斯坦估计，一辆中型内燃发动机汽车的生产成本为 1.5 万美元，而一辆可比电动汽车的生产成本达到 2.4 万美元。这一差异的关键在于电池，其占电动汽车成本的一半。内燃发动机仅占传统汽车成本的 15%。

目前，国家下发补贴有助于让消费者买得起电动汽车，同时也帮助生产成本较高的制造商。但是这个补贴制度将进行改革，转向把重点放在配额和积分上。

Unit 12 参观科技园 A Visit to Hi-Tech Park

> 跨越发展鸿沟，重振全球发展事业。
>
> We need to bridge the development divide and revitalize global development.
>
> 摒弃冷战思维，实现和平共处、互利共赢。
>
> We need to discard Cold War mentality and seek peaceful coexistence and win-win outcomes.

课文 A

SECTION Ⅰ: Dialogue 参观科技园 At the Hi-tech Park

Interpret the following dialogue from Chinese into English and vice versa.

A：您好，我是科技园区的业务经理，我能为您做点什么吗？

B：I want to know something about your hi-tech park. What about your industrial zone?

A：产业区最早于 1996 年投入使用，占地面积为 $117,500m^2$，包括 45 个工业地块。

B：That's great. Your park is really large.

A：我们研发中心的服务和研究可以辅助各企业的运作和发展。

B：Are there any other support facilities apart from those main parts?

A：园区中还设有教育培训中心、保卫处、医院以及火灾救援中心等。

B：What about the public facilities?

A：对水电供应和垃圾处理，我们也都有独立完备的设施。

B：Wonderful. Do you have any requirements on companies applying to enter the park?

A：首先，公司入园是基于企业的科技水平。

B：Of course，our company is hi-tech related. Are there any other requirements?

A：公司还要能促进新兴技术领域内产品的发展。

B：Well，our company is then quite a qualified one.

A：很好，非常期待和贵公司合作。

B：And I think it will be a pleasure to cooperate with you.

相关词汇

公共服务及高新产业类英语

infrastructure 基础设施

infrastructure development 基础设施建设

public facilities 公共设施

water supply 供水

electricity supply 供电

gas 煤气

heating system 供热

sewerage system 污水系统

drainage 排水系统

waste treatment 垃圾处理

emerging industry 新兴产业

sunrise industry 朝阳产业

emerging market 新兴市场

innovation 创新

innovative progress 开拓进展

renovation 革新

the commercialization of research findings 科技成果转化

environment-friendly 环保

ecological conservation 生态保护

shopping centre 商业区

entertainment facilities 娱乐设施

municipality 市政当局

municipal 市的；市政的

innovatively skilled sci-tech workers 创新型科技人才

human resources strategy 人才战略

talent fostering/staff development 人才培养

personnel training 人才培训

versatile professionals 复合型人才

SECTION Ⅱ：Warm-ups for Interpretation

➢ **Tongue twister.**

Once upon a barren moor.

There dwelt a bear also a boar.
The bear could not bear the boar.
The boar thought the bear a bore.
At last the bear could bear no more.
Of that boar that bored him on the moor.
And so one morn he bored the boar.
That boar will bore the bear no more.

从前，在一块荒地上住着一头熊，那里还住着一头野猪。熊不能忍受那头野猪，熊认为那头野猪很讨厌。最后，熊再也忍受不了那头在荒地上令他厌烦的野猪了。于是有一天早上，他烦死了住在沼地上的野猪，野猪也不再忍受这头熊的欺负了！

➢ **Interpret the following proverbs from Chinese into English.**

1. 不劳无获。
2. 二人同心，其利断金。
3. 做贼心虚。
4. 拙匠常怨工具差。
5. 闻其歌知其鸟，听其言知其人。

➢ **Interpret the following sentences from Chinese into English.**

1. 作为一个高度综合的高科技园区，它汇聚了以下功能：工业生产、研发设施、医疗教育机构及娱乐设施。
2. 该中心为园区承租者提供广泛的服务及各种便利设施，包括免费停车场、自助餐厅及 24 小时安全保障。
3. 园区绿地覆盖率超过 40%，我们十分重视有利于生态环境的先进设计标准。
4. 园区目标产业的选择标准是：能加强研发功能、能利用当地技术资源和材料，能发展相应的辅助产业，能与各大学和政府研究机构合作。
5. 我科技园区有强大的政府支持和完备的高科技产业链。

➢ **Interpret the following paragraphs from Chinese into English and vice versa.**

1. 另外还有 143 平方千米的配套协作区，为开发区及投资商的进一步发展提供了广阔的空间。目前，开发区已经形成了以制药业、信息技术、光机电一体化、新材料等为主的产业格局。

2. Equipment Manufacturing Industrial Area Specializes in high-speed rail transportation equipment, motor vehicles and key components, precise processing and forming equipment, medical facilities and intelligent equipment, etc. The industrial projects that have settled down in Qingdao National Hi-Tech Industrial Development Zone include the 350km/h D-trains project invested by China South Locomotive & Rolling Stock Corporation Ltd., the biggest manufacturing and R&D base in China, the forging manipulator project and the industrial robot's project.

SECTION Ⅲ: Speech

Interpret the following speech from Chinese into English.

尊敬的女士们、先生们、朋友们：

非常高兴能够借此机会向各位朋友介绍青岛国家高新技术产业开发区的情况。

青岛国家高新技术产业开发区成立于 1992 年，是中国第一批国家级高新技术产业开发区之一。高新区位于青岛市胶州湾北部，总规划面积为 63 平方千米。

2006 年，经国家批准，高新区在青岛胶州湾北部实现扩区。

2007 年，青岛市正式提出环绕胶州湾发展的新阶段发展战略。在这个战略规划中，高新区处于至关重要的位置。为加快战略实施，青岛市于 11 月调整高新区管理体制和布局，成立了新的高新区管理委员会实施统一管理。

SECTION Ⅳ: Speech

Interpret the following speech from English into Chinese.

Qingdao Hi-Tech Zone's primary aim is to become the pioneering zone of system and mechanism innovation, a cluster zone of high-tech industry, a demonstration zone of ecological conservation. Qingdao Hi-Tech Zone is also the key area of a new round economic development of Qingdao.

Qingdao Hi-Tech Zone is focused on developing hi-tech and environment-friendly industries with low resource consumption.

A well-established infrastructure is available here. Pipe network facilities like water supply, drainage, sewage, electricity, gas, heat, communication and cable TV are available to the enterprises in the zone. Integrated pipeline in the hi-tech zone is laid by underground tunnel, which will incorporate electricity, communication, heat, water, reclaimed water and industrial reserved tunnel. The pipelines of gas, drainage and sewage are directly buried along the road. Currently, the integrated pipelines network in the hi-tech zone is one of the most compacted and longest ones in China, and the maintenance and supervision of the network can be done underground.

The Living Service Center provides supporting service facilities including accommodation, restaurants and entertainment facilities for technicians and workers of the enterprises settled in the zone, The first phase of the apartment project accommodates 4,000 people.

Scientists and Technicians Apartment provides upscale renting apartments for senior management staffs and talented scientists and technicians. At the same time, it facilitates people's living with other modern conveniences such as health care and information services, etc.

As a nationally-acclaimed science park, Qingdao Hi-Tech Zone is indeed an industrial property that can represent Qingdao's resolute ideals and thrust into the high technological frontiers of China.

参考译文

SECTION Ⅰ: Dialogue

A: Hello, I am Operation Manager of the Hi-Tech Park. What can I do for you?

B: 我想了解一下你们高科园区的情况。你们的产业区怎么样?

A: The industrial zone was first put into use in 1996. It covers an area of 117,500m^2, and includes 45 industrial lots.

B: 真不错，你们的园区规模确实很大。

A: Services and researchers of our R & D Centre may support the operations and development of the enterprises.

B: 除了那些主要部分外，还有没有其他辅助设施呢?

A: There are also educational and training centers, a security office, a hospital, a fire and rescue center, and so on.

B：其他公共设施怎么样？

A：For water and power supply，as well as waste treatment，we also have independent and complete establishments.

B：棒极了。你们对申请入园的公司有什么要求吗？

A：First，the selection of the companies in the park is based on their relationship with technologies.

B：当然，我们公司与高科技相关。还有其他要求吗？

A：The companies should also promote the development of products in the areas of new and emerging technologies.

B：嗯，那么我们公司是非常符合这些要求的。

A：Good. We are eager to work with your company.

B：我也认为与你们的合作将会很愉快。

SECTION Ⅱ：Warm-ups for Interpretation

➢ **Interpret the following proverbs from Chinese into English.**

1. No work，no money.
2. If two people are of the same mind，their sharpness can cut through metal.
3. A bad conscience is a snake in one's heart.
4. A bad workman quarrels with his tools.
5. A bird is known by its note，and a man by his talk.

➢ **Interpret the following sentences from Chinese into English.**

1. As a fully integrated hi-tech park，it incorporates the following functions：industrial，research & development facilities，medical and educational institutions and recreational facilities.
2. The center provides a wide range of services and nearby facilities to tenants of the park such as free parking lots，cafeteria and 24-hour security.
3. The park with a green cover over 40% emphasizes advanced design standards for an ecological environment.
4. The criteria for selection of target industries in the park are to strengthen research

and development functions, use locally available technical resources and materials, develop suitable supporting industries and collaborate with universities and public research institutes.

5. Our hi-tech park has strong government supports and complete high technology industry chains.

➢ **Interpret the following paragraphs from Chinese into English and vice versa.**

1. In addition, there is a 143km^2 support area, providing ample space for future development. We now have a good mix of companies in pharmaceutical manufacturing, information technology, in opto-mechatronics as well as in new materials.
2. 装备制造产业区主要发展高速轨道交通装备、汽车及关键零部件、精密加工及成形设备、医疗设备、智能化装备等。落户青岛国家高新技术产业开发区的产业项目包括中国最大的制造研发基地——中国南车股份有限公司投资的350千米/小时动车组项目、锻造操作机项目和工业机器人项目。

SECTION Ⅲ: Speech

Ladies and gentlemen, dear friends,

I am very pleased to take this opportunity to introduce you the city of Qingdao and its national Hi-Tech Industrial Development Zone.

Qingdao National Hi-Tech Industrial Development Zone was formally established in 1992 and is among the first batch of dedicated, hi-tech industrial development zones in China. Located in the north of Qingdao Jiaozhou Bay, it has a total planning area of 63 km^2.

In 2006, approved by the Central Government, Qingdao Hi-Tech Zone was expanded in the north of Jiaozhou Bay.

In 2007, Qingdao Municipal Government put forward the strategy of promoting the development in and around Jiaozhou Bay. Obviously, Qingdao Hi-Tech Zone occupies an important place. In November 2007, Qingdao Municipal Government made major adjustments to managerial system of Qingdao Hi-Tech Zone to speed up the implementation of the strategy and from then a new administrative committee was established.

SECTION Ⅳ: Speech

青岛高新区的基本目标是成为体制和机制创新的先行区、高新产业的集聚区、生态文明的示范区，同时成为青岛新一轮经济发展的重点区域。

青岛高新区大力发展科技含量高、资源消耗小、环境影响少的产业。

高新区可以提供完善的基础设施服务。入园企业可享有给水、雨水、污水、电力、天然气、热力、通信、有线电视等管网设施服务。高新区市政管道采用综合管沟的方式铺设，将电力、通信、热力、给水、中水和工业预留管道全部纳入综合管沟，燃气、排水、污水管道沿道路直埋铺设。目前，高新区内建有中国密度最高，距离最长的综合管廊，基本实现了所有公用管线地下集中管理。

生活服务中心可为入区企业的科研技术人员和蓝领工人提供居住、餐饮、休闲、娱乐等配套完善的生活服务设施，一期可容纳 4,000 人入住。

科技人员公寓将提供面向高级管理人员和科技人才的高档租赁公寓，同时建设便民生活、医疗保障、信息服务等配套服务设施。

作为一个在国内享有盛赞的科技园，青岛高新区确实是一大产业，可以体现青岛进入中国高科技前沿阵地的坚定理想和强劲攻势。

课文 B

SECTION Ⅰ: Dialogue　参观高科园 At the Hi-tech Park

Interpret the following dialogue from English into Chinese and vice versa.

A: Welcome to our hi-tech park. May I help you?

B: 我对你们科技园区非常感兴趣，可否请您介绍一下园区的基本情况。

A: Our hi-tech park was established in 1992, and it covers 63km^2. It focuses on the development of high and new technology.

B: 园区的环境如何？这对我很重要。

A: At present, we have completed a series of standard industrial workshops. And the green cover in the park is over 47%.

B: 良好的环境有利于更好地工作，对吧？

A: I agree. An international school and a recreation center are also under construction now.

B：听说贵科技园有很强大的经济支持，是吗？

A：Yes. The Bank of China and HSBC have pledged to provide us with long-term assistance to support our development.

B：如果我想申请入园，要履行哪些程序呢？

A：You should submit a formal application about what you want to do in the park. Then you will have an interview with our general manager.

B：那么各方面的收费情况怎样？

A：We can make another 10% discount on the basis of our offer. I bet this offer is very tempting.

B：不错，我会考虑在你们的科技园进行投资。

A：Great. We sincerely welcome you to collaborate with us.

B：好的，我也希望我们能尽快合作。

SECTION Ⅱ：Warm-ups for Interpretation

➤ **Tongue twister.**

How may saws could a see-saw saw if a see-saw could saw saws?
如果一块跷跷板能锯木锯的话，一块跷跷板能锯多少把锯？

➤ **Interpret the following proverbs from English into Chinese.**

1. Accidents will happen.
2. Every little makes a nickle.
3. He who rides on a tiger can never dismount.
4. Don't bite the hand that feeds you.
5. Two's company, three is a crowd.

➤ **Interpret the following sentences from English into Chinese.**

1. The hi-tech park focuses on the integration of industry, education, and R & D. The park provides a one-stop service for enterprises, a beautiful area for work and life.
2. There is only a 30 minutes' drive from Qingdao National Hi-Tech Industrial Development Zone to Qingdao downtown which has sound facilities of finance, education,

scientific research, medical care, residence, sports, recreation, etc.

3. We have a management system of international standards.
4. The first phase of the Hi-Tech Zone covers 15 square kilometers. It has been well-planned. Within the area, there is an industrial zone in the east, a residential area in the west, and an area for public utilities in-between.
5. We have taken full advantage of the preferential policies and achieved impressive results. There are already multinational companies from the US, Japan, Germany, UK, Canada and Holland, settling down in our area.

➢ **Interpret the following paragraphs from English into Chinese and vice versa.**

1. Enterprise Accelerator project mainly serves the advanced manufacturing and high-growth enterprises such as precision machinery and electronics information to implement research and development and commercialize achievements. It is the booster and accelerator for hi-tech enterprises to start businesses. After completion, it will fully satisfy the personalized needs of high-growth enterprises in aspects of space expansion, research and development and innovation and marketing management, etc. It accommodates more than 50 different kinds of high-growth enterprises settling in and developing.
2. 高科技园区一直关注的问题是如何促进园内企业的发展。我们根据客户的需要提供各种支持，最主要的包括人力资源管理、调查潜在商机和创新性解决方案。同时，我们还为客户提供本地及跨地区、跨国的战略联系，资源募集等方面的咨询。

SECTION Ⅲ: Speech

Interpret the following speech from Chinese into English.

女士们、先生们：

首先感谢你们来参加展会。在此我想介绍一下科技园区的情况。

我们的科技园区建于 2000 年 6 月，是一个国家级园区，用于发展高新技术。园区的两大主导产业是信息技术以及现代生物技术。

园区的主要产业由两大国家级基地支持，即生物技术基地和国家 IT 产业基地。

为推动园区的腾飞，各金融机构已保证提供进一步支持。大部分贷款将投入到园区建设以及高科技成果的商品化。

日前，园区中已有68家研究机构和1,500家高科技公司。我们科技园区正努力成为世界闻名的高科技产业中心。

到2017年，本科技园区将成为我国顶尖科技园区之一。我们诚挚欢迎各位与我方合作，在科技园区进行投资。

谢谢。

SECTION Ⅳ: Speech

Interpret the following speech from English into Chinese.

Hi, welcome to Coco-Cola, Qingdao branch. Before you visit our production assembly line, just glance at the brief description of the enterprise.

The flagship product of the Coca-Cola company is the coke which was originally intended as a patent medicine which helps to reduce the stress. The company produces concentrates which result in iconic products such as Diet Coke, Coke Zero, Coca-Cola Vanilla, etc. The Coca-Cola Company is the world's largest beverage company and one of the top FMCG companies in the world owing to its product range and distribution. The company owns the market of more than 500 nonalcoholic beverage brands, which they group into the following category clusters: sparkling soft drinks, water, enhanced water and sports drinks; juice and dairy beverages, tea, coffee, and energy drinks. The company markets four of the world's top five non-alcoholic soft-drink brands that are Diet Coke, Coca-Cola, Fanta, and Sprite. The company sells its finished beverage products in more than 200 countries.

All FMCG products are furnished to consumers in all over the world, through the network of company-owned and distribution operations, as well as independent bottling partners, distributors, and retailers—the world's largest beverage distribution system. The company is also known for its innovative way of distribution and promotion: this is one of the reasons why the products are much popular within youngsters. 60 billion servings of all beverages consumed worldwide every day. The company's main operating segments are Europe, Middle East, Africa, Latin America, North America, Asia Pacific, etc. The company takes its commitment to sustainability very seriously. 89% of bottling partners and 90% of direct suppliers achieved compliance with supplier guiding principles.

1.7 million women enabled through 5by20 initiative and gained economic empowerment.

参考译文

SECTION Ⅰ: Dialogue

A：欢迎来到我们的高科技园区。我可以帮您做点什么吗？

B：I am quite interested in your hi-tech park. Would you please give me some idea of this park?

A：我们的科技园成立于 1992 年，占地 63 平方千米。园区注重高新技术的发展。

B：What about the environment of the park? This is very important to me.

A：目前，我们已建成了一系列标准的工业厂房。园区的绿地覆盖率也超过 47%。

B：A good environment is good for work，right?

A：我同意。目前有一所国际学校和一个娱乐中心也在建设之中。

B：I've heard that your hi-tech park has a powerful financial back-up，doesn't it?

A：是的。中国银行和汇丰银行已承诺提供长期帮助来支持我们的发展。

B：Well，if I want to apply for your park，what procedures should I follow?

A：你要就自己想在园区内做的事情提交一份正式申请，然后要和我们的总经理会面。

B：And what about the charges and fees?

A：我们将在报价基础上再打九折。我们的优惠肯定是很诱人的。

B：Good. I will consider investing in your park.

A：好极了。我们真诚地欢迎您与我们合作。

B：OK. I also hope we will work together soon.

SECTION Ⅱ: Warm-ups for Interpretation

➢ **Interpret the following proverbs from English into Chinese.**

1. 天有不测风云。
2. 积少成多，滴水成流。
3. 骑虎难下。
4. 不要恩将仇报。

5. 二人为伴，三人不欢。

➢ **Interpret the following sentences from English into Chinese.**

1. 科技园区注重产业、教育和研发的整合。园区为引入的企业提供一条龙服务，也是一个适合工作和生活的美丽之地。
2. 青岛高新区距青岛中心城区大约 30 分钟车程，在这里你可轻松享受青岛主城区完善的居住、教育、休闲、娱乐等配套设施。
3. 我们的经济区域有国际标准的管理体制。
4. 高新区一期占地 15 平方千米，这里规划合理，井井有条。区内东部是工业区，西部是生活区，中部为公共建筑区。
5. 我们充分利用国家的各项优惠政策，取得了很大成就。已经有美国、日本、德国、英国、加拿大、荷兰的跨国公司前来落户。

➢ **Interpret the following paragraphs from English into Chinese and vice versa.**

1. 企业加速器项目主要面向以精密机械、电子信息为主的先进制造类高成长企业，用于企业研发和成果转化，是高科技企业起步发展的助推器和加速器。建成后将充分满足高成长企业在空间拓展、研发创新、市场营销等方面的个性化需求，可容纳 50 家以上各类高成长企业入驻发展。
2. Contributing to the development of park businesses is a constant concern of the hi-tech park. It provides customized support, most notably, in human resource management, in researching business opportunities, and in innovative solutions. It also provides references for strategic contacts and resource recruitment locally and throughout the world.

SECTION Ⅲ: Speech

Ladies and gentlemen,

First, thank you for attending our exhibition. Here I would like to present you some information on our hi-tech park.

Our hi-tech park was established in June 2000 as a national-level park designated for the development of high technology. The park's two leading industries are information technology and modern biotechnology.

The park's main industries are supported by two national-level bases, namely, the Biotech Industry Base, and the National IT Industry Base.

To fuel the park's take-off, the financial institutions have pledged to provide further assistance. Most of the loans will be put into the park's construction and the commercialization of its hi-tech fruits.

At present, there are 68 research institutions and 1,500 hi-tech firms within the park. Our park is striving to become a world-renowned center for hi-tech industries.

By 2017 our hi-tech park will be one of the nation's top hi-tech parks. And we sincerely welcome all of you to work with us, and invest in our park.

Thanks.

SECTION Ⅳ: Speech

所有产品均通过公司自有渠道、分销业务网、独立运营的装瓶合作伙伴、分销商和零售商(世界上最大的饮料分销系统)供给世界各地的消费者。该公司还以其创新的分销和推广方式著名，这也是产品备受年轻人追捧的原因之一。全球每天消费600亿份该公司的饮料。公司主营业务涵盖欧洲、中东、非洲、拉丁美洲、北美、亚太等地区。公司非常重视对可持续发展的承诺。89%的装瓶合作伙伴和90%的直接供应商均遵守《供应商指导原则》。170万女性通过“5by20”倡议项目获得支持及经济援助。

Unit 13 商务谈判 Business Negotiation

迈向命运共同体，必须坚持合作共赢、共同发展。东南亚朋友讲"水涨荷花高"，非洲朋友讲"独行快，众行远"，欧洲朋友讲"一棵树挡不住寒风"，中国人讲"大河有水小河满，小河有水大河满"。这些说的都是一个道理，只有合作共赢才能办大事、办好事、办长久之事。

To build a community of common destiny, we need to seek win-win cooperation and common development. Our friends in Southeast Asia say that the lotus flowers grow taller as the water rises. Our friends in Africa say that if you want to go fast, walk alone; and if you want to go far, walk together. Our friends in Europe say that a single tree cannot block the chilly wind. And Chinese people say that when big rivers have water, the small ones are filled; and when small rivers have water, the big ones are filled. All these sayings speak to one same truth, that is, only through win-win cooperation can we make big and sustainable achievements that are beneficial to all.

课文 A

SECTION Ⅰ: Dialogue 议价 Negotiating on Price

Interpret the following dialogue from English into Chinese and vice versa.

A: I have seen your exhibits in the showroom and studied your catalog. I'm particularly interested in your racing bicycles. I think some of the models will sell well in the States.

B：谢谢您对我们的产品感兴趣。我们的自行车在世界市场上确实很有竞争力。请问，您比较喜欢哪些车型？

A：Here's a list of my requirements. I'd like to have your lowest quotation, CIF New York.

B：谢谢您的询价。请告诉我们您的订货量，以便我们计算报价。

A：OK. But could you give me an indication of the prices first?

B：好的。这是我们最新的价目单，请过目。

A：My goodness. I'm really surprised at the listed prices you have.

B：您觉得我们的价格太高吗？

A：Well, they're much more than what we expected. In fact, you'll find your prices comparatively unfavorably with those of other suppliers. Their quotations are lower than yours.

B：我们的报价有根有据。我们的赛车都是新产品，比老车型轻多了。轻型铝合金赛车只有 10 千克重。而且，我们在各地的分公司会提供良好的售后服务，你们根本不用担心技术问题。另外，我们还提供各种配件，包括润滑油。

A：I know that your R & D takes the lead in world bicycle industry and your research and service costs are high. But we're large dealers in racing bicycles and I'm sure there's a promising market in our area for moderately priced bicycles of the models mentioned. This will slash your costs, right?

B：您说得对。折扣的大小取决于订单的大小。如果你们能保证跟我们长期合作，并且订货量大，比如，半年达到 1,000 件，那我们会给贵方九二折。另外，订货量每增加 100 件，我们再降一个百分点。

A：What if we place an order for over 2,000 pieces for 12 months, with a guarantee? May I suggest we sign a contract at a 16% discount on your quoted prices? That would help introduce your products to our customers. You know, when we're launching a new product on the market, we usually start with low prices, so as to make it more competitive.

B：八四折似乎有点太高了，那样我们就没什么利润了。我们给您打八八折如何？这可是我们的底价。不然，我们就没什么利润可言了。

A：It's unwise for either of us to stick to one's own price. Let's meet each other halfway to conclude the business. What about a structured deal? I mean 16% for the first six months and 12% for the next six months.

B：那就前半年八六折，后半年八八折吧。我们只能让到这个地步了。

A：Good. What if we pay within 10 days from receipt of invoice?

B：我们通常按实际价格打九折。

A：Sounds great! Now shall we come to the next issue?

相关词汇

常用商务类相关词汇

professional ethics　职业道德

peak season/high season/in season　旺季

slack season/low season/out of season　淡季

promising market/potential market　潜在市场

freight　运费

net price　净价

quotation/offer　报价

inquiry　询盘(询价)

warranty　保修

price list　价目单

discount/allowance　折扣

turnover　营业额

down payment　预付款

wholesale price　批发价

retail price　零售价

spot price　现货价格

current price/prevailing price　现行价格(时价)

world (international) market price　国际市场价格

sales volume　销售量

revenue　收入；利润

purchasing power　购买力

large dealer　大宗产品经营商

hard sell　强行推销

consultative selling　咨询性销售

entrust　委托

delivery　交货

shipment　装运

purchase contract　购货合同

sample contract　合同草案

sales contract　销售合同

valid contract　有效合同

void contract　无效合同

general terms and conditions　一般交易条件

sole agency　独家代理

general sales agent　销售总代理

sales rep.　销售代表

marketing strategy　销售策略

strong market　强市场

weak market　疲软

specifications　规格

pamphlet　宣传手册

SECTION Ⅱ: Warm-ups for Interpretation

➢ **Tongue twister.**

The driver was drunk and drove the doctor's car directly into the deep ditch.
司机喝醉了，把医生的车直接开沟里了。
If you can't can any candy can,
how many candy cans can a candy canner can?
if he can can candy cans.
如果你不能罐制任何糖果罐头，而假如一个糖果罐头制造商能罐制糖果罐头，那么他能罐制多少糖果罐头？

➢ **Interpret the following proverbs from English into Chinese.**

1. A blind man who leans against a wall imagines that it's the boundary of the world.
2. Be swift to hear, slow to speak.
3. Great minds think alike.
4. Knowledge is power.
5. Gifts blind the eyes.

➢ **Interpret the following sentences from English into Chinese.**

1. I have read your brochure and am very impressed by your scope of business, especially the variety of machine tools you manufacture.
2. Here's our CIF. US Pacific Coastal City price list. We may adjust the prices according to the quantity you want.
3. This deal promises big returns for both sides. Let's hope it's the beginning of a long and prosperous relationship.
4. But my knowledge of the auto parts market tells me that your offer is very unattractive. Besides, I need time to build up my confidence in the quality of your stuff.
5. We'd like you to give training to our technical staff in Shanghai, and we'd like you to pay the fee for after-sales service.

➢ **Interpret the following paragraphs from English into Chinese and vice versa.**

1. As this is the first deal between us, I hope we can trade on customary terms, that is

to say, letter of credit payable against sight draft. I know you may have some difficulty. Payment by L/C is a bit complicated and expensive, and you have to put a deposit in your bank. But we also have some difficulty in collecting the payment on time. I would like to accommodate you if I could, but we only accept D/P only if the amount is under \$3,000. Your case is different. I regret to say we could only accept confirmed, irrevocable L/C.

2. 英国是中国在欧洲的第二大贸易伙伴。去年英国对华出口额达 37.2 亿英镑，比前年增长 17%。中国对英国的出口达到创纪录水平。许多中国企业现在把英国灵活、开放的经济看作进军更大的欧洲市场的理想跳板。

SECTION Ⅲ: Speech

Interpret the following speech from Chinese into English.

优秀的推销员在销售过程中总是很有计划。咨询性销售是一个有计划的过程，可以清楚地分为四步。

1. 了解客户需求；
2. 帮助客户选择合适的产品；
3. 表明这样才能满足他们的要求；
4. 顾客购买后，要让他们确信货物会准时、完好无损地送达，并保证他们对货物完全满意。

同时，一位优秀的推销员要讲职业道德，应该自始至终以顾客需求为中心。职业推销员总是把顾客的利益放在首位，必须真心诚意地了解并满足顾客的需求。不要刻意夸大顾客购买了自己的产品后会得到的利益。产品销售后，回访顾客也很重要。这样可以传递善意，保证顾客真的对自己购买的产品称心如意。

此外，一位优秀的推销员知道如果稍不留意就会有损形象。因此，你们要为自己和自己的产品树立正面形象；穿着上不要给人留下负面印象；讲话时语速不应太快，也不能太慢，声音更不能过大；坚定有力的握手传达了你的力量和诚意；微笑会让顾客敞开心扉，讲出他们对所需产品的真实想法。

最后一点，要充满自信。自信的推销员能提高销量。有了自信，成功就不远了。

SECTION Ⅳ: Speech

Interpret the following speech from English into Chinese.

Basic Principles of World Trade Organization

1. Non-discrimination: It has two major components: the most favored nation (MFN) rule and the national treatment policy. Both are embedded in the main WTO rules on goods, services, and intellectual property. The MFN rule requires that a WTO member must apply the same conditions on all trade with other WTO members.

2. Reciprocity: It reflects both a desire to limit the scope of free-riding that may arise because of the MFN rule and a desire to obtain better access to foreign markets.

3. Transparency: The WTO members are required to publish their trade regulations, to respond to requests for information by other members, and to notify changes in trade policies to the WTO.

4. Fair competition: Not allowed to take unfair trade practices to compete, such as dumping and subsidies.

参考译文

SECTION Ⅰ: Dialogue

A：我参观了你们的展室，也看过你们的产品目录。我对你们的赛车很感兴趣。有些车型可能在美国很有市场。

B：Thank you for your interest in our bicycles. Our products are really competitive in the world market. What type in particular you're interested in?

A：这是我们的询价单，请报最低成本、保险加运输到纽约的到岸价。

B：Thank you for your inquiry. Would you please tell us what quantity you require so that we can work out the offers?

A：好的。不过您能否先给我们一个参考价格？

B：Sure. This is our latest price list. Here you are.

A：天哪！你们的要价真叫我吃惊。

B：Is it a little bit too high?

A：这个价格大大超出了我们的预料。事实上，跟其他厂家的价格相比，你们在价格上没有优势可言。他们的报价比你们要低。

B：Ours are well-calculated in fact. These are all newly designed models, a lot lighter than the old ones. Those made from light aluminum alloy only weighs about 10 kilos. Besides, our local offices provide efficient after-sales services and you don't have to worry about technical problems. Any parts of the bicycle, even lubricants, are provided for our customers.

A：我知道贵方的研发在全球自行车制造领域里占领先地位，你们在研究和售后服务方面投入的费用不低。我们是赛车的大经销商，如果价格适中，贵方的赛车在美国会大有销路。这样，贵方的成本就会降低，对吗？

B：You're right. Discount depends on the size of the order. If you guarantee future business and volume sales, say 1,000 pieces over a six-month period, we'll give you an 8% discount. An additional 1% discount for each additional 100 pieces ordered.

A：那如果我们保证一年内订货超过 2,000 件呢？以贵方报价的八四折签约如何？那样有助于贵方产品在我地的销售。因为在市场上推广新产品的时候，通常以低价开始销售会更有竞争力。

B：That seems a little bit too much. I don't know how we can make a profit with those numbers. How about we are to allow you a discount of 12%? That's our minimum price. Otherwise, I'm afraid it would leave us a much lower margin.

A：我们双方都各执己见是不明智的。不如各让一半，做成这笔生意。那分阶段怎么样？就是说，前半年八四折，后半年八八折。

B：Well, I suggest 14% for the first six months and 12% for the next six months. It's the best I can do.

A：行。那如果我们在收到发票 10 日内付款，会有什么优惠呢？

B：We often allow a special discount of 10% of the net price.

A：不错！现在我们来谈下个问题。

SECTION Ⅱ: Warm-ups for Interpretation

➢ **Interpret the following proverbs from English into Chinese.**

1. 坐井观天。
2. 多听少说。

3. 英雄所见略同。
4. 知识就是力量。
5. 拿了手短，吃了嘴软。

➢ **Interpret the following sentences from English into Chinese.**

1. 我已看过贵公司的宣传手册，贵公司的经营范围，特别是贵公司生产的机床产品，给我留下了极为深刻的印象。
2. 这是我方的美国太平洋沿岸城市到岸价的价目单。我们还可以根据您所想要的数量调整价格。
3. 生意保证能让双方都获得丰厚利润。希望这是我们长期愉快合作的一个良好开端。
4. 从我对汽车零部件市场所掌握的信息来看，贵方的报价没有吸引力。此外我还需要时间来树立对贵方产品质量的信心。
5. 我们希望贵方能给我们上海的技术人员提供培训，并且承担售后服务的费用。

➢ **Interpret the following paragraphs from English into Chinese and vice versa.**

1. 因为这是我们的第一笔生意，希望我们在付款方面按照惯例行事，也就是说使用即期信用证付款。我知道你们恐怕有自己的难处：信用证付款程序有点复杂，费用也高，而且你们还要付押金。但我们也存在不能按时收回货款的困难。如果可能的话，我也想给你们破例，但是数额在 3,000 美元以下我们才接受付款交单。你们的情况不同。因此，很遗憾我们只能接受保兑的、不可撤销信用证。
2. The UK is China's second largest European trading partner. British exports to China last year, at £3.72 billion, were up 17% on the year 2000. China's exports to Britain are at an all-time high. Many Chinese enterprises now regard Britain's flexible and open economy as an ideal launching pad into the wider European market.

SECTION Ⅲ: Speech

Good sales people(善于营销的人) plan their approach to selling. Consultative selling is a planned process with four clearly defined phases.

1. discovering the customer's needs;
2. helping the customer to select the right product;
3. showing how this satisfies their requirements; and

4. serving the customer after the sale by ensuring that goods are delivered on time and in good condition and that the customer is happy with their purchase.

Good sales people are also ethical in their sales. You should always concentrate on the customer's needs. A professional sales person puts the customer's interests first. You must make a genuine attempt to discover the customer's needs and fulfill them. Don't exaggerate the benefits that will be gained from buying your products. After-sales follow-up is important in creating goodwill and ensuring that the customer is really satisfied with what they have bought.

In addition, a good sales person is conscious of the fragile nature of their sales image. Try to create right image for yourself and the product. Do not dress in clothes that would create the wrong impression. Avoid speaking too fast or too slowly, and never too loudly. A good firm handshake communicates your strength and honesty. Smiling encourages the customer to tell you what they really want.

Last of all, be confident. A confident sales person creates sales. Be confident and you will be successful.

SECTION Ⅳ: Speech

世界贸易组织基本原则

1. 无歧视待遇原则：此原则由两个主要组成部分：最惠国(MFN)原则和国民待遇政策。两者都包含在世贸组织关于商品、服务和知识产权的主要规则中。最惠国原则要求世贸组织成员国在与其他成员国贸易往来时使用相同条件。

2. 互惠原则：避免因最惠国原则而可能出现的不担风险取利现象，也利于成员国更好进入国外市场。

3. 透明原则：世贸组织成员需公开其贸易法规，回应其他成员的信息请求，并向世贸组织汇报贸易政策的变化。

4. 公平竞争原则：禁止非公平性贸易活动参与竞争，比如倾销和补贴。

课文 B

SECTION Ⅰ: Dialogue 保险、交货和支付条款 Warranty, Delivery and Terms of Payment

Interpret the following dialogue from Chinese into English and vice versa.

A：费尔莫先生，我们已经谈妥了价格和订货量的问题，现在我们该谈保修问题了吧？这些型号的赛车保修期多长？

B：It's six months. But I can make an exception in your case and give you a one-year warranty period.

A：也就是说，在一年时间内如果任何一辆车出了问题，你们会免费维修。这很好。但是，如果一年后出了问题怎么办呢？因为赛车不同于普通的自行车，在训练和比赛中什么事情都可能发生。

B：Well, we have a special scheme: It's $400 or so for a year's cover. And we guarantee to carry out any repairs on site within 24 hours provided the bicycles are used within the city. If you phone our local office before 10 o'clock in the morning, we usually come out to your place the same day. Outside the city it will obviously take longer. Of course you can send the faulty bikes to our local office.

A：明白了。那交货日期呢？我们希望你们能在 31 日之前履行第一批订单。我们这批货要的很急，因为现在是赛车的销售旺季。

B：You mean in 25 days? We usually deliver within 40 days from receipt of your order—30 days at most. But if you decide now and let me have a firm order with a 10% deposit, I think we can promise to get the vehicles to you by the 5th next month—that'll be 30 days. We'll give your order top priority. And remember you can have a 10% discount of net price provided we receive the full amount in 10 days from now.

A：我知道了。我回办公室就把我们的决定告诉你。现在我们谈谈如何付款吧？

B：In our export business, we demand payment by confirmed, irrevocable Letter of Credit payable against documents.

A：你们也使用其他付款方式，如托收、汇款和银行担保书等吗？使用信用证就意味着增加我们的进口成本，因为我们去银行开信用证，是要付一笔押金的。你们能否破例接受承兑交单或者付款交单呢？

B：I'm afraid we cannot accommodate you there. We have been doing business with all other buyers on 100% confirmed，irrevocable L/C. I suggest you consult your bank and see if they can reduce the required deposit to a minimum amount.

A：谢谢。请问你们会提供哪些单据呢？

B：Together with the draft，we'll send you a complete set of Bills of Lading，an invoice，an export license，an insurance policy，a certificate of origin，and a certificate of inspection.

A：我们需要一式三份的发票，要有签字；保险单一式两份，包括海洋险和战争险，投保金额为发票金额的110%。

B：No problem. We'll do that. And now let's iron out the remaining details.

SECTION Ⅱ：Warm-ups for Interpretation

➤ **Tongue twister.**

Badmin was able to beat Bill at billiards，but Bill always beat Badmin badly at badminton.

巴德民打台球能打败比尔，但是打羽毛球比尔总是打败巴德民。

Mr. See owned a saw and Mr. Soar owned a seesaw.

Now See's saw sawed Soar's seesaw before Soar saw See.

席先生拥有一把锯子，而索尔先生有一个跷跷板。

可是在索尔先生看见席先生之前，席先生先的锯子已经锯断了索尔先生的跷跷板。

➤ **Interpret the following proverbs from Chinese into English.**

1. 善有善报。
2. 烈火炼真金。
3. 问心无愧，高枕无忧。
4. 静水流深。
5. 他山之石，可以攻玉。

➤ **Interpret the following sentences from Chinese into English.**

1. 我们很有兴趣在你们的保税区投资技术密集型的项目。

2. 请给我一个有效期为 90 天的 CIF 报价，目的港为洛杉矶，报价含 5%的佣金。
3. 这是我方的底盘，对不起，我们不准备接受还盘。
4. 如果价格再优惠一点，我们将增加订货量。
5. 七五折的折扣我们难以接受，因为那样我们就没多少利润了。

➢ **Interpret the following paragraphs from Chinese into English and vice versa.**

1. 世贸组织的性质是谈判，而世贸组织所做的一切都是谈判的结果。当国家间面临贸易壁垒并希望降低这些壁垒时，谈判有助于贸易自由化。但是，世贸组织的作用不仅仅是使贸易自由化，同时在某些情况下它的准则会支持现有的贸易壁垒——如为了保护消费者。世贸组织还帮助制造商和出口商了解国外市场是否对他们开放。
2. I propose that payment be made by installment, that is, after each shipment we will send you through our bank and yours the Bills of Lading, an invoice, an export license, an insurance policy, a certificate of origin, and a certificate of inspection. As long as the documents are in order you should effect payment without delay. To ensure the payment, your bank should give us a written letter to the effect that they will guarantee the payment if the buyer fails to do so. They can either give one letter of guarantee for the whole transaction or give separate letters of guarantee for separate installments. Either way, the letter should reach us two months before shipment is due.

SECTION Ⅲ: Speech

Interpret the following speech from Chinese into English.

要想在谈判中有备无患，必须做好以下三点。

1. 知道自己在谈判中所处的地位。

每场谈判中，总有一方处于优势地位，而另一方处于劣势地位。那么你所处的地位呢？在任何谈判中，总是更希望达成协议的一方让步更多——正是因为他们更希望完成交易，所以他们会尽量避免对方终止谈判。

2. 知道对方认为他们在谈判中所处的地位。

只知道自己在谈判中所处的地位还不够。还需知道对方认为他们在谈判中处于怎样的地位。正如扑克玩家所知，如果牌出得适时，即使不是高手有时也会赢。如果你在谈判中并不处于优势地位，但你发现对方害怕交易失败，那么此时可以利用他的担心，态度变得强硬起来，也绝对不会有问题。

3. 衡量自己的谈判方式。

你性格乐观还是争强好胜？虽然这不太好说，但我研究律师 25 年，发现那些天生争强好胜、无所畏惧、为人处世非常粗暴过分的人通常是最适合谈判的人选。大家都怕他们，不想惹恼他们，因此就让他们称心如意。要想谈判完全成功，激发自己性格中蛮横粗暴的一面还是有好处的。别忘了，谈判就是一场游戏。

SECTION Ⅳ: Speech

Interpret the following speech from English into Chinese.

Leveraging the contrast effect is also a powerful tool in negotiations. You might ask for more than you realistically expect, accept rejection, and then shade your offer downward. Your counterpart is likely to find a reasonable offer even more appealing after rejecting an offer that's out of the question. Additionally, offering several equivalent offers that aim higher than your counterpart is likely to accept will elicit reactions that can help you frame a subsequent set that, thanks in part to the contrast effect, are more likely to hit the mark.

Building a team is critical to negotiations in business. To prevent conflicts among diverse, strong-minded team members from overshadowing group goals, negotiation teams should spend at least twice as much time preparing for upcoming talks as they expect to spend at the table. Because the other side will be ready and willing to exploit any chinks in your team's armor, it's important to hash out your differences in advance.

参考答案

SECTION Ⅰ: Dialogue

A: Mr. Fillmore, we've settled questions of price and quantity. What about warranty?

What's the warranty period of these bicycles?

B：保修期 6 个月。但我可以给您破例延长到一年。

A：So free repairs if any bicycle has a fault within a one-year period. Sounds good. But what happens if a bicycle breaks down after a year? You know, racing bikes are really different from ordinary ones, and you never know what will happen in training or racing.

B：嗯，我们有一个特别的维修方案，费用是每年 400 美元左右。在市区内，我们保证在 24 小时内到达指定地点进行现场维修。如果你在早上 10 点以前致电我们，我们一般当日到达。在市区以外，那自然需要的时间稍长。当然，你也可以把车送到我们的服务处。

A：I see. When will you make the delivery? We'd like you to execute the first order by the 31st. It's all very urgent in our particular case. This is the peak season for racing bicycles in our market, you know.

B：你的意思是在 25 日内交货？我们通常是在收到订单 40 日内交货——最快 30 日内。但是，如果你现在就做决定，给我们确认订单，并缴纳 10%的定金，那我们可以保证在下个月 5 日把货交到你们手里，也就是 30 天时间。我们会优先处理你们的订单。不要忘了，10 日内支付全部货款我们会给 10%的实价折扣。

A：I see. I'll let you know our decision after I get back to my office. Now shall we come to the terms of payment?

B：我们的出口业务要求可兑保的、不可撤销的即期跟单信用证。

A：Do you also use other modes of payment, such as payment by collection, or by remittance, or bankers' letter of guarantee? You know a Letter of Credit means increasing the cost of our import. When we open a Letter of Credit, we have to pay a deposit. Would it be possible for you to make an exception and accept D/A or D/P?

B：这个我们恐怕不能破例。我们和其他买家一直毫无例外地采用可兑保的、不可撤销的即期跟单信用证。我建议你去咨询下银行，看看他们能否将押金降低到最低限度。

A：Thank you for your suggestion. Could you tell me what documents you will provide?

B：我们会连同汇票一起，寄给你们一整套单据，包括提货单、发票、出口许可证、保险单、产地证明及检验证书。

A：We need a signed invoice in triplicate and the insurance policy in duplicate, covering marine and war risks, for the invoice value of the goods plus 10%.

B：好的，我们会照办。现在我们谈谈其他细节问题。

SECTION Ⅱ：Warm-ups for Interpretation

➢ **Interpret the following proverbs from Chinese into English.**

1. Virtue is its own reward.
2. The fire is the test of gold.
3. A clear conscience is a soft pillow.
4. Still waters run deep.
5. By other's faults, wise men correct their own.

➢ **Interpret the following sentences from Chinese into English.**

1. We are greatly interested in investing in technology-intensive projects in your free trade zone.
2. I'd like to hear your quotation on a C. I. F. Los Angeles basis valid for 90 days, with an inclusion of a 5% agent's commission in your quotation.
3. This is our floor offer and you'll have to excuse me, we're not prepared for any counter-offer.
4. We'll place a larger order if the price is more favorable.
5. A 25% discount would be too much for us, for it would slash our profit margin.

➢ **Interpret the following paragraphs from Chinese into English and vice versa.**

1. The WTO was born out of negotiations, and everything the WTO does is the result of negotiations. When countries have faced trade barriers and wanted them lowered, the negotiations have helped to liberalize trade. But the WTO is not just about liberalizing trade, and in some situations its rules support maintaining trade barriers—for example to protect consumers. The WTO also helps producers and exporters know that foreign markets will remain open to them.
2. 我建议采用分期付款的方式。也就是说，每次装运之后，我们将通过我方银行和你方银行把提货单、发票、出口许可证、保险单、产地证明，还有检验证书寄给你方。只要这些单据符合要求，你方就要按时付款。为了保证顺利付款，你方银行应向我们出具一份担保书，大意是如果买方未能付款，他们保证付款。你方银行可以为整笔交易出具一份担保书，也可以为每批交易分别出具一份担保书。无论采取何种形式，担保书必须在装运前两个月到达我方。

SECTION Ⅲ: Speech

To get ready for any negotiation, you must do three things.

1. Know your bargaining position.

In every negotiation, someone is in a stronger position and someone is in a weaker position. Where are you? In any negotiation, the side that needs the deal more is the side that gives up the most—precisely because they need the deal and can't afford to have the other side walk away from the table.

2. Know how the other side perceives its position.

It isn't enough to know what your real bargaining position is. You also have to consider how each side perceives its position. As any poker player knows, sometimes a mediocre hand can be a winning hand if it's played properly. If your negotiating position isn't great but you see the other side is worried about losing the deal, you can't go wrong by coming on strong and playing to the other side's fears.

3. Assess your bargaining style.

Are you aggressive or passive by nature? I hate to say it, but in 25 years of studying lawyers, I've found that those who are naturally aggressive, fearless and downright ornery tend to make the best negotiators. People are afraid of them, want to avoid their nasty behaviors and give them what they want. To truly succeed at negotiating, it helps if you can find your inner Rottweiler. Remember, it's a game.

SECTION Ⅳ: Speech

在谈判中利用对比效应也是非常有效的。你提出的要求可以比自己实际期望的高，然后接受对方的回绝，再适当降低你的要求。此时，对方在回绝了刚才非常过分的要求后，会觉得这个要求还比较合理，从而乐于接受。另外，还可以提出几个等效要求，比对方所能接受的限度稍高。由此而引发的效应则有助于你在接下来的谈判中更容易获得成功。这在某种程度上可以说是得益于对比效应产生的效果。

组建谈判团队在商务谈判中也非常重要。为避免团队成员由于意见分歧、各执己见而产生矛盾冲突，影响整个团队达成一致的目标，谈判团队的所有成员应为即将进行的谈判做准备。准备的时间应至少为预计在谈判中所用时间的两倍。因为一旦谈判团队中出现分歧，就会被对方不失时机地加以利用，所以预先解决分歧非常重要。

Unit 14 参观规划局 A Visit to the Urban Planning Bureau

我们要虚心学习借鉴人类社会创造的一切文明成果，但我们不能数典忘祖，不能照抄照搬别国的发展模式，也绝不会接受任何外国颐指气使的说教。

We should modestly draw on the achievements of all other cultures, but never forget our own origin. We must not blindly copy the development models of other countries nor accept their dictation.

课文 A

SECTION Ⅰ: Dialogue 在规划局 At the Urban Planning Bureau

Interpret the following dialogue from Chinese into English and vice versa.

A：你好，贝克先生。我叫张大维，你可以叫我大卫。欢迎到青岛市规划局参观。

B：Hi, David. Nice meeting you. Oh, I'm very impressed by your fancy office building, as magnificent as the Empire State Building.

A：谢谢。是的，我们规划局在市政建设、城市规划方面投入了大量资金，以美化青岛这个大都市的形象。

B：Fantastic! I have witnessed your well-designed express way network, magnificent buildings, nice hotels and the beautiful landscaping.

A：是的。这些年来，我们的城市规划专家，包括一些国外专家以及其他著名建筑师为我们城市的规划和建设做出了杰出的贡献。在这里我还要感谢你对我们提出的建议。

B：Oh, it's my honor to do something for the city and for the friendship between our two sister cities.

A：哦，贝克先生，来杯咖啡怎么样？卡布其诺还是橙汁？

B：Actually，I prefer Chinese green tea. You know，I have been addicted to it for a couple of years. I have a lot of Chinese friends in Long Beach. We often get together in China Tea House.

A：好的。我的助手会给你泡从黄山采的上等绿茶。现在，我们来谈一下我们的合作项目吧。

B：Sure. That's what I come here for today. I have brought with me the sketch plan for Qingdao Jiaodong International Airport. I think this is considered as the most magnificent new airport project in China.

A：你的工作效率太高了。想不到这么短时间内就设计好了这么大的工程。棒极了。

B：Let's discuss some details. Look at the area of the aprons at Terminal 3. What do you think of the dimension of this area?

A：我觉得停747是够宽敞了。不过，考虑到将来要停靠空客A380，这个停机坪还需扩大面积，应和其他国际上的A380停机坪保持一致。

B：Oh，very thoughtful. I didn't consider that before. Great idea. What do you think of the wing maintenance stands?

A：我想你这个设计已经很理想了。面积充足，设计新颖，也很实用。

B：Thank you for your nice compliments. You're pulling my legs.

A：哦，你的绿茶来了。喝完茶我们再谈下一个环节。

相关词汇

基础设施相关词汇

terminal　航站楼
hangar　机库
runway　跑道
apron　停机坪
maintenance stands　维修坪
departure zone　起飞区
touchdown zone　降落区
urban transit system　城市交通系统
light rail　轻轨
unban planning　城市规划
sewage　污水
sewer　污水管
sewage treatment plant　污水处理厂
Combined Sewer Systems (CSS)
混合下水道排污体系
industrial waste　工业污水

storage reservoir 水库；蓄水库
distribution reservoir 水库；配水库
distribution pipes 配水管网
sewerage system 污水系统；排污体系
rainfall 降水
domestic waste 生活污水
waste treatment/waste disposal 垃圾处理
treatment plant 处理厂
blueprint 蓝图
landfill 垃圾填埋区
landscape 景观设计

SECTION Ⅱ: Warm-ups for Interpretation

➢ **Tongue twister.**

Don't trouble troubles until trouble troubles you! If you trouble troubles, triple troubles trouble you!

不要自找麻烦。如果你自找麻烦，更多的麻烦会找你。

I wish to wish, I dream to dream, I try to try, and I live to live, and I'd die to die, and I cry to cry but I don't know why.

我希望许愿，我梦想着梦想，我试着去尝试，我活着为了活着，我为了死而死，我哭了又哭，但我不知道为什么。

➢ **Interpret the following proverbs from Chinese into English.**

1. 各守本分。
2. 心急吃不了热豆腐。
3. 决不要灰心。
4. 覆水难收。
5. 饥不择食。

➢ **Interpret the following sentences from Chinese into English.**

1. 根据青岛城市发展规划，我们正在大力改善城市交通体系，包括发展轨道交通，修建新的道路，完善交通路网，扩大公共交通运输能力。
2. 信息高速公路是一种大规模的全国范围，乃至全球范围的电子通信网络系统，可以传送任何形式的记录信息。
3. 有的“轻轨”系统与城市铁路几乎没有相似之处，可以被列为通勤铁路或城内铁路。

4.“欧洲之星”列车穿越英伦海峡海底隧道，是世界上最长的海底隧道。

5. 立交桥和地下通道组成了立体交叉道。

➢ **Interpret the following paragraphs from Chinese into English and vice versa.**

1. 2021年年末，我们的基础设施投资400多亿元，城市供水能力237万立方米/日，新增城市道路868.94千米，新增桥梁135座，用气普及率达93.93%，城市绿地覆盖率为33.73%。

2. As the nation's earliest established special economic zone, Shenzhen has very close economic contacts with the inner land provinces. Especially after the returning of Hong Kong to the motherland, the number of passengers coming and leaving Shenzhen is increasing rapidly. Shenzhen Airport claims to be one of the ten largest airports in the country. For the convenience of the passengers, Shenzhen Airport Administration set up 4 well-furnished change rooms. The passengers can change their clothes, tidy themselves up in the easy and pleasant surroundings, so as to leave a good first impression on the relatives and friends who come to meet them at the airport.

SECTION Ⅲ: Speech

Interpret the following speech from English into Chinese.

Urban rail transit in the People's Republic of China encompasses a broad range of urban and suburban electric passenger rail mass transit systems, including subway, light rail, tram and even maglev. Some classifications also include non-rail bus rapid transport.

Several Chinese cities had urban electric tramways in the early 20th century, which were dismantled in the 1950s-1970s. Nanjing had an urban railway from 1907 to 1958.

Today China boasts both the world's longest and second longest metro systems. Out of the top 10 busiest metro systems in the world 4 of them are in China.

The first subway in China was built in Beijing in 1969. The Tianjin Metro followed in 1984. Since 2000, the growth of rapid transit systems in Chinese cities has accelerated. The Shanghai Metro despite being the world longest only started operating in 1993.

From 2009 to 2015, China plans to build 87 mass transit rail lines, totaling 2,495 km, in 25 cities at the cost of 988.6 billion *yuan*. Of the new metro systems to be built between now and 2015, 16% will be in the Pearl River Delta, 25% in the Yangtze River Delta and 24% in the Jingjinji region. As of 2012, China averages 270 km of new rapid transit mileage per year.

Hong Kong's MTR is the combination of the former KCRC and the MTR corporation. The MTR now has investment and management stakes in the rapid transit systems of several mainland Chinese cities.

SECTION Ⅳ: Speech

Interpret the following speech from Chinese into English.

我代表市南区人民政府的领导和工作人员欢迎各位来到市南区城市规划管理局参观，相信市南区会给您留下深刻印象。

我们局是市南区人民政府的规划管理部门，业务上受市规划局指导，主要有以下几项职责。

首先，根据城市规划，制订本区的经济和社会发展计划，编制一般地区的详细规划和开发建设规划。

其次，执行国家城市规划管理的有关法律、法规、规章和政策，负责本区的城市建设规划管理。

再次，我们局负责本区范围内城市建设工作的管理档案。除此之外，还根据有关法规对违法建设进行查处。

最后，我们城市规划管理局还要完成市南区政府以及各上级部门交给本局的其他任务。

参考答案

SECTION Ⅰ: Dialogue

A: Hi, Mr. Baker. My name is Dawei Zhang. You may call me David. Welcome to Qingdao Municipal Urban Planning Bureau.

B: 你好，大卫。见到你很高兴。哇，你们的办公大楼太漂亮了，和帝国大厦一样壮观。

A：Thank you. Yes, we have great investment on city planning and infrastructure facilities to enhance the beauty of this metropolitan city.

B：太棒了！我已经看到了四通八达的高速路，林立的高楼大厦，高档宾馆和配套的景观。

A：Yes. In the past several decades of years, our city planners, architects, including some international experts have made great contributions to the city planning and its infrastructure construction. Here, we pay our great thanks to your great ideas.

B：我很荣幸能为我们两座城市的友谊做点什么。

A：Oh, Baker, how about a cup of coffee? Cappuccino or Tropicana?

B：其实我更喜欢中国绿茶。我爱上绿茶已经两三年了。我在长滩也有很多中国朋友。我们经常在中国茶馆喝茶。

A：OK. My assistant will get you the best green tea from the top of Mount Huang. Let's get down to our business for our joint program.

B：好的。我今天来的目的就是谈业务。我带来了新机场"青岛胶东国际机场"的初步设计草图。我想这个新机场是中国最大最壮观的机场了吧！

A：How efficient you are. You've done such a great design for such a huge project within such a short period. That's amazing.

B：下面我们来讨论一些细节问题吧。你看一下这个 3 号航站楼的停机坪。你觉得它的规模怎么样？

A：I think that's big enough for jet 747. Considering Airbus A380, we have to widen the apron, by keeping the same size as other international airport.

B：嗯，你想得太周到了。在这之前，我没想到这个问题。好主意。那你看这个机翼维修坪怎么样？

A：In my opinion, your design is perfect, quite novel and practical. The space is big enough for any maintenance in future.

B：谢谢你的夸奖。你在跟我开玩笑吧。

A：Oh, here is your tea. Go ahead before we move to the next point.

SECTION Ⅱ: Warm-ups for Interpretation

➢ **Interpret the following proverbs from Chinese into English.**

1. The cobbler should stick to his last.

2. A watched pot never boils.
3. Never say die.
4. Don't cry over spilt milk.
5. Beggars can't be choosers.

➢ **Interpret the following sentences from Chinese into English.**

1. In the implementation of our urban development plan, Qingdao will spare no efforts to improve the city's transport system by developing rail transport, building new roads, improving transport network and expanding public transport capacity.
2. Information superhighway is a large-scale nationwide, or worldwide, electronic communications network system, capable of transmitting just about any form of recorded data.
3. Some "light rail" systems bear little similarity to urban rail, and could alternatively be classified as commuter rail or even inter-city rail.
4. The Channel Tunnel used by Eurostar services holds the record for having the longest undersea section anywhere in the world.
5. An overpass and underpass together form a grade separation.

➢ **Interpret the following paragraphs from Chinese into English and vice versa.**

1. By the end of 2021, we had invested over 40 billion *yuan* in the urban infrastructure. Our water supply capacity was more that 2.37 million cubic meters per day. There were 868.94 kilometers of new roads in the city and 135 new bridges. Our gas utilization had reached 93.93%. Our green coverage was 33.73%.
2. 深圳作为全国最早的特区，与内地经济往来极为密切，特别是在香港回归后，人员往来大为增加。深圳机场是全国十大机场之一。为方便旅客，深圳机场设置了4间设备齐全的更衣室。室内设备齐全。旅客可以在轻松愉快的环境中更换衣服，整理仪容，给前来迎接的亲朋好友留下良好的第一印象。

SECTION Ⅲ: Speech

中国城市轨道交通系统，涵盖了众多城市内部或城市与城郊之间各种以电力驱动的客运城市轨道交通系统，包括地铁、轻轨、有轨电车及磁悬浮等，有时快速公交也被包括在内。

中国有些城市自 20 世纪初便已铺设了有轨电车轨道，但大多在 20 世纪 50～70 年代被拆除。南京在 1907—1958 年就有市区内的铁路。

目前，中国同时拥有世界上第一长和第二长的地铁网络。全世界最繁忙的 10 大地铁线路中，4 条都在中国。

中国的第一条地铁是北京地铁，于 1969 年建成。随后，天津地铁于 1984 年建成。2000 年后，中国的城市轨道交通系统开始快速成长。上海地铁于 1993 年开通，但已成为世界上规模最大的地铁网络。

2009—2015 年，中国准备在全国 25 个城市以 9886 亿元建成总长 2495 千米的 87 条轨道交通线路。从现在起截至 2015 年，中国新建的地铁系统中有 16％集中在珠江三角洲，有 25％集中在长江三角洲，24％集中在京津冀地区。至 2012 年，中国以每年新建 270 千米的速度建设其轨道交通网络。

港铁(公司)由前九广铁路(公司)和香港地铁(有限公司)合并而成，而港铁也已参与中国内陆部分城市轨道交通系统的投资和管理。

SECTION Ⅳ: Speech

I would like to extend my warm welcome to you on behalf of the administrators and the People's Government of Shinan District on your visit to the Shinan District Town Planning Administrative Bureau. I am sure this visit will leave you with positive impression.

Our bureau is a planning department under the People's Government of the Shinan District. With its business submitted to the direction of the City Planning Bureau of the Municipal Government, the Bureau takes the following as its main functions.

First, according to the municipality's program for city planning work, we formulate a plan for socio-economic development in Shinan District, work out detailed plans and plans of development and construction for ordinary regions.

Second, our bureau follows those laws, rules, regulations, and policies concerning urban planning and management stipulated by the State; it is also responsible for the management of the district's urban construction and planning.

Third, we are responsible for managing those archives regarding urban construction work within this district. Besides, we monitor and deliver punishments on those illegal construction projects according to the related laws and regulations.

Finally, we undertake other projects assigned by the Shinan District Government, and higher authorities at various levels.

课文 B

SECTION Ⅰ: Dialogue　讨论工程细节 Discuss about the Details on the Project

Interpret the following dialogue from Chinese into English and vice versa.

A: 吉姆，绿茶怎么样？

B: It's great. Its flavor makes me feel good. This is the best green tea I've ever had.

A: 吉姆，我们下午到新机场看一下。为节省时间我们一起在餐厅吃工作餐。午饭前还有点时间，我们一起检查一下下水道及排污管道的设计。

B: Yes, let's use every minute. Time is money. Okay, this is the draft for sewer and drain system. Combined sewer systems (CSS) for the new airport are designed to collect storm water runoff, domestic sewage, and industrial wastewater in the same pipe and bring it to the publicly owned treatment works (POTW) facilities.

A: 这个方法对我来说太新颖了，技术上没有问题吗？

B: Don't worry about it. Combined sewers are used across New York State, also in my city Long Beach. It has been applied there for 10 years and more.

A: 这种体系用在市区，在机场也适用吗？

B: No problem. CSS fits an airport much better than the urban area. During rain events, when storm water enters the sewers, the capacity of the sewer system may be exceeded and the excess water will be discharged directly to a waterbody.

A: 这会不会造成河道污染？

B: That's not a problem. This is mainly because the sewer is over-flown with storm water. Do you have more questions?

A: 那我们还得和市环保局合作，对吧？

B: You have to. In the States, we do the same with various governmental organizations.

A: 这个没问题。我们城市规划局负责这方面的工作。新机场是中央批准的国家项目，由市长直接监管。因此，其他部门必须和我们互相配合。

B: I'm proud of you living in China. In America, it's not that easy. Such a huge project needs a public hearing, and debated and approved by the Congress.

A: 我承认这一点。在别的国家做不到的事情，在中国就可能做得到。这是我们集体主义体制的优点。

B: Yes. Every coin has two sides. So far so good. We have been through with the blueprint of the design.

A: 如果想起新问题，我们在去机场场址的路上再聊。

B: OK. How time flies. It's near 12 o'clock.

A: 我没注意看表。我们得赶快去吃午饭。

SECTION Ⅱ: Warm-ups for Interpretation

➢ **Tongue twister.**

He wanted to desert his dessert in the desert!

他要把甜点扔到沙漠里!

When I went to Warsaw, I saw a saw that could outsaw any saw that I ever saw. Now, if you go to Warsaw and see a saw that could outsaw the saw I saw, I'd like to see your saw saw.

我去华沙的时候看见了一把我从未见过的可以锯开任何锯子的锯子。如果你现在要去华沙见到我看见的那种能锯掉别的锯的锯子，那我想看看你的锯怎么锯那把锯。

➢ **Interpret the following proverbs from English into Chinese.**

1. A close mouth catches no flies.
2. He who plays with fire gets burnt.
3. In the end, things will mend.
4. Many hands make light work.
5. Be slow to promise and quick to perform.

➢ **Interpret the following sentences from English into Chinese.**

1. Simply put, for a region to become a world-class communications hub, its fixed line and wireless infrastructure must be able to connect with the greatest number of people over the widest distance all the time.

2. Many travelers cross beneath the Channel using the Channel Tunnel, first proposed in the early 19th century and finally opened in 1994, connecting the UK and France by rail.
3. The London terminus is St. Pancras International, with the other British calling points being Ebbsfleet International and Ashford International in Kent.
4. Railroads also use balloon loops and flying junctions instead of flat junctions, as a way to reverse direction and to avoid trains conflicting with those on other tracks.

➢ **Interpret the following paragraphs from English into Chinese and vice versa.**

1. Qingdao is a city that has both an international harbor and light industry. The population has been continuously growing. Due to the prosperous economy, the amount of garbage has been growing. To match the urbanization development and the real needs of the city, the transporting of garbage mainly uses sealed compressive environmental protection vehicles. And the container compressive environmental protection vehicles can also assist. The total number of vehicles is 298, and they will be responsible for the cleaning and transporting of garbage in the city.
2. 我们已经建成了广州新白云国际机场，它是中国大陆三大枢纽机场之一。目前，与广州直航的亚洲城市有17个。广州还将在近年内开辟9～12条通往亚洲各国，特别是通往西亚和南亚地区的国际航线。

SECTION Ⅲ: Speech

Interpret the following speech from English into Chinese.

Good morning. I'm Dave Sheldon, Senior Director of Innovations and Partnership Programs, at the Council for Excellence in Government, and I'd like to welcome you to the first National Environmental Innovations Symposium.

As you can imagine from my title, I am extremely pleased to be partnering with the EPA and ECOS to bring you these two days devoted to learning about innovations in environmental governance. This symposium fits in very nicely with the mission of the Council: to improve the performance of government. The Council, a non-partisan, non-profit organization in Washington DC, has a number of programs aimed at encouraging practitioners in government to share their successes and learn from their mistakes.

First, our leadership development work helps federal government managers see how they can innovate and create change for their agencies.

Second, our technology consortium is looking at how the advancements and innovations in the technology sector are allowing governments at all levels to provide more meaningful service to citizens, both individually and through partnerships.

And finally, as a partner with the Ford Foundation and the Kennedy School at Harvard University in the Innovations in American Government Awards program, we seek out and recognize innovative government at all levels.

SECTION Ⅳ: Speech

Interpret the following speech from Chinese into English.

女士们，先生们，大家上午好。现在我来给大家简要介绍一下我市日夜发展的青岛地铁。

自 2010 年以来，山东省沿海城市青岛已经建成了六条地铁线路，全长 246 千米，使该市跻身中国地铁线路长度前 10 名。

青岛的日客流量目前超过 120 万人次，是过去十年中国地铁发展最快的城市之一。

官员们在 12 月 7 日的新闻发布会上表示，青岛将加大力度，在“十四五”(2021-2025)期间加快建设该市地铁网络。

建造七条新地铁线路的项目已于今年 9 月获得批准。这些线路的总长度为 139 千米，耗资 1000 亿元人民币(157.3 亿美元)。

该市推进“地铁＋”综合交通系统建设，以改善地铁线路与汽车、公交与铁路的连通性。

当局还将探索建设城市地铁网络的低碳方法。将应用一系列节能技术，鼓励使用氢能、光伏发电等清洁能源。

参考译文

SECTION Ⅰ: Dialogue

A: How do you like the green tea, Jim?

B: 棒极啦！茶的味道使我感到舒服极啦。这是我喝过的最好喝的绿茶。

A: Jim, we are to visit the new airport this afternoon. For time saving sake, we just have a work lunch together in our cafeteria. Since we still have some time before lunch, let's check the sewage and drainage system design.

B: 好的。我们抓紧时间，时间就是金钱。这是机场排污系统的草图。新机场设计采纳混合下水道排污体系，可将暴雨带来的雨水与生活污水以及工业废水一同排入市政污水处理厂处理。

A: Wow, this is new to me. But is this new tech mature?

B: 这个不用担心。这种混合下水道排污体系已经在纽约州和我居住的城市长滩市使用了十几年了。

A: But this system is utilized in downtown areas. Is it applicable to such a big airport?

B: 没问题。这种混合下水道排污体系更适合机场。下雨时，大量雨水流入下水道，下水道里的雨水过多时就会直接排到河道中。

A: Can this cause any water pollution?

B: 这不是问题。这主要是因为排入下水道的水是暴雨造成的雨水。还有别的问题吗？

A: So we have to consult it with Qingdao Municipal Environmental Protection Bureau?

B: 必须的。在美国，我们也得和政府各种部门打交道。

A: That's a piece of cake. We, the Urban Planning Bureau, are responsible for this state program approved by the central government. And the good thing is that our mayor is supervising the project himself. It's natural other governmental organizations have to coordinate with us.

B: 住在中国真好，替你感到骄傲。在我们美国，这种大项目必须经过听证会，国会通过辩论，最后才能批准。

A: I quite agree. What can not be done in other countries could be done in China. This is the pros of our collectivism system.

B：是的。任何事情都有两方面。不错。我们已经核对完了设计图纸。

A：If we come across a new idea, we will talk it over on the way to the project site.

B：好吧，时间过得真快，马上到12点了。

A：Oh, I did not notice the time. Let's hurry to have lunch.

SECTION Ⅱ: Warm-ups for Interpretation

➢ **Interpret the following proverbs from English into Chinese.**

1. 病从口入，祸从口出。
2. 玩火者必自焚。
3. 车到山前必有路。
4. 人多好办事。
5. 不轻诺，诺必果。

➢ **Interpret the following sentences from English into Chinese.**

1. 简言之，一个地区如果要成为世界级的通信中心，那么它的无线和固定通信基础设施就必须能够时刻在最大范围内与最多人群互相连接。
2. 19世纪初首次提出建设英伦海峡海底隧道，并于1994年建成，是英法之间铺设的一条铁路隧道。现在许多从海底横渡英吉利海峡的人都走英伦海峡海底隧道。
3. 伦敦的终点站是圣潘克拉斯车站，列车也会在艾贝斯费特国际车站和肯特的阿萨福德国际火车站稍作停留。
4. 铁路还用环形回车道和立体交汇线路而非平面交汇线路使列车转向，以避免不同线路上的列车相撞。

➢ **Interpret the following paragraphs from English into Chinese and vice versa.**

1. 青岛市是一个兼具国际港湾及发达轻工业的城市，人口不断增长。随着社会经济的繁荣，本市垃圾量也与日俱增。为配合本市都市化发展及实际需要，清运垃圾以密封压缩式环保车为主，另以子母压缩式环保车为辅，车辆总数为298辆，负责全市清运工作。
2. As one of the three hub airports in China, the new Guangzhou Baiyun International Airport has been built and put into operation. Currently there are direct flights link-

ing Guangzhou with 17 Asian cities, and a further 9 to 12 routes to Asian cities will be established in recent years, especially to West and South Asia.

SECTION Ⅲ: Speech

早上好。我是政府杰出成就理事会“创新合作项目”的高级主管，戴夫·谢尔顿。欢迎大家参加首届“全国环境创新研讨会”。

以我所担任的职务，大家可以知道，我非常高兴能够与美国国家环境保护局及美国环境保护委员会一起给您带来为期两天的、以了解环境管理创新为主题的研讨会。本次研讨会很好地体现出美国环境保护委员会的使命：提高政府的工作表现。“美国环境保护委员会”成立于华盛顿，是一个无党派的非营利性组织，经常策划组织各种项目，旨在鼓励政府职员分享成功经验或从失败中吸取教训。

首先，我们的领导才能有助于各联邦政府的管理人员了解到如何才能为他们所在的各级政府带来创新或新的变化。

其次，我们的技术联盟正在研究技术的发展和革新将如何使各级政府通过自身或联合其他组织更好地为美国人民服务。

最后，我们和福特基金会、哈佛大学肯尼迪政府学院一起参与了“美国政府创新奖”项目，共同发掘并表彰各级创新型政府。

SECTION Ⅳ: Speech

Good morning, ladies and gentlemen, let me give you a brief idea about the metro system in the town.

The coastal city of Qingdao, Shandong province has since 2010 built six metro lines that span 246 kilometers, placing the city among China's top 10 in terms of the length of metro lines.

The daily passenger flow in Qingdao is currently in excess of 1.2 million, making it one of the cities with the fastest subway development in China in the past decade.

Qingdao will make more efforts to accelerate the construction of the city's subway network during the 14th Five-Year Plan (2021-2025) period, officials said at a news conference on Dec 7, 2021.

The project to build seven new metro lines was approved this September. These lines will span a combined 139 kilometers and cost 100 billion yuan ($15.73 billion) to build.

The city has promoted the construction of a "metro+" comprehensive transportation system to improve the connectivity between metro lines and cars, buses and railways.

Authorities will also explore low-carbon approaches to constructing the city's subway network. A series of energy-saving technologies will be applied and the use of clean energy such as hydrogen power and photovoltaic power will be encouraged.

Unit 15 教育 Education

中国的教育体系旨在培养中国特色社会主义的建设者和继承者。

China's education system aims to train builders and inheritors of socialism with Chinese characteristics.

党和全社会需要弘扬尊重教师、重视教育的社会规范。要努力提高教师的政治、社会和职业地位，使他们享有应有的社会声望，通过传授知识和教育人民，为党和人民的事业作出更大的贡献。

The Party and the entire society need to promote the social norms of respecting teachers and valuing education. Efforts should be made to enhance the political, social and professional status of teachers so they can enjoy their due social prestige and make greater contributions to the cause of the Party and the people by imparting knowledge and educating people.

课文 A

SECTION Ⅰ: Dialogue 参观校园 Touring the Campus

Interpret the following dialogue from English into Chinese and vice versa.

A: Good morning, is this the Foreign Affairs Office? I'm Tamil Baker from Missouri State University. And this is Steve Robinette, our exchange student to Qingdao University.

B: 早上好。我是李洁。我们主任让我带你俩参观一下校园。咱们走吧。

A: You have a big campus with so many buildings! Can you tell me what that red mansion is next to this block?

B：哦，那是我们刚建好的留学生教学大楼，一共 12 层，配有现代化教室、高级语音室、视听室、报告厅等。

A：Great! How many overseas students do you have on campus?

B：哦，共有 1000 多名留学生。

A：Do you have enough apartments to hold them?

B：当然有。你看小山坡下的那两栋高楼是专门给留学生盖的。每个房间都配有壁橱、写字台、台灯、中央空调、电视、冰箱、微波炉、电脑和无线网络。

A：Wonderful! Well equipped.

B：我们前面这个湖是人工的，曾经是当地居民吃水用的水库。

A：Wow, there are ducks and swans, too.

B：是的。有一些老师和学生照料它们，保护它们，每天都喂它们。

A：Cool! This makes the campus look much more lively and beautiful.

B：的确如此！你参观过其他中国大学吗？

A：Yes, it was sometime 3 years ago when we toured Xiamen University. It is a good university. Their gymnasium is the first class.

B：我们也有 CBA 标准的体育馆，是青岛双星队的主场。我带你去看。

A：What is this structure for, Li?

B：我们的图书馆。很多学生都在这里看书，楼里也有我们的机房，学生经常上网查资料。

A：Look ahead of you. You see that huge building with a sloped roof?

B：这就是我跟你说的体育馆。我们进去看一下。

A：How time flies! It's about time Jim finished his lecture in the office building. We should meet him there. Thank you for showing us around.

B：不客气。随时都愿意为您效劳。

相关词汇

常用教育类相关词汇

auditorium　礼堂

conference room　会议室

multimedia room　多媒体室

audio-visual room　视听室

recording room　录音室

lecture hall　阶梯教室

multifunction classroom 多功能教室
fountain 喷水池
reservoir 水库
academic 学术的
admission office 招生办
graduate school 研究生院
students union 学生会
dormitory 宿舍
canteen 食堂
cafeteria 自助餐厅
gymnasium 体育馆
undergraduate 大学生；本科生
postgraduate 研究生
master 硕士
doctor 博士
staff 全体员工
faculty 教师
discipline 学科
elective course 选修课
compulsory course 必修课
liberal arts 文科
adjunct professor 兼职教授
tenure professor 终生教授
associate professor 副教授
assistant professor 助理教授
enrollment 注册入学人数
extra-curricular 课外的
minor 辅修科目
major 主修科目
student union 学生会
exchange of students 学生交换
short-term training course 短训班
faculty, students and staff 师生员工
dean 院长
provost 教务长
department head 系主任
enthusiasm in learning Chinese 学汉语热
Chinese character 汉字
radical 偏旁
stroke 笔画

SECTION Ⅱ: Warm-ups for Interpretation

➢ **Tongue twister.**

A Finnish fisher named Fisher failed to fish any fish one Friday afternoon and finally he found out a big fissure in his fishing net.

一个名叫费希尔的芬兰渔民在一个星期五的下午未能捕到任何鱼，结果他发现他的渔网有一个大口。

A loyal warrior will rarely worry why we rule.

一个忠诚的战士很少会担心我们为什么要统治。

> **Interpret the following proverbs from English into Chinese.**

1. Learn not, and know not.
2. Early sow, early mow.
3. Money breeds money.
4. One today is worth two tomorrow.
5. Faith will move mountains.

> **Interpret the following sentences from English into Chinese.**

1. The admission of undergraduates, graduates with master and PHD by this elite university is very much favored by the faculty and staff of the organization.
2. This university has long become a renowned institute of higher learning with a strong teaching staff and prestigious academic strength and is now well on its way to becoming a world-class quality university.
3. Our school is facilitated with advanced modern teaching equipment: the language laboratories of various sizes, classrooms equipped with computers, multimedia classrooms and a satellite-TV reception system.
4. Our university stresses on the international cooperation and maintains exchange programs with more than 20 universities in the US, Canada, England, France, Germany and Australia.
5. The majority educators, however, agree that quality education is not only a key task of the education circles, but also a responsibility of the whole nation.

> **Interpret the following paragraphs from English into Chinese and vice versa.**

1. Today, I am going to talk about the role of the university in the 21st century. I have chosen not one, but several different roles which will be important for universities in the future. First, the university will take on an even larger role in assisting pre-college education in preparing students for study and work. Second, partnership with corporations and businesses will become a greater part of university involvement. The next century will see an expansion of partnerships of this type, particularly with research universities. Finally, the university will play a world role as a result of convenient communication worldwide, greater opportunities for trade, and the develop-

ment of multinational corporations.

2. 美国的教育体系体现了美国人对自由、民主社会的追求。反过来，教育又帮助塑造他们理想中的社会。一个民主国家的存亡有赖于其所有公民的智慧和参与。

SECTION Ⅲ: Speech

Interpret the following speech from Chinese into English.

随着中国加入世界贸易组织和改革开放步伐加快，中国经济成就举世瞩目，越来越多的海外学者、学生及商界人士希望更多地了解中国。

为此，我校的国际交流中心，本着友好交往、增进了解、加强合作的原则，向海内外各界人士提供各种层次的汉语言文化培训课程。

目前，国际交流中心致力于短期汉语强化课程，全面介绍中国政治、经济、文化等各方面的内容。

所有课程均由本大学的资深教授执教。许多授课教师都具有十分丰富的国际教学经验。

国际交流中心开设的这些课程受到广大海外学者的欢迎，研修这些课程的人数大幅增加。

为了满足学员的求知欲望，中心不断增设新的课程，如太极、武术、书法、中国历史等。有的培训班给学员提供学习按摩、针灸、拔罐、刮痧等课程。所有这些课程都受到了学生的欢迎。

SECTION Ⅳ: Speech

Interpret the following speech from English into Chinese.

Qingdao University is situated in Qingdao-a famous coastal city in eastern China. The university sits at the foot of the Fushan Mountains, overlooking the Yellow Sea's sandy beaches. The breathtaking views and the comfortable seaside climate make Qingdao University a great place to study.

Qingdao University is comprised of 25 colleges and 100 majors with undergraduate programs covering literature, history, philosophy, natural sciences, law, economics, management, engineering, medical science, education, art, and more. There are 35 doctoral programs and 175 master's programs. Current enrollment is over 43,000 students.

Qingdao University attaches great importance to international exchanges and cooperation, taking a welcoming policy as the important developmental strategy of the university as it moves toward internationalization. Qingdao University is proud to have international exchange programs with more than 130 universities in more than 20 countries and regions, including the United States, the United Kingdom, Germany, Russia, Canada, Australia, Japan, Korea, Singapore, and many more.

Each year Qingdao University invites about 50 long-term and 100 short-term international professors and instructors to teach on campus. There are also opportunities for approximately 500 Chinese students, scholars, and administrative staff members to study, teach, or work abroad. The number of faculty, staff, and students involved in international academic exchange has significantly increased in recent years.

Qingdao University began recruiting international students in 1987. It is one of the universities approved by the Ministry of Education to enroll international students and is also an authorized HSK Test Center (the primary Chinese proficiency test). Designated as an "Education Center of Chinese Language and Culture" by the Overseas Chinese Bureau of the State Council, Qingdao University has become one of a dozen universities in China which offer quality courses in Chinese language and culture.

Qingdao University offers a wide range of disciplines. It also has a Chinese Language College specializing in teaching Chinese as a foreign language, which gives it obvious advantages in international education. In recent years, there is a growing number of international students who apply to study in Qingdao University. Apart from enrolling international students to various majors, the university also offers special courses such as Chinese Language Undergraduate Courses, Chinese Language Training Courses, Master of Teaching Chinese Language and MBBS via English Media program to those students.

参考译文

SECTION Ⅰ: Dialogue

A：早上好，这里是外事处吗？我是美国密苏里州立大学的泰米·贝克。这是我们密大派往青大的交流生，斯蒂芬·罗宾内特。

B： Good morning. I'm Li Jie. Yes, our director asked me to show you around the campus. Here we go.

A： 你们的校园真大，这么多楼！你能告诉我旁边的红楼是什么楼吗？

B： Oh, that's a twelve-storied teaching building for overseas students. It is equipped with modern classrooms, advanced language labs, video rooms and lecture halls and so on.

A： 太好了！你们学校有多少留学生？

B： More than 1,000.

A： 那你们有足够的宿舍吗？

B： I bet. Look at the two tall towers at the foot of the hill. They are specially built for the overseas students. Each apartment is facilitated with a closet, a desk, a table lamp, central heating, a plasma, a fridge, a microwave, a PC and the WiFi.

A： 棒极了！设备齐全。

B： In front of us, there is an artificial lake, used to be a reservoir for the local residents to fetch drinking water.

A： 湖上还有鸭子和大雁呢！

B： Yes, some faculty and our students take care of them, feed them and protect them.

A： 真好！这给校园增加了活力，使校园更漂亮了。

B： Precisely. Have you ever visited other Chinese universities before?

A： 是的，大约3年前我参观过厦门大学。那是个好大学。学校的体育馆设施一流。

B： We, too, have a standard gymnasium for China Basketball Association. It's the host court for Qingdao Double Star Team. I'll show you there.

A： 李，这是什么建筑？

B： That's our library. A lot of students study here. There is a computer service center here inside the building. Students spend plenty of time on the Internet for information.

A： 你看我们前面，那个带斜坡楼顶的楼是干什么的？

B： This is the gym I mentioned. Let's enter and have a trip there.

A： 时间过得真快！吉姆在办公楼的讲座快结束了。我们到那儿和他会面，谢谢你带我们参观你们的校园。

B： You are welcome. Honor is mine.

SECTION Ⅱ: Warm-ups for Interpretation

➢ **Interpret the following proverbs from English into Chinese.**

1. 不学无术。
2. 早种早收。
3. 钱生钱，利滚利。
4. 把握一个今天，胜似两个明天。
5. 精诚所至，金石为开。

➢ **Interpret the following sentences from English into Chinese.**

1. 这所名牌大学录取的本科生、硕士研究生和博士研究生都深受学校教职工的好评。
2. 这所大学已经发展成为师资雄厚、学术声名远播的著名学府，并正在向世界知名高水平大学迈进。
3. 我们学校装备了现代化的教学设施：有不同规格的语言实验室、计算机教室、多媒体教室，配置有先进的地面卫星接收系统。
4. 我们学校注重国际合作，积极开展对外学术交流，目前与美国、加拿大、英国、法国、德国、澳大利亚等 20 国的多所高等院校保持良好的校际交流关系。
5. 然而绝大多数教育工作者认为素质教育不仅仅是教育领域的重要任务，也是全民族的责任。

➢ **Interpret the following paragraphs from English into Chinese and vice versa.**

1. 今天，我打算谈谈大学在 21 世纪的作用。我所要谈的是大学今后将发挥多个重要作用。第一，大学在帮助开展大学预科教育中将发挥更大的作用，为学生进一步学习和工作做准备。第二，与公司、行业展开合作将是大学事务的重要参与部分。这种合作，特别对研究性大学来说，在下个世纪将会进一步扩大。最后，由于全球范围的便捷通信，更多的贸易机会和跨国公司的发展，大学将发挥世界性作用。
2. Education in the United States has been shaped by the American belief in a free, democratic society. In turn, education has helped to shape that society. The survival of a democracy depends upon the intelligent participation of all its citizens.

SECTION Ⅲ: Speech

In response to the rapid development of China's economy, and thanks to its accession to the WTO and the reform and opening-up policy, an ever-increasing number of foreign scholars, students and business people wish to learn more about China.

Because of this, the International Academic Exchange Centre of our university offers varieties of training courses for all levels of Chinese language and Chinese culture to overseas learners based on the principles of promoting friendly exchanges and enhancing mutual understanding and cooperation.

At present, the International Academic Exchange Centre is dedicated to offering a Short-term Intensive Chinese Training Program and then giving a comprehensive introduction to Chinese politics, economy, culture, etc.

All courses are taught by senior professors and many of them have rich international teaching experience.

These courses have gained great popularity since they were first introduced. There has been a great increase in the number of overseas students.

To meet students' needs, our center keeps adding new courses such as taiji, martial arts, calligraphy, Chinese history, etc. Some training programs offer courses like massage, acupuncture, cupping, coining and so on. All the courses are favored by overseas students.

SECTION Ⅳ: Speech

青岛大学位于中国东部沿海名城——青岛。学校坐落于黄海之滨、浮山之麓，环境优美，气候宜人。

目前，学校设有25个学院、100个本科专业，涵盖文学、历史学、哲学、理学、工学、医学、经济学、管理学、法学、教育学、艺术学等学科门类。现有博士点35个，硕士点175个，在校生43,000余人。

青岛大学重视国际交流与合作，提出开放办学战略，形成了国际化办学特色。学校与美国、英国、德国、俄罗斯、加拿大、澳大利亚、日本、韩国、新加坡等20多个国家和地区的130余所高校建立了交流合作项目。

学校每年聘请长期外国专家和教师50余名，短期外国专家、教授百余名。每年派往国外高校学习、研修、教学和工作的学生、学者和管理人员近500人。近年来，参与国际学术交流与合作的师生人数显著增多。

青岛大学自1987年起开始招收留学生，是教育部批准的具有招收留学生资格的高校之一，是HSK考试考点。并被中国国务院侨务办公室确立为“国家华文教育基地”，成为全国十余所承担华文教育任务的高校之一。

青岛大学学科门类齐全，并设有擅长对外汉语教学的汉语言学院，留学生教育优势明显。近年来，申请到青岛大学学习的留学生日益增多。青岛大学除各专业均招收外国留学生外，还专门为留学生开设了特色课程，如汉语言专业本科班、汉语言进修班、汉语国际教育专业硕士及青岛大学临床医学英语授课课程MBBS。

Unit 16 参观城市 City Touring

真正的友谊使人们彼此接近，无论他们相距多远。

True friendship brings people close however far apart they may be.

一起起航，我们可以乘风破浪，勇敢跋涉一万里。

By setting sail together, we could ride the wind, break the waves, and brave the journey of ten thousand miles.

课文 A

SECTION Ⅰ: Dialogue 游八大关 At Badaguan Scenic Resort

Interpret the following dialogue from Chinese into English and vice versa.

A: 我们到八大关景区了。

B: It's such a lovely place. What does Badaguan mean?

A: 简而言之，“八大关”由三个汉字组成。“八”表示“eight”，“大”表示“big”，“关”的意思是“pass”或“fort”。

B: You mean eight big passes?

A: 是的。城市规划师用中国古代军事要塞的名字来命名这里的八条街。

B: It's hard to believe that I found German houses here.

A: 哦，这里的确有德国建筑。八大关景区因有众多欧式风格的花园式别墅和建筑而出名。

B: The area is very lush with trees forming canopies along most streets and plenty of parkland and scenic walks along the coast.

A：是的。无论何时，这里都是一个散步的好去处。许多新婚夫妇都来这里拍婚纱照。

B：Oh, yes. I see a couple of young guys are taking photos over there near the sea. Can't they get cold on such a windy day with their wedding gowns?

A：为了记录这一重要时刻，冒一点险也是值得的。如果我年轻10岁，我也会这么做。

B：You're kidding, Liang. Actually, my hometown San Diego also has such a beautiful place teeming with residents and literally dozens of brides and grooms getting their photos taken on weekends.

A：对啊！我们两国的文化有许多相似之处。

B：The tree-lined streets are amazing and beaches make it like a paradise in the beautiful city of Qingdao.

A：哦，没错。我很喜欢这里的樱花树。

B：Scenes are so beautiful. It's worth a walk through when you are off business.

A：詹姆斯，说实话，我经常晚饭后来这里散步。现在我们去栈桥吧。

B：Alright. Here we go.

相关词汇

与城市有关的英语词汇

metropolis　大都市

metropolitan　大都会；大城市人

cosmopolis　国际都市

cosmopolitan　世界性的；周游世界的人

skyscraper　摩天大楼

newsstand　报摊

church　教堂

cathedral　大教堂

chapel　小礼拜堂

theater　剧院

museum　博物馆

zoo　动物园

fairground/fun fair　游乐园

stadium　体育场

gallery　画廊

Laoshan Scenic Area　崂山风景区

Badaguan Scenic Resort　八大关景区

Qingdao Beer Museum　青岛啤酒博物馆

Qingdao Catholic Church　青岛天主教堂

the Pier　栈桥

Qingdao Underwater World　青岛海底世界

Qingdao Olympic Sailing Center（Regatta Center）　青岛奥帆中心

Qingdao Naval Museum 青岛海军博物馆
Qingdao Polar Ocean World 青岛极地海洋世界
Old Stone Man Beach (Shilaoren Beach) 石老人沙滩
Tsingtao Brewery 青岛啤酒厂
Golden Beach 金沙滩
Guest House 青岛迎宾馆
city proper 城市市区
downtown 市中心
suburb 市郊
vicinity 附近地区
landmark 地标
avenue 大街；林荫大道
boulevard 林荫大道
street 街道；马路
road 公路

SECTION Ⅱ: Warm-ups for Interpretation

➢ **Tongue twister.**

How can a clam cram in a clean cream can?
一只蛤蜊怎么可以塞满干净的奶油罐头?
Birdie birdie in the sky laid a turdie in my eye.
If cows could fly I'd have a cow pie in my eye.
空中小鸟扔下了一只龟让我看见了。如果牛可以飞的话，我眼睛里可以吃一张牛饼。

➢ **Interpret the following proverbs from Chinese into English.**

1. 宁为清贫，不为浊富。
2. 自寻苦恼。
3. 严以律己，宽以待人。
4. 物以类聚，人以群分。
5. 谎言终究要败露。

➢ **Interpret the following sentences from Chinese into English.**

1. 澳门，南海之滨一颗闪耀的明珠，以她的风采、沧桑和辉煌吸引着全世界的目光。
2. 纽约市的主要部分是个岛屿，只能通过隧道或桥才能接近它。
3. 苏州因城内水道遍布而享有“东方威尼斯”的美誉。
4. 上海系江南名城，远东巨埠，内联九州，外通四海，物华天宝，人杰地灵。

5. 20 世纪 80 年代华尔街重整旗鼓，纽约市重获世界金融中心的地位。

➢ **Interpret the following paragraphs from Chinese into English and vice versa.**

1. 位于太湖和大运河岸边的江苏同里，离著名旅游城——苏州仅 18 千米。古镇周围环绕着 5 个湖泊，镇上多条河流将古镇分为 15 个部分，40 多座反映各朝代风格的石桥连接其中。该镇保留了许多具有明清两代特色的建筑。河水从屋前流过，居民通常坐船互相拜访。在这里，旅游者能欣赏到典型的江南水乡的景色——小桥、流水、人家的和谐相容。
2. Like all large cities throughout the world, New York has old problems to solve and new ones to face. Slums must be cleared and new houses must be built. Traffic congestion continues to trouble the city's already over-crowded streets. Not only must new highways be constructed, but also old road must be repaired. Caring for the sick, providing for the needy, and helping new comers to adjust to big city life are additional tasks that the City of New York must perform. Protecting the health and safety of New Yorkers requires an army of police, firemen, as well as doctors and nurses. In spite of all these, millions of visitors continue to flock to the city every year. New Yorkers are working hard to meet their city's needs and to keep it a world center of culture, industry and commerce.

SECTION Ⅲ: Speech

Interpret the following speech from Chinese into English.

女士们、先生们：

想喝啤酒，就来青岛吧。1903 年起，青岛沦为德国殖民地，随后又被日本占领。战后，殖民者才把青岛归还中国。青岛啤酒的发展非常成功，然而其承传过程却颇具趣味性。如果你对酿酒过程、工业建筑或只对啤酒感兴趣，不妨来啤酒博物馆一游。无论是殖民时期的古老建筑，还是世界上现存的最早的西门子发电机；无论是工人翻动平铺在地面的大麦的场景，还是工人酿酒的全息投影，都会让你感到充满乐趣。你还可免费享用生啤，与瓶装啤酒的味道进行对比。这里确实值得一游。

青岛啤酒博物馆设立在青岛啤酒最早的厂房中，展览包括三部分：(1)青岛啤酒百年历史和文化，(2)啤酒生产工艺，(3)现代啤酒厂的生产过程。所有展览都经过精心设计，品质较高。老厂房本身就是一座精美的历史建筑。

啤酒厂周围及啤酒厂内有许多值得拍照的东西，如殖民时期的老建筑、“啤酒瓶”喷泉、排列在现代啤酒厂房顶的巨型“啤酒罐”及馆内的诸多展品。

博物馆展现了中国的标志性啤酒——青岛啤酒的历史。参观结束后，还有机会品尝青岛啤酒并购买纪念品。

SECTION Ⅳ: Speech

Interpret the following speech from English into Chinese.

Paris, the capital of France, has a total of 2 million inhabitants who live in Paris proper, and almost 11 million people who live in greater Paris, which is one of Europe's largest metropolitan areas. Like London, Paris is a city that sits on a river, the Seine, 145 km from the river's mouth on the English Channel.

As a city of world importance and the business, historic, cultural, diplomatic, religious, educational, artistic, and tourist center of France, Paris owes its prosperity in large part to its favorable position on the Seine, which has been a major commercial artery since the Roman period.

Along the banks on both sides are seen buildings that tell the history of Paris. On the lower banks, sheltered by ancient trees, fishermen wait long hours for a catch. Upon the street level are stands of well-worn books, where students rub shoulders with grey-haired scholars in browsing and searching.

But it would be even better to go down the Seine in a boat. It will pass the Cathedral of Notre Dame, well known to foreign readers thanks to Victor Hugo's novel. Further on you will find on your right the Louvre, the great palace which houses da Vinci's Mona Lisa, whose faint smile has charmed viewers for centuries.

And still further on the left, you will find the Eiffel Tower, which was built in 1889 to celebrate the centenary of the French Revolution. There are over 150 art galleries and museums in the city and an uncounted number of cafés and restaurants lining every street and boulevard.

After dark, the city's theatres and concert halls host world-leading productions of theatre and dance, while many classical concerts take place in fine architectural settings.

Paris is a beautiful city. One sees marble statues, fountains, Roman Columns, everywhere. It is the pride of France, and of civilized humanity.

参考译文

SECTION Ⅰ: Dialogue

A：Here we are at Badaguan Scenic Resort.

B：这儿真漂亮。“八大关”是什么意思？

A：Let me put it simply. Badaguan is a combination of three Chinese characters. Ba means eight. Da refers to big, and Guan stands for pass or fort.

B：你是说“eight big passes”？

A：Yes. City planners used these Chinese ancient military fortress buildings to name the eight avenues in this area.

B：这里竟然有德国风格的建筑，真令人难以置信。

A：Oh, yes. Badaguan is famous for its garden-like villas and European-styled buildings.

B：这里街道两旁绿树成荫，随处可见庭院绿地，滨海步行道风景秀丽。

A：Yes. It is a favorite walking spot on any day of the week. It's frequented by lots of wedding couples for their wedding pics.

B：哦，真的。我看到海边那儿就有一对年轻人在拍婚纱照呢。今天这么大风，他们穿着婚纱会冻感冒吧？

A：Worth a risk to record this moment of significance. I would do it too, if I were 10 years younger.

B：梁，你在开玩笑吧。其实，我家乡圣地亚哥也有这样一个风景优美的地方。每到周末，许多居民和新婚夫妇也会去那里拍照。

A：Yes. Our culture has a lot of similarities.

B：幽静的林荫道，美丽的海滩，八大关让人仿佛置身天堂。

A：Oh, yes. For me, I like the sakura trees here.

B：真是风景如画。如果不忙，来这儿散散步还真不错。

A：Honestly, I often come here after dinner, James. Let's move to the pier.

B：好吧。我们走。

SECTION Ⅱ: Warm-ups for Interpretation

➢ **Interpret the following proverbs from Chinese into English.**

1. A clear fast is better than a dirty breakfast.
2. Nobody's enemy but his own.
3. Pardon all men, but never yourself.
4. Birds of a feather flock together.
5. Lies have short legs.

➢ **Interpret the following sentences from Chinese into English.**

1. Macao, a sparkling pearl in the south coast of China, catches the world's attention for her charm, her experiences of various changes and her bright achievements.
2. The main part of New York is an island and you have to approach it either by tunnel or bridge.
3. With numerous narrow waterways covering the town, Suzhou enjoys the fame as the "Oriental Venice".
4. Shanghai is a famous port city in Southeast China and in the Far East. Linked with all the places in China and major ports throughout the world, this metropolis is known as a land of attractive resources and magical power and a birthplace of creative minds and gifted talents.
5. The 1980s saw a rebirth of Wall Street, and New York City reclaimed its role as the center of the world-wide financial industry.

➢ **Interpret the following paragraphs from Chinese into English and vice versa.**

1. Lying on the bank of Taihu Lake and Grand Canal, Tongli in Jiangsu Province is 18 km away from the famous tourist city of Suzhou. This ancient town is surrounded by five lakes and divided into 15 parts by crisscross river courses. They are linked by more than 40 bridges that were built in varied styles of different dynasties. The town maintains many buildings featuring the architecture of the Ming and Qing dynasties. With waters flowing in front of houses, residents most often visit each other by boat. Here, tourists can enjoy the typical riverside scenery of south China, which

features a harmonious combination of small bridges, murmuring streams and dwellings.

2. 和世界上许多大城市一样，纽约既要解决老问题，也要面对新问题。既要拆除贫民窟，又要建造新房。交通堵塞仍然是已经拥挤不堪的街道的大麻烦。不但要造新的高速公路，而且要整修旧道路。照顾病者，接济穷人，帮助新来者适应大城市的生活是纽约必须做的额外工作。保障纽约人的健康与安全需要大量的警察、消防人员、医生和护士。尽管如此，纽约每年仍然有数以百万计的来访者。纽约人正在努力奋斗以适应城市作为世界文化、工业和商务中心的需求。

SECTION Ⅲ: Speech

Ladies and gentlemen,

Think of beer, come to Tsingtao. Started by German colonials in 1903, stolen by the Japanese and returned to China after the war. This is a true success story, with an interesting heritage. If you have an interest in brewing, industrial architecture or just beer you will enjoy this. From the colonial buildings, to the oldest surviving Siemens engine, floor malting to holographic brewers. Enjoy a free taste of raw beer and compare it to the finished product. A worthwhile visit.

The Museum derived from the oldest beer factory. The exhibitions contain three parts: (1) history of Tsingtao Beer, (2) the way how beer is made, (3) current brew factory production. The exhibitions are well-designed and with high quality. The building, the old factory itself is a beautiful historical architecture.

There are many great photos ops in and around the brewery including some of the old colonial architecture, the "beer bottle" fountain, huge "cans" of beer perched atop the modern brewery building and some of the many exhibits inside.

Here you will learn about the history of the iconic beer of China. And at the end of the tour you get a chance to sample beer and buy souvenirs.

SECTION Ⅳ: Speech

在法国首都巴黎，有两百万居民住在巴黎市中心，另有约 1,100 万人住在大巴黎地区，那是欧洲最大的都市区之一。和伦敦一样，巴黎也是坐落在一条河上，即塞纳河，离英吉利海峡的河口 145 千米。

作为举足轻重的世界级城市，以及法国的商业、历史、文化、外交、宗教、教育、艺术和旅游中心，巴黎的繁荣，很大程度上得益于其位于塞纳河有利的地理位置。自罗马时期，塞纳河就已经是一条主要商业干线。

两岸的建筑诉说着巴黎的历史。在河的下游，古树垂荫，钓鱼人为鱼儿上钩等上几个小时。岸上摆着一排排旧书摊，大学生和白发学者擦肩接踵，在其中翻阅寻找。

最好沿塞纳河泛舟而下。游船经过巴黎圣母院，维克多·雨果的名作早已使它闻名四海。再往前，在右侧的岸上，你会看到宏伟的罗浮宫。里面收藏着达·芬奇的《蒙娜丽莎》，她嘴角浅浅的微笑，让多少世纪以来的观赏者为之陶醉。

再往前划，你可以看到左侧的艾菲尔铁塔。那是 1889 年为纪念法国大革命一百周年而建造的。这座城市共有 150 多座美术馆和博物馆，无数咖啡馆和餐馆布满每条街道和林荫大道。

入夜以后，城市的剧院和音乐厅里上演着世界一流的戏剧和舞蹈，许多经典音乐会也在一些富丽堂皇的建筑中演出。巴黎是美丽的城市，这里到处是大理石雕像、喷泉和罗马式圆柱。它是法国的骄傲，也是人类文明的骄傲。

课文 B

SECTION Ⅰ: Dialogue 参观城市 A Tour in the City

Interpret the following dialogue from English into Chinese and vice versa.

A: I'm a little surprised by Qingdao. It's such a metropolitan city. I guess I expected to see more pagodas and traditional architectures.

B: 很多西方人都到北京看传统的中国建筑。北京有紫禁城、颐和园、天坛、地坛、长城等，但青岛没有那么长的历史。

A: What do you mean? I thought I read somewhere that Qingdao is the birthplace of Taoism.

B: 对。但和北京比起来，青岛就是一座新城了。

A: I see what you mean. Peking was the capital of China for about a thousand years or more.

B: 对。明、清两朝都曾在北京建都。青岛曾是德国的殖民地。现在，它是轻工业和电子产业基地。

A：I didn't realize that. No wonder it looks so modern.

B：你看这片区域。这里是大学城，还有许多科研机构。

A：How many universities do you have in the town?

B：青岛的大学没有波士顿、纽约和洛杉矶那么多，但我们有 25 所大学，还有一些国家级科研机构。

A：Education and science always play an important role for the civilization.

B：我们前面就是高新区了。这里有许多“财富 500 强”投资的企业，如杜邦公司、卡特彼勒公司、高通公司、通用公司等都在这里有投资。

A：What's that huge tower over there near the sea?

B：是 2008 年北京奥运会比赛用的帆船中心。青岛是 14 年前北京奥运会的伙伴城市。那届奥运会办得不错。谁能想到两个星期前北京又成功地举办了北京冬奥会和残奥会。

A：Exactly. I feel proud of Beijing. Beijing is the only city in the world to have sponsored two Olympic Games—the Summer Olympics Games and Winter Olympics Games.

B：谢谢你。我们有信心为世界奉献一场简约、安全、精彩的奥运盛会。北京冬奥会、冬残奥会的主题口号是“一起向未来”。我们确实做到了并赢得了世界的赞扬。

A：Why don't you lead me to see the regatta spot now?

B：好主意！我们马上就去。

A：Qingdao is really a city full of vigor and vitality.

B：谢谢。祝你在青岛过得愉快。

A：I bet.

SECTION Ⅱ：Warm-ups for Interpretation

➢ **Tongue twister.**

Bobby Bippy bought a bat.
Bobby Bippy bought a ball.
With his bat Bob banged the ball.
Banged it bump against the wall.
But so boldly Bobby banged it,
That he burst his rubber ball.

"Boo!" cried Bobby!

Bad luck ball,

Bad luck Bobby, bad luck ball.

Now to drown his many troubles,

Bobby Bippy's blowing bubbles.

鲍勃·比皮买了一个球拍。鲍勃·比皮买个一个球。鲍勃用他的球拍击球，把球猛的打到了墙上。

但是鲍勃用的力气太大了，以至于把球打爆了。"波!"鲍勃哭了。倒霉的球，倒霉的鲍勃，倒霉的球。

现在，为了解决他的麻烦，鲍勃·波比开始吹起了泡泡。

➢ **Interpret the following proverbs from English into Chinese.**

1. Misfortune tests the sincerity of friends.
2. Do as you would be done by.
3. He who is ashamed of asking is ashamed of learning.
4. Of nothing comes nothing.
5. Love me, love my dog.

➢ **Interpret the following sentences from English into Chinese.**

1. Tornados, hurricanes, cyclones, tsunami, landslide, mudslide, earthquakes and volcano eruptions are natural catastrophes in both Atlantic and Pacific zones.
2. Hong Kong is an ideal shopping center that attracts tourists from all over the world. Many five-star hotels have been established on Hong Kong Island and Kowloon. The adjacent islands have been developed into beautiful resorts and recreational facilities.
3. Many big cities offer a unique atmosphere and history. The Great Wall and the Palace Museum of Beijing, and the cable cars of San Francisco are part of the unusual atmosphere of those cities.
4. The Thames is the longest river in England. It has shaped the history of the country. Without it, there would have been no London as we know it today.
5. Cambridge is one of the most important and beautiful towns not only in Britain, but also in Europe. Visitors all over the world are attracted by the quality of its buildings, in particular those belonging to the University and the unique atmosphere

caused by the combination of rivers and gardens.

➤ **Interpret the following paragraphs from English into Chinese and vice versa.**

1. Vancouver is Canada's third largest metropolitan city. Known as Canada's gateway to the Pacific Ocean, Vancouver is linked by shipping services with the Pacific countries. Manufactured goods from Asia keep flowing into this natural ice-free harbor throughout the year. A multi-national, multi-cultural society, Vancouver is largely British in character with obvious traditional Chinese influence. Its Chinatown is the second largest Chinese community in North America, second only to San Francisco of the United States.
2. 以东方明珠闻名于世的上海是中国通向世界的东大门。早在唐宋时期，上海便是中国东部的一座外贸商镇，与日本、朝鲜和东南亚各国之间有着商贸往来。到了清朝乾隆、嘉庆年间，上海成了中国东南部的大都市和海运中心。那时，申城里万商云集，浦江上千帆斗艳，好一派繁荣兴旺的景象！自 20 世纪 50 年代起，上海取代广州，成了中国的外贸中心，至今仍保持着这一龙头地位。今天这座著名的国际港口城市已发展成为中国重要的经济、金融、贸易、科技、信息和文化中心。

SECTION Ⅲ: Speech

Interpret the following speech from Chinese into English.

中国有这么一句俗语，“上有天堂，下有苏杭”。

这句话毫无夸张之意，苏杭这两座邻近上海的历史名城以其秀丽的景色每年吸引了数以万计的海内外游客。

例如，中国南方园林建筑艺术之典范，迷人的苏州造景园林在有限的空间里造就了无数自然景观。

园林的池塘、河水、石头、花朵、树木给游客带来了如诗般的意境，是赴苏州观光必游之处。

苏杭附近的上海进入 21 世纪后正在迅速发展为世界经济、金融和贸易中心之一。

上海金融业的发展尤为引人注目，已经逐渐成为一个具有相当规模与影响力的金融市场体系。

浦东新区近年来的崛起使这块黄金宝地成了海外投资的热点，投资总额已经达到了

830亿美元。

上海这颗璀璨的东方明珠以其特有的魅力召唤富有远见卓识的金融家和企业家来此大展宏图。

SECTION Ⅳ: Speech

Interpret the following speech from English into Chinese.

Australia's premier city, Sydney, is the oldest colony in Australia, the economic powerhouse of the nation and the country's capital in everything but name. Its unique setting, with hundreds of miles of coastline, a breathtaking harbor and mountainous parklands is complemented by a warm tropical climate.

Sydney harbor is the defining characteristic of the city. Its dramatic cliffs, rocky islands and stunning bays and beaches make it one of the most beautiful stretches of water in the world. You can catch a ferry to enjoy the beauty of it, but the best way to experience the 20 kilo harbor is to go sailing.

Australia's most recognizable symbol is the Sydney Opera House. Its famous sail-and shell-like roofs are so unique that the house has been photographed a zillion times and appeared on an army of cheap T-shirts and every other Sydney postcard.

The Opera House hosts theatre, classical music, ballet and film, as well as the seasonal opera performances. Although some visitors are disappointed by the interior of the house, it's a truly memorable place to see a performance or to sit at one of its outdoor cafés with a cup of white wine and watch harbor life go by.

Sydney is famous for its beaches. One of city's best beaches, Bondi, is a magnet for travelers who love its proximity to the city. Also one of Australia's busiest, it has a thriving beach culture and many fine cafés, restaurants and bars. The coastal walk along Bondi is spectacular.

Sydney is one of the biggest cities in the world—but fortunately most of the interesting things are concentrated in a relatively compact area around one of the finest urban harbors in the world. Come to Sydney, otherwise you will miss the most attractive metropolis on the southern hemisphere.

参考译文

SECTION Ⅰ: Dialogue

A: 青岛让我感到有点惊讶。这是一座大都市。我还以为会看到许多中式宝塔寺庙和中国传统风格的建筑。

B: Most people from West go to Beijing for that. They have Forbidden City, Summer Palace, Altar of Heaven, Temple of Earth and the Great Wall. But you know, Qingdao really isn't that old.

A: 怎么讲？我曾在哪里看到过说青岛是道教的发源地。

B: That's true. But compared to Beijing, it's a brand-new city.

A: 我明白你的意思了。北京曾经在一千多年的时间里一直是中国的首都。

B: Yes. Beijing was the capital for both Ming and Qing Dynasties. But Qingdao used to be the colony of Germany. And now it's a base for light industry covering electronic products.

A: 我刚了解到这些。难怪青岛这么具有现代气息。

B: Look at this zone. It's a location for universities and scientific institutions.

A: 青岛有多少大学？

B: Not as many as in Boston, New York and Los Angeles. But we do have 25 universities and some national scientific institutions.

A: 教育和科学对一个城市的文明总是起着至关重要的作用。

B: Ahead of us, is the New Hi-Tech Zone, where you'll see a lot of foreign investments from Fortune 500, such as Dupont, Caterpillar, Qualcomm and GM.

A: 海边的那座高楼是什么？

B: That's the Regatta Center of the Olympics 2008 Beijing. You know, Qingdao is the co-sponsor of the Olympic Games, that was 14 years ago. It was a good one. Who can imagine that Beijing has just successfully held the Winter Olympic and Paralympic Games two weeks ago?

A: 确实如此。我为北京感到骄傲，北京市是全世界唯一举办过夏季和冬季奥运会的城市。

B：Thank you. We were confident that China would present a streamlined, safe and splendid Games to the world. The official motto for Beijing 2022 is "Together for a Shared Future". Indeed, we did it. It has won the universal applause from all over the world.

A：为什么不领我去看看青岛奥帆中心呢？

B：Great idea! Let's hit the road right away.

A：青岛真是一座充满活力的城市。

B：Thank you. I wish you will have a happy stay here.

A：一定的。

SECTION Ⅱ: Warm-ups for Interpretation

➢ **Interpret the following proverbs from English into Chinese.**

1. 患难见真情。
2. 推己及人。
3. 耻于问即耻于学。
4. 巧妇难为无米之炊。
5. 爱屋及乌。

➢ **Interpret the following sentences from English into Chinese.**

1. 龙卷风、飓风、旋风、海啸、山体滑坡、泥石流、地震和火山喷发是发生在环大西洋地区和环太平洋地区的自然灾害。
2. 香港是购物天堂，吸引了各国游客。五星级酒店遍布港岛和九龙。周围的岛屿被开发成美丽的度假胜地和游乐场所。
3. 许多大城市有一种独特的氛围和历史渊源，如北京的长城和故宫，旧金山的有轨电车，构成了这两座城市与众不同的氛围。
4. 泰晤士河是英格兰最长的河流，它塑造了该国的历史。没有它，就不会有我们今天所了解的伦敦。
5. 剑桥不仅是英国，而且是欧洲最重要和最美丽的城镇之一。其建筑特色吸引着全世界的游览者，尤其是剑桥大学的建筑物以及河流与花园交融的独特氛围。

➢ **Interpret the following paragraphs from English into Chinese and vice versa.**

1. 温哥华是加拿大的第三大城市。作为加拿大通往太平洋的门户，其航运业将太平洋沿岸各国同加拿大联系起来。亚洲的产品一年四季源源不断地运往这座天然不冻港。温哥华是一个多民族、多文化的城市，虽然以英国文化为主要特征，但也深受中国传统的影响。这里的"中国城"规模仅次于美国的旧金山，为整个北美地区的第二大华人社区。
2. Known to the world as the Oriental Pearl, Shanghai is China's major eastern gate to the outside world. As early as the Tang and Song dynasties, Shanghai functioned as a foreign trade port in East China and had mercantile ties with Japan, Korea and Southeast Asia. During the reigns of Emperor Qianlong (1736-1796) and Emperor Jiaqing (1796-1821) of the Qing Dynasty, Shanghai turned into a navigation hub and metropolis in southeast China, which attracted numerous merchants and countless ships to the Huangpu River. What a spectacle of prosperity during that period! In the 1950s, Shanghai replaced Guangzhou as China's foreign trade center and has remained so ever since. Today, this well-known international port has developed into China's important center of economy, finance, trade, science and technology, information and culture.

SECTION Ⅲ: Speech

A Chinese saying goes like this: "Just as there is a paradise in Heaven, there are Suzhou and Hangzhou on earth."

This saying is no exaggeration about the scenic beauty of the two historic cities near Shanghai which attract millions of tourists from home and abroad every year.

For example, the charming landscaped gardens of Suzhou, typical of China's southern garden architecture, contain numerous created landscape scenes within limited space.

The ponds, water, stones, flowers and trees of these gardens create a poetic mood for tourists and therefore, a visit to these gardens is a must for every tourist visiting Suzhou.

Shanghai, in the vicinity of Suzhou and Hangzhou, upon entering the 21st century, is developing rapidly into one of the world's economic, financial and trade centers.

The development of Shanghai's financial industry is particularly spectacular, with a fairly large and influential system of a financial market coming into shape.

The rise of Pudong New Area in recent years has turned this most valuable place into a hot destination of overseas investment, with a total investment volume reaching US$83 billion.

Shanghai, the brilliant Oriental Pearl with its unique charm, invites financiers and entrepreneurs with broad visions to this city, where they will readily materialize their ambitions.

SECTION Ⅳ: Speech

澳大利亚最重要的城市——悉尼，是澳大利亚最早的殖民地和国家经济中心。不是首都，胜似首都。该市拥有独特的地理位置，数百英里的海岸线，摄人心魄的海湾和山峦起伏的地形，还有温暖的热带气候。

悉尼海湾是该市最有特色的景点。雄伟的峭壁、嶙峋的小岛、美得令人窒息的海湾和沙滩使它成为世界上最美丽的水域之一。你可以乘坐渡轮领略悉尼海湾的动人之处，不过要感受长达 20 千米的海湾魅力，最好还是出帆远航。

澳大利亚最具辨识度的标志是悉尼歌剧院。著名的帆船贝壳形屋顶非常独特，因此这幢建筑留影于无数的照片，也大量出现在廉价 T 恤衫和悉尼风景明信片上。

歌剧院举行各种表演，包括戏剧、古典音乐、芭蕾、电影和季节性的歌剧表演。尽管一些游客对歌剧院的内部感到失望，但在这里看一场演出，或是坐在它附近的露天咖啡吧喝一杯白酒，看着海湾生活的流逝，仍然是让你难以忘怀的经历。

悉尼的沙滩举世闻名。邦代是悉尼最好的沙滩之一，它像一块磁石，吸引着喜欢将海滩和城市生活融为一体的人。拥有自己沙滩文化的邦代也是澳大利亚最热闹的沙滩之一，沙滩上有许多不错的咖啡吧、餐厅和酒吧。沿着邦代散步，景色非常壮观。

悉尼是世界上最大的城市之一，幸运的是该市许多景点都集中在这个最好的城市港湾周围。来悉尼吧，不然你将错过南半球最迷人的国际大都市。

Unit 17 体育健身 Sports

体育不仅可以提高人民健康水平，还可以促进各国人民相互了解和友谊。

Sports can not only build up our health, but also boost friendship and mutual understanding between peoples of different countries.

世界各国与其在190多条小船上，不如同在一条大船上，共同拥有更美好未来，所以我们提出了"一起向未来"的北京冬奥会口号。中方将为奥林匹克运动和推动构建人类命运共同体做出新的更大贡献。

Instead of riding separately in some 190 small boats, countries around the world should stay together in one giant vessel and sail toward a brighter future. That is why we put forth "Together for a Shared Future" as the official motto for the Beijing 2022 Games. China will make new and bigger contributions to the Olympic Movement and the building of a community with a shared future for mankind.

体育强则中国强，国运兴则体育兴。

A country prospers if its sports is thriving; a country is flourishing when its sports is popular.

课文 A

SECTION Ⅰ: Dialogue 谈论乒乓球 Talk about Ping Pong

Interpret the following dialogue from Chinese into English and vice versa.

A：约翰，你最近一次打网球是什么时候？

B：Probably when I was in high school. Lately I have been playing ping pong.

A：是吗？打乒乓球是我最喜欢的运动之一。

B：Is ping pong popular in China?

A：是的，非常流行。很多人都打得很好。

B：How long have you been playing?

A：我 12 岁就开始打乒乓球了。

B：You must be good. Did you bring your paddles with you?

A：没有。我得租一副乒乓球拍。然后我们一起打吧。

B：I'd like to. But I'm not very good. I just started taking lessons last year.

A：嗯，我也一直没打。因此现在打得也没那么好了。好了。我们先热热身吧。

B：Alright. You start serving please.

A：注意，我发球啦。

B：Jesus. I missed your ball. How did you make the spinning?

A：噢，就是练习的问题。你练多了，你也能做到。

B：I got it. Let's go and practice some bowling there.

相关词汇

常用体育英语相关词汇

track and field/athletics　田径运动

field events　田赛

high jump　跳高

pole vault　撑杆跳高

long jump　跳远

triple jump　三级跳远

javelin　标枪

shot put　铅球

discus　铁饼

hammer　链球

decathlon　十项全能

pentathlon　五项全能

track events　竞赛

marathon (race)　马拉松赛跑

100 meters (100-metre dash)　100 米

110 meters hurdles　110 米栏

4 × 100 meters relay (sprint relay)　4 × 100 米接力

ball games　球类运动

soccer　足球

football　橄榄球

basketball　篮球

volleyball　排球

ping pong　乒乓球

spin 旋球
badminton 羽毛球
tennis 网球
baseball 棒球
golf 高尔夫球
cricket 板球
squash 壁球
hockey 曲棍球
ice hockey 冰球
paddle 乒乓球拍
club 高尔夫球杆
racket 羽毛球拍；网球拍
bat 棒球棍
goalkeeper 足球守门员
goalie 冰球守门员
forward 前锋
center 中锋
guard 后卫
swimming 游泳
freestyle 自由泳
backstroke 仰泳
breaststroke 蛙泳
butterfly 蝶泳
Winter Games 冬季比赛项目
speed skating 速度滑冰
short track speed skating 短道速滑
figure skating 花样滑冰
curling 冰壶

SECTION Ⅱ: Warm-ups for Interpretation

➢ **Tongue twister.**

You know New York. You need New York. You know you need unique New York.
你知道纽约。你需要纽约。你知道你需要独特的纽约。
I need not your needles; they're needless to me; for kneading of noodles, were needless, you see.
我不需要你的针，对我来说没用。你知道对揉面来说它们是没用的。

➢ **Interpret the following proverbs from English into Chinese.**

1. By falling we learn to go safely.
2. Kill not the goose that lays the golden eggs.
3. A clear conscience laughs at false accusations.
4. Every family has a skeleton in the closet.
5. Where there's life, there's hope.

➢ **Interpret the following sentences from English into Chinese.**

1. In 1896, in Athens, Greece held the first modern Olympic Games. Since then a world of sports was born, and also produced a new kind of global, unified sports and cultural pattern.
2. Extreme sports allow and encourage individual creativity in the innovation of new maneuvers and in the stylish execution of existing techniques.
3. Volleyball is an Olympic sport in which two teams separated by a high net use their hands, arms or (rarely) other parts of their bodies to hit a ball back and forth over the net.
4. Bridge is not only an entertainment game, but a sports game; it is more instructive than interesting.
5. Warm-up exercises are important for promoting flexibility and preventing injury.

➢ **Interpret the following paragraphs from English into Chinese and vice versa.**

1. New Zealanders are traditionally keenly interested in sports of all kinds, and the temperate climate encourages most forms of outside recreation. Although rugby probably remains the major national winter sport, football, netball, hockey, rugby league and skiing are increasingly popular. The principal summer sports include cricket, softball, tennis, athletics, swimming, surfing and boating, while golf and horseracing are enjoyed throughout the year.
2. 体育是美国文化的重要组成部分。美国的四大专业体育联盟是美国职业棒球大联盟、美国篮球协会、美国橄榄球联盟和美国冰球联盟。四大联盟均受到美国各媒体的广泛关注，且被认为是各自项目在世界上最顶尖的比赛。只有篮球和棒球(冰球在较小程度上)在别的国家也有大量的球迷。

SECTION Ⅲ: Speech

Interpret the following speech from English into Chinese.

Dear fellow Olympians,

Your Excellency, Xi Jinping, President of the People's Republic of China,

Your Excellencies, Antonio Guterres, Secretary-General of the United Nations, and Abdulla Shahid, President of the UN General Assembly,

President of the Organising Committee, Cai Qi,

Your Excellencies,

Dear Olympic friends,

Welcome to the Olympic Winter Games Beijing 2022.

To all our Chinese friends: a very happy new year.

Xin Chun Kuai Le! Hu Nian Da Ji! (Happy New Year! Best wishes for the Year of the Tiger!)

This Year of the Tiger is also an Olympic Year. Both the Year of the Tiger and the Olympic Year stand for ambition, courage and strength.

Today, thanks to this ambition, China is a winter sport country. Well over 300 million people are engaged in winter sports in about 2,000 ski resorts and ice rinks.

This extraordinary achievement opens a new era for global winter sport. It will raise the global participation to new levels, benefiting the Chinese people as well as winter sport enthusiasts around the world.

We can only write this new chapter in sporting history, because of our gracious hosts—the Chinese people, whom we thank wholeheartedly for welcoming us all so warmly. Xie Xie Ni Men, Zhong Guo Peng You. (Thank you, our Chinese friends!)

A special thanks goes to all the volunteers. You make us feel at home from the very first moment we arrived. Your smiling eyes are warming our hearts. Thank you, volunteers.

Unfortunately, the global pandemic is still a reality for all of us. Therefore, our gratitude is even deeper for the Beijing 2022 Organising Committee, the public authorities and all the Chinese people. Thank you for making these Olympic Winter Games happen, and making them happen in a safe way for everyone. We all could only get here because of the countless medical workers, doctors, scientists, everybody in China and around the world who is going beyond the call of duty. Thank you for your outstanding efforts and solidarity.

In the same spirit, our heart goes out to all the athletes who because of the pandemic could not make their Olympic dream come true.

Dear fellow Olympians, your Olympic stage is set. You have arrived here after overcoming so many challenges, living through great uncertainty. But now your moment has come: the moment you have been longing for, the moment we all have been longing for.

Now your Olympic dream is coming true, in magnificent venues, supported by hundreds of millions of new Chinese winter sport fans. You the Olympic athletes; you will show how the world would look like, if we all respect the same rules and each other. Over the next two weeks, you will compete with each other for the highest prize. At the same time, you will live peacefully together under one roof in the Olympic Village. There will be no discrimination for any reason whatsoever.

In our fragile world, where division, conflict and mistrust are on the rise, we show the world, yes, it is possible to be fierce rivals, while at the same time living peacefully and respectfully together. This is the mission of the Olympic Games: bringing us together in peaceful competition. Always building bridges, never erecting walls. Uniting humankind in all our diversity. This mission is strongly supported by the United Nations General Assembly. It adopted the Olympic Truce Resolution by consensus of all 193 UN Member States. The resolution explicitly mentions you, the Olympic athletes, welcoming how you promote peace and human understanding through the Olympic ideal. In this Olympic spirit of peace, I appeal to all political authorities across the world: observe your commitment to this Olympic Truce. Give peace a chance.

Dear athletes, we all are standing with you. We all are supporting you. We all are cheering you on.

May this encourage you to go faster, to aim higher, to become stronger-together. In this way, you will inspire the world in this Olympic Year with the same ambition, courage and strength like the Year of the Tiger.

Now, I have the honour of inviting the President of the People's Republic of China, His Excellency Xi Jinping, to declare opening of the 24th Olympic Winter Games Beijing 2022.

SECTION Ⅳ: Speech

Interpret the following speech from Chinese into English.

马拉松是一项长跑比赛项目，其标准长度为 42.195 千米(26 英里 385 码)。马拉松比赛通常在公路上进行。这个比赛项目的确立是为了纪念希腊士兵菲迪皮茨，他传奇般地从马拉松战场跑到雅典送信。

1896 年举行的第一届现代奥林匹克运动会上就设立了马拉松项目，但直到 1921 年，马拉松比赛的标准长度才正式确立。全世界每年举行的马拉松比赛超过500次。大型的赛事通常有数以万计的参与者，多数人以健身休闲为目的。

参考译文

SECTION Ⅰ：Dialogue

A： John，when was the last time you played tennis?

B： 可能是高中时候吧。我最近一直打乒乓球。

A： Really? Ping pong is one of my favorite sports.

B： 乒乓球在中国很流行?

A： Yes，extremely popular. Many people are good at it.

B： 你打乒乓球多长时间了?

A： Since I was 12.

B： 那你一定打得很好了。你现在带拍子了吗?

A： No. I'll need to rent some. We'll have to play together.

B： 好啊，但我打得不太好。我去年才开始学打乒乓球。

A： Well，I'm out of practice. So I'm not that good myself. OK. Let's start doing some warm-up exercise.

B： 好，你先发球吧。

A： Attention. Watch my ball.

B： 糟糕，没接住你的球。你是怎么发旋球的?

A： Oh，just a matter of practice. You can do it，too，if you practice a lot.

B： 明白了。我们现在去练练保龄球吧。

SECTION Ⅱ：Warm-ups for Interpretation

➢ **Interpret the following proverbs from English into Chinese.**

1. 吃一堑，长一智。
2. 杀鸡取卵。

3. 白日不做亏心事，夜半敲门心不惊。
4. 家家有本难念的经。
5. 留得青山在，不怕没柴烧。

➢ **Interpret the following sentences from English into Chinese.**

1. 1896 年，希腊雅典举行了第一届现代奥林匹克运动会。从此一种世界性的体育活动诞生了，同时产生了一种新的世界性的、统一的体育文化形态。
2. 极限运动允许并鼓励个人在花样翻新和现有技巧上进行创新。
3. 排球是奥运会比赛项目，两只队伍被高网分开，各队球员使用手臂或(极少使用)身体的其他部位将球轮流击打过网。
4. 桥牌不仅是一项娱乐活动，也是一项竞技运动；不仅有趣，更富有教育意义。
5. 准备活动有助于提高柔韧性，防止受伤。

➢ **Interpret the following paragraphs from English into Chinese and vice versa.**

1. 新西兰人喜爱多种多样体育活动。当地宜人的气候也适合人们进行各种形式的户外运动。尽管橄榄球可能仍然是主要的全国性冬季运动项目，但是足球、触网球、曲棍球以及橄榄球比赛和滑雪运动也越来越普及。夏季的主要运动项目有板球、垒球、网球、田径、游泳、冲浪和划船，高尔夫球和赛马是一年四季都受欢迎的运动。
2. Sports in the United States is an important part of the country's culture. The four major professional sports leagues in the United States are Major League Baseball (MLB), the National Basketball Association (NBA), the National Football League (NFL), the National Hockey League (NHL); all four enjoy massive US media exposure and are considered the preeminent competitions in their respective sports in the world, although only basketball and baseball (and to a lesser extent hockey) have substantial followings in other nations.

SECTION Ⅲ: Speech

奥林匹克运动员们，尊敬的中华人民共和国习近平主席，尊敬的联合国秘书长古特雷斯，联合国大会主席沙希德，北京冬奥组委主席蔡奇，各位来宾，奥林匹克运动的朋友们：

欢迎参加北京2022年冬奥会！祝中国朋友们新年快乐，新春快乐，虎年大吉！

今年是虎年，也是奥运年，虎年和奥运年都代表着雄心、勇气和力量。如今，正是凭借着这份雄心，中国已是一个冬季运动之国。在中国，有超过3亿人在约2,000座滑雪场和溜冰场上参与冬季体育运动。中国在冬季运动方面取得的非凡成就，开启了全球冬季运动的新时代，将使全球冬季运动参与度登上新台阶，让中国人民和全球各地的冬季运动爱好者从中受益。

今天，我们之所以能够书写体育运动史的这一全新篇章，要归功于我们热情的东道主，也就是全体中国人民。我衷心地感谢中国人民的热情款待。谢谢你们，中国朋友！

我们要特别感谢全体志愿者。从我们抵达的第一刻起，你们就给了我们宾至如归的感受。你们眼中的微笑温暖着我们的心。谢谢你们，志愿者！

遗憾的是，目前全球疫情仍然是我们要面对的现实，因此，我们要感谢北京冬奥组委、中国政府部门和全体中国人民，感谢你们让本届冬奥会能够成功举办，感谢你们让所有的人都能够安全地参与本届冬奥会。我们之所以能够在这里相聚，得益于中国及世界各地无数的医护人员、科研人员以及所有人员的主动奉献。谢谢你们的辛勤付出与团结协作。

基于同样的精神，我们也欣喜地看到，疫情并没有阻碍运动员们实现奥运梦想。奥林匹克运动员们，奥运舞台已经为你们搭好，你们克服了重重困难，经历了诸多不确定因素，最终来到了这里。现在，你们即将迎来自己的时刻，这是你们一直长久期待的时刻，也是我们都长久期待的时刻。现在，你们将在中国数亿新冬季运动爱好者的支持下，在恢宏的运动场馆内，实现你们的奥运梦想。作为奥林匹克运动员，你们将向世人展示，如果我们遵守同一规则，并且彼此尊重，世界将会是怎样的一番景象。在未来的两周时间里，你们将为最高荣誉展开激烈角逐，与此同时，也将在奥运村的同一个屋檐下和谐共处，在奥运村里，不会有任何理由的歧视存在。

我们所在的这个世界是脆弱的，分裂、冲突和猜疑正在日益升级。我们要向世界证明，是的，竞争激烈的对手也能够和平共处、彼此尊重。这就是奥林匹克运动会的使命，让人们在和平竞争当中团结一心。奥运会总是搭建沟通的桥梁，绝不会筑起一道道高墙。奥运会让我们保留多样性的同时，把我们团结在一起。这一崇高使命，得到了联合国大会的强力支持。联合国大会以173个会员国全体协商一致通过了《奥林匹克休战决议》。决议当中明确提到了奥林匹克运动员，感谢你们借助奥林匹克理想，促进世界和平与人类的相互理解。本着奥林匹克和平精神，我呼吁全球各国政府，遵守你们对奥林匹克休战的承诺，给和平一个机会。

亲爱的运动员们，我们与你们站在一起，我们都在支持着你们，我们都在为你们加油喝彩！愿这样的支持能够鼓励你们团结一致，共同实现更快、更高、更强。如此一来，你们将在这个奥运年，以虎年的雄心、勇气和力量来鼓舞全世界的人们。

现在，我荣幸地邀请中华人民共和国主席习近平宣布北京2022年第24届冬季奥林匹克运动会开幕。

SECTION Ⅳ: Speech

The marathon is a long-distance running event with an official distance of 42.195 kilometers (26 miles and 385 yards), usually run as a road race. The event was instituted in commemoration of the fabled run of the Greek soldier Pheidippides, a messenger from the Battle of Marathon to Athens.

The marathon was one of the original modern Olympic events in 1896, though the distance did not become standardized until 1921. More than 500 marathons are held throughout the world each year, with the vast majority of competitors being recreational athletes as larger marathons can have tens of thousands of participants.

课文 B

SECTION Ⅰ: Dialogue 谈论体育运动 Talk about Sports

Interpret the following dialogue from English into Chinese and vice versa.

A：Mr. Li, nice to meet you.

B：再次见到你很高兴，理查德先生。旅途一切还好吧？

A：Good, but I am still a bit tired from the jet lag. Don't worry. I will be alright soon. I think some exercises will do me good.

B：那就好。因为知道您喜欢运动，所以就为您安排了设有健身房和游泳池的凯宾斯基酒店。酒店里还有体育馆，您可以去那里打篮球、打羽毛球等。

A：Great! You know, I take an hour of aerobic exercise at home every day. I am happy that I can do aerobic exercise and rehabilitation gymnastics here.

B：我每天也去健身房，那里有教练指导所有的健身活动。

A：Ah，no wonder you have a strong build.

B：当然。像我一样，越来越多的中国人开始热衷于通过运动来强身健体。

A：And sports bring us a lot of fun，right?

B：是的，我非常同意。

A：By the way，does the gym offer traditional Chinese exercises?

B：是的，他们开有气功和太极拳课程。每两天上一次课。

A：Terrific! I would like to learn Taiji. I am fascinated by it.

B：没问题。我们可以一起去。

A：Thank you. I just can't wait. Mr. Li，thank you for what you've done for me. You're really my hand.

B：不客气。今天上午你好好休息，下午 2 点我们一起到健身房运动好吗?

A：OK. I'll be in the lobby at 2 pm.

SECTION Ⅱ：Warm-ups for Interpretation

➢ **Tongue twister.**

A tutor who tooted a flute tried to tutor two tooters to toot. Said the two to their tutor，"Is it harder to toot or to tutor two tooters to toot?"

一个吹笛的导师尝试教两个吹笛者吹笛。那两个学吹笛的问导师："吹笛难，还是教两个学吹笛的人吹笛难呢?"

➢ **Interpret the following proverbs from Chinese into English.**

1. 自助者天助。
2. 光明磊落，胜券在握。
3. 妄自尊大，腹中空空。
4. 小事聪明，大事糊涂。
5. 耳听为虚，眼见为实。

➢ **Interpret the following sentences from Chinese into English.**

1. 上下楼梯可比什么健身器材都要好。
2. 日益流行的健身热潮正风靡整个中国。
3. 这座城市的体育设施远远不能满足人民日益增长的需要。

4. 中国球员在削球、抽球、推挡、扣杀以及几乎所有的技术方面都是无与伦比的。
5. 极限运动要求参与者把高超的运动技巧与极大的冒险精神完美地结合起来。

➢ **Interpret the following paragraphs from Chinese into English and vice versa.**

1. 对大多数外国人来说，板球运动似乎极其无聊。但英格兰人却认为板球与木棍之间的撞击声是世界上最动听的音乐。全英板球队是最重要的一支队伍，队员包括职业运动员和业余爱好者，都选拔自英格兰各地的球队。最有影响力的板球国际赛事是英格兰和澳大利亚之间的比赛，两国每年轮流举办。
2. The idea of the Olympic Village comes from Pierre de Coubertin. Up until the 1924 Summer Olympic Games, National Olympic Committees rented locations around the host city to house participants, which was expensive. For the 1924 Summer Olympics, the organizers built cabins near the Stade Olympique de Colombes to allow the athletes to easily access the Games' venues. The Olympic Village of the 1932 Summer Olympics served as the model of today's Olympic Villages, and it consisted of a group of buildings with rooms to lodge athletes, and buildings with other accommodations. Only athletes, trainers and officials are allowed to room at the Village, though family members and former Olympic athletes are allowed inside with proper checks. Press and media are barred.

SECTION Ⅲ: Speech

Interpret the following speech from English into Chinese.

Welcome to the Beijing Martial Art Palace to practice martial art for body-building. But I have no intention of persuading anyone, and am not prepared to convince anyone, either. You know, exercising for your health and fitness is a matter of personal choice; it's an investment for one's future.

Of course, if you're looking for a place where you can build up your body, reduce your weight, make new friends and learn about Chinese culture, this is the very place for you. All you need to do is fill out a form and get a membership card. It takes only a few minutes.

Here you enjoy and learn this ancient form of combat. The Palace, a creation of the Chinese Martial Art Association, puts on fabulous performances to thrill the visitor—not only martial artists in action but also Peking Opera and acrobatics shows.

If you want to get in on the action yourself, the Chinese Martial Art Association has the best teaching team available any time upon request: nothing less than the best professional martial artists, excellent coaches with unique skills and perfect martial art performers in China, gathering under one roof.

If you prefer to learn the art on your own home turf, the Chinese Martial Art Association will send its first-class coaches to train you or your group, no matter where you live.

If you are in the market looking for martial art equipment or literature, the Chinese Martial Art Association is well supplied with all that you need, at excellent prices. We also have a well-stocked bookstore selling printed information, videotapes and DVD disks on everything you are interested in knowing about Chinese martial art.

Ladies and gentlemen, this is the place for you, and we are here for you.

SECTION Ⅳ: Speech

Interpret the following speech from Chinese into English.

北京冬季残奥会火炬传递开始

北京 2022 年冬季残奥会火炬接力于周三在北京开始，这是奥运会正式开幕前两天。

中国国务院副总理、中共中央政治局委员孙春兰，在天坛举行的启动仪式上从大锅上点燃火炬，然后将其交给平昌冬季残奥会轮椅冰壶冠军陈建新。

9 名代表携带了从 9 个地点收集的火焰，一个是来自被公认为残奥会发源地的斯托克德维尔村，其他 8 个地点来自北京和张家口地区。9 个火焰聚集在一起，形成了北京冬季残奥会的官方火焰。

北京 2022 年组委会主席蔡琦在致辞中表示，主办方将兑现“两届同样精彩的奥运会”的承诺，举办一届“精简、安全、精彩”的奥运会。

“2008 年，残奥会圣火在北京天坛点燃。现在，这新的火焰标志着一个历史性奥运会的到来。北京是有史以来第一个举办夏季和冬季残奥会的城市”，国际残奥委会主席安德鲁帕森斯在视频消息中说。

来自中央党政机关、北京、河北、北京 2022 年组委会、火炬手、运动员、志愿者代表等约 400 人出席了仪式。

火炬接力将持续到周五，565 名火炬手将参加北京，延庆和张家口比赛区的传递。

参考译文

SECTION Ⅰ: Dialogue

A：李先生，很高兴见到你。

B：Nice to meet you again，Mr. Richard. How was your trip?

A：还好，但是因为时差的关系感觉还有点累。别担心，我很快就会恢复的。我想做点运动会有好处。

B：That's good. Since we know you like sports，we have booked Kempinski Hotel which is facilitated with fitness center and swimming pool. In fact，they also have a gymnasium. You can play basketball and badminton in it.

A：太棒了！你知道，我每天都会在家进行一小时的有氧运动。我很高兴可以在这做有氧运动和康复操。

B：I also go to a gym everyday. There all activities are supervised by the coach.

A：啊，难怪您的体格很强壮。

B：You bet. Like me，more and more Chinese are becoming sports enthusiasts to build up their health.

A：而且运动也给我们带来很多快乐，不是吗?

B：Yes，I couldn't agree with you more.

A：顺便问一下，那家健身房有中国传统的健身运动吗?

B：Yes，they have Qigong and Taiji. Classes are offered every other day.

A：太好了！我想学太极，它让我着迷。

B：No problem. You can join me.

A：谢谢。我都等不及了。李先生，谢谢你的帮助，真是帮了我大忙了。

B：You're welcome. Just relax this morning and we can do exercise in the gym at 2 this afternoon. Is that good for you?

A：好。下午 2 点我在大厅等你。

SECTION Ⅱ: Warm-ups for Interpretation

➢ **Interpret the following proverbs from Chinese into English.**

1. God helps those who help themselves.
2. A clear conscience is a sure card.
3. He that is full of himself is very empty.
4. Penny wise, pound foolish.
5. Words are but wind, but seeing is believing.

➢ **Interpret the following sentences from Chinese into English.**

1. Walking up and down stairs would beat any exercise machine.
2. A growing keep-fit fervor is sweeping over China.
3. The sports facilities in the city are far from enough to meet the growing demand.
4. Chinese are unmatchable in chopping, driving, pushing shot, smashing and nearly in all techniques.
5. Extreme sports require participants to well combine excellent athletic skill with pronounced risk.

➢ **Interpret the following paragraphs from Chinese into English and vice versa.**

1. To most foreigners, cricket seems a dreadful boring game. But English people think the sound of a wooden cricket ball striking against a wooden cricket bat is just about the most beautiful sound in the world. The All-England cricket team is the most important one. Its players, who may be either amateur or professional, are chosen from the country cricket teams. The most important international matches are those played between England and Australia, and are held one year in one country, the next year in the other.
2. 奥运村的理念是由皮埃尔·德·顾拜旦提出的。直到1924年举办夏季奥运会的时候，奥委会才开始在主办城市附近为参赛人员租借住宿的场所，当时耗费了大笔租金。1924年奥运会期间，主办者还在"哥伦布奥林匹克体育场"附近建起了临时的简易小屋，方便运动员到各个比赛场馆参加比赛。1932年夏季奥运会为运动员们建了很多供住宿的小屋，还建了各种辅助设施。现代的奥运村就是仿照1932年奥运村的模式建立的。现在，只有运动员、教练员和裁判员才可以在奥运村住宿。这些人员的家属和前奥运运动员在经过相应检查后，也可进入奥运村。新闻媒体及记者则禁止入内。

SECTION Ⅲ：Speech

欢迎各位来北京武术宫习武健身。我不想劝说任何人，也不打算说服任何人，因为健身是每个人自己的事，是为将来投资的。

当然了，如果您在寻找可以健身、减肥、结交朋友以及了解中国文化的场所，您找对了地方。您只需在这里填写一张登记表，再拿一张会员卡即可。这些事只需几分钟即可办完。

您在这里可以欣赏古代格斗术，您也可以在这里习武。由中国武术协会创立的武术宫为您准备了精彩的、扣人心弦的表演节目——您除了可以观赏武术家的表演外，还可以观赏京剧节目和杂技表演。

倘若您想有一种身临其境的体验，中国武术协会将随时派出最好的教学人员，我们这里有中国顶尖的武林高手、身怀绝技的优秀教头和无懈可击的武术表演家。

无论您身居何处，您若想在自家门口学习武术，中国武术协会都可派出一流教员，指导个人或团体皆可。

如果您在市场上寻找武术器具或资料，中国武术协会也为您准备好了一切，价格从优。我们还有货物齐全的书店，出售您感兴趣的一切有关中华武术的图书资料、录像带和 DVD 光盘。

女士们，先生们，这里是您的理想之地，我们愿为您效劳。

SECTION Ⅳ：Speech

Winter Paralympic torch relay starts in Beijing

The torch relay for the Beijing 2022 Paralympic Winter Games started in Beijing on Wednesday, two days before the Games officially opens.

Chinese Vice Premier Sun Chunlan, also a member of the Political Bureau of the Communist Party of China Central Committee, lit the torch from a cauldron at the launch ceremony held at the Temple of Heaven, and then handed it over to Chen Jianxin, wheelchair curling champion at the Pyeongchang Winter Paralympics.

Nine representatives carried the flames collected in Stoke Mandeville, a village north-west of London that is recognized as the birthplace of the Paralympic Games, and eight other locations in Beijing and Zhangjiakou, then the nine flames gathered to form the Beijing Winter Paralympic official flame.

Beijing 2022 organizing committee president Cai Qi said in a speech that organizers will fulfill its promise of "two equally wonderful Olympic Games" and host a "streamlined, safe and splendid" Games.

"In 2008, the Paralympic flame was lit in the Temple of Heaven in Beijing. Now this new flame signals the arrival of a historic Games. Beijing is the first ever city to host the summer and winter editions of the Paralympics," International Paralympic Committee president Andrew Parsons said in a video message.

Around 400 people attended the ceremony, including those from central Party and government organs, Beijing, Hebei Province and Beijing 2022 organizing committee, and representatives of torch bearers, athletes, and volunteers.

The torch relay gets underway until Friday, and 565 torchbearers will participate in the Beijing, Yanqing and Zhangjiakou competition zones.

Unit 18 购物 Shopping

"国之称富者，在乎丰民。"中国经济得到长足发展，人民生活水平大幅提高，但我们深知，满足人民对美好生活的向往还要进行长期艰苦的努力。中国明确提出要推动人的全面发展、全体人民共同富裕取得更为明显的实质性进展，将为此在各方面进行努力。中国要实现共同富裕，但不是搞平均主义，而是要先把"蛋糕"做大，然后通过合理的制度安排把"蛋糕"分好。

"The wealth of a country is measured by the abundance of its people." Thanks to considerable economic growth, the Chinese people are living much better lives. Nonetheless, we are soberly aware that to meet people's aspiration for an even better life, we still have much hard work to do in the long run. China has made it clear that we strive for more visible and substantive progress in the well-rounded development of individuals and the common prosperity of the entire population. We are working hard on all fronts to deliver this goal. The common prosperity we desire is not egalitarianism. To use an analogy, we will first make the pie bigger and then divide it properly through reasonable institutional arrangements.

脱贫只是迈向幸福生活的第一步，是新生活、新事业的起点。

Getting rid of poverty is just the first step towards a happy life, it is a starting point for a new life and new endeavor.

课文 A

SECTION Ⅰ: Dialogue 在鞋店 At a Shoe Shop

Interpret the following dialogue from Chinese into English and vice versa.

A：先生，请问您要买些什么？

B：My friend is just looking. But I'd like to buy a pair of casual shoes.

A：好的。你喜欢系带的平底鞋吗？

B：I think I'd prefer loafers. You know my Chinese friends and I are going to climb Mount Lao tomorrow. They will fit me good on foot.

A：好的。请稍坐片刻。我给您拿我们这儿的平底鞋。您穿多大号？

B：I'm afraid I don't know my size in American measurements. You'd better measure my feet.

A：好的。我量一下……您穿 8.5 码，中等宽度的鞋。您喜欢什么颜色？

B：Well, I'd better get light brown.

A：我们这儿有三款平底鞋。浅棕色的穿起来很舒服，而且很耐脏。另一款也很漂亮。

B：Let me try on the other ones… I think they're a little too fancy.

A：那试一下这双绒革面的吧。给您。

B：Ah, you are right. They are very comfortable. And the price tag seems quite reasonable. I think I'll take them.

A：好的。我给您包起来。您还需要买什么？

B：Do you have a kind of sunbonnet or something to protect the sunshine?

A：有的。我们有多种应季的太阳帽。这顶怎么样？

B：Oh, it looks cool. The sandy color is my favorite, too. I'll buy this one, please.

A：出于友谊，赠您一支手杖以备明天登山用。

B：Wow, you are very thoughtful. Chinese people are the best in the world. Thanks a million!

A：不客气。谢谢惠顾。

相关词汇

常用购物类相关词汇

shopping center 商业中心区
department store 百货商店
bricks-and-mortar shop/real shop 实体店
show window 橱窗
price tag 标价签
wrap up 包装
free of charge 不收费
all sold out/out of stock 售空
antique shop 古玩店
handicrafts 手工艺品
embroidery 刺绣品
scroll of calligraphy and painting 字画卷轴
traditional Chinese painting 国画
souvenir 纪念品
confectionery 糖果糕点
cosmetics 化妆品
stationery 文具
fabrics 纺织品
men's wear 男装
women's wear 女装
sports goods/athletic equipment 体育用品
dress shoes 正式场合穿的鞋子
casual shoes 休闲鞋
loafers 平底鞋
athletic shoes 运动鞋
hiking shoes 登山鞋
boots 靴子
sandals 凉鞋
slippers 拖鞋
clogs 木屐
browser 浏览器
cyber economy 网络经济
B to B (Business to Business) 企业间的电子交易
B to C (Business to Customer) 企业对消费者的电子交易
C to C (Customer to Customer) 消费者之间的电子交易
electronic mall 电子购物中心
electronic money 电子货币
e-banking 网上银行
e-wallet 电子钱包
Electronic Commerce (EC) 电子商务
Electronic Data Interchange (EDI) 电子数据交换
e-consumer 电子消费者
online service 在线服务
personal marketing 个性化营销

SECTION Ⅱ: Warm-ups for Interpretation

➢ **Tongue twister.**

Nine nice night nurses nursing nicely.

9个为人友善的夜班护士正在精心护理病人。

He said that he is an iron and steel man from Pittsburgh. Yes. His wife irons and he steals.

他说他是个来自美国匹兹堡的钢铁大王。是的，他的妻子熨衣服而他偷东西。

➢ **Interpret the following proverbs from Chinese into English.**

1. 意志就是力量。
2. 距离产生美。
3. 王婆卖瓜，自卖自夸。
4. 教学相长。
5. 光阴一去不复返。

➢ **Interpret the following sentences from Chinese into English.**

1. 网上购物和电子商务在发达国家和发展中国家都很流行。
2. 中国有着各种各样新奇独特、极具特色的商品，你绝不会为带什么东西回去而失望或发愁。
3. 在中国的大部分商店里，人们是可以讨价还价的。有时，讨价还价比购物本身更有趣。
4. 在这个现金充裕、时间紧张的社会里，网上购物无疑成了一个理想的购物途径。
5. 消费者往往十分注重商品的价格，希望自己购买的食品及其他物品物有所值。

➢ **Interpret the following paragraphs from Chinese into English and vice versa.**

1. 在中国，商品的定价通常有三种。第一种是国家制定的固定价格，第二种是国家制定的调节价格，第三种是市场价格。大部分旅游商品都属于第三种——市场价格。
2. Department stores are large establishments that offer a wide selection of merchandise including fashion clothing, house wares, luggage and jewelry. They normally offer good quality merchandise, well-known brands and the latest fashions, but not low

quality products at bargain prices. They frequently have seasonal sales with attractive discounts. At such times, you can get high quality or fashion merchandise at bargain prices. For example, in November, the Thanksgiving Day sale is one of the biggest shopping days of the year.

SECTION Ⅲ: Speech

Interpret the following speech from Chinese into English.

女士们、先生们：

网上购物(有时被称为"电子零售"，英文叫 e-tail 或 e-shopping)是电子商务的一种，消费者可直接通过互联网购买商品或服务。网店(虚拟商店)在英文中有许多不同的叫法，如 e-web-store、e-shop、e-store、Internet shop、web-shop、web-store、online store、online storefront 和 virtual store。

移动电子商务(或移动商务)指的是通过网上零售商的移动优化网站或网络应用购物。

网络商店促使人们在网上像在实体店和购物中心那样购买商品和服务。这一过程被称为企业对消费者的网上购物模式(B2C)。而企业与企业之间购买商品和服务的过程被称为企业对企业的网上购物模式(B2B)。现在世界上最大的网上零售企业有阿里巴巴、亚马逊和易趣。

SECTION Ⅳ: Speech

Interpret the following speech from English into Chinese.

The business battle generated so much buzz in China that it accelerated the growth of e-commerce. Once eBay withdrew from China, it was an open field, and Alibaba has a huge lead.

Alibaba has become the world's largest shopping mall. Its two shopping platforms, Taobao and Tmall, connect retailers with consumers.

Alibaba collects most of its revenue from commissions and advertising.

Beijing housewife Zhang Jiazhi, 32, swears by the storefronts on Taobao. Using her smartphone, Zhang shops for products for her 2-year-old daughter. Taobao is an important part of her life, for shopping and sheer pleasure, she says.

"Products sold in real shops are more expensive than the ones sold in Taobao shops. I heard you can buy any products in ordinary supermarkets in America, but we don't have so many to choose from in Chinese supermarkets," Zhang says.

Zhang does want Alibaba to do more to crack down on counterfeit goods, something it has pledged it would.

"I, and most of my friends, only trust baby products from America or European countries," she says, after a string of fake infant formula incidents. "It's easy to buy these imported products in Taobao. But you must have sharp eyes, because there are many counterfeits, too."

During its road show this week to persuade U. S. investors to buy the stock, Alibaba executives said they expect the average spending per buyer to increase over time.

On a single day in November 2013—the equivalent of Cyber Monday in the USA—Tmall and Taobao customers spent a record-shattering \$5.7 billion.

"This is the largest e-commerce company in what will be the largest e-commerce market in the world," Bernstein Research analyst Carlos Kirjner says. "Everything about it is: Wow."

参考译文

SECTION Ⅰ: Dialogue

A: May I help you, sir?

B: 我的朋友只是随便看看。不过我想买双休闲鞋。

A: Very good. Would you prefer loafers of shoes with laces?

B: 我想平底鞋比较好。我和我的中国朋友明天要去爬崂山，步行穿平底鞋会很舒服。

A: Fine. Please take a seat and I'll show you what we have. What size do you take?

B: 恐怕我也不知道我穿美码多大号的鞋。你最好量一下我脚的尺寸。

A: Certainly. Let me see... You wear an eight and half B. Would you prefer any particular color?

B: 嗯，浅棕色的吧。

A: Here are three different models. This light brown pair is very comfortable, and you don't have to worry about keep them shined. The other pair is very attractive.

B: 我试一下另一款吧……我觉得价格有点贵。

A: Here, try on the suede ones.

B: 啊，不错。这双很舒服。而且价格也合理。我就要这双吧。

A: Very good, I'll wrap them up for you. Anything else you want?

B: 你们有太阳帽吗？或者其他遮阳的东西？

A: Sure. We've got variety of sun hats available at this time of the season. How is this one?

B: 哦，看起来很时髦，而且是我最喜欢的浅黄色了。我买这顶帽子。

A: To be friendly, here is a cane as a gift for your jogging on Mount Lao tomorrow.

B: 哇，你想得真周到。中国人最好了。谢谢！

A: You are warmly welcome.

SECTION Ⅱ: Warm-ups for Interpretation

➢ **Interpret the following proverbs from Chinese into English.**

1. Will is power.
2. Absence makes the heart grow fonder.
3. Every cook praises his own broth.
4. Teaching others teaches yourself.
5. Lost time is never found again.

➢ **Interpret the following sentences from Chinese into English.**

1. Cyber shopping and electronic commerce have been overwhelming both in developed and developing nations.
2. China abounds with various unusual and characteristic goods, and you will never feel disappointed or worried about what to bring back.
3. Bargaining is usually allowed in most of the stores in China, and sometimes it is even more enjoyable than the purchase itself.
4. In this cash-rich, time-poor society, shopping online no doubt has become an ideal

solution.

5. Consumers are generally very price-conscious and want value for their money in their purchases of food and other items.

➢ **Interpret the following paragraphs from Chinese into English and vice versa.**

1. In China, commodities are usually priced in three ways. First, fixed prices by the state; second, regulatory prices by the state; and third, market prices. Most of the tourist merchandises fall under the third category of market prices.
2. 百货商店是提供流行服装、家居用品、箱包及珠宝首饰等众多商品的大型场所。通常它们提供的是优质商品、知名品牌商品及最新时装，而非廉价劣质货。它们常常会举办一些价格诱人的季节性特卖活动，此时你可以以低廉的价格购买高品质或时尚的商品。譬如，11 月份的感恩节特卖就是一年中的大型特卖活动之一。

SECTION Ⅲ: Speech

Ladies and gentlemen,

Online shopping (sometimes known as e-tail from "electronic retail" or e-shopping) is a form of electronic commerce which allows consumers to directly buy goods or services from a seller over the Internet using a web browser. Alternative names are: e-web-store, e-shop, e-store, Internet shop, web-shop, web-store, online store, online storefront and virtual store.

Mobile commerce (or m-commerce) describes purchasing from an online retailer's mobile optimized online site or App.

An online shop evokes the physical analogy of buying products or services at a bricks-and-mortar retailer or shopping center. The process is called business-to-consumer (B2C) online shopping. In the case where a business buys from another business, the process is called business-to-business (B2B) online shopping. The largest of these online retailing corporations are Alibaba, Amazon, and eBay.

SECTION Ⅳ: Speech

商业大战在中国引起了轩然大波，同时也加速了电子商务的发展。易趣撤出中国的时候，电子商务是一片充满机会的开放领域，而阿里巴巴则成为这一领域的一大巨头。

阿里巴巴现已成为世界上最大的网上零售商。其两大网上购物平台淘宝和天猫，将零售商和消费者联系在一起。

阿里巴巴的收入主要来自佣金和广告费。

北京一位 32 岁的母亲，张家芝(音译)非常信赖淘宝上的网店。她用手机在淘宝上给两岁的女儿买东西。她说，无论购物还是消遣，她都去淘宝，淘宝已成为她生活中重要的一部分。

“淘宝网店上卖的东西比实体店里卖的东西便宜多了。我听说在美国的超市可以买到任何东西，但在中国的超市，可买到的东西没有那么多。”张家芝说。

她很希望阿里巴巴能更有力地打击产品造假，阿里巴巴也曾对此有过承诺。

她说：“我和我的大多数朋友都只信任美国和欧洲的婴儿产品。在淘宝上买这些东西就很容易，但你必须仔细辨别，因为上面也有很多假货。”此前，中国曾曝光多起婴儿奶粉造假事件。

本周阿里巴巴在美国举行路演，其高管在说服美国投资者购买该公司股份时说，他们预计消费者在网上的消费会逐年递增。

2013 年“双十一”(相当于美国的“网络星期一”)那一天，天猫和淘宝创下 57 亿美元的单日销售记录。

“这是未来世界上最大的电子商务市场中最大的电子商务公司。它带给人们的是一声声惊叹：哇。”伯恩斯坦研究公司的分析师卡洛斯·柯基纳说。

课文 B

SECTION Ⅰ: Dialogue 在纪念品店 At a Souvenir Shop

Interpret the following dialogue from Chinese into English and vice versa.

A：先生，请问您要买什么？

B：Yes, I'd like to buy a gift for my wife.

A：您想好买什么了吗？

B：No, I don't. But, I want something she couldn't get in America.

A：这可能很难找到。您想买什么价位的礼物？

B：About 50 bucks.

A：让我想想……她有什么爱好吗？

B：Well，she likes to play bingo with neighbors.

A：我建议您买麻将，打麻将和玩宾戈游戏类似。她肯定喜欢这个礼物，因为在美国买不到麻将。

B：I guess she will like it. Perhaps her Chinese friends in our community might teach her how to play it.

A：你决定了要买副麻将吗？

B：Why not. It's an ideal gift for her. How much does it cost?

A：120 元，约 20 美元。再给她买个礼物怎么样？我们还有画着凤凰和牡丹的雨伞。

B：That's a good gift. It's beautiful. But I'm afraid it's too big for my luggage.

A：我疏忽这个问题了……啊，有了。青岛啤酒的杯子怎么样？

B：That's a good idea，a good reminder of Qingdao，too.

A：我们有玻璃杯和瓷杯。当然，瓷杯要贵一点。

B：I'll take a porcelain one. After all，she is my wife.

SECTION Ⅱ：Warm-ups for Interpretation

➢ **Tongue twister.**

Ripe white wheat reapers reap ripe white wheat right.

成熟的白小麦收割者收获成熟的白小麦。

➢ **Interpret the following proverbs from English into Chinese.**

1. Tall trees catch much wind.
2. Wise men are silent；fools talk.
3. You cannot see the wood for the trees.
4. Absence sharpens love，presence strengthens it.
5. The cheap buyer takes bad meat.

➢ **Interpret the following sentences from English into Chinese.**

1. Handicrafts make ideal souvenirs and gifts. Things like cloisonné made in Beijing and porcelain made in Jingdezhen are all highly recommended.

2. American whiskey, fashion jeans, children's clothing, plush bath towels and fine bed linens are all popular items for shoppers from other countries.
3. The emergence of electronic business has created enormous and exciting challenges for business managers. Internet commerce immediately opens global and more efficient markets.
4. There are various kinds of special merchandise available for your choice, such as Chinese silk, tea, paintings and calligraphy, jade and pearls, and handicrafts.
5. You can find many bargains in the US if you know where to shop and how to take advantage of the competitive sales.

➢ **Interpret the following paragraphs from English into Chinese and vice versa.**

1. Take, for example, the way that I recently bought my car. First I went to an Internet site listing cars, their features and their prices, both wholesale and retail. I did all my research. And then I went to an auto dealership and asked for this particular price. The transaction lasted less than 30 minutes. No hassle. Easy. Simple. I was informed. I went in. I was an informed buyer.
2. 在中国购物既有趣又颇具挑战性。讨价还价在中国很常见，尤其是在小商店里或路边的小摊子上。若你还的价格被接受了，就应该将东西买下来。仔细检查所购买的商品，以确保没有任何瑕疵。

SECTION Ⅲ: Speech

Interpret the following speech from English into Chinese.

Ladies and gentlemen,

Let me give you some ideas of shopping online.

Summer is definitely my favorite season of the year. I love to be outdoors, enjoying the warm weather and spending as much time with my family as possible. So why would I want to interrupt my fun in the sun to run errands at the grocery store to pick up household staples when I can have them conveniently delivered right to my doorstep?

With just a few quick clicks of my mouse on some shopping websites. I can get great deals on all my household essentials and have them shipped to me for free, when I spend

$50 or more.

You may not know it, but I'm a total neat and clean freak when it comes to my home. "A place for everything and everything in its place" is my motto. I hate dishes left in the sink at night, laundry in the hamper and the worst is dirty floors.

So when I logged onto some shopping websites, I was looking to stock up on cleaning supplies. I found loads products at great, low prices.

It was great not having to look through flyers to search for the best deals on items or go to the store to check if a product was available. I was also able to check out customer reviews on the items I was interested in getting before buying them. I should also note that I did my cleaning supply shopping spree on a Friday night around 10: 30 pm while sitting in my home office in my comfy pajamas. I was shopping when I could fit it into my agenda and not on a store schedule. I could also do without having to drag two kidlets around with me who constantly ask "are you done shopping yet?"

SECTION Ⅳ: Speech

Interpret the following speech from Chinese into English.

一百多年来，这家购物中心一直为数以百万的顾客提供便捷的一站式家庭购物。现在它作为一家国际折扣零售公司，为顾客提供了种类繁多的日用商品。

这家购物中心致力于为顾客节省时间和开支，并提供一种独特的购物体验。通过高效运作和大量销售，它能够以“天天平价”的价格供应高质量的名牌商品。

购物中心以这家折扣店内36个日用品部门为特色。如拥有各式配件的完整的服饰部门、种类繁多的精美珠宝部门、草坪和花园商店、大型的健康美容部门，甚至还有药房。此外，食品杂货类还有面包房、冷冻食品、肉类、奶制品以及蔬菜水果。

为了提供舒适悠闲的购物氛围，购物中心特别加宽了购物走道，在店里各处安装了指示牌，并提供24小时服务。广场内还设有客户服务台和扫描式记账器，以提供快速高效的结账服务。

购物中心平均建筑面积为10万到22万平方英尺。根据不同的规模和客户需要，每家广场雇用200～550名员工，他们在自己的岗位上尽心尽力地为客户服务。

参考译文

SECTION Ⅰ: Dialogue

A: May I help you, sir?

B: 我想给我的妻子买个礼物。

A: Do you have anything particular in mind?

B: 还没有，但我想买点美国没有的东西。

A: That might be pretty difficult to find. About how much do you like to spend?

B: 50 美元左右的吧。

A: Let me think… does she have any hobbies?

B: 嗯，她喜欢和邻居一起玩宾戈游戏。

A: I suggest you buy a Chinese mahjong, a game similar to bingo. She must like it as she can't get it in America.

B: 我想她会喜欢的。可能我们小区里的中国朋友会教她打麻将呢。

A: Are you sure to get one?

B: 当然。她会中意这个礼物的。多少钱?

A: It's 120 *yuan*, about 20 bucks in dollars. Why don't buy another gift for her? We do have an umbrella with a local phoenix and peony on it.

B: 这个礼物也很好。这把伞很漂亮，但我觉得恐怕太大了，我的行李箱装不下。

A: I hadn't thought of that problem… Ah, here is something. How about a Qingdao brewery drinking mug?

B: 这个主意好，还有纪念意义呢。

A: We have glass ones or porcelain ones. The porcelain is, of course, a little bit more expensive.

B: 我买个瓷杯。毕竟是要送给妻子的。

SECTION Ⅱ: Warm-ups for Interpretation

➢ **Interpret the following proverbs from English into Chinese.**

1. 树大招风。

2. 智者沉默寡言，愚者滔滔不绝。
3. 只见树木不见林。
4. 相聚爱益切，离别情更深。
5. 便宜无好货。

➢ **Interpret the following sentences from English into Chinese.**

1. 手工艺品是理想的纪念品和礼品，北京的景泰蓝和景德镇的瓷器等都是值得大力推荐的。
2. 美国威士忌、时尚牛仔裤、儿童服装、长毛绒浴巾及优质床单、枕套等都是广受海外购物者青睐的东西。
3. 电子商务的出现给公司经理人员带来了巨大而又激动人心的挑战。因特网商务即刻打开了全球性的更有效率的市场。
4. 可供选择的独特商品有很多，如中国的丝绸、茶叶、书画作品、玉石珍珠及手工艺品等。
5. 如果你知道该在哪里购物，以及如何利用竞争销售的话，就可以在美国找到很多便宜商品。

➢ **Interpret the following paragraphs from English into Chinese and vice versa.**

1. 以我本人最近购车一事为例。首先我找到一个网站，上面列有不同车型及其性能和价格，既有批发又有零售。所有的市场调查我都做了。然后我去一家汽车商行询价。整个交易用不了 30 分钟就完成了。没有激烈的无休止的讨价还价，既简单又方便。我了解了车市行情，走进车行时已是一个懂行的买主了。
2. Shopping in China is both interesting and challenging. Bargaining is very common in China, especially in the small shops or on the roadside stands. You should buy the item if your counter offer is accepted. Check your purchase carefully to ensure there are no flaws.

SECTION Ⅲ: Speech

女士们、先生们：

请允许我与您分享网上购物的一些建议。

夏季是一年中我最喜欢的季节。我喜欢外出游玩，享受温暖的天气，并尽量抽时间多陪伴家人。那么，要是能很方便地让人把东西直接送到家门口，又何必我自己虚掷这大好时光奔走于杂货店购买各种生活必需品呢？

只需登录购物网站，花 50 美元左右就能买到所有的生活必需品，非常划算，还能免费送货上门。

您可能还不知道，我对家的干净整洁程度要求很高。我的座右铭是："各得其所"。我不喜欢晚上把没洗的盘子堆在厨房水槽里，也不喜欢把脏衣服堆在篮子里，最讨厌的是脏乎乎的地面。

因此，当我登录一些购物网站时，就想找一些清洁用品。结果我找到了许多价格超低的产品。

不用浏览商品传单找那些最划算的商品，也不用去商店查看某件商品是否到货。这真是太棒了。在购买我感兴趣的商品前，我还可以查看其他消费者的评论。还应该提到的是，我是在某个周五晚上十点半左右疯狂购买了这些清洁用品，当时我穿着舒适的睡衣坐在我的家庭办公室里。我不是根据商店的时间安排，而是从工作中挤时间购物的。我购物的时候也不必在身边带着两个孩子，他们不停地问："你买完东西了吗？"

SECTION Ⅳ: Speech

For more than a century, this supercenter has been providing one-stop family shopping convenience for millions of customers. It is now an international discount retailer offering a wide variety of general merchandise.

This supercenter is designed to save customers' time and money, while providing a unique shopping experience. Through efficient operations and high-volume sales, it offers "Every Day Low Prices" on top-quality, name-brand merchandise.

Supercenter features 36 general merchandise departments including a complete apparel department with accessories, an extensive fine jewelry department, a lawn & garden center, a large health & beauty aids department and even a pharmacy department. In addition, grocery areas generally feature a bakery, frozen food section, meat & dairy, and vegetables & fruits.

Designed to provide a pleasant and hustle-free shopping experience, this supercenter is enhanced with wide aisles, helpful signing throughout the store and 24-hour service. This supercenter is also equipped with a customer service desk and scanning registers for fast, efficient checkout service.

Supercenter average between 100,000 and 220,000 square feet of retail space. Depending on size and customer needs, they employ between 200 and 550 associates, each dedicated to exceptional customer service.

Unit 19 风味小吃 Local Delicacies

我们要牢记人民对美好生活的向往就是我们的奋斗目标，坚持以人民为中心的发展思想，努力抓好保障和改善民生各项工作，不断增强人民的获得感、幸福感、安全感，不断推进全体人民共同富裕。

We must remain committed to the people-centered philosophy of development, strive to guarantee and improve living standards, make steady progress towards enhancing our people's sense of gain, happiness and security, and realize common prosperity for all our people.

我们要着力提升发展质量和效益，更好满足人民多方面日益增长的需要，更好促进人的全面发展、全体人民共同富裕。

We must focus on improving the quality and efficiency of development to better meet the growing expectation of our people in all areas, and further promote well-rounded personal development and common prosperity for all.

课文 A

SECTION Ⅰ: Dialogue 在饭店 At the Restaurant

Interpret the following dialogue from English into Chinese and vice versa.

A: Mr. Liang, nice to see you again. It's very kind of you to have invited me to such a fancy restaurant.

B: 我也很高兴再次与您相见，您能光临是我们的荣幸。

A：Chinese people are known for their hospitality. Now I've experienced it by myself.

B：您是用筷子还是刀叉呢？

A：I think I'll try chopsticks and see if I can handle it. When I'm in China, I will do as Chinese do.

B：好的。那您是喝红酒还是啤酒呢？或者喝茅台？

A：I will taste a little bit Maotai. I've heard about it when I was attending a Chinese National Day party in Chinese Embassy in Oslo. Thank you.

B：好的。现在我们来尝尝菜肴吧。这是红烧牛肉，那是糖醋里脊。

A：Very savory. Sweet and sour pork is my favorite. Chinese cooking is famous all over the world.

B：你喜欢就好。这是红烧鲍鱼，请趁热吃。

A：Great! It's tender and tasty. Do you know how it is cooked?

B：我不会做饭，我只是在某种程度上是个美食家。

A：Oh, then you must know a lot of local specialty food in China. What's coming?

B：这是青岛当地的一道名菜，海鲜鱼丸汤。吃这道菜时喝上一口茅台酒特别香。

A：That's a good idea. The dish looks good, smells nice and tastes good, too. Thank you again for such a nice dinner!

B：不客气。

相关词汇

常用饮食类英语相关词汇

cookery　烹饪术
cuisine　烹饪
delicacy　美食
gourmet　美食家
dietician　美食家
foodie　吃货
recipe　食谱
stir-frying/sautéing　煸炒
quick-frying　爆炒
pan-frying　煎
plain-frying　清炒
scalding　烫
stewing　炖
steaming　清蒸
braising　红烧
roasting　焙
grilling　铁扒
quick-boiling　氽

stewing in gravy 汁卤
pickling 腌
marinating 卤制
dressing with starchy sauce 勾芡
dicing/filleting/slicing/shredding 切丁/柳/片/丝
steamed bun filled with roast pork 叉烧包
appetizer 凉菜；开胃菜
staple 主食
pan-fried cake with sesame and green onion 葱油饼
dim sum 广东茶点
fried twisted stick 油条
chive pie (Chinese chive taco) 韭菜盒子
glutinous rice dumpling in soup 汤圆
Xiaolongpao 小笼包
Kungpao chicken 宫保鸡丁
Sweet and sour pork 糖醋里脊
fried shrimp 炸虾仁
sliced noodles/seafood noodles/spicy hot noodles 刀削面/乌龙面/麻辣面
rice dumpling wrapped in reed leaves/rice dumpling/zongzi 粽子
shark fin soup 鱼翅汤
hot pot 火锅
cream of mushroom with chicken 鸡茸蘑菇汤
thick soup of minced fish and egg-white 凤凰鱼蓉羹
consommé of abalone 鲍鱼清汤
mapo tofu 麻婆豆腐
sautéed crab meat and roes 炒蟹粉
shrimps with egg white 芙蓉虾仁
crisp rice with sea cucumber 锅巴海参
stewed sliced fish in wine sauce 糟溜鱼片
squirrel-shaped mandarin fish 松鼠桂鱼
shrimp with colorful vegetables 虾仁什锦菜
stir-fried pork shreds and cabbage with fungus and scrambled eggs 炒木须肉
sautéed mushrooms and bamboo shoots 炒双冬
egg fry rice 蛋炒饭
egg roll 春卷
poached eggs 荷包蛋
fried eggs 炒鸡蛋
steamed eggs 鸡蛋糕
boiled eggs 煮鸡蛋
instant frozen foods 速冻食品
seasonings/ingredients/condiments 调味品/原料/佐料
chili sauce/oyster sauce/fish sauce/sesame oil 辣椒油/蚝油/鱼露/香油
sesame sauce 芝麻酱
peanut butter 花生酱
tomato sauce 番茄酱
ginger/vinegar/soy sauce/yellow rice wine/tomato sauce 生姜/醋/酱油/黄酒
ground mustard/curry powder 芥末粉/咖喱粉
fennel/cassia bark/the five spices powder/cloves 茴香/桂皮/五香粉/丁香

SECTION Ⅱ: Warm-ups for Interpretation

➢ **Tongue twister.**

If you must cross a course cross cow across a crowded cow crossing, cross the cross coarse cow across the crowded cow crossing carefully.

如果你必须穿过一条牛总是穿过的那条拥挤的牛穿过的十字路口的路线的话，穿越那一条拥挤的坑坑洼洼的牛道十字路口时一定要小心。

Rory the warrior and Roger the worrier were reared wrongly in a rural brewery.

勇士罗瑞和忧虑的罗杰是在乡村的啤酒厂里用不适当的方式培养出来的。

➢ **Interpret the following proverbs from English into Chinese.**

1. The leopard cannot change its spots.
2. Put the cart before the horse.
3. Diamond cut diamond.
4. Share and share alike.
5. One swallow does not make a summer.

➢ **Interpret the following sentences from English into Chinese.**

1. Four scores and seven years ago my grandfather was an average farmer in a remote area not far from the Yangtze River, growing kales, okra, taro, bukchoi, leek, chives, broccoli, cilantro and those kinds of vegetables.
2. Typical hot pot dishes include thinly sliced meat, leafy vegetables, mushrooms, wontons, and seafood. The cooked food is usually eaten with a dipping sauce. In many areas, hot pot meals are often eaten in the winter.
3. Spaghetti, macaroni, vermicelli and tofu were considered to be brought back to Italy by Marco Polo during the silk road in Yuan Dynasty.
4. A good wine, or a vintage champagne, is like a person you've met whose personality you don't forget.
5. Wonton is a type of dumpling commonly found in a number of Chinese cuisines, similar to the Jewish kreplach or Italian ravioli.

➢ **Interpret the following paragraphs from English into Chinese and vice versa.**

1. Generally speaking, dinners are much less formal and elaborate in the United States than in China. In China, the number of different dishes served at each meal is really impressive. It is impossible to finish everything. In the United States, when guests come to a home for dinner, the hostess, or host, usually serves one main dish with a couple of vegetables, a bread, maybe a salad or soup and one dessert. Guests may very likely consume all or most of what is offered.
2. 在漫长的历史发展过程中，中餐逐渐分化为南北两大口味。一般来说，南方菜讲究鲜嫩，而北方由于天气寒冷油重一些，菜中常加醋和大蒜。北方的主食是面条、饺子以及其他用面粉做的食物，而大多数南方人则以米饭为主食。

SECTION Ⅲ: Speech

Interpret the following speech from Chinese into English.

尊敬的各位来宾：

欢迎来到这里品尝上海小吃。众所周知，中国的饮食文化绚烂多彩，各地的小吃更是各有特色，美不胜收。

上海的小吃品种繁多，其特色是制作精美，风味独特。在上海，小吃是人们日常生活中的重头戏。寻找这些小吃的最佳地点是南京路和豫园商业区。

今天邀请各位在此品尝小吃是为了让大家在更舒适的环境中享受美食，在大快朵颐的同时了解上海的小吃文化。

大家将品尝到数十种小吃。这里我只将其中最有代表性的几种推荐给大家。

首先是南翔汤包，这种汤包个头小，但味道鲜美。包子皮薄如蝉翼，却饱含醇香的汤汁，吃的时候不要一口吞下以免烫嘴。

再有就是香脆的蟹壳黄，它看起来像煮熟的螃蟹。总之，请大家好好品尝。

SECTION Ⅳ: Speech

Interpret the following speech from English into Chinese.

Eating in China is quite different from eating in North America. In my country, people often go outside eating in large restaurants. The menus offer a wide choice with excellent seafood like lobsters and clam, and also a range of ethnic foods.

However, most restaurants in China have their own features. Some mainly serve the dishes of Sichuan Cuisine like hot pot series, and some offer delicate local snacks. People with different tastes can find their favorite foods in different places.

In America and Canada, people often drink beer or wine with dinner. But in China, most restaurants offer free tea for customers. That is very nice and I love Chinese tea. It makes my stomach warm and comfortable.

All in all, I like Chinese food just as I love this country. I will recommend the tasty food here to my friends and family. I'm sure they will love them too.

参考译文

SECTION Ⅰ: Dialogue

A: 梁先生，很高兴再见到您。非常感谢您邀请我到这么豪华的饭店。

B: Nice to see you too and it's a pleasure to have you here.

A: 中国人以好客闻名，今天我亲身体验到了这一点。

B: Would you like to use chopsticks or a knife and fork?

A: 我想试试筷子，入乡随俗嘛。

B: Well. Would you like wines or beer? We also have Maotai.

A: 我想尝尝你们的茅台。我在奥斯陆的中国大使馆参加国庆宴会的时候听说过茅台。谢谢。

B: OK. Now let's try the food. This is braised beef and that is sweet and sour pork.

A: 非常鲜美。我喜欢糖醋里脊。中国的烹饪世界闻名啊。

B: I'm glad you like it. Here's the braised abalone. Please enjoy it while it's piping hot.

A: 不错，又嫩又鲜。您知道这是怎么做的吗？

B: I'm not much of a cook. I'm a kind of gourmet only.

A: 哦，那你一定知道很多本地的美食了。这道菜是什么？

B: Oh, this is a local specialty food in Qingdao. It's called fish ball soup. It's especially tasty if you have it with a sip of Maotai.

A：这个主意不错。这道菜色香味俱全。再次感谢您招待我这么丰盛的一餐！

B：You are welcome!

SECTION Ⅱ: Warm-ups for Interpretation

➢ **Interpret the following proverbs from English into Chinese.**

1. 江山易改，本性难移。
2. 本末倒置。
3. 强中更有强中手。
4. 有福同享，有难同当。
5. 一燕不成夏。

➢ **Interpret the following sentences from English into Chinese.**

1. 八十七年前，我爷爷只是长江附近偏远山区的一个普通农民，种植小油菜、秋葵、芋头、白菜、葱、韭菜、西兰花、香菜等蔬菜。
2. 典型的火锅宴包括薄肉片、各种带叶的蔬菜、蘑菇、馄饨和海鲜，各种食物在煮熟后蘸酱吃。火锅在许多地区是冬季里的一道佳宴。
3. 据说，在元朝"丝绸之路"贸易兴盛之时，马可·波罗通过"丝绸之路"将实心面、空心面、粉条和豆腐带回了意大利。
4. 遇到一瓶上等葡萄酒，或者是一瓶精制香槟，就像遇到一个个性令你难以忘怀的人。
5. 中国许多地方都吃馄饨，它形似饺子，与犹太菜肴中的三角馄饨或意式小方饺类似。

➢ **Interpret the following paragraphs from English into Chinese and vice versa.**

1. 一般说来，美国人的晚餐远不如中国人的晚餐那么正式和复杂。在中国，吃一顿饭的菜肴的数目确实让人惊讶，要吃完所有的菜简直是不可能的。在美国，如果客人到家里来吃晚餐，主人通常是上一道主菜，加上几种蔬菜，一份面包，可能还有色拉或汤以及餐后甜点，客人很可能会吃完或几乎吃完全部食物。
2. In the course of the historical development, the Chinese dishes gradually developed into Southern and Northern tastes. In general, the southern dishes emphasize fresh-

ness and tenderness. Due to the cold weather, northern dishes are relatively oily, and the use of vinegar and garlic tends to be quite popular. As far as staple food is concerned, people in North China favor noodles. Dumplings and other staple food made from flour while the majority in the South almost consume rice daily.

SECTION Ⅲ: Speech

Respected guests,

Welcome to taste Shanghai snacks here. As we all know, the culture of Chinese food is colorful and so are the snacks all over China.

Of great varieties, Shanghai snacks are delicate and exquisite in shape with unique flavor. Snacks are a big deal in Shanghai and the best place to find them is Nanjing Road and Yuyuan Bazaar area.

Today you are invited here to taste these snacks and enjoy them in a comfortable environment and learn about the related culture at the same time.

We have prepared more dozens of snacks for you to sample. Here I just recommend some typical ones to you.

The first item is called Nanxiang Juicy Dumplings (xiaolongpao), relatively small and delicious with a thin and translucent wrapper, filled with mashed meat and tasty juice. Don't swallow the whole because the juice inside is a bit hot.

Our crab-brown baked cake is a must-try too. It looks like a cooked brown crab. Please try these specialty snacks now.

SECTION Ⅳ: Speech

中国的餐饮习惯和北美不一样。在我的国家，人们通常去大饭店吃，菜单提供的海鲜选择很多，如龙虾、蛤蜊以及一系列的民族菜肴。

中国的餐馆大多有自己的特色，一些餐馆提供川菜如火锅，另一些餐馆主要提供当地的小吃等。口味不同的人可以在不同的饭店满足自己的需要。

在美国和加拿大，人们在吃饭时经常会喝啤酒或红酒。然而，中国大部分餐馆为顾客提供免费的茶水。这很好，我很喜欢中国茶，它让我的胃暖暖的，很舒服。

总之，我喜欢中国的食物就如同我爱这个国家一样。我将向我的朋友和家人推荐这里好吃的食物。我相信他们也同样会爱上中国食物。

课文 B

SECTION Ⅰ: Dialogue 谈论小吃 Talk about Local Specialty Food

Interpret the following dialogue from English into Chinese and vice versa.

A：I've been in Qingdao for several days and I found the food here is very tempting.

B：很高兴你喜欢这里的饭菜。你最喜欢的是什么呢？

A：Umm，yellow croaker fish jiaozi is my favorite.

B：这是青岛的特色小吃之一啊。我也很喜欢。我们青岛人还喜欢吃鲅鱼饺子。

A：Oh，why do you like to eat mackerel jiaozi?

B：年轻人给丈母娘送鲅鱼已经成了当地的一种风俗，而且多数家庭在五月这个时节都会包鲅鱼饺子。

A：Oh，this is really something new to me. We eat Spanish mackerel in Europe，but I have never had jiaozi with mackerel filling. Before I came here，I've heard of China as a "Kingdom of Cuisine". But many dishes are delicious beyond my expectation.

B：是的，中国人对"吃"很讲究，我们从"色、香、味"三个方面来评价烹饪水平。

A：Really? Then I think Squirrel-shaped Mandarin Fish is a perfect combination of the three.

B：是的，不过松鼠桂鱼是苏州菜，不是青岛菜。因为是名菜，所以在全国各地都吃。其实桂鱼就是鳜鱼，做这道菜最难的是刀工。

A：I agree. I can't figure out how they make the dish look like a squirrel.

B：你吃过青岛的小吃吗？很能引起你的食欲。

A：Snacks? I haven't got such a chance to try them but I would like to.

B：那我们一起去尝尝吧？

A：I'd love to. Where can we get Qingdao snacks? I didn't find any near Kempinski Hotel.

B：我和你一起去小吃一条街。

A：Great! Just a minute. I must take my phone.

B：好的，我在楼下等你。

SECTION Ⅱ: Warm-ups for Interpretation

➢ **Tongue twister.**

The great Greek grape growers grow great Greek grapes.

这个伟大的希腊优秀葡萄种植者种出了优质的希腊大葡萄。

I saw a kitten eating chicken in the kitchen.

我看见一只小猫在厨房吃鸡肉。

➢ **Interpret the following proverbs from Chinese into English.**

1. 身正不怕影子斜。
2. 痛快一时，痛苦一世。
3. 若要人不知，除非己莫为。
4. 早起的鸟儿有虫吃。
5. 忧虑伤身。

➢ **Interpret the following sentences from Chinese into English.**

1. 炒锅主要用来炒菜，但也可用于蒸、炸、焖、炖、熏制食物，还可以用它来煲汤。
2. 杭州的龙井茶为我国绿茶中极品，以虎跑泉水冲饮，清香扑鼻，甘醇无比。
3. 我不太擅长烹饪，但你不妨尝尝我包的饺子。虽然不太好看，但都是我自己擀的皮、调的馅，也很充饥。
4. 如今，很多中国人都开始吃生鱼片、寿司和泡菜。其实我受不了配生鱼片吃的芥末的味道。
5. 享誉全球的青岛啤酒色泽清凉透明、口味香醇爽口。

➢ **Interpret the following paragraphs from Chinese into English and vice versa.**

1. 美国人的饮食习惯正在发生诸多变化。美国人那种丰盛的、一成不变的肉制品加土豆的传统餐，早已为世人所熟知。而今，我们美国人可以有多种不同的选择，除了传统的家常菜外，我们可以享受到各种民族风味餐、营养合理的保健餐，以及方便可口的快餐。
2. Welsh food has a long-established reputation for distinctiveness and quality. From

unique cheeses and wines, famous Welsh beef and lamb to fresh fish and seafood, Wales has them all. In hotels around Wales, you will be served with the most mouthwatering breakfast—local eggs and bacon combined with the more unusual ingredients—Laver bread and Cockles. Afternoon tea can be served with Bara Brith (a fruit bread) or Welsh cakes. The traditional meat for dinner in the evening is Welsh Lamb.

SECTION Ⅲ: Speech

Interpret the following speech from Chinese into English.

上海菜虽有四百多年的历史，但它却是中国十大菜系中最年轻的一类。上海菜以前被称之为“本帮菜”，始现于明清时期。

上海菜的常见做法有用酒糟、烤、蒸、炸等。19 世纪下半叶，上海成为国内一个主要的贸易港口，本帮菜采用了很多其他菜系的烹饪方法，发生了巨大变化。

上海菜经常使用酱油调味。糖是上海菜的重要成分，尤其常与酱油一起使用。上海菜另一个特点是米饭比面条或其他小麦制品更常见。

上海菜保留原料的原始风味。它以清淡为目标，与其他一些菜系相比，味道更柔和，略带甜味。酸甜口是典型的上海味道。上海菜中食材经过精心雕琢和色彩搭配，十分诱人。

上海菜还包括多种引起人们食欲的小吃，到上海的游客都对这些小吃赞不绝口。

SECTION Ⅳ: Speech

Interpret the following speech from English into Chinese.

To my surprise, I found many fast food chains like McDonald's, Kentucky Fried Chicken, Pizza Hut, Starbucks, Taco Bell, Papa Jones, Subway, Burger King, Wendy's in China. This reminds me of how we Americans eat when we are in a hurry.

You'll find all types of restaurants in the United States. If you're in a hurry, you can grab some "junk food" at a grocery store, or you can bite to eat at one of those many fast food chains.

Some of these places have tables, but many don't. People can eat in their cars or take their food home, to their offices or to parks. If you prefer sitting down but don't want to spend much, you can try a cafeteria.

At all of these places, you pick and choose your own food and then pay at a cash register, but you usually have to clear the table when you finish.

Coffee shops are usually less expensive and more casual than fine restaurants. So are pizza places, sandwich shops and family restaurants. But the name of a restaurant won't necessarily tell you much about the kind of place it is or the food it serves.

Like most fast food restaurants and cafeterias, many restaurants don't serve alcoholic beverages. This is often because they want people to feel comfortable bringing their children.

参考译文

SECTION Ⅰ: Dialogue

A: 到青岛已经好多天了，我发现这里的饭菜很诱人。

B: I'm glad to hear you enjoy the food. What do you like most?

A: 嗯，我最喜欢黄花鱼饺子。

B: That is a typical Qingdao snack. I also like it. We people in Qingdao eat mackerel fish jiaozi, too.

A: 哦，你们为什么喜欢吃鲅鱼饺子？

B: It has become a local custom that young married couples send mackerel to their parents-in-law as a filial piety present. Many families also wrap mackerel fish jiaozi in May during this season.

A: 哦，我以前不知道这一风俗。我们在欧洲也吃鲅鱼，但从没吃过鲅鱼馅的饺子。来中国之前，我就听说中国是"烹饪王国"，很多菜好吃得超出了我的想象。

B: Yes, we Chinese people have been paying a lot of attention to what to eat, and we judge cooking from three elements known as color, aroma and taste.

A: 真的吗？我觉得松鼠桂鱼是三者的完美结合。

B: That's right. But the Squirrel-shaped Mandarin Fish is a Suzhou local special dish. It's not a Qingdao dish. But it is popular in many places. In fact, Mandarin Fish is Chinese perch. And the most difficult part to make this dish is the slicing technique.

A：对呀，我简直想不出来他们是怎样把菜做得像松鼠的。

B：Have you tasted the snacks in Qingdao? They are also very appetizing.

A：小吃？我很感兴趣，但至今还没有机会品尝。

B：Then let's go to try some?

A：我很乐意去。我们在哪里能吃到青岛小吃？我在凯宾斯基宾馆附近没看见过。

B：I will go with you to the food corner.

A：那太好了。请等我一下，我得带上手机。

B：OK, I will wait for you downstairs.

SECTION Ⅱ: Warm-ups for Interpretation

➢ **Interpret the following proverbs from Chinese into English.**

1. A clean hand wants no washing.
2. Short pleasure, long lament.
3. The day has eyes, the night has ears.
4. The early bird catches the worm.
5. Care killed a cat.

➢ **Interpret the following sentences from Chinese into English.**

1. Woks are most often used for stir frying, but can also be used in other Chinese cooking techniques, such as in steaming, deep frying, braising, stewing, smoking, or making soup.
2. Hangzhou's Longjing Tea, the best of China's green tea, requires the water from the Tiger Spring to bring out its fragrance and delicacy.
3. I am not much of a cook. You can eat the jiaozi I wrapped. It can feed you. I made the wrapping and the filling myself though they don't look so nice-looking.
4. These days majority of the Chinese people start eating sashimi, sushi and kimchi. Actually I can not stand the odor of the wasabi for sashimi.
5. The world-famous Tsingtao Beer features a clear and cool spring water with a richly

satisfying aroma and a refreshing and pleasant taste.

➤ **Interpret the following paragraphs from Chinese into English and vice versa.**

1. Many changes are taking place in Americans' food styles. The United States is traditionally famous for its very solid and unchanging diet of meat and potatoes. Now we have many different alternatives to choose from: various ethnic foods, nutrition-balanced health food, and convenient and delicious fast food, in addition to the traditional home-cooked meal.
2. 威尔士饮食以其特色和品质而声名远扬。独特的奶酪、酒、著名的威尔士牛羊肉和新鲜的鱼类和海鲜，在这里应有尽有。在威尔士的酒店里，早餐一般都会为你奉上当地的鸡蛋和咸猪肉，且加入了较为独特的配料——莱弗面包和乌蛤，这准让你垂涎三尺。下午茶是茶、巴拉伯里斯水果面包或威尔士蛋糕的组合。传统的晚餐肉菜是威尔士羊肉。

SECTION Ⅲ: Speech

Although its history spans some 400 years, Shanghai cuisine is the youngest among the ten major cuisines in China. Shanghai cuisine was originally called "Benbang" and originated in the Ming and Qing dynasties.

Shanghai dishes are often pickled in wine, baked, stewed and deep-fried. In the later part of 19th century after Shanghai became a major domestic and international trading port, Benbang dishes underwent substantial changes and adopted certain elements of other types of cuisine.

Shanghai cuisine often uses soy sauce for seasoning. Sugar is an important ingredient in Shanghai cuisine, especially when used in combination with soy sauce. Another characteristic is the use of rice is more commonly served than noodles or other wheat products.

Shanghai cuisine retains the original flavors of raw ingredients. It aims at lightness in flavor and is mellower and slightly sweet in taste compared to some other Chinese cuisines. Sweet and sour is a typical Shanghai taste. An attractive presentation is also important in Shanghai cooking, with ingredients carefully cut and presented with a view to harmonizing colors.

SECTION Ⅳ: Speech

我很惊奇地发现在中国也有如此多的快餐连锁店，像麦当劳、肯德基、必胜客、星巴克、塔可钟、棒约翰、赛百味、汉堡王、温蒂汉堡等。这让我想起美国人在忙碌时就餐的情景。

在美国，你可以找到任何一种餐馆。如果你十分忙碌，可以去食品店随手买些“方便食品”，也可以到众多快餐店中的一家去买些食物充饥。

这类快餐店有的有桌子，有的甚至连桌子都没有，人们买完快餐后，有的拿到自己的车里去吃，有的拿回家吃，有的拿到办公室或公园去吃。如果你既想坐在餐桌前吃又不愿多破费，那么你可以去自助餐馆。

在这些地方，你可以先挑选自己喜欢的食物，然后到收银台付钱。不过通常用完餐后，你得把自己的餐桌清理干净。

咖啡馆的价位通常比高级餐馆低，也更为随意。比萨饼店、三明治店和家庭餐馆都属于这个档次。当然一个餐馆的名称不一定能向你透露很多有关这家餐馆和食物的情况。

同大多数快餐店和自助餐馆一样，许多餐饮店不供应酒，这样做是为了方便带孩子去餐馆的客人。

Unit 20 名胜古迹 Places of Interest

我们应该向世界推广具有鲜明中国特色的传统文化产业。

We should promote traditional cultural industries with distinctive Chinese features to the rest of the world.

要做出更多努力来保护我国的文化遗产，并保护我们祖先留给我们的宝贵宝藏。

We should make more efforts to conserve the country's cultural heritage and protect the valuable treasure left to us by our ancestors.

应该更多地弘扬优良的中国传统文化，为经济社会发展和人民的生活质量做出贡献。

The fine traditional Chinese culture should be promoted more to contribute to economic and social development and people's quality life.

课文 A

SECTION Ⅰ: Dialogue 参观上海博物馆 A Visit to the Shanghai Museum

Interpret the following dialogue from English into Chinese and vice versa.

A：Fine weather today，isn't it?

B：是的，天气很好。今天我带您参观上海博物馆。

A：Honestly speaking，I don't have a good knowledge of history.

B：那你有什么特别的喜好呢?

A：I enjoyed old works of art，but I'm sorry to say I don't know much about the museum.

B：那我尽量满足您的兴趣。

A：What will we begin with?

B：如果不介意的话，我想先带您参观青铜器和玉器的展厅。您可以从它们身上看到我们的祖先在几千年前就是优秀的艺术家。

A：I like these carvings of early hunters and farmers. They give you a vivid picture of life in China thousands of years ago.

B：是的，我同意您的说法。我们继续往前参观，去看明朝的画作。我记得您说您喜欢书画作品。

A：All right. Let's go to the Ancient Painting Gallery.

B：请走这边，名画作品在二楼展出。

A：OK. Great! I like these landscape and figure paintings.

B：对，它们都很好看，大多数都是名家的作品。

A：Well, thank you so much for showing me around.

B：不用谢。希望下次有机会和您一起参观更多的展览。

相关词汇

名胜古迹类相关词汇

natural attraction/scenery　自然景观
places of historic figures and cultural heritage　人文景观
places of interest　名胜古迹
ancient architectural complex　古建筑群
grotto　石窟
pagoda　塔
glazed tile　琉璃瓦
bronze ware　青铜器
cloisonné enamel　景泰蓝
celadon　青瓷
enamel　珐琅；瓷釉
tapestry　挂毯
The Forbidden City　故宫
The Palace of Heavenly Purity　乾清宫
Palace of Earthly Tranquility　坤宁宫
Imperial Garden　御花园
Echo Wall　回音壁
Imperial Mountain Summer Resort　避暑山庄
Hall of Prayer for Good Harvest　祈年殿
Summer Palace　颐和园
Palace Museum　故宫博物院
Meridian Gate　午门
Big Wild Goose Pagoda　大雁塔
Stone Forest　石林
Grand Canal　大运河
Sun Moon Lake　日月潭
Terra Cotta Warriors　陕西秦始皇陵兵马俑

Patala Palace　布达拉宫
Taj Mahal　泰姬陵
Pyramids　金字塔
Great Barrier Reef　大堡礁
Notre Dame de Paris　巴黎圣母院
Leaning Tower of Pisa　比萨斜塔
Grand Canyon　大峡谷

SECTION Ⅱ: Warm-ups for Interpretation

➢ **Tongue twister.**

I have got a date at a quarter to eight. I'll see you at the gate, so don't be late.
差一刻八点我有个约会，咱们在大门会面，你可不要迟到哦。
Mr. Tongue Twister tried to train his tongue to twist and turn, and twit and twat to learn the letter T.
绕口令先生努力训练他的舌头去“扭”、“翻”、“转”来“学“T”的发音。

➢ **Interpret the following proverbs from Chinese into English.**

1. 多多益善。
2. 井底之蛙，所见不广。
3. 画饼充饥。
4. 天下没有免费的午餐。
5. 众口难调。

➢ **Interpret the following sentences from Chinese into English.**

1. 花园建于明朝嘉靖年间，是江南一带最大的园林，园内的莲花池与楼堂亭阁相映成趣。
2. 五月归来不看山，黄山归来不看岳。
3. 长城、兵马俑、大三巴牌坊、泰姬陵、金字塔、大峡谷和自由女神像等闻名世界的观光胜地令人叹为观止，吸引了大量游客。
4. 这座殿堂的建筑艺术集中代表了我国宋朝时期的建筑风格。
5. 桂林山水甲天下，阳朔山水甲桂林。

➢ **Interpret the following paragraphs from Chinese into English and vice versa.**

1. 泰山海拔 1545 米，是我国四大名山之一。其巅峰玉皇顶为峡谷和险峰所环绕。沿石梯而上，登山远眺，只见山外有山，景外有景。泰山壮观的自然风光和历史名胜，激发了历代文人雅士书法家为之舞文弄墨，创作了无数经典佳作。他们留下的石刻碑文，令游客目不暇接，叹为观止。

2. The Potala Palace in downtown Lhasa is a 41-hectare complex which came under construction during Songtsan Gambo's 7th-century reign. It was built to honor the marriage of this 33rd King to Princess Wencheng of the Tang Dynasty. The palace is 13 stories and has over ten thousand pillars. Housed in this castle-like palace are a wealth of Buddhist statues, murals, religious scriptures, and treasures. As a precious legacy of Tibetan culture, the Potala Palace is now the most widely recognized symbol of Tibet. It is a UNESCO-endorsed world cultural heritage site.

SECTION Ⅲ: Speech

Interpret the following speech from English into Chinese.

Ladies and gentlemen,

Here we are at Datong Yungang Grottoes. The Yungang Grottoes are ancient Chinese Buddhist temple grottoes near the city of Datong in the province of Shanxi. They are excellent examples of rock-cut architecture and one of the three most famous ancient Buddhist sculptural sites of China. The others are Longmen and Mogao.

The site is located about 16 km west of the city of Datong, in the valley of the Shi Li river at the base of the Wuzhou Shan mountains. They are an outstanding example of the Chinese stone carvings from the 5th and 6th centuries. The site is in all composed of 252 grottoes with more than 51,000 Buddha statues and statuettes. In 2001, the Yungang Grottoes were made a UNESCO World Heritage Site. The Yungang Grottoes are considered by UNESCO to be a "masterpiece of early Chinese Buddhist cave art", representing the successful fusion of Buddhist religious symbolic art from south and central Asia with Chinese cultural traditions.

Within the city of Datong, there are a few surviving sites of historical interest such as the Nine-Dragon Wall, the Huayan Monastery, and the Shanhua Temple. Further afield is the Hanging Temple built into a cliff face near Mount Heng. Most of the historical sites in this region date to the Tang and Ming dynasties, but the Hanging Temple dates to the

Northern Wei dynasty (386-534).

SECTION Ⅳ: Speech

Interpret the following speech from Chinese into English.

非常欢迎各位来到上海做客，请允许我就上海的情况向各位做简要介绍。上海简称“沪”或“申”，占地 6341 平方千米，其中浦东开发新区占地 523 平方千米。

作为一座历史文化悠久的沿海开放城市，上海已成为长江三角洲的门户。在中央政府的直接管辖下，上海逐渐发展为中国最大的经济贸易中心和工业基地。

近年来，无数现代化建筑在上海拔地而起，如东方明珠电视塔、上海博物馆、上海大剧院、金茂大厦等都成为了上海的新景点。

上海不光是作为国际化大都市而闻名于世，其独特的人文历史也吸引了无数的中外游客。

上海市内和周边有不少景点，如位于市中心的景色秀丽的豫园，以独特的水乡风光吸引了中外游客的江南水乡周庄。

希望各位在上海度过一段美好而快乐的时光。

参考译文

SECTION Ⅰ: Dialogue

A：今天天气不错啊。

B：Yes, the weather is really lovely. And today I will be your guide for the tour of the Shanghai Museum.

A：坦白地说，我对历史并不太了解。

B：Then what are your special interests?

A：我喜欢古代的艺术品，但我不太了解这个博物馆。

B：Well, I'll try and help you the best I can.

A：我们从哪里开始呢？

B：If you don't mind, I prefer to show you around the hall where the bronze vessels and jade exhibited. You can see from them that our ancestors were magnificent craftsmen thousands of years ago.

A：我喜欢早期猎户和农民的雕刻。这些雕刻将几千年前的中国生动地展现在人们眼前。

B：Yes, I agree. Let's move on for the exhibition of Ming paintings. I remember that you said you liked paintings.

A：好的，我们去古代名画展厅吧。

B：This way please. The paintings are on the second floor.

A：好的。太好了，我喜欢这些山水画和人物画。

B：Yes, they are beautiful, and for most of them were works of great masters.

A：非常感谢您带我到处参观。

B：You are welcome. I hope we have another chance to see more exhibitions and more museums together.

SECTION Ⅱ: Warm-ups for Interpretation

➢ **Interpret the following proverbs from Chinese into English.**

1. Plenty is no plague.
2. The frog in the well knows nothing of the great ocean.
3. Fine words butter no parsnips.
4. There's no such thing as a free lunch.
5. He who pleased everybody died before he was born.

➢ **Interpret the following sentences from Chinese into English.**

1. This garden, which was constructed during the reign of Emperor Jia Jing of the Ming Dynasty, is the largest garden of its kind in Southern China. Its lotus ponds mirror the mansions, halls, towers and pavilions on the edge, offering visitors picturesque views.
2. Trips to China's five great mountains render trips to other mountains unnecessary, and a trip to Huangshan renders trips to the five great mountains unnecessary.
3. Tourists are always tempted by those world miraculous sight-seeing spots like the Great Wall, the Terracotta Warriors, Ruins of St. Paul, Taj Mahal, the Pyramid,

the Grand Canyon and the Statue of Liberty.

4. The architecture of this hall represents the architectural style of China's Song Dynasty.

5. Guilin landscape tops those elsewhere, and Yangshuo landscape tops that of Guilin.

➢ **Interpret the following paragraphs from Chinese into English and vice versa.**

1. Rising to 1,545 meters above sea level, Mount Tai is one of China's four renowned great mountains. Yuhuangding, Mount Tai's highest peak, stands over deep valleys and above other perilous peaks. Following a stone staircase all the way up and looking in the distance, one will enjoy the views of mountains beyond mountains and scenery beyond scenery. Mount Tai's natural scenery and historical sites have inspired writers, scholars and calligraphers of various dynasties to produce numerous great works of all time. The tourists will marvel at a dazzling exhibition of their inscriptions carved in stones.

2. 坐落在拉萨市中心的布达拉宫，占地 41 公顷，是 7 世纪松赞干布统治时期建造的。它最初是第 33 任赞普松赞干布为迎娶文成公主而兴建的。这座宫殿共 13 层，有一万多根梁柱。这座城堡式的宫殿是座宝藏，内有许多佛像、壁画、经文和珍宝。布达拉宫是西藏文化的宝贵遗产，现已被普遍认为是西藏的象征，被联合国教科文组织列为世界文化遗产。

SECTION Ⅲ: Speech

女士们、先生们：

今天在我们眼前的就是大同云冈石窟。云冈石窟位于山西大同附近，展现了中国古代佛教石窟艺术。云冈石窟是石雕艺术的典范，和龙门石窟、莫高窟一起同为中国最著名的三大古代佛教石窟雕塑群。

云冈石窟距大同市约 16 千米，位于武周山山麓、十里河畔的山谷中，是中国五、六世纪石刻艺术的杰出典范。云冈石窟共有 252 个窟龛、51000 多座佛像。2001 年，云冈石窟被联合国教科文组织列入世界遗产名录，并被称为“中国早期佛教雕刻艺术的杰作”。其雕刻技艺继承了中国的文化传统，又成功地融合了中、南亚象征佛教的宗教艺术。

在大同市内，还现存着几处历史古迹，如九龙壁、华严寺、善化寺等。还有建在离市区稍远的恒山峭壁间的悬空寺。这些历史古迹大都建于唐朝和明朝，而悬空寺建于北魏时期(公元 386-534 年)。

SECTION Ⅳ: Speech

Welcome to Shanghai. Please allow me to make a brief introduction of Shanghai. Shanghai, is also named "Hu" or "Shen" in short. It occupies a total area of 6,341 square kilometers, including Pudong New Area which occupies 523 square kilometers.

Shanghai, as an open city on the coast and famous historical and cultural city, is a gate to the Yangtze River Delta. With the direct jurisdiction of the central government, it gradually developed into the largest economic and trade center and industrial base in China.

In recent years, a number of modern buildings have been added to the city, such as the Oriental Pearl TV Tower, Shanghai Museum, Shanghai Grand Theatre and Jin Mao Building. They have become new scenic sights in Shanghai.

Shanghai is well-known in the world not only for its prosperous cosmopolitan feature but also for its rich humanistic resources.

There are numerous scenic spots within and near the city. For example, the beautiful Yuyuan Garden which is located in the center of the city, and the water town Zhouzhuang which attracts tourists from home and abroad with its special characteristics.

Wish all of you a happy and pleasant stay in Shanghai.

课文 B

SECTION Ⅰ: Dialogue

Interpret the following dialogue from English into Chinese and vice versa.

A: Hi, Mr. Liang. Which places of interest are we going to see today?

B: 我们去参观市郊的诸城恐龙化石遗址。它是 20 世纪中国发现的最大的、最丰富的恐龙遗址。

A: That's great! I really enjoy learning about some Chinese history while sightseeing. When did people discover this site?

B：是 1960 年发现并开始挖掘的。

A：It must be a grand and amazing place.

B：是的。它是 20 世纪 80 年代在诸城发现的，是世界上最大的鸭嘴龙化石。

A：I see. I can't wait. How long can we get there?

B：大约一个半小时。

A：Are we driving or flying?

B：哦，我们坐商务车去。

A：Oh, that would be convenient. We can drive straight to the site.

B：是的。我们请了最好的司机确保你的安全。

A：Thank you. Very thoughtful. Have you ever visited this dinosaur fossil site before?

B：是的。这是我第二次去。

A：What's the name of the dinosaur fossil site? How can this place have such a big groups of dinosaurs?

B：是诸城恐龙化石遗址。科学家认为火山喷发导致恐龙灭绝，后来洪水把恐龙化石冲到了诸城。诸城是一片长满草的湿地。

A：When was the site open to public?

B：恐龙博物馆始建于 1995 年，于 1997 年竣工。

A：I'm expecting to see it. It has been 20 years since I saw the Jurassic Park.

SECTION Ⅱ：Warm-ups for Interpretation

➢ **Tongue Twister.**

The two-twenty-two train tore through the tunnel.

二二零二号火车飞奔穿梭过隧道。

To begin to toboggan first buy a toboggan, but don't buy too big a toboggan. Too big a toboggan is too big a toboggan to buy to begin to toboggan.

刚开始滑雪先买个雪橇，但不要买太大的雪橇。刚开始滑雪买一个大雪撬是太大啦。

➢ **Interpret the following proverbs from English into Chinese.**

1. Fear is often greater than the danger.
2. It is better to give than to take.

3. A true friend is known in the day of adversity.
4. The child is father of the man.
5. He who does not advance falls backward.

➢ **Interpret the following sentences from English into Chinese.**

1. The 7,000-kilometer-long "Silk Road", whose history dates back to the second century B. C., is a trade thoroughfare linking Asia and Europe.
2. The castle, the very best in Europe, has a long history dating back to the ancient Roman times.
3. Places of historic interest and scenic beauty across China have become tourist destinations, such as the Yungang Grottoes in Datong, the Imperial Palace in China's capital Beijing and the beautiful landscape of Guilin in the South, to name just a few.
4. Tourists from all over the world are drawn to a wealth of historical relics, fascinating scenery and interesting local cultures along the "Silk Road".
5. Perhaps the most spectacular feature of the Grand Canyon, its "Red Wall" limestone cliff, stands about half way up the chasm and is practically vertical.

➢ **Interpret the following paragraphs from English into Chinese and vice versa.**

1. There are many places of interest around the Sun Moon Lake, such as Wenwu Temple, Peacock Park, Lalu Island, Syuentzang Temple, Ci En Pagoda and so on. Wenwu Temple is located at the mountain slope of Tanpeishan. This temple is devoted to Confucius, a great scholar in ancient China, and Yuefei and Guanyu, a great warrior in ancient China. The temple consists of three halls, the front, central and rear halls. It is spacious and decorated with multiple colors with gold as the main color. The architecture is of traditional Chinese palace style. It is majestic and grand-looking. At the center of Sun Moon Lake is Lalu Island, which marks the boundary. And Cien Pagoda, on the peak of Chinlung Mountain, is the highest point in Sun Moon Lake Area at an altitude of 1,000 meters. The pagoda is of Chinese style of 9 levels.
2. 曲阜地处山东省西南部，春秋时期曾为鲁国国都，是中国古代伟大的思想家、教育家孔子的故乡。孔府曾是孔子嫡长子孙的府第，收藏了公元 1534 年至 1948 年的 9000 多卷档案，还有大批历史文物、古代服饰、器皿等。孔庙有 2000 多座石碑、

100 多座汉代以来的石雕像。孔林是孔子及其后裔的墓地。

SECTION Ⅲ: Speech

Interpret the following speech from Chinese into English.

青岛海军博物馆建于 1988 年，1989 年起对外开放，是中国第一个专门介绍海洋军事的博物馆。其占地面积约 4 万平方米。

青岛海军博物馆东邻鲁迅公园、南接小青岛，西望青岛海湾。

海军博物馆共有三大展区：海军服装和礼品展区、武器装备展区及位于海上的海上展舰区。

室内展室展出了约 1200 张照片，记述了中国古代海军史、中国近代海军史，并展示了各个时期的海军制服、军衔肩章。展室还展出了约 230 件外国海军赠送给中国海军的各种礼品。

武器装备展区有现已退役的各种战舰、飞机、导弹、两栖坦克等多种武器装备。

海上展舰区停泊着已退役的驱逐舰、导弹护卫舰及多艘潜艇等海军舰艇。

海军博物馆确实值得一去。

SECTION Ⅳ: Speech

Interpret the following speech from English into Chinese.

The Terracotta Army or the "Terracotta Warriors and Horses" is a collection of terracotta sculptures depicting the armies of Qin Shi Huang, the first Emperor of China. It is a form of funerary art buried with the emperor in 210-209 BC and whose purpose was to protect the emperor in his afterlife.

The figures, dating from approximately the late third century BC, were discovered in 1974 by local farmers in Lintong District, Xi'an, Shaanxi province. The figures vary in height according to their roles, with the tallest being the generals. The figures include warriors, chariots and horses. Estimates from 2007 were that the three pits containing the Terracotta Army held more than 8,000 soldiers, 130 chariots with 520 horses and 150 cavalry horses, the majority of which remained buried in the pits nearby Qin Shi Huang's mausoleum. Other terracotta non-military figures were found in other pits, including officials, acrobats, strongmen and musicians.

The Terracotta Army was discovered on 29 March 1974 to the east of Xi'an in Shaanxi province by farmers digging a water well approximately 1.6 kilometers east of the Qin Emperor's tomb mound at Mount Li, a region riddled with underground springs and watercourses. For centuries, occasional reports mentioned pieces of terracotta figures and fragments of the Mausoleum of the First Qin Emperor-roofing tiles, bricks and chunks of masonry. This discovery prompted Chinese archaeologists to investigate, revealing the largest pottery figurine group ever found in China.

参考译文

SECTION Ⅰ: Dialogue

A: 梁先生，你好。今天我们去参观什么名胜古迹呢？

B: We are going to take you to the Zhucheng dinosaur fossil site in the suburbs. It's perhaps the greatest treasury of dinosaur fossils found in the 20th century.

A: 那太好了！我很喜欢在观光的同时了解中国的历史。这个遗址是什么时候发现的？

B: It was discovered and excavated ever since 1960.

A: 它一定很壮观。

B: Of course. It's the world's largest hadrosaur fossil found in Zhucheng in the 1980s.

A: 我明白了。我等不及去看了。我们多久能到那里？

B: About one and a half hour.

A: 我们开车去还是坐飞机去？

B: Oh, we're going to take a station-wagon.

A: 哦，那很方便。我们可以直接开到遗址那儿。

B: Yes. We'll have our best driver to ensure your security.

A: 谢谢。你们想得真周到。你曾经去过这个恐龙化石遗址吗？

B: Yes, this is my second trip.

A: 这个遗址叫什么名字？那儿怎么会有这么多恐龙？

B: It is named Zhucheng. Scientists believe a volcano eruption may have killed the dinosaurs, and a subsequent flood carried the fossils to Zhucheng. You know, Zhucheng has been a wetland covered in grass.

A：遗址是什么时候对外开放的呢？

B：The fossil museum was built in 1995, and completed in 1997.

A：我期待着去看一看。“侏罗纪公园”是20年前看的了。

SECTION Ⅱ：Warm-ups for Interpretation

➢ **Interpret the following proverbs from English into Chinese.**

1. 杞人忧天。
2. 施比受更有福。
3. 疾风知劲草，患难知友情。
4. 三岁看到老。
5. 不进则退。

➢ **Interpret the following sentences from English into Chinese.**

1. 连接亚欧两大洲的贸易通道“丝绸之路”全程长达7000千米，其历史可以追溯到公元前2世纪。
2. 古堡为欧洲之最，其历史悠久，可追溯到古罗马时代。
3. 全国各地的名胜古迹都是游客向往的地方，如大同的云冈石窟、首都北京的故宫、南方桂林的山水。
4. 丝绸之路沿途的大批历史文物、引人入胜的自然风景以及富有情趣的地方文化吸引着来自世界各地的游人。
5. 也许大峡谷最引人注目的特色是“红墙”石灰石悬崖，它耸立在峡谷的半空中，几乎是垂直的。

➢ **Interpret the following paragraphs from English into Chinese and vice versa.**

1. 日月潭及其周边有很多景点，如文武庙、孔雀园、光华岛、玄奘寺、慈恩塔等。文武庙位于潭北山腰上，因供奉孔子(文圣)、岳飞及关羽(武胜)而得名。殿宇沿山势而建，分前、中、后三殿，占地广阔，色彩以金黄色为主，为中国宫殿式庙宇，气势雄伟。华光岛位于日月潭中心，为日月潭分界。慈恩塔位于青龙山顶，塔顶高度达海拔 1000 米，为日月潭最高点，是中国宝塔式建筑，共九层。

2. Qufu, in southwestern Shandong Province, was the capital of the state of Lu during the Spring and Autumn Period (770-476 BC) and the hometown of Confucius, a great thinker and educator. Confucius' Mansion was the residence of Confucius' eldest male descendants for generations. The mansion holds more than 9,000 volumes of archives dating from 1534 to 1948 and many cultural relics, ancient costumes and utensils. Confucius' Temple is famous for its 2,000 stone steles and more than 100 portrait stones from the Han Dynasty. Confucius' Cemetery houses tombs for Confucius and his descendants.

SECTION Ⅲ: Speech

Qingdao Navy Museum was built in 1988, and opened in 1989. It was the first specialized Navy Museum in China. It covers about 40,000 square meters.

It's located west of Lu Xun Park, north of the Little Qingdao Isle, and west faces to the Qingdao Bay.

The Navy Museum has three main exhibit areas: military uniform and gifts exhibition hall, weapons and equipment exhibition area, and the ship and Naval Warfare history galleries on the sea area.

The indoor exhibition hall displays about 1200 pictures to show ancient and modern Chinese navy history, uniforms, badges, and about 230 gifts from friendly exchanges with other countries.

The weapons and equipment exhibition area has retired battle ships, aircraft, missiles, amphibious tanks and more.

The sea area has retired destroyer, missile frigate ship, submarines and more.

A visit to the museum is very tempting and rewarding.

SECTION Ⅳ: Speech

秦始皇兵马俑即兵马俑，是中国第一个皇帝——秦始皇的卫队的陶俑雕塑。它是公元前 210—209 年随秦始皇一起被埋葬的陪葬品，是为了在秦始皇死后也保卫他。

兵马俑的历史可追溯至公元前 3 世纪末。当地的农民于 1974 年在陕西西安市临潼区发现了秦始皇兵马俑。兵俑因职位不同而身高各异，最高的兵俑是将军。兵马俑中有武士俑、战车和陶马。2007 年，人们估计 3 个俑坑共有 8000 多兵俑、130 辆战车、520 匹陶马和 150 匹战马。大部分兵马俑依然埋葬在秦始皇陵附近的俑坑中。在其他俑坑中还发现了除军队以外的其他秦俑，如各级行政官员、杂技演员、大力士和乐师等。

1974 年 3 月 29 日，陕西农民在西安以东打井时意外发现了兵马俑。兵马俑位于地下温泉、水道广布的骊山秦始皇陵以东约 1.6 千米处。几百年来，不时有消息称，在此发现了部分兵马俑及秦陵的片瓦碎石——房屋的瓦片、砖块、石块等。这一发现立刻吸引了大批中国考古学家到现场调查研究，从而将迄今为止在中国发现的最大的陶俑群公诸于世。

Appendix

附录 1　2021 年世界 500 强公司企业名称

排名	公司名称（中英文）	国家
1	沃尔玛(WALMART)	美国
2	国家电网有限公司(STATE GRID)	中国
3	亚马逊(AMAZON. COM)	美国
4	中国石油天然气集团有限公司(CHINA NATIONAL PETROLEUM)	中国
5	中国石油化工集团有限公司(SINOPEC GROUP)	中国
6	苹果公司(APPLE)	美国
7	CVS Health 公司(CVS HEALTH)	美国
8	联合健康集团(UNITEDHEALTH GROUP)	美国
9	丰田汽车公司(TOYOTA MOTOR)	日本
10	大众公司(VOLKSWAGEN)	德国
11	伯克希尔—哈撒韦公司(BERKSHIRE HATHAWAY)	美国
12	麦克森公司(MCKESSON)	美国
13	中国建筑集团有限公司(CHINA STATE CONSTRUCTION ENGINEERING)	中国
14	沙特阿美公司(SAUDI ARAMCO)	沙特阿拉伯
15	三星电子(SAMSUNG ELECTRONICS)	韩国
16	中国平安保险(集团)股份有限公司(PING AN INSURANCE)	中国
17	美源伯根公司(AMERISOURCEBERGEN)	美国
18	英国石油公司(BP)	英国
19	荷兰皇家壳牌石油公司(ROYAL DUTCH SHELL)	荷兰

续表

排名	公司名称(中英文)	国家
20	中国工商银行股份有限公司(INDUSTRIAL & COMMERCIAL BANK OF CHINA)	中国
21	Alphabet 公司(ALPHABET)	美国
22	鸿海精密工业股份有限公司(HON HAI PRECISION INDUSTRY)	中国
23	埃克森美孚(EXXON MOBIL)	美国
24	戴姆勒股份公司(DAIMLER)	德国
25	中国建设银行股份有限公司(CHINA CONSTRUCTION BANK)	中国
26	美国电话电报公司(AT & T)	美国
27	开市客(COSTCO WHOLESALE)	美国
28	信诺(CIGNA)	美国
29	中国农业银行股份有限公司(AGRICULTURAL BANK OF CHINA)	中国
30	嘉德诺(CARDINAL HEALTH)	美国
31	托克集团(TRAFIGURA GROUP)	新加坡
32	中国人寿保险(集团)公司(CHINA LIFE INSURANCE)	中国
33	微软(MICROSOFT)	美国
34	嘉能可(GLENCORE)	瑞士
35	中国铁路工程集团有限公司(CHINA RAILWAY ENGINEERING GROUP)	中国
36	沃博联(WALGREENS BOOTS ALLIANCE)	美国
37	EXOR 集团(EXOR GROUP)	荷兰
38	安联保险集团(ALLIANZ)	德国
39	中国银行股份有限公司(BANK OF CHINA)	中国
40	克罗格(KROGER)	美国
41	家得宝(HOME DEPOT)	美国
42	中国铁道建筑集团有限公司(CHINA RAILWAY CONSTRUCTION)	中国
43	摩根大通公司(JPMORGAN CHASE)	美国
44	华为投资控股有限公司(HUAWEI INVESTMENT & HOLDING)	中国
45	威瑞森电信(VERIZON COMMUNICATIONS)	美国
46	安盛(AXA)	法国
47	福特汽车公司(FORD MOTOR)	美国
48	本田汽车(HONDA MOTOR)	日本

续表

排名	公司名称(中英文)	国家
49	通用汽车公司(GENERAL MOTORS)	美国
50	Anthem 公司(ANTHEM)	美国
51	三菱商事株式会社(MITSUBISHI)	日本
52	道达尔能源公司(TOTALENERGIES)	法国
53	德国电信(DEUTSCHE TELEKOM)	德国
54	宝马集团(BMW GROUP)	德国
55	日本电报电话公司(NIPPON TELEGRAPH AND TELEPHONE)	日本
56	中国移动通信集团有限公司(CHINA MOBILE COMMUNICATIONS)	中国
57	Centene 公司(CENTENE)	美国
58	日本邮政控股公司(JAPAN POST HOLDINGS)	日本
59	京东集团股份有限公司(JD. COM)	中国
60	上海汽车集团股份有限公司(SAIC MOTOR)	中国
61	中国交通建设集团有限公司(CHINA COMMUNICATIONS CONSTRUCTION)	中国
62	房利美(FANNIE MAE)	美国
63	阿里巴巴集团控股有限公司(ALIBABA GROUP HOLDING)	中国
64	美国康卡斯特电信公司(COMCAST)	美国
65	中国五矿集团有限公司(CHINA MINMETALS)	中国
66	中国第一汽车集团有限公司(CHINA FAW GROUP)	中国
67	恒力集团有限公司(HENGLI GROUP)	中国
68	正威国际集团有限公司(AMER INTERNATIONAL GROUP)	中国
69	中国华润有限公司(CHINA RESOURCES)	中国
70	山东能源集团有限公司(SHANDONG ENERGY GROUP)	中国
71	日本伊藤忠商事株式会社(ITOCHU)	日本
72	中国宝武钢铁集团有限公司(CHINA BAOWU STEEL GROUP)	中国
73	意大利忠利保险公司(ASSICURAZIONI GENERALI)	意大利
74	中国邮政集团有限公司(CHINA POST GROUP)	中国
75	雪佛龙(CHEVRON)	美国
76	戴尔科技公司(DELL TECHNOLOGIES)	美国
77	美国银行(BANK OF AMERICA)	美国

续表

排名	公司名称(中英文)	国家
78	塔吉特公司(TARGET)	美国
79	雀巢公司(NESTLÉ)	瑞士
80	美国劳氏公司(LOWE'S)	美国
81	马拉松原油公司(MARATHON PETROLEUM)	美国
82	花旗集团(CITIGROUP)	美国
83	现代汽车(HYUNDAI MOTOR)	韩国
84	俄罗斯天然气工业股份公司(GAZPROM)	俄罗斯
85	东风汽车公司集团有限公司(DONGFENG MOTOR)	中国
86	Facebook 公司(FACEBOOK)	美国
87	皇家阿霍德德尔海兹集团(ROYAL AHOLD DELHAIZE)	荷兰
88	索尼(SONY)	日本
89	联合包裹速递服务公司(UNITED PARCEL SERVICE)	美国
90	中国人民保险集团股份有限公司(PEOPLE'S INSURANCE CO. OF CHINA)	中国
91	中国南方电网有限责任公司(CHINA SOUTHERN POWER GRID)	中国
92	中国海洋石油集团有限公司(CHINA NATIONAL OFFSHORE OIL)	中国
93	法国农业信贷银行(CRÉDIT AGRICOLE)	法国
94	强生(JOHNSON & JOHNSON)	美国
95	日立(HITACHI)	日本
96	家乐福(CARREFOUR)	法国
97	法国巴黎银行(BNP PARIBAS)	法国
98	博世集团(BOSCH GROUP)	德国
99	乐购(TESCO)	英国
100	日本永旺集团(AEON)	日本
101	国家能源投资集团有限责任公司(CHINA ENERGY INVESTMENT)	中国
102	汇丰银行控股公司(HSBC HOLDINGS)	英国
103	美国富国银行(WELLS FARGO)	美国
104	通用电气公司(GENERAL ELECTRIC)	美国
105	法国电力公司(ELECTRICITÉ DE FRANCE)	法国
106	州立农业保险公司(STATE FARM INSURANCE)	美国

续表

排名	公司名称(中英文)	国家
107	中国电力建设集团有限公司(POWERCHINA)	中国
108	英特尔公司(INTEL)	美国
109	中国医药集团有限公司(SINOPHARM)	中国
110	哈门那公司(HUMANA)	美国
111	日本生命保险公司(NIPPON LIFE INSURANCE)	日本
112	中粮集团有限公司(COFCO)	中国
113	德国邮政敦豪集团(DEUTSCHE POST DHL GROUP)	德国
114	三井物产株式会社(MITSUI)	日本
115	中国中信集团有限公司(CITIC GROUP)	中国
116	日产汽车(NISSAN MOTOR)	日本
117	慕尼黑再保险集团(MUNICH RE GROUP)	德国
118	意大利国家电力公司(ENEL)	意大利
119	第一生命控股有限公司(DAI-ICHI LIFE HOLDINGS)	日本
120	西班牙国家银行(BANCO SANTANDER)	西班牙
121	国际商业机器公司(INTERNATIONAL BUSINESS MACHINES)	美国
122	中国恒大集团(CHINA EVERGRANDE GROUP)	中国
123	美国邮政(U. S. POSTAL SERVICE)	美国
124	北京汽车集团有限公司(BEIJING AUTOMOTIVE GROUP)	中国
125	卢克石油公司(LUKOIL)	俄罗斯
126	中国电信集团有限公司(CHINA TELECOMMUNICATIONS)	中国
127	中国兵器工业集团有限公司(CHINA NORTH INDUSTRIES GROUP)	中国
128	宝洁公司(PROCTER & GAMBLE)	美国
129	SK 集团(SK)	韩国
130	意昂集团(E. ON)	德国
131	百事公司(PEPSICO)	美国
132	腾讯控股有限公司(TENCENT HOLDINGS)	中国
133	艾伯森公司(ALBERTSONS)	美国
134	巴斯夫公司(BASF)	德国
135	联邦快递(FEDEX)	美国

续表

排名	公司名称(中英文)	国家
136	大都会人寿(METLIFE)	美国
137	交通银行股份有限公司(BANK OF COMMUNICATIONS)	中国
138	晋能控股集团有限公司(JINNENG HOLDING GROUP)	中国
139	碧桂园控股有限公司(COUNTRY GARDEN HOLDINGS)	中国
140	中国航空工业集团有限公司(AVIATION INDUSTRY CORP. OF CHINA)	中国
141	房地美(FREDDIE MAC)	美国
142	绿地控股集团股份有限公司(GREENLAND HOLDING GROUP)	中国
143	Phillips66 公司(PHILLIPS 66)	美国
144	洛克希德－马丁(LOCKHEED MARTIN)	美国
145	华特迪士尼公司(WALT DISNEY)	美国
146	ADM 公司(ARCHER DANIELS MIDLAND)	美国
147	瑞士罗氏公司(ROCHE GROUP)	瑞士
148	厦门建发集团有限公司(XIAMEN C & D)	中国
149	太平洋建设集团有限公司(PACIFIC CONSTRUCTION GROUP)	中国
150	西门子(SIEMENS)	德国
151	中国中化集团有限公司(SINOCHEM)	中国
152	Engie 集团(ENGIE)	法国
153	英国法通保险公司(LEGAL & GENERAL GROUP)	英国
154	松下(PANASONIC)	日本
155	信实工业公司(RELIANCE INDUSTRIES)	印度
156	布鲁克菲尔德资产管理公司(BROOKFIELD ASSET MANAGEMENT)	加拿大
157	英杰华集团(AVIVA)	英国
158	中国太平洋保险(集团)股份有限公司(CHINA PACIFIC INSURANCE GROUP)	中国
159	联想集团有限公司(LENOVO GROUP)	中国
160	万科企业股份有限公司(CHINA VANKE)	中国
161	中国化工集团有限公司(CHEMCHINA)	中国
162	招商银行股份有限公司(CHINA MERCHANTS BANK)	中国
163	招商局集团有限公司(CHINA MERCHANTS GROUP)	中国
164	瓦莱罗能源公司(VALERO ENERGY)	美国

续表

排名	公司名称(中英文)	国家
165	丸红株式会社(MARUBENI)	日本
166	引能仕控股株式会社(ENEOS HOLDINGS)	日本
167	丰田通商公司(TOYOTA TSUSHO)	日本
168	苏黎世保险集团(ZURICH INSURANCE GROUP)	瑞士
169	宏利金融(MANULIFE FINANCIAL)	加拿大
170	物产中大集团股份有限公司(WUCHAN ZHONGDA GROUP)	中国
171	厦门国贸控股集团有限公司(XIAMEN ITG HOLDING GROUP)	中国
172	荷兰全球保险集团(AEGON)	荷兰
173	波音(BOEING)	美国
174	中国保利集团有限公司(CHINA POLY GROUP)	中国
175	联合利华(UNILEVER)	英国
176	广州汽车工业集团有限公司(GUANGZHOU AUTOMOBILE INDUSTRY GROUP)	中国
177	中国建材集团有限公司(CHINA NATIONAL BUILDING MATERIAL GROUP)	中国
178	保德信金融集团(PRUDENTIAL FINANCIAL)	美国
179	空中客车公司(AIRBUS)	荷兰
180	三菱日联金融集团(MITSUBISHI UFJ FINANCIAL GROUP)	日本
181	巴西国家石油公司(PETROBRAS)	巴西
182	惠普公司(HP)	美国
183	雷神技术公司(RAYTHEON TECHNOLOGIES)	美国
184	软银集团(SOFTBANK GROUP)	日本
185	英国保诚集团(PRUDENTIAL)	英国
186	富腾公司(FORTUM)	芬兰
187	东京电力公司(TOKYO ELECTRIC POWER)	日本
188	Seven & I 控股公司(SEVEN & I HOLDINGS)	日本
189	厦门象屿集团有限公司(XMXYG)	中国
190	Stone X 集团(STONEX GROUP)	美国
191	Alimentation Couche-Tard 公司(ALIMENTATION COUCHE-TARD)	加拿大
192	LG 电子(LG ELECTRONICS)	韩国
193	高盛(GOLDMAN SACHS GROUP)	美国

续表

排名	公司名称(中英文)	国家
194	中国光大集团股份公司(CHINA EVERBRIGHT GROUP)	中国
195	俄罗斯石油公司(ROSNEFT OIL)	俄罗斯
196	兴业银行股份有限公司(INDUSTRIAL BANK)	中国
197	安赛乐米塔尔(ARCELORMITTAL)	卢森堡
198	中国铝业集团有限公司(ALUMINUM CORP. OF CHINA)	中国
199	西斯科公司(SYSCO)	美国
200	河钢集团有限公司(HBIS GROUP)	中国
201	上海浦东发展银行股份有限公司(SHANGHAI PUDONG DEVELOPMENT BANK)	中国
202	巴西 JBS 公司(JBS)	巴西
203	法国兴业银行(SOCIÉTÉ GÉNÉRALE)	法国
204	摩根士丹利(MORGAN STANLEY)	美国
205	印度国家银行(STATE BANK OF INDIA)	印度
206	泰国国家石油有限公司(PTT)	泰国
207	HCA 医疗保健公司(HCA HEALTHCARE)	美国
208	东京海上日动火灾保险公司(TOKIO MARINE HOLDINGS)	日本
209	沃达丰集团(VODAFONE GROUP)	英国
210	迪奥公司(CHRISTIAN DIOR)	法国
211	丰益国际(WILMAR INTERNATIONAL)	新加坡
212	印度石油公司(INDIAN OIL)	印度
213	友邦保险集团有限公司(AIA GROUP)	中国
214	万喜集团(VINCI)	法国
215	起亚公司(KIA)	韩国
216	埃尼石油公司(ENI)	意大利
217	日本 KDDI 电信公司(KDDI)	日本
218	诺华公司(NOVARTIS)	瑞士
219	雷诺(RENAULT)	法国
220	陕西煤业化工集团有限责任公司(SHAANXI COAL & CHEMICAL INDUSTRY)	中国
221	思科公司(CISCO SYSTEMS)	美国
222	韩国电力公司(KOREA ELECTRIC POWER)	韩国

续表

排名	公司名称(中英文)	国家
223	西班牙电话公司(TELEFÓNICA)	西班牙
224	中国民生银行股份有限公司(CHINA MINSHENG BANKING)	中国
225	江西铜业集团有限公司(JIANGXI COPPER)	中国
226	韩国浦项制铁公司(POSCO)	韩国
227	拜耳集团(BAYER)	德国
228	加拿大鲍尔集团(POWER CORP. OF CANADA)	加拿大
229	Orange 公司(ORANGE)	法国
230	特许通讯公司(CHARTER COMMUNICATIONS)	美国
231	中国远洋海运集团有限公司(CHINA COSCO SHIPPING)	中国
232	默沙东(MERCK)	美国
233	ELO 集团(ELO GROUP)	法国
234	陕西延长石油(集团)有限责任公司(SHAANXI YANCHANG PETROLEUM (GROUP))	中国
235	和硕(PEGATRON)	中国
236	百威英博(ANHEUSER-BUSCH INBEV)	比利时
237	美洲电信(AMÉRICA MÓVIL)	墨西哥
238	百思买(BEST BUY)	美国
239	浙江吉利控股集团有限公司(ZHEJIANG GEELY HOLDING GROUP)	中国
240	中国船舶集团有限公司(CHINA STATE SHIPBUILDING)	中国
241	Talanx 公司(TALANX)	德国
242	美国纽约人寿保险公司(NEW YORK LIFE INSURANCE)	美国
243	印度石油天然气公司(OIL & NATURAL GAS)	印度
244	电装公司(DENSO)	日本
245	MS & AD 保险集团控股有限公司(MS & AD INSURANCE GROUP HOLDINGS)	日本
246	Equinor 公司(EQUINOR)	挪威
247	艾伯维(ABBVIE)	美国
248	中国华能集团有限公司(CHINA HUANENG GROUP)	中国
249	日本制铁集团公司(NIPPON STEEL CORPORATION)	日本
250	加拿大皇家银行(ROYAL BANK OF CANADA)	加拿大

续表

排名	公司名称(中英文)	国家
251	台积公司(TAIWAN SEMICONDUCTOR MANUFACTURING)	中国
252	德国联邦铁路公司(DEUTSCHE BAHN)	德国
253	大众超级市场公司(PUBLIX SUPER MARKETS)	美国
254	好事达(ALLSTATE)	美国
255	浙江荣盛控股集团有限公司(ZHEJIANG RONGSHENG HOLDING GROUP)	中国
256	力拓集团(RIO TINTO GROUP)	英国
257	墨西哥石油公司(PEMEX)	墨西哥
258	埃森哲(ACCENTURE)	爱尔兰
259	德国艾德卡公司(EDEKA ZENTRALE)	德国
260	中国联合网络通信股份有限公司(CHINA UNITED NETWORK COMMUNICATIONS)	中国
261	住友商事(SUMITOMO)	日本
262	美国利宝互助保险集团(LIBERTY MUTUAL INSURANCE GROUP)	美国
263	美国国际集团(AMERICAN INTERNATIONAL GROUP)	美国
264	英国葛兰素史克公司(GLAXOSMITHKLINE)	英国
265	法国 BPCE 银行集团(GROUPE BPCE)	法国
266	圣戈班集团(SAINT-GOBAIN)	法国
267	英国劳埃德银行集团(LLOYDS BANKING GROUP)	英国
268	瑞士再保险股份有限公司(SWISS RE)	瑞士
269	俄罗斯联邦储蓄银行(SBERBANK)	俄罗斯
270	泰森食品(TYSON FOODS)	美国
271	韩华集团(HANWHA)	韩国
272	德国大陆集团(CONTINENTAL)	德国
273	必和必拓集团(BHP GROUP)	澳大利亚
274	伍尔沃斯集团(WOOLWORTHS GROUP)	澳大利亚
275	前进保险公司(PROGRESSIVE)	美国
276	赛诺菲(SANOFI)	法国
277	马来西亚国家石油公司(PETRONAS)	马来西亚
278	百时美施贵宝公司(BRISTOL-MYERS SQUIBB)	美国

续表

排名	公司名称(中英文)	国家
279	青山控股集团有限公司(TSINGSHAN HOLDING GROUP)	中国
280	美国全国保险公司(NATIONWIDE)	美国
281	辉瑞制药有限公司(PFIZER)	美国
282	山东魏桥创业集团有限公司(SHANDONG WEIQIAO PIONEERING GROUP)	中国
283	卡特彼勒(CATERPILLAR)	美国
284	中国机械工业集团有限公司(SINOMACH)	中国
285	美国教师退休基金会(TIAA)	美国
286	英格卡集团(INGKA GROUP)	荷兰
287	印尼国家石油公司(PERTAMINA)	印度尼西亚
288	美的集团股份有限公司(MIDEA GROUP)	中国
289	邦吉公司(BUNGE)	美国
290	费森尤斯集团(FRESENIUS)	德国
291	意大利联合圣保罗银行(INTESA SANPAOLO)	意大利
292	乔治威斯顿公司(GEORGE WESTON)	加拿大
293	国家电力投资集团有限公司(STATE POWER INVESTMENT)	中国
294	巴西淡水河谷公司(VALE)	巴西
295	西班牙 ACS 集团(ACS)	西班牙
296	多伦多道明银行(TORONTO-DOMINION BANK)	加拿大
297	马士基集团(MAERSK GROUP)	丹麦
298	蒂森克虏伯(THYSSENKRUPP)	德国
299	法国布伊格集团(BOUYGUES)	法国
300	三菱电机股份有限公司(MITSUBISHI ELECTRIC)	日本
301	中国能源建设集团有限公司(CHINA ENERGY ENGINEERING GROUP)	中国
302	瑞银集团(UBS GROUP)	瑞士
303	Finatis 公司(FINATIS)	法国
304	甲骨文公司(ORACLE)	美国
305	Energy Transfer 公司(ENERGY TRANSFER)	美国
306	大和房建(DAIWA HOUSE INDUSTRY)	日本
307	中国航天科技集团有限公司(CHINA AEROSPACE SCIENCE & TECHNOLOGY)	中国

续表

排名	公司名称(中英文)	国家
308	江苏沙钢集团有限公司(JIANGSU SHAGANG GROUP)	中国
309	浙江恒逸集团有限公司(ZHEJIANG HENGYI GROUP)	中国
310	陶氏公司(DOW)	美国
311	盛虹控股集团有限公司(SHENGHONG HOLDING GROUP)	中国
312	美国运通公司(AMERICAN EXPRESS)	美国
313	日本明治安田生命保险公司(MEIJI YASUDA LIFE INSURANCE)	日本
314	森宝利公司(J. SAINSBURY)	英国
315	安徽海螺集团有限责任公司(ANHUI CONCH GROUP)	中国
316	通用动力(GENERAL DYNAMICS)	美国
317	德意志银行(DEUTSCHE BANK)	德国
318	日本出光兴产株式会社(IDEMITSU KOSAN)	日本
319	Iberdrola 公司(IBERDROLA)	西班牙
320	中国航天科工集团有限公司(CHINA AEROSPACE SCIENCE & INDUSTRY)	中国
321	耐克公司(NIKE)	美国
322	伊塔乌联合银行控股公司(ITAÚ UNIBANCO HOLDING)	巴西
323	采埃孚(ZF FRIEDRICHSHAFEN)	德国
324	广达电脑公司(QUANTA COMPUTER)	中国
325	日本三井住友金融集团(SUMITOMO MITSUI FINANCIAL GROUP)	日本
326	美国诺斯洛普格拉曼公司(NORTHROP GRUMMAN)	美国
327	沃尔沃集团(VOLVO)	瑞典
328	苏宁易购集团股份有限公司(SUNING. COM GROUP)	中国
329	麦德龙(METRO)	德国
330	联合服务汽车协会(UNITED SERVICES AUTOMOBILE ASSN.)	美国
331	损保控股有限公司(SOMPO HOLDINGS)	日本
332	阳光龙净集团有限公司(YANGO LONGKING GROUP)	中国
333	安达保险公司(CHUBB)	瑞士
334	中国电子信息产业集团有限公司(CHINA ELECTRONICS)	中国
335	贺利氏控股集团(HERAEUS HOLDING)	德国
336	金川集团股份有限公司(JINCHUAN GROUP)	中国

续表

排名	公司名称(中英文)	国家
337	西班牙对外银行(BANCO BILBAO VIZCAYA ARGENTARIA)	西班牙
338	小米集团(XIAOMI)	中国
339	仁宝电脑(COMPAL ELECTRONICS)	中国
340	迪尔公司(DEERE)	美国
341	法国邮政(LA POSTE)	法国
342	德国中央合作银行(DZ BANK)	德国
343	泰康保险集团股份有限公司(TAIKANG INSURANCE GROUP)	中国
344	中国太平保险集团有限责任公司(CHINA TAIPING INSURANCE GROUP)	中国
345	巴克莱(BARCLAYS)	英国
346	国泰金融控股股份有限公司(CATHAY FINANCIAL HOLDING)	中国
347	日本三菱重工业股份有限公司(MITSUBISHI HEAVY INDUSTRIES)	日本
348	Rajesh Exports 公司(RAJESH EXPORTS)	印度
349	中国中车集团有限公司(CRRC GROUP)	中国
350	雅培公司(ABBOTT LABORATORIES)	美国
351	中国兵器装备集团有限公司(CHINA SOUTH INDUSTRIES GROUP)	中国
352	中国华电集团有限公司(CHINA HUADIAN)	中国
353	长江和记实业有限公司(CK HUTCHISON HOLDINGS)	中国
354	中国电子科技集团有限公司(CHINA ELECTRONICS TECHNOLOGY GROUP)	中国
355	意大利邮政集团(POSTE ITALIANE)	意大利
356	法国国营铁路集团(SNCF GROUP)	法国
357	印度塔塔汽车公司(TATA MOTORS)	印度
358	富士通(FUJITSU)	日本
359	雪松控股集团有限公司(CEDAR HOLDINGS GROUP)	中国
360	西北互助人寿保险公司(NORTHWESTERN MUTUAL)	美国
361	Dollar General 公司(DOLLAR GENERAL)	美国
362	路易达孚集团(LOUIS DREYFUS)	荷兰
363	上海建工集团股份有限公司(SHANGHAI CONSTRUCTION GROUP)	中国
364	融创中国控股有限公司(SUNAC CHINA HOLDINGS)	中国
365	株式会社爱信(AISIN)	日本

续表

排名	公司名称(中英文)	国家
366	KB 金融集团(KB FINANCIAL GROUP)	韩国
367	住友生命保险公司(SUMITOMO LIFE INSURANCE)	日本
368	英美烟草集团(BRITISH AMERICAN TOBACCO)	英国
369	Exelon 公司(EXELON)	美国
370	可口可乐公司(COCA-COLA)	美国
371	中国核工业集团有限公司(CHINA NATIONAL NUCLEAR)	中国
372	怡和集团(JARDINE MATHESON)	中国
372	麦格纳国际(MAGNA INTERNATIONAL)	加拿大
374	霍尼韦尔国际公司(HONEYWELL INTERNATIONAL)	美国
375	敬业集团有限公司(JINGYE GROUP)	中国
376	加拿大丰业银行(BANK OF NOVA SCOTIA)	加拿大
377	菲尼克斯医药公司(PHOENIX PHARMA)	德国
378	瑞士信贷(CREDIT SUISSE GROUP)	瑞士
379	加拿大永明金融集团(SUN LIFE FINANCIAL)	加拿大
380	赛默飞世尔科技公司(THERMO FISHER SCIENTIFIC)	美国
381	雷普索尔公司(REPSOL)	西班牙
382	3M 公司(3M)	美国
383	TJX 公司(TJX)	美国
384	山东钢铁集团有限公司(SHANDONG IRON & STEEL GROUP)	中国
385	Travelers 公司(TRAVELERS)	美国
386	Migros 集团(MIGROS GROUP)	瑞士
387	欧莱雅(L'ORÉAL)	法国
388	富邦金融控股股份有限公司(FUBON FINANCIAL HOLDING)	中国
389	第一资本金融公司(CAPITAL ONE FINANCIAL)	美国
390	新希望控股集团有限公司(NEW HOPE HOLDING GROUP)	中国
391	荷兰国际集团(ING GROUP)	荷兰
392	特斯拉(TESLA)	美国
393	法国达飞海运集团(CMA CGM)	法国
394	巴拉特石油公司(BHARAT PETROLEUM)	印度

续表

排名	公司名称(中英文)	国家
395	SAP 公司(SAP)	德国
396	深圳市投资控股有限公司(SHENZHEN INVESTMENT HOLDINGS)	中国
397	Coop 集团(COOP GROUP)	瑞士
398	现代摩比斯公司(HYUNDAI MOBIS)	韩国
399	英美资源集团(ANGLO AMERICAN)	英国
400	鞍钢集团有限公司(ANSTEEL GROUP)	中国
401	三菱化学控股(MITSUBISHI CHEMICAL HOLDINGS)	日本
402	西门子能源(SIEMENS ENERGY)	德国
403	山西焦煤集团有限责任公司(SHANXI COKING COAL GROUP)	中国
404	日本钢铁工程控股公司(JFE HOLDINGS)	日本
405	海尔智家股份有限公司(HAIER SMART HOME)	中国
406	日本瑞穗金融集团(MIZUHO FINANCIAL GROUP)	日本
407	铜陵有色金属集团控股有限公司(TONGLING NONFERROUS METALS GROUP)	中国
408	Medipal 控股公司(MEDIPAL HOLDINGS)	日本
409	武田药品公司(TAKEDA PHARMACEUTICAL)	日本
410	瑞士 ABB 集团(ABB)	瑞士
411	首钢集团有限公司(SHOUGANG GROUP)	中国
412	铃木汽车(SUZUKI MOTOR)	日本
413	法国威立雅环境集团(VEOLIA ENVIRONNEMENT)	法国
414	佳能(CANON)	日本
415	新华人寿保险股份有限公司(NEW CHINA LIFE INSURANCE)	中国
416	三星人寿保险(SAMSUNG LIFE INSURANCE)	韩国
417	关西电力(KANSAI ELECTRIC POWER)	日本
418	Enbridge 公司(ENBRIDGE)	加拿大
419	美敦力公司(MEDTRONIC)	爱尔兰
420	东芝(TOSHIBA)	日本
421	纬创集团(WISTRON)	中国
422	菲利普一莫里斯国际公司(PHILIP MORRIS INTERNATIONAL)	美国
423	艾睿电子(ARROW ELECTRONICS)	美国

续表

排名	公司名称（中英文）	国家
424	施耐德电气（SCHNEIDER ELECTRIC）	法国
425	潍柴动力股份有限公司（WEICHAI POWER）	中国
426	巴西布拉德斯科银行（BANCO BRADESCO）	巴西
427	菲尼克斯集团控股公司（PHOENIX GROUP HOLDINGS）	英国
428	海亮集团有限公司（HAILIANG GROUP）	中国
429	CHS 公司（CHS）	美国
430	中国通用技术（集团）控股有限责任公司（CHINA GENERAL TECHNOLOGY）	中国
431	北京建龙重工集团有限公司（BEIJING JIANLONG HEAVY INDUSTRY GROUP）	中国
432	日本电气公司（NEC）	日本
433	浙江省交通投资集团有限公司（ZHEJIANG COMMUNICATIONS INVESTMENT GROUP）	中国
434	普利司通（BRIDGESTONE）	日本
435	中国大唐集团有限公司（CHINA DATANG）	中国
436	英国电信集团（BT GROUP）	英国
437	上海医药集团股份有限公司（SHANGHAI PHARMACEUTICALS HOLDING）	中国
438	利安德巴塞尔工业公司（LYONDELLBASELL INDUSTRIES）	荷兰
439	广西投资集团有限公司（GUANGXI INVESTMENT GROUP）	中国
440	日本中部电力（CHUBU ELECTRIC POWER）	日本
441	CRH 公司（CRH）	爱尔兰
442	住友电工（SUMITOMO ELECTRIC INDUSTRIES）	日本
443	Financière de l'Odet 公司（FINANCIÈRE DE L'ODET）	法国
444	新疆广汇实业投资（集团）有限责任公司（XINJIANG GUANGHUI INDUSTRY INVESTMENT）	中国
445	X5 零售集团（X5 RETAIL GROUP）	荷兰
446	捷普公司（JABIL）	美国
447	林德集团（LINDE）	英国
448	Enterprise Products Partners 公司（ENTERPRISE PRODUCTS PARTNERS）	美国
449	马自达汽车株式会社（MAZDA MOTOR）	日本
450	CJ 集团（CJ CORP.）	韩国
451	中国中煤能源集团有限公司（CHINA NATIONAL COAL GROUP）	中国

续表

排名	公司名称(中英文)	国家
452	SK 海力士公司(SK HYNIX)	韩国
453	慧与公司(HEWLETT PACKARD ENTERPRISE)	美国
454	达能(DANONE)	法国
455	Achmea 公司(ACHMEA)	荷兰
456	龙湖集团控股有限公司(LONGFOR GROUP HOLDINGS)	中国
457	United Natural Foods 公司(UNITED NATURAL FOODS)	美国
458	英国森特理克集团(CENTRICA)	英国
459	斯巴鲁公司(SUBARU)	日本
460	广州市建筑集团有限公司(GUANGZHOU MUNICIPAL CONSTRUCTION GROUP)	中国
461	LG 化学公司(LG CHEM)	韩国
462	阿斯利康(ASTRAZENECA)	英国
463	亿滋国际(MONDELEZ INTERNATIONAL)	美国
464	德国勃林格殷格翰公司(BOEHRINGER INGELHEIM)	德国
465	维亚康姆 CBS 公司(VIACOMCBS)	美国
466	卡夫亨氏公司(KRAFT HEINZ)	美国
467	KOC 集团(KOÇ HOLDING)	土耳其
468	广州医药集团有限公司(GUANGZHOU PHARMACEUTICAL HOLDINGS)	中国
469	新加坡奥兰国际有限公司(OLAM INTERNATIONAL)	新加坡
470	华润置地有限公司(CHINA RESOURCES LAND)	中国
471	云南省投资控股集团有限公司(YUNNAN PROVINCIAL INVESTMENT HOLDING GROUP)	中国
472	蒙特利尔银行(BANK OF MONTREAL)	加拿大
473	三星 C & T 公司(SAMSUNG C & T)	韩国
474	万洲国际有限公司(WH GROUP)	中国
475	Dollar Tree 公司(DOLLAR TREE)	美国
476	安进(AMGEN)	美国
477	康帕斯集团(COMPASS GROUP)	英国
478	Coles 集团(COLES GROUP)	澳大利亚
479	美国合众银行(U. S. BANCORP)	美国

续表

排名	公司名称(中英文)	国家
480	爱立信公司(ERICSSON)	瑞典
481	华阳新材料科技集团有限公司(HUAYANG NEW MATERIAL TECHNOLOGY GROUP)	中国
482	巴西银行(BANCO DO BRASIL)	巴西
483	Performance Food Group 公司(PERFORMANCE FOOD GROUP)	美国
484	Netflix 公司(NETFLIX)	美国
485	诺基亚(NOKIA)	芬兰
486	紫金矿业集团股份有限公司(ZIJIN MINING GROUP)	中国
487	BAE 系统公司(BAE SYSTEMS)	英国
488	珠海格力电器股份有限公司(GREE ELECTRIC APPLIANCES)	中国
489	吉利德科学公司(GILEAD SCIENCES)	美国
490	Synnex 公司(SYNNEX)	美国
491	联合信贷集团(UNICREDIT GROUP)	意大利
492	霍尔希姆公司(HOLCIM)	瑞士
493	曼福集团(MAPFRE GROUP)	西班牙
494	阿弗瑞萨控股公司(ALFRESA HOLDINGS)	日本
495	美国礼来公司(ELI LILLY)	美国
496	Truist Financial 公司(TRUIST FINANCIAL)	美国
497	中国再保险(集团)股份有限公司(CHINA REINSURANCE (GROUP))	中国
498	澳洲联邦银行(COMMONWEALTH BANK OF AUSTRALIA)	澳大利亚
499	伟创力公司(FLEX)	新加坡
500	来德爱(RITE AID)	美国

附录 2　世界货币

	货币名称		货币符号	辅币进位制
	中文	英文		
中国香港	港元	Hong Kong Dollars	HKD	1HKD=100cents(分)
中国澳门	澳门元	Macao Pataca	MOP	1MOP=100avos(分)
中国	人民币元	Renminbi Yuan	CNY	1CNY=10 jiao(角) 1 jiao=10 fen(分)
朝鲜	圆	Korean Won	KPW	1KPW=100 分
越南	越南盾	Vietnamese Dong	VND	1VND=10 角 =100 分
日本	日圆	Japanese Yen	JPY	1JPY=100 sen(钱)
老挝	基普	Laotian Kip	LAK	1LAK 1LAK=100 ats(阿特)
柬埔寨	瑞尔	Cambodian Riel	KHR	1KHR=100 sen(仙)
菲律宾	菲律宾比索	Philippine Peso	PHP	1PHP=100 centavos(分)
马来西亚	马元	Malaysian Dollar	MYR	1MYR=100 cents(分)
新加坡	新加坡元	Singapore Dollar	SGD	1SGD=100 cents(分)
泰国	泰铢	Thai Baht (Thai Tical)	THP	1THP=100 satang(萨当)
缅甸	缅元	Burmese Kyat	BUK	1BUK=100 pyas(分)
斯里兰卡	斯里兰卡卢比	Sri Lanka Rupee	LKR	1LKR=100 cents(分)
马尔代夫	马尔代夫卢比	Maldives Rupee	MVR	1MVR=100 larees(拉雷)
印度尼西亚	盾	Indonesian Rupiah	IDR	1IDR=100 cents(分)
巴基斯坦	巴基斯坦卢比	Pakistan Rupee	PRK	1PRK=100 paisa(派萨)
印度	卢比	Indian Rupee	INR	1INR=100 paise(派士)
尼泊尔	尼泊尔卢比	Nepalese Rupee	NPR	1NPR=100 paise(派士)
阿富汗	阿富汗尼	Afghani	AFA	1AFA=100 puls(普尔)
伊朗	伊朗里亚尔	Iranian Rial	IRR	1Irr=100 dinars(第纳尔)
伊拉克	伊拉克第纳尔	Iraqi Dinar	IQD	1IQD=1000 fils(费尔)
叙利亚	叙利亚镑	Syrian Pound	SYP	1SYP=100 piastres(皮阿斯特)
黎巴嫩	黎巴嫩镑	Lebanese Pound	LBP	1LBP=100 piastres(皮阿斯特)

续表

	货币名称		货币符号	辅币进位制
	中文	英文		
约旦	约旦第纳尔	Jordanian Dinar	JOD	1JOD=1,000 fils(费尔)
沙特阿拉伯	亚尔	Saudi Arabian Riyal	SAR	1SAR= 100qurush(库尔什) 1qurush=5 halals(哈拉)沙特里
科威特	科威特第纳尔	Kuwaiti Dinar	KWD	1KWD=1,000 fils(费尔)
巴林	巴林第纳尔	Bahrain Dinar	BHD	1BHD=1,000 fils(费尔)
卡塔尔	卡塔尔里亚尔	Qatar Riyal	QAR	1QAR=100 dirhams(迪拉姆)
阿曼	阿曼里亚尔	Oman Riyal	OMR	1OMR=1,000 baiza(派沙)
阿拉伯也门	也门里亚尔	Yemeni Riyal	YER	1YER=100 fils(费尔)
民主也门	也门第纳尔	Yemeni Dinar	YDD	1YDD=1,000 fils(费尔)
土耳其	土耳其镑	Turkish Pound (Turkish Lira)	TRL	1TRL=100 kurus(库鲁)
塞浦路斯	塞浦路斯镑	Cyprus Pound	CYP	1CYP=1,000 mils(米尔)
澳大利亚	澳大利亚元	Australian Dollar	AUD	1AUD=100 cents(分)
新西兰	新西兰元	New Zealand Dollar	NZD	1NZD=100 cents(分)
斐济	斐济元	Fiji Dollar	FJD	1FJD=100 cents(分)
所罗门群岛	所罗门元	Solomon Dollar	SBD	1SBD=100 cents(分)
欧元区国家	欧元	Euro (1)	EUR	1EUR=100 euro cents(生丁)
冰岛	冰岛克朗	Icelandic Krona	ISK	1ISK=100 aurar(奥拉)
丹麦	丹麦克朗	Danish Krone	DKK	1DKK=100 ore(欧尔)
挪威	挪威克朗	Norwegian Krone	NOK	1NOK=100 ore(欧尔)
瑞典	瑞典克朗	Swedish Krona	SEK	1SEK=100 ore(欧尔)
俄罗斯	卢布	Russian Ruble	SUR	1SUR=100 kopee(戈比)
波兰	兹罗提	Polish Zloty	PLZ	1PLZ=100 groszy(格罗希)
匈牙利	福林	Hungarian Forint	HUF	1HUF=100 filler(菲勒)
瑞士	瑞士法郎	Swiss Franc	CHF	1CHF=100 centimes(分)
英国	英镑	Pound	GBP	1GBP=100 new pence(新便士)
罗马尼亚	列伊	Rumanian Leu	ROL	1ROL=100 bani(巴尼)
南斯拉夫	南斯拉夫新第纳尔	Yugoslav Din	YUD	1YUD=100 paras(帕拉)
保加利亚	列弗	Bulgarian Lev	BGL	1BGL=100 stotinki(斯托丁基)

续表

	货币名称		货币符号	辅币进位制
	中文	英文		
阿尔巴尼亚	列克	Albanian Lek	ALL	1All=100 quintars(昆塔)
加拿大	加元	Canadian Dollar	CAD	1CAD=100 cents(分)
美国	美元	U. S. Dollar	USD	1USD=100 cent(分)
墨西哥	墨西哥比索	Mexican Peso	MXP	1MXP=100 centavos(分)
危地马拉	格查尔	Guatemalan Quetzal	GTQ	1GTQ=100 centavos(分)
萨尔瓦多	萨尔瓦多科朗	Salvadoran Colon	SVC	1SVC=100 centavos(分)
洪都拉斯	伦皮拉	Honduran Lempira	HNL	1HNL=100 centavos(分)
尼加拉瓜	科多巴	Nicaraguan Cordoba	NIC	1NIC=100 centavos(分)
哥斯达黎加	哥斯达黎加科朗	Costa Rican Colon	CRC	1CRC=100 centavos(分)
巴拿马	巴拿马巴波亚	Panamanian Balboa	PAB	1PAB=100 centesimos(分)
古巴	古巴比索	Cuban Peso	CUP	1CUP=100 centavos(分)
巴哈马联邦	巴哈马元	Bahaman Dollar	BSD	1BSD=100 cents(分)
牙买加	牙买加元	Jamaican Dollars	JMD	1JMD=100 cents(分)
海地	古德	Haitian Gourde	HTG	1HTG=100 centimes(分)
多米尼加	多米尼加比索	Dominican Peso	DOP	1DOP=100 centavos(分)
特立尼达和多巴哥	特立尼达多巴哥元	Trinidad and Tobago Dollar	TTD	1TTD=100 cents(分)
巴巴多斯	巴巴多斯元	Barbados Dollar	BBD	1BBD=100 cents(分)
哥伦比亚	哥伦比亚比索	Colombian Peso	COP	1COP=100 centavos(分)
委内瑞拉	博利瓦	Venezuelan Bolivar	VEB	1VEB=100 centimos(分)
圭亚那	圭亚那元	Guyanan Dollar	GYD	1GYD=100 cents(分)
苏里南	苏里南盾	Surinam Florin	SRG	1SRG=100 cents(分)
秘鲁	新索尔	Peruvian Sol	PES	1PES=100 centavos(分)
厄瓜多尔	苏克雷	Ecuadoran Sucre	ECS	1ECS=100 centavos(分)
巴西	新克鲁赛罗	Brazilian New Cruzeiro GBRC	BRC	1BRC=100 centavos(分)
玻利维亚	玻利维亚比索	Bolivian Peso	BOP	1BOP=100 centavos(分)
智利	智利比索	Chilean Peso	CLP	1CLP=100 centesimos(分)
阿根廷	阿根廷比索	Argentine Peso	ARP	1ARP=100 centavos(分)

续表

	货币名称		货币符号	辅币进位制
	中文	英文		
巴拉圭	巴拉圭瓜拉尼	Paraguayan Guarani	PYG	1PYG=100 centimes(分)
乌拉圭	乌拉圭新比索	New Uruguayan Peso	UYP	1UYP=100 centesimos(分)
埃及	埃及镑	Egyptian Pound	EGP	1EGP=100 piastres(皮阿斯特)=1,000 milliemes(米利姆)
利比亚	利比亚第纳尔	Libyan Dinar	LYD	1LYD=100 piastres(皮阿斯特)=1,000 milliemes(米利姆)
苏丹	苏丹镑	Sudanese Pound	SDP	1SDP=100 piastres(皮阿斯特)=1,000 milliemes(米利姆)
突尼斯	突尼斯第纳尔	Tunisian Dinar	TND	1TND=1,000 milliemes(米利姆)
阿尔及利亚	阿尔及利亚第纳尔	Algerian Dinar	DZD	1DZ=100 centimes(分)
摩洛哥	摩洛哥迪拉姆	Moroccan Dirham	MAD	1MAD=100 centimes(分)
毛里塔尼亚	乌吉亚	Mauritania Ouguiya	MRO	1MRO=5 khoums(库姆斯)
塞内加尔	非共体法郎	African Financial Community Franc	XOF	1XOF=100 centimes(分)
上沃尔特	非共体法郎	African Financial Community Franc	XOF	1XOF=100 centimes(分)
科特迪瓦	非共体法郎	African Financial Community Franc	XOF	1XOF=100 centimes(分)
多哥	非共体法郎	African Financial Community Franc	XOF	1XOF=100 centimes(分)
贝宁	非共体法郎	African Financial Community Franc	XOF	1XOF=100 centimes(分)
尼泊尔	非共体法郎	African Financial Community Franc	XOF	1XOF=100 centimes(分)
冈比亚	法拉西	Gambian Dalasi	GMD	1GMD=100 bututses(分)
几内亚比绍	几内亚比索	Guinea-Bissau peso	GWP	1GWP=100 centavos(分)
几内亚	几内亚西里	Guinean Syli	GNS	辅币为科里 cauri，但 50 科里以下舍掉不表示；50 科里以上进为一西里。
塞拉里昂	利昂	Sierra Leone Leone	SLL	1SLL=100 cents(分)

续表

	货币名称		货币符号	辅币进位制
	中文	英文		
利比里亚	利比里亚元	Liberian Dollar	LRD	1LRD=100 cents(分)
加纳	塞地	Ghanaian Cedi	GHC	1GHC=100 pesewas(比塞瓦)
尼日利亚	奈拉	Nigerian Naira	NGN	1NGN=100 kobo(考包)
喀麦隆	中非金融合作法郎	Central African Finan-Coop Franc	XAF	1XAF=100 centimes(分)
乍得	中非金融合作法郎	Central African Finan-Coop Franc	XAF	1XAF=100 centimes(分)
刚果	中非金融合作法郎	Central African Finan-Coop Franc	XAF	1XAF=100 centimes(分)
加蓬	中非金融合作法郎	Central African Finan-Coop Franc	XAF	1XAF=100 centimes(分)
中非	中非金融合作法郎	Central African Finan-Coop Franc	XAF	1XAF=100 centimes(分)
赤道几内亚	赤道几内亚埃奎勒	Equatorial Guinea Ekuele	GQE	1GQE=100 centimes(分)
南非	兰特	South African Rand	ZAR	1ZAR=100 cents(分)
吉布提	吉布提法郎	Djibouti Franc	DJF	1DJF=100 centimes(分)
索马里	索马里先令	Somali Shilling	SOS	1SOS=100 cents(分)
肯尼亚	肯尼亚先令	Kenya Shilling	KES	1KES=100 cents(分)
乌干达	乌干达先令	Uganda Shilling	UGS	1UGS=100 cents(分)
坦桑尼亚	坦桑尼亚先令	Tanzania Shilling	TZS	1TZS=100 cents(分)
卢旺达	卢旺达法郎	Rwanda Franc	RWF	1RWF=100 cents(分)
布隆迪	布隆迪法郎	Burnudi Franc	BIF	1BIF=100 cents(分)
扎伊尔	扎伊尔	Zaire Rp Zaire	ZRZ	1ZRZ=100 makuta(马库塔)
赞比亚	赞比亚克瓦查	Zambian Kwacha	ZMK	1ZMK=100 nywee(恩韦)
马达加斯加	马达加斯加法郎	Franc de Madagascar	MCF	1MCF=100 cents(分)
塞舌尔	塞舌尔卢比	Seychelles Rupee	SCR	1SCR=100 cent(分)
毛里求斯	毛里求斯卢比	Mauritius Rupee	MUR	1MUR=100 centimes(分)
津巴布韦	津巴布韦元	Zimbabwe Dollar	ZWD	1ZWD=100 cents(分)

附录3 世界主要港口

英文港口名称	中文港口名称	所属国家	所属地区
Aalborg	奥尔堡	丹麦	西北欧
Aalesund	奥勒松	挪威	北欧
Aarhus	奥尔胡斯	丹麦	西北欧
Abadan	阿巴丹	伊朗	波斯湾
Aberdeen	阿伯丁郡	英国	欧洲
Abidjan	阿比让	科特迪瓦	西非
Abu Dhabi	阿布扎比	阿联酋	波斯湾
Acajutla	阿卡胡特拉	萨尔瓦多	中南美
Acapulco	阿卡普尔科	墨西哥	中南美
Accra	阿克拉	加纳	西非
Adelaide	阿德莱德	南澳洲	澳新
Aden	亚丁	也门	红海
Agadir	阿加迪尔	摩洛哥	地中海
Agana	阿加尼亚	关岛	西太平洋
Alexandria	亚历山大	埃及	地中海
Algeciras	阿尔赫西拉斯	西班牙	地中海
Algiers	阿尔及尔	阿尔及利亚	地中海
Amsterdam	阿姆斯特丹	荷兰	欧洲
Ancona	安科纳	意大利	地中海
Annaba	安纳巴	阿尔及利亚	地中海
Antofagasta	安托法加斯塔	智利	中南美
Antwerp	安特卫普	比利时	西北欧
Apapa	阿帕帕	尼日利亚	西非
Apia	阿皮亚	西萨磨亚群岛	澳新
Aqaba	亚喀巴	约旦	红海
Arica	阿里卡	智利	中南美

续表

英文港口名称	中文港口名称	所属国家	所属地区
Arkhangelsk	阿尔汉格尔斯克	俄罗斯	亚欧
Aseb	阿萨布	埃塞俄比亚	非洲
Ashdod	阿什杜德	以色列	地中海
Assab	阿萨布	埃塞俄比亚	红海
Athens	雅典	希腊	地中海
Atlanta	亚特兰大	美国	北美洲
Auckland	奥克兰	新西兰	澳新
Avonmouth	阿芬默斯	英国	西北欧
Bahia Blanca	布兰卡港	阿根廷	中南美
Bahrain	巴林	巴林	波斯湾
Balboa	巴尔博亚	巴拿马	中南美
Baltimore	巴尔的摩	美国	美东
Banana	巴纳纳	扎伊尔	西非
Bandar Abbas	阿巴斯港	伊朗	波斯湾
Bandar Khomeini	霍梅尼港	伊朗	波斯湾
Bandar Seri Begawan	斯里巴加湾市	文莱	东南亚
Bangkok	曼谷	泰国	暹罗湾
Banjarmaisn	马辰	印尼	东南亚
Banjul(banthurst)	班珠尔	冈比亚	西非
Bar	巴尔	黑山共和国	欧洲
Barcelona	巴塞罗那	西班牙	地中海
Barranquilla	巴兰基利亚	哥伦比亚	中南美
Basra	巴士拉	伊拉克	波斯湾
Bassein	勃生	缅甸	孟加拉湾
Bata	巴塔	赤道几内亚	西非
Beira	贝拉	莫桑比克	东非
Beirut	贝鲁特	黎巴嫩	地中海
Belawan	乌拉湾	印尼	东南亚
Belem	贝伦	巴西	南美

续表

英文港口名称	中文港口名称	所属国家	所属地区
Belfast	贝尔法斯特	英国	西北欧
Belize	伯利兹	伯利兹	中南美
Belmopan	贝尔莫潘	伯利兹	中南美
Benghazi	班加西	利比亚	地中海
Berbera	伯贝拉	索马里	东非
Bergen	卑尔根	挪威	西北欧
Berne	伯尔尼	瑞士	欧洲
Bilbao	毕尔巴鄂	西班牙	西北欧
Birkenhead	伯肯黑德	英国	西北欧
Bissau	比绍	及内比亚绍	西非
Bizerta	比塞大	突尼斯	地中海
Boma	博马	扎伊尔	西非
Bombay	孟买	印度	波斯湾
Bordeaux	波尔多	法国	西北欧
Boston	波士顿	美国	北美
Bourgas	布尔加斯	保加利亚	地中海
Bremen	不莱梅	德国	西北欧
Bremenhaven	不来梅哈芬	德国	西北欧
Brest	布雷斯特	法国	西北欧
Bridgetown	布里奇顿	巴巴多斯	中南美
Brindisi	布林迪西	意大利	地中海
Brisbane	布里斯班	德国	西北欧
Bristol	布里斯托尔	英国	西北欧
Buenaventura	布埃纳文图拉	哥伦比亚	南美
Buenos Aires	布宜诺斯艾利斯	阿根廷	南美
Burnie	伯尼	澳大利亚	澳大利亚
Busan	釜山	南韩	南韩
Bushire	布什尔	伊朗	中东
Butterworth	巴特沃斯	马来西亚	东南亚

续表

英文港口名称	中文港口名称	所属国家	所属地区
Cabinda	卡宾达	安哥拉	西非
Cadiz	加的斯	西班牙	西北欧
Cagliari	卡利亚里	意大利	欧洲
Calcutta	加尔各答	印度	印度次大陆
Callao	卡亚俄	秘鲁	南美
Cam Pha	锦普	越南	东南亚
Cambridge	坎布里奇	美国	美东
Cape Town	开普敦	南非	西非
Caracas	加拉加斯	委内瑞拉	中南美
Cardiff	加的夫	英国	西北欧
Cartagena	卡塔赫纳	西班牙	欧洲
Casablanca	卡萨布兰卡	摩洛哥	西非
Cayenne	卡宴	圭亚那	中南美
Cebu	宿务	菲律宾	东南亚
Charleston	查尔斯顿	美国	北美
Charlotte	夏洛特	美国	北美
Charlotte Aamalie	夏洛特阿马利亚	维尔京群岛(美属)	中美
Chennai	钦奈	印度	印度次大陆
Cheribon	井里文	印尼	东南亚
Chiba	千叶	日本	亚洲
Chicago	芝加哥	美国	北美
Chimbote	钦博特	秘鲁	南美
Chittagong	吉大港	孟加拉	印度次大陆
Chongjin(Seishin)	清律	朝鲜	亚洲
Christchurch	克赖斯特彻奇	新西兰	澳新线
Christiansted	克里斯琴斯特德	维尔京群岛(美属)	中美
Churchill	彻奇尔	加拿大	北美
Cienfuegos	西恩付戈斯	古巴	中南美
Cleveland	克利夫兰	美国	北美

续表

英文港口名称	中文港口名称	所属国家	所属地区
Coatzacoalcos	夸察夸尔科斯	墨西哥	北美
Cochin	科钦	印度	印度次大陆
Colombo	科伦坡	斯里兰卡	印度次大陆
Colon	科隆	巴拿马	中南美
Columbus	哥伦布	美国	北美
Conakry	科纳克里	几内亚	非洲
Constanza	康斯坦察	罗马尼亚	地中海
Copenhagen	哥本哈根	丹麦	西北欧
Corinto	科林托	尼加拉瓜	中南美
Cork	科克	爱尔兰	西北欧
Cotonou	科托努	贝宁	非洲
Cristobal	克里斯托巴尔	巴拿马	中南美
Crotone	克努托内	意大利	欧洲
Grande	克鲁斯格兰德	智利	中南美
Cumana	库马纳	委内瑞拉	南美
Dacca	达卡	孟加拉	印度次大陆
Dakar	达喀尔	塞内加尔	非洲
Dalian	大连	中国	亚洲
Dallas	达拉斯	美国	北美
Damietta	达米埃塔	埃及	地中海
Dammam	达曼	沙特阿拉伯	地中海
Danang	岘港	越南	东南亚
Dar El-Beida	达尔贝达	摩洛哥	非洲
Dar Es Salaam	达累斯萨拉姆	坦桑尼亚	非洲
Darwin	达尔文	澳大利亚	澳新线
Detroit	底特律	美国	北美
Djakarta(Jakarta)	雅加达	印尼	东南亚
Djibouti	吉布提	吉布提	红海
Doha	多哈	卡塔尔	地中海

续表

英文港口名称	中文港口名称	所属国家	所属地区
Douala	杜阿拉	喀麦隆	非洲
Dover	多佛尔	英国	西北欧
Dubai	迪拜	阿联酋	地中海
Dublin	都柏林	爱尔兰	西北欧
Dunedin	达尼丁	新西兰	澳新线
Dunkirk	敦刻尔克	法国	西北欧
Durban	德班	南非	非洲
Durres	都拉斯	阿尔巴尼亚	欧洲
Dusseldorf	杜赛尔多夫	德国	西北欧
DutchHarbour	荷兰港	美国	北美
East Canada	东加拿大	加拿大	北美
East London	东伦敦	南非	非洲
Ensenada	恩塞纳达	墨西哥	中南美
Felixstowe	费力克斯托	英国	欧洲
Fort de France	法兰西堡	马提尼克岛	中南美
Fos	福斯	法国	欧洲
Frankfurt	法兰克福	德国	西北欧
Fredericia	腓特烈西亚	丹麦	北欧
Fredrikstad	腓特烈斯塔	挪威	北欧
Freeport	弗里波特	巴哈马	中南美
Freetown	弗里敦	塞拉利昂	西非
Fremantle	佛里曼特尔	西澳洲	澳新线
Fukuoka	福冈	日本	亚洲
Fukuyama	福山	日本	亚洲
Funafuti	富纳富提	图瓦卢	澳新线
Funchal	丰沙尔	马德拉群岛	西非
Fuzhou	福州	中国	亚洲
Gdansk	格但斯克	波兰	西北欧
Gdynia	格丁尼亚	波兰	西北欧

续表

英文港口名称	中文港口名称	所属国家	所属地区
Geelong	吉朗	澳大利亚	澳新线
Gela	杰拉	意大利	地中海
Gemlik	盖姆利克	土耳其	中东
Genoa(Genova)	热那亚	意大利	地中海
Georgetown	乔治敦	美国	北美
Ghent	根特	比利时	西北欧
Gibraltar	直布罗陀	直布罗陀	西北欧
Gijon	希洪	西班牙	欧洲
Gioia Tauro	焦亚陶罗	意大利	地中海
Glasgow	格拉斯哥	英国	西北欧
Godthab	戈特霍布	格陵兰	北美
Gothenburg	哥德堡	瑞典	西北欧
Grangemouth	格兰杰默斯	英国	西北欧
Guadalajara	瓜达拉哈拉	墨西哥	中南美
Guam	关岛	马利亚纳群岛	澳新线
Guangzhou	广州	中国	亚洲
Guayaquil	瓜亚基尔	厄瓜多尔	南美
Guaymas	瓜伊马斯	墨西哥	北美
Gwadur	瓜达尔	巴基斯坦	印度次大陆
Hai Kou	海口	中国	亚洲
Haifa	海法	以色列	中东
Haiphong	海防	越南	东南亚
Hakata	伯方	日本	亚洲
Hakodate	涵馆	日本	亚洲
Halifax	哈立法克斯	美国	北美
Halmstad	哈尔姆斯塔德	瑞典	北欧
Hamburg	汉堡	德国	西北欧
Hamilton	哈密尔顿	加拿大	北美
Hanoi	河内	越南	东南亚

续表

英文港口名称	中文港口名称	所属国家	所属地区
Haugesund	豪格松	挪威	西北欧
Havana	哈瓦那	古巴	中南美
Helsinborg	赫尔辛堡	瑞典	西北欧
Helsingo	赫尔辛格	丹麦	西北欧
Helsinki	赫尔辛基	芬兰	西北欧
Hiroshima	广岛	日本	亚洲
Ho Chi Ming City	胡志明市	越南	东南亚
Hobart	霍巴特	澳大利亚	澳新线
Hodeidah	荷台达	也门	中东
Honalulu	檀香山	美国	北美
Hong Kong	香港	中国	亚洲
Hongay	鸿基	越南	东南亚
Honiara	霍尼亚拉	所罗门群岛	澳新线
Horta	澳尔塔	亚速尔群岛(葡属)	西非
Houston	休斯敦	美国	北美
Huangpu	黄埔	中国	亚洲
Hudaydak Al	荷台达	也门	西亚
Hull	赫尔	英国	西北欧
Hungnam	兴南	朝鲜	东亚
Ilo	伊洛	秘鲁	南美
Immingham	伊明赫姆船坞	英国	西北欧
Inchon	仁川	南韩	亚洲
Iquique	伊基克	智利	南美
Iskenderun	伊斯肯德伦	土耳其	地中海
Istanbul	伊斯坦布尔	土耳其	中东
Izmir	伊兹密尔	土耳其	中东
Jacksonvile	捷克逊维尔	美国	北美
Jakarta	雅加达	印尼	东南亚
Jebel Ali	杰贝阿里	阿联酋	中东

续表

英文港口名称	中文港口名称	所属国家	所属地区
Jeddah	吉达	沙特阿拉伯	中东
Jogjakarta	日惹	印尼	东南亚
Johannesburg	约翰内斯堡	南非	南非
Johore Bahru	柔佛巴鲁	马来西亚	东南亚
Kagoshima	鹿儿岛	日本	亚洲
Kakinada	卡基纳达	印度	印度次大陆
Kaliningrad	加里宁格勒	俄罗斯	西北欧
Kampong Saon	磅逊	柬埔寨	东南亚
Kanazawa	金泽	日本	亚洲
Kandla	坎德拉	印度	印度次大陆
Kansas City	堪萨斯城	美国	北美
Kaoshiung	高雄	台湾	亚洲
Karachi	卡拉奇	巴基斯坦	印度次大陆
Katakia	拉塔基亚	叙利亚	西亚
Kavieng	卡维恩	巴布亚新几内亚	澳新线
Kawasaki	川崎	日本	亚洲
Keelung	基隆	台湾	亚洲
Kholmsk	霍尔姆斯克	俄罗斯	西北欧
Khor Fakkan	豪尔费坎	阿联酋	地中海
Khorramshahr	霍拉姆沙赫尔	伊朗	波斯湾
Kiel	基尔	德国	北欧
Kiev	基辅	俄罗斯	欧洲
Kingston	金斯顿	牙买加	中南美
Kismayu	基斯马尤	索马里	东非
Kobe	神户	日本	亚洲
Kompong Som	磅逊	柬埔寨	亚洲
Koper	科佩尔	斯洛文尼亚	地中海
Kota Kinabalu	亚庇(哥打基)	马来西亚	东南亚
Kotka	科特卡	芬兰	西北欧

续表

英文港口名称	中文港口名称	所属国家	所属地区
Kuala Lumpur	吉隆坡	马来西亚	东南亚
Kuantan	关丹	马来西亚	东南亚
Kuching	古晋	马来西亚	东南亚
Kudat	库达特	马来西亚	东南亚
Kukura	小仓	日本	亚洲
Kure	吴港	日本	亚洲
Kuwait	科威特	科威特	波斯湾
Kwangyang	光阳	南韩	亚洲
La Conuna	拉科鲁尼亚	西班牙	欧洲
La Guaira	拉瓜伊拉	委内瑞拉	中南美
La Paz	拉巴斯	墨西哥	中南美
La Plata	拉普拉塔	阿根廷	中南美
La Rouchelle	拉罗歇尔	法国	欧洲
La Spezia	拉斯佩齐亚	意大利	欧洲
Labuan	拉布安(纳闽)	马来西亚	东南亚
Lae	莱城	巴布亚新几内亚	澳新线
Laem Chabang	林查班	泰国	东南亚
Lagos	拉各斯	尼日利亚	非洲
Lancaster	兰凯斯特	英国	欧洲
Las Palmas	拉斯帕尔马斯	加纳利群岛	西非
Lattajua	拉塔基亚	叙利亚	地中海
Launceston	朗塞斯顿	澳大利亚	澳新线
Lautoka	劳托卡	斐济群岛	澳新线
Leghorn(Livormo)	来航	意大利	欧洲
Leningrad	圣彼得堡	俄罗斯	欧洲
Lianyungang	连云港	中国	亚洲
Libreville	利伯维尔	加蓬	非洲
Limassol	利马索尔	塞浦路斯	地中海
Limon	利蒙	哥斯达黎加	南美洲

续表

英文港口名称	中文港口名称	所属国家	所属地区
Lisbon	里斯本	葡萄牙	西北欧
Liverpool	利物浦	英国	西北欧
Lome	洛美	多哥	非洲
London	伦敦	英国	西北欧
Londonderry	伦敦德里	英国	西北欧
Long Beach	长滩	美国	北美
Los Angeles	洛杉矶	美国	北美
Lourenco-Marques	洛伦索一马贵斯(马普托)	莫桑比克	东非
Luanda	罗安达	安哥拉	非洲
Lubeck	卢贝克	德国	西北欧
Lyttelton	利特尔顿	新西兰	澳新线
Macao	澳门	中国	亚洲
Madang	马丹	巴布亚新几内亚	澳新线
Madras	马德拉斯	印度	印度次大陆
Madrid	马德里	西班牙	地中海
Mahe	马希	印度	印度次大陆
Majunga	马任加	马达加斯加	东非
Makasar	望加锡	印尼	东南亚
Malabo(Santa Isabel)	马拉博	赤道几内亚	西非
Malacca	马六甲	马来西亚	东南亚
Male	马累	马尔代夫	波斯湾
Malindi	马林迪	肯尼亚	东非
Malmo	马尔默	瑞典	西北欧
Malta	马耳他	马耳他	地中海
Manama，Al	麦纳麦	巴林	亚洲
Manchester	曼彻斯特	英国	西北欧
Manila	马尼拉	菲律宾	东南亚
Manta	曼塔	厄瓜多尔	南美
Manzanillo	曼萨尼约	墨西哥	中美

续表

英文港口名称	中文港口名称	所属国家	所属地区
Manzanillo(P)	曼萨尼约角	巴拿马	中美
Maputo	马普托	莫桑比克	非洲
Maracaibo	马拉开波	委内瑞拉	中南美
Marseilles	马赛	法国	欧洲
Massawa	马萨瓦	埃塞俄比亚	红海
Matadi	马塔迪	扎伊尔	非洲
Matanzas	马但萨斯	古巴	南美洲
Melbourne	墨尔本	澳大利亚	澳新线
Memphis	孟菲斯	美国	北美
Menado	万鸦老	印尼	东南亚
Mersin	梅尔辛	土耳其	地中海
Messina	墨西拿	意大利	地中海
Mexico City	墨西哥城	墨西哥	中美
Miami	迈阿密	美国	北美
Middlesbrough	米德尔斯伯勒	英国	欧洲
Midland	米德兰	加拿大	北美
Milford	米尔福德港	英国	欧洲
Miri	米里	马来西亚	东南亚
Mobile	莫比尔	美国	北美
Mogadiscio	摩加迪沙	索马里	东非
Moji	门司	日本	亚洲
Mokha	穆哈	也门	红海
Momasa	蒙巴萨	肯尼亚	非洲
Monrovia	蒙罗维尔	利比里亚	非洲
Monterrey	蒙特雷	墨西哥	中美
Montevideo	蒙得维的亚	乌拉圭	南美
Montreal	蒙特利尔	美国	北美
Moscow	莫斯科	俄罗斯	欧洲
Mostaganem	穆斯塔加奈	阿尔及利亚	非洲

续表

英文港口名称	中文港口名称	所属国家	所属地区
Moulmein	毛淡棉	缅甸	东南亚
Mozambique	莫桑比克	莫桑比克	东非
Mukalla	木卡拉	也门	红海
Mumbai	孟买	印度	印度次大陆
Murmansk	摩尔曼斯克	俄罗斯	西北欧
Muscat	马斯喀特	阿曼	地中海
Mutsamudu	木察木杜	科摩罗	东非
Nagasaki	长崎	日本	东亚
Nagoya	名古屋	日本	东亚
Naha	那坝	日本	东亚
Nakhodka	纳霍德卡	俄罗斯	欧洲
Nampo	南浦	朝鲜	亚洲
Nanjing	南京	中国	东亚
Nantes	南特	法国	欧洲
Nantong	南通	中国	东亚
Naoetsu	直江津	日本	东亚
Napier	内皮尔	新西兰	澳新线
Naples	那不勒斯	意大利	欧洲
Nassau	拿骚	巴哈马联邦	中南美
Nauru	瑙鲁	瑙鲁	澳新线
Nelson	内尔逊	新西兰	澳新线
New Orleans	新奥尔良	美国	北美
Newark	纽瓦克	美国	北美
Newcastle	纽卡斯尔	英国	西北欧
Newport	纽波特	英国	西北欧
New York	纽约	美国	北美
Nicosia	新潟	日本	东亚
Ningbo	宁波	中国	东亚
Norfolk	诺福克	美国	北美

续表

英文港口名称	中文港口名称	所属国家	所属地区
Noro	诺劳	所罗门群岛	澳新线
Nouakchott	努瓦克肖特	毛利塔尼亚	非洲
Noumea	努美阿	新喀里多尼亚	澳新线
Novorossiysk	诺沃西比尔斯克（新西伯利亚）	俄罗斯	亚欧
Oakland	奥克兰	美国	北美
Oranjestad	奥腊涅斯塔德	安的列斯	中南美
Osaka	大阪	日本	东亚
Oslo	奥斯陆	挪威	西北欧
Padang	巴东	印尼	东南亚
Paita	派塔	秘鲁	中南美
Palembang	巨港	印尼	东南亚
Panama City	巴拿马城	巴拿马	中南美
Papette	帕皮提	塔希提岛	澳新线
Paramaribo	帕拉马里博	苏里南	中南美
Paranagua	巴拉那瓜	巴西	中南美
Penang	槟城	马来西亚	东南亚
Perth	珀斯	澳大利亚	澳新线
Perth	珀斯	英国	北欧线
Philadeiphia	费城	美国	北美
Phnom Penh	金边	柬埔寨	东南亚
Phoenix	费尼克斯	美国	北美
Piraeus	比雷艾夫斯	希腊	地中海
Ponce	蓬塞	波多黎各	中南美
Pondicherry	本地治里	印度	印度次大陆
Pontianak	坤甸	印尼	东南亚
Port Elizabeth	伊丽莎白港	南非	非洲
Port Suez	苏伊士港	埃及	地中海
Portland	波特兰	美国	北美

续表

英文港口名称	中文港口名称	所属国家	所属地区
Portsmouth	朴次茅斯	英国	西北欧
Priolo	辟利洛	意大利	地中海
Puntarenas	彭塔雷纳斯	哥斯达黎加	中南美
Qingdao	青岛	中国	东亚
Quebec	魁北克	加拿大	北美
Rabat	拉巴特	摩洛哥	西非
Rabaul	腊包尔港	巴布亚新几内亚	澳新线
Rangoon	仰光	缅甸	东南亚
Ravenna	拉佛纳	意大利	欧洲
Recife	累西腓	巴西	南美
Reykjavik	雷克雅未克	冰岛	西北欧
Rio de Janeiro	里约热内卢	巴西	南美
Rostock	罗斯托克	德国	西北欧
Rotterdam	鹿特丹	荷兰	欧洲
Sabang	沙璜	印尼	东南亚
Sakaiminato	境港	日本	东亚
Sakata	酒田	日本	东亚
Salalah	塞拉莱	阿曼	地中海
Salvador	萨尔瓦多	巴西	南美
San Antonio	圣安东尼奥	智利	南美
San Diego	圣迭戈	美国	北美
San Francisco	旧金山	美国	北美
Sandwich	桑德威奇	英国	欧洲
Santiago	圣地亚哥	佛得角	西非
Santos	桑托斯	巴西	南美
Savannah	萨凡纳	美国	北美
Savona	萨沃纳	意大利	欧洲
Seattle	西雅图	美国	北美
Semarang	三宝垄	印尼	东南亚

续表

英文港口名称	中文港口名称	所属国家	所属地区
Shanghai	上海	中国	东亚
Sharjah	沙迦	阿拉伯酋长联合国	地中海
Shekou	蛇口	中国	东亚
Shimizu	清水	日本	东亚
Shuidong	水东	中国	东亚
Sibu	诗巫	马来西亚	东南亚
Sihanoukville	西哈努克城	柬埔寨	东南亚
Singapore	新加坡	新加坡	东南亚
Skikda	斯克基达	阿尔及利亚	非洲
Sofiya	索非亚	保加利亚	地中海
Songkhla	宋卡	马来西亚	东南亚
Southampton	南安普敦	英国	欧洲
Split	斯普利特	南斯拉夫	地中海
St. John	圣约翰	加拿大	北美
St. Lawrence	圣劳伦斯	加拿大	北美
ST. Louis	圣路易斯	美国	北美
St. Petersburg	圣彼得堡	俄罗斯	亚欧
Stockholm	斯德哥尔摩	瑞典	西北欧
Surabaya	泗水	印尼	东南亚
Suva	萨瓦	斐济群岛	澳新线
Swansea	斯旺西	英国	西北欧
Sydney	悉尼	澳大利亚	澳新线
Szczecin	什切青	波兰	西北欧
Tabaco	塔巴科	菲律宾	东南亚
Tacoma	塔科马	美国	北美
Taibei	台北	中国	东亚
Takoradi	塔利拉迪	加纳	非洲
Tangier	丹吉尔	摩洛哥	地中海
Taranto	塔兰托	意大利	欧洲

续表

英文港口名称	中文港口名称	所属国家	所属地区
Thamesport	泰晤士港	英国	欧洲
Thessalonikli	塞萨洛尼基	希腊	地中海
Tianjin	天津	中国	东亚
Tijuana	蒂华纳	墨西哥	中美
Timaru	蒂马鲁	新西兰	澳新线
Tjirebon	井里汶	印尼	东南亚
Tokyo	东京	日本	东亚
Toronto	多伦多	美国	北美
Toulor	土伦	法国	地中海
Toyama	富山	日本	东亚
Trazon	特拉布宗	土耳其	地中海
Trieste	德里亚斯特	意大利	欧洲
Trujillo	特鲁希略	洪都拉斯	中美
Tsuruga	敦贺	日本	东亚
Tumaco	图马科	哥伦比亚	中南美
Tunis	突尼斯	突尼斯	非洲
Turku	图尔库	芬兰	西北欧
Tuticorin	杜蒂戈林	印度	印度次大陆
Ulsan	蔚山	南韩	亚洲
Valenxia	瓦伦西亚	西班牙	地中海
Valletta	瓦莱塔	马耳他	南欧
Varna	瓦尔纳	保加利亚	地中海
Vasa	瓦沙	芬兰	西北欧
Venice	威尼斯	意大利	欧洲
Visby	维斯比	瑞典	西北欧
Vladivostok	符拉迪沃斯托克	俄罗斯	亚欧
Wellington	惠灵顿	新西兰	澳新线
Wenzhou	温州	中国	东亚
Wewak	威瓦克	巴布亚新几内亚	澳新线

续表

英文港口名称	中文港口名称	所属国家	所属地区
Wonsan	元山	朝鲜	东亚
Xiamen	厦门	中国	东亚
Yantai	烟台	中国	东亚
Yokohama	横滨	日本	东亚
Zhanjiang	湛江	中国	东亚
Zhuhai	珠海	中国	东亚

附录 4　世界主要商船公司名称

公司名称	简称	缩写
澳大利亚国家航运公司	澳国航运	ANL
美国总统轮船私人有限公司	美国总统	APL
邦拿美船务有限公司	邦拿美	BNML
波罗的海航运公司	波罗的海	BOL
中波轮船股份公司	中波	C-P
南美邮船公司	南美邮船	CLAN S. A.
南美智利国家航运公司	智利航运	CCNI
中日国际轮渡有限公司	中日轮渡	CHINJIF
天敬海运	天敬海运	CK
法国达飞轮船公司	达飞轮船	CMA
京汉海运有限公司	京汉海运	CO-HEUNG
中国远洋集装箱运输有限公司	中远集运	COSCO
朝阳商船有限公司	朝阳商船	CHOYANG
达贸国际轮船公司	达贸国际	DELIMAS
德国胜利航运公司	德国胜利	SENATOR
埃及国际轮船公司	埃及船务	EIL
长荣海运股份有限公司	长荣海运	EVERGREEN
远东轮船公司	远东轮船	FESCO
金发船务有限公司	金发船务	GFNG
浩洲船务公司	浩洲船务	HCSC
韩进海运有限公司	韩进海运	HANJIN
香港航运有限公司	香港海运	HKMSH
香港明华船务有限公司	香港明华	HKMW
赫伯罗特船务有限公司	赫伯罗特	HAPPAG-LLOYD
现代商船有限公司	现代商船	HYUNDAI
上海海隆轮船有限公司	海隆轮船	HNT

续表

公司名称	简称	缩写
金华航运有限公司	金华航运	JH
川崎汽船株式会社	川崎汽船	K LINE
高丽海运株氏会社	高丽海运	KMTC
七星轮船有限公司	七星轮船	SSCL
上海育海航运公司	育海航运	SYH
上海中福轮船公司	中福轮船	SZFSC
墨西哥航运有限公司	墨西哥航运	TMM
上海天海货运有限公司	天海货运	TMSC
东航船务有限公司	东航船务	TOHO
宁波泛洋船务有限公司	宁波泛洋	TOS
阿拉伯联合国家轮船公司	阿拉伯轮船	UASC
立荣海运股份有限公司	立荣海运	UNIGLORY
环球船务有限公司	环球船务	UNIWD
万海航运股份有限公司	万海航运	WANHAI
伟航船务有限公司	伟航船务	WH
阳明海运股份有限公司	阳明海运	YANGMING
以星轮船船务有限公司	以星轮船	ZIM
浙江远洋运输公司	浙江远洋	ZOSCO
联丰船务有限公司	联丰船务	LIFEN
意大利邮船公司	意大利邮船	LT
马来西亚国际航运有限公司	马来西亚航运	MISC
商船三井有限公司	商船三井	MOL
地中海航运公司	地中海航运	MSC
马士基海陆有限公司	马士基海陆	MAERSK SEALAND
民生神原海运有限公司	民生神原	MSKM
太古船务代理有限公司	太古船代	NGPL
铁行渣华船务有限公司	铁行渣华	P & O NEDLLOYD
新加坡海皇轮船有限公司	海皇轮船	NOL
北欧亚航运有限公司	北欧亚航运	NORASIA

续表

公司名称	简称	缩写
宁波远洋运输公司	宁波远洋	NOSCO
南星海运株式会社	南星海运	NS
沙特阿拉伯国家航运公司	沙特航运	NSCSA
日本邮船有限公司	日本邮船	NYK
东方海外货柜航运有限公司	东方海外	OOCL
萨姆达拉船务有限公司	萨姆达拉	SAMUDERA
太平船务有限公司	太平船务	PIL
泛洋商船株式会社	洋商船	POBU
瑞克麦斯轮船公司	瑞克麦斯	RICKMERS
美商海陆联运(中国)有限公司	美商海陆	vS/L
南非国家轮船有限公司	南非轮船	SAF
东映海运有限公司	东映海运	SBL
上海国际轮渡有限公司	国际轮渡	SFCO
中海发展股份有限公司	中海发展	CSD
长锦有限公司	长锦公司	SINKO
上海市锦江航运有限公司	锦江船代	JINJIANG
中外运(集团)总公司	中外运	SINOTRANS
志晓船务有限公司	志晓船务	SSC

附录 5　世界主要贸易组织

世界贸易组织(WTO)。

国际经贸组织：经济合作暨发展组织（OECD)、半导体国际组织(GAMS)、联合国(UN)、联合国贸易暨发展会议（UNCTAD)、联合国粮农组织（FAO)、国际农业发展基金（IFAD)、世界海关组织（WCO)、世界知识产权组织（WIPO)、国际电信联盟(ITU)、国际货币基金组织（IMF)、世界银行（WB)、七大工业国（G7)、国际标准组织(ISO)。

区域经贸组织：北美自由贸易协定（NAFTA)、美洲自由贸易区（FTAA)、东南亚国家协会(ASENA)、东盟自由贸易区（AFTA)、欧洲联盟（EU)。

中东非洲主要区域经贸暨金融组织：伊斯兰开发银行（IDB)、阿拉伯联盟（AL)、阿拉伯社会经济发展基金（AFESD)、阿拉伯货币基金会（AMF)、阿拉伯海湾国家合作理事会（GCF)、阿拉伯单一经济理事会（CAEU)、阿拉伯马格里布联盟（AMU)、非洲经济发展阿拉伯银行（ABEDA)、经济合作组织（ECO)、非洲开发银行（BAD)、西非开发银行（WADB)、马诺河联盟（MRU)、西部非洲国家经济共同体（ECOWAS)、东南非洲特惠贸易区（PTAESAS)、东南非共同市场(COMESA)、南部非洲关税同盟（SACU)、南部非洲发展共同体（SADC)、共同货币区（CMA)、中部非洲国家经济共同体（ECCAS)、中部非洲国家经济联盟（CACEU)、中非国家开发银行（BDEAC)、西非经济货币联盟（UEMOA)。

中南美洲主要区域经贸暨金融组：拉丁美洲和加勒比海经济委员会（ECLAC)、中美洲共同市场(CACM)、加勒比海共同市场（CARICOM)、拉丁美洲经济组织（SELA)、拉丁美洲一体化协会（LAIA)、加勒比海国家协会（ACS)、南方共同市场（MERCOSUR)、三国集团（G3)、美洲开发银行（IDB)、中美洲经济整合银行（CABEI)。

附录 6　世界主要快递公司翻译

四大国际快递公司

1. FedEx(联邦快递)
2. UPS(联合包裹)
3. DHL 快递(敦豪物流)
4. TNT 快递(天地快递)

其他知名的国际快递公司有

1. OCS(欧西爱斯)
2. SAGAWA(佐川急便)
3. DPEX(迪比翼)
4. ZMS(威鹏达)
5. AAE(美亚快递)
6. SF Express(顺丰快递)

附录 7　国际商务装运条款

Group C, Main Carriage Paid		C 组　主要运费已付
CFR	Cost and Freight	货价＋运费
CIF	Cost, Insurance, and Freight	货价＋保费＋运费
CPT	Carriage Paid To (location)	运费付至目的地
CIP	Carriage and Insurance Paid To (location)	运费、保险费付至目的地
Group D, Arrival		D 组　抵达
DAF	Delivered at Frontier	边境交货
DES	Delivered ex Ship	目的港船上交货
DEQ	Delivered ex Quay	目的港码头交货
DDU	Delivered Duty Unpaid	未完税交货
DDP	Delivered Duty Paid	完税后交货
Group E, Departure		E 组　启运
EXW	EX Works	工厂交货
Group F, Main Carriage Unpaid		F 组　主要运费未付
FCA	Free Carrier	货交承运人
FAS	Free Alongside Ship	装运港船边交货
FOB	Free on Board	装运港船上交货

附录 8 商务英语常用缩略语

AAR	against all risk	全险，对所有危险承担责任
A/C	account current; account	账户，往来户口
Acc.	acceptance; accepted	受领支票，接受，承兑
ad.	advertisement	广告
agcy.	agency	代理处
agt.	agent	代理人；委托购买；销售人
Amt.	amount	金额
A/P	authority of purchase	购买委托书
AR; A/R	all risks; account receivable	全险；应受款
a/s	after sight	见票即付
atty.	attorney	代理人；律师
a. v.	according to the value	照价
av.	average	平均
a. w.	all wool	纯羊毛
A/W	actual weight	净重
bal.	balance	差额；收支平衡数
BB	bill book; bank book	票据簿；存款簿
B/C	bill for collection	托收票据
BD	bank draft	汇票
B/E	bill for exchange	汇票
b. f.	bona fide	凭信用记账
bk.	bank; book	银行，账簿
B/L	bill of lading	提货单
B/N	bank note	纸币；钞票
b. o.	branch office	支行；分行
B/P	bills payable	应付票据
B/P	bill purchased	购入授权
b. p.	bill of parcels	包裹单
B/R	bill of sale	卖据

Bs/E	bills of exchange	汇票
b. s.	balance sheet	资产负债表
BTT	bank telegraph transfer	银行电汇
CA	credit advice	信用通知
canc.	cancelled	取消
cap.	capital	资本
C/B	clean bill	纯净提单；光票
CBD	cash before delivery	现金先汇
CC	chamber of commerce	商会
certif.	certificate	证；证明书
CFR；CNF	C & F(cost and freight)	成本加运费
chgd.	charged	收费
CIF	cost，insurance and freight	到岸价格
ck.	check	支票
cl.	collection	收款
cld.	cleared	办妥出港手续
C/N	credit note	贷方票
CO	certificate of origin	产地证明书
c/o	care of	由……转变
COD	cash on delivery	货到付款
com.	commission	佣金
Cr.	credit	贷方；信用
cub.	cubic	立方
cy.	currency	通货；货币
D/A	document against acceptance	承兑取单汇票
D/D	demand draft	即期汇票
d. d.	days after date	期后……日
dd/s	delivered sound	已交付
ddt.	deduct	折扣
dept.	department	部门
diff.	difference	差额
disc.	discount	折扣；贴现

div.	dividend	股息
D/L	demand loan	活期放款
D/N	debit note	收款单
D/O	delivery order	提货单
doc.	document	票据；文件
doz.	dozen	打
D/P	document against payment	付款取单汇票
d/st	days after sight	见票后一日即付
Entd.	entered	已入账；记账
E-I	Export-Import	进出口
enc.；encl.	enclosure	附函；附件
est.	estimated	估计的
ETA	estimated time of arrival	估计到达时间
ETD	estimated time of departure	估计离开时间
exch.	exchange	汇兑；兑换
ec div.	ex dividend	不带股息
exec.	executive	执行人员
exp.	export	出口
ext.	extra；extract；extention	特别；摘要；延期
ext.	extension	(电话)分机
f. a. a.	free of all average	不负赔偿责任
FAQ	fair average quality	平均良好品质；中等品
FAS	free alongside ship	船边交换价格
FB	freight bill	运费清单
FBE	foreign bill of exchange	外国汇票
F/D	free docks	船坞交换
F/D	forward delivery	定期交换
FGA	free of general average	共同海损不包在内
fig.	figure	图；数字
fin.	finance，financial	财政
FO	foreign office；for orders	外国公司；遵照指定
FOB	free on board	船上交货价格；离岸价格

FOQ	free on quay	码头交货价格
FOR	free on rail	铁路上交货价格
FOS	free on steamer	轮船交货价格
FPA	free of particular average	单独海损不赔偿；平安险
FP	floating policy；fine paper	预约保险；薄纸
F/P	fire policy	火险单
fr.	franc	法郎
frt.	freight	运费
ft.	foot；flat	尺；无利息
FX	foreign exchange	外汇
GA	general average	共同海损
gds.	goods	货物
GM	general manager	总经理
g. m. b.	good merchantable brand	畅销名牌
gr. wt.	gross weight	毛重
GT	gross ton	总吨数
HO	home office	本部；本国总部
incr.	increased	增加
info.	information	资料
insce.	insurance	保险
insp.	inspection	检查
inst.	instant；instalment	本月的；分期付款
int.	interest	利息
inv.	invoice	发票
invt.	inventory	财产目录；卸货表
IOU	I owe you	借据
I/P	insurance policy	保险单
JA	joint account	共同户口
J	journal	分类账
L/A	letter of authorization	授权书
L&G	loss and gain	损益
L/C	letter of credit	信用证

Led.	ledger	总账
L/G	letter of guarantee	保证书
L/H	letter of indemnity	赔偿信
LT	long ton	英吨
max.	maximum	最大限度
mem.	memorandum	备忘录
Messrs.	messieurs	诸位先生
mfg.	manufacturing	制造
mfr.	manufacturer	制造商
Mgr.	manager	经理
min.	minimum	最小限度
m. i. p.	marine insurance policy	海运保险单
mk.	mark	码头；西德马克
mkt.	market	市场
MO	money order	汇兑；邮汇
MO	mail order	邮购
mph	miles per hour	每小时航速
M/R	Mate's receipt	大副收货单
M/S	months after sight	见票后几个月付款
M/T	mail transfer	邮汇
MT	metric ton	公吨
MV	marine vessel	轮船
no.	numbers	数量；号码
NOP	not otherwise provide for	不另作规定
N/P	no payment	拒绝付款
NP	Notary Public	公证人
nt. wt.	net weight	净重
OD	overdraft	透支
o. r. d.	owner's risk damage	损毁自负
orig.	original	正本
OT	on track	卡车上交货价格
PA	particular average	单独海损

P/A	power of attorney	委任状
P&L	profit and loss	损益
pat.	patent	专利
p. c.	percent	百分之……
pc.	piece	件；块；台
pcl.	parcel	包裹
pd.	paid	已付
pkg.	package	包装
pkt.	packet	包装；包裹
pm.	premium	保险费
PMO	post money order	邮班汇票
P/O	payment order	付款汇票
p. o. c.	port of call	中途停靠港
POD	pay on delivery	收获付款
POR	payable on receipt	收货时付款
PP	parcel post	包裹邮件
p. p.	postpaid	邮资已付
pr.	pair	双；对
Pr.	price	价格
PS	post scripture	再启者；附述
pt.	payment	付款
Q/D	quick dispatch	快单
R/A	refer to acceptor	请与承兑人接洽
R/D	refer to drawer	请与开票人接洽
rect.	receipt	收据
ref.	reference	参阅
reg.	registered	已注册的
rep.	representative	代表
RI	re-insurance	再保险
RM	remittance	汇款
rpt.	report	报告
R. R.	railroad	铁路

R/T	radio telegraphy	无线电报
s. a.	subject to approval	须经批准
SB	sales book	销货簿
SD	sight draft	即期汇票
S/D	sea damaged	海损
shtg.	shortage	短少
sig.	signature	签名
SN	shipping note	装船通知
SOS	save our soul	求救信号
specs.	specifications	规格
SR	shipping receipt	装船收据
SS	steamship	轮船；汽船
stg.	sterling	英镑
T/A	trade acceptance	贸易承兑
tempt.	temperature	温度
Tg.	telegraph	电报
TL	total loss	全损
TLO	total loss only	仅担保全损
TMO	telegraph money order	电汇
U/A	underwriting account	保险账户
U/W	underwriter	保险商
val.	value	价值
ves.	vessel	船舶
WPA	with particular average	负责单独海损；水渍险
W/B	waybill	运货单
whf.	wharf	码头

附录 9　部门名称及职位的翻译

(1) UN Principal Organizations　联合国主要组织

General Assembly(President)　联合国大会

Security Council(Membership)　安理会

Economic and Social Council　联合国经济及社会理事会

Secretariat　联合国秘书处

Secretary-General　联合国秘书长

Deputy-Secretary General　联合国常务秘书长

Under-Secretary-General　联合国副秘书长

Programmes and Specialized Agencies　联合国组织与专门机构

Food and Agriculture Organization (FAO) 联合国粮食及农业组织(粮农组织)

International Civil Aviation Organization (ICAO) 国际民用航空组织(民航组织)

International Labour Organization (ILO) 国际劳工组织(劳工组织)

International Maritime Organization (IMO) 国际海事组织(海事组织)

International Trade Centre(ITC) 国际贸易委员会

Intergovernmental Panel on Climate Change(IPCC) 国际气候变化委员会

International Atomic Energy Agency (IAEA) 国际原子能组织

United Nations Industrial Development Organization (UNIDO) 联合国工业发展组织

International Telecommunication Union (ITU) 国际电信联盟

Joint United Nations Programme on HIV/AIDS (UNAIDS) 联合国艾滋病规划署

Special Court for Sierra Leone(SCSL) 塞拉利昂特别法庭

United Nations Conference on Trade and Development(UNCTAD) 联合国贸易和发展会议

United Nations Commission on International Trade Law(UNCITRAL) 联合国国际贸易法委员会

United Nations Capital Development Fund(UNCDF) 联合国资本开发基金

United Nations Development Assistance Framework(UNDAF) 联合国发展援助框架

United Nations Development Group(UNDG) 联合国发展集团

United Nations Development Programme(UNDP) 联合国开发计划署
United Nations Department of Public Information (UNDPI) 联合国新闻部
United Nations Environment Programme (UNEP) 联合国环境规划署
United Nations Educational Scientific and Cultural Organization (UNESCO) 联合国教科文组织
United Nations Fund for International Partnerships (UNFIP) 联合国国际伙伴关系基金
United Nations Population Fund (UNFPA) 联合国人口基金
United Nations Human Settlements Programme (UN-Habitat) 联合国人类住区规划署
Office of the United Nations High Commissioner for Human Rights (OHCHR) 联合国人权事务高级专员办事处
United Nations High Commissioner for Refugees (UNHCR) 联合国难民事务高级专员公署
United Nations Human Rights Council (UNHRC) 联合国人权理事会
United Nations International Children's Emergency Fund (UNICEF) 联合国儿童基金会
United Nations Interregional Crime and Justice Research Institute (UNICRI) 联合国区域间犯罪和司法研究所
United Nations Institute for Disarmament Research (UNIDIR) 联合国裁军研究所
United Nations Institute for Training and Research (UNITAR) 联合国训练研究所
United Nations Office on Drugs and Crime (UNODC) 联合国毒品和犯罪问题办公室
United Nations Office for Project Services (UNOPS) 联合国项目事务厅
United Nations Research Institute For Social Development (UNRISD) 联合国社会发展研究所
United Nations University(UNU) 联合国大学
United Nations Volunteers (UNV) 联合国志愿人员组织
UN Women (UN Women) 联合国妇女署
United Nations World Tourism Organization (UNWTO) 联合国旅游组织
Universal Postal Union (UPU) 万国邮政联盟
World Food Programme (WFP) 世界粮食计划署
World Health Organization (WHO) 世界卫生组织
World Intellectual Property Organization (WIPO) 世界知识产权组织
World Meteorological Organization (WMO) 世界气象组织
World Trade Organization (WTO) 世界贸易组织

（2）中国政府各部委、各直属机构名称的翻译

中华人民共和国国务院 State Council of the People's Republic of China

中华人民共和国外交部 Ministry of Foreign Affairs

中华人民共和国国防部 Ministry of National Defense

中华人民共和国国家发展计划委员会 State Development Planning Commission

中华人民共和国国家经济贸易委员会 State Economic and Trade Commission

中华人民共和国教育部 Ministry of Education

中华人民共和国科学技术部 Ministry of Science and Technology

中华人民共和国国防科学技术工业委员会 Commission of Science，Technology and Industry for National Defense

中华人民共和国国家民族事务委员会 State Ethnic Affairs Commission

中华人民共和国公安部 Ministry of Public Security

中华人民共和国国家安全部 Ministry of State Security

中华人民共和国监察部 Ministry of Supervision

中华人民共和国民政部 Ministry of Civil Affairs

中华人民共和国司法部 Ministry of Justice

中华人民共和国财政部 Ministry of Finance

中华人民共和国人事部 Ministry of Personnel

中华人民共和国劳动和社会保障部 Ministry of Labour and Social Security

中华人民共和国国土资源部 Ministry of Land and Resources

中华人民共和国建设部 Ministry of Construction (Infra-structure)

中华人民共和国交通部 Ministry of Communications

中华人民共和国信息产业部 Ministry of Information Industry

中华人民共和国水利部 Ministry of Water Resources

中华人民共和国农业部 Ministry of Agriculture

中华人民共和国对外贸易经济合作部 Ministry of Foreign Trade and Economic Cooperation

中华人民共和国文化部 Ministry of Culture

中华人民共和国卫生部 Ministry of Health

中华人民共和国审计署 National Audit Office

中华人民共和国海关总署 General Administration of Customs

国家税务总局 State Administration of Taxation

中华人民共和国国家工商行政管理总局 State Administration for Industry and Commerce
中华人民共和国国家质量监督检验检疫总局 General Administration of Quality Supervision, Inspection and Quarantine
国家环境保护总局 State Environmental Protection Administration
中国民用航空总局 General Administration of Civil Aviation of China
国家体育总局 General Administration of Sports
中华人民共和国国家统计局 National Bureau of Statistics
国家林业局 State Forestry Administration
国家药品监督管理局 State Drug Administration
中华人民共和国国家知识产权局 State Intellectual Property Office
中华人民共和国国家旅游局 National Tourism Administration
国家宗教事务局 State Administration of Religious Affairs
国务院侨务办公室 Overseas Chinese Affairs Office of the State Council
国务院港澳事务办公室 Hong Kong and Macao Affairs Office of the State Council
国务院法制办公室 Legislative Affairs Office of the State Council
国务院经济体制改革办公室 Economic Restructuring Office of the State Council
国务院研究室 Research Office of the State Council
国务院台湾事务办公室 Taiwan Affairs Office of the State Council
国务院新闻办公室 Information Office of the State Council
新华通讯社 Xinhua News Agency
中国科学院 Chinese Academy of Sciences
中国社会科学院 Chinese Academy of Social Sciences
中国工程院 Chinese Academy of Engineering
国务院发展研究中心 Development Research Center of the State Council
国家行政学院 National School of Administration
中国地震局 China Seismological Bureau
中国气象局 China Meteorological Administration
中国证券监督管理委员会 China Securities Regulatory Commission
中国保险监督管理委员会 China Insurance Regulatory Commission
全国社会保障基金理事会 National Council for Social Security Fund
国家自然科学基金委员会 National Natural Science Foundation
国家粮食局 State Administration of Grain

国家安全生产监督管理总局 State Administration of Work Safety

国家烟草专卖局 State Tobacco Monopoly Administration

国家外国专家局 State Administration of Foreign Experts Affairs

国家海洋局 State Oceanic Administration

国家测绘局 State Bureau of Surveying and Mapping

国家邮政局 State Post Bureau

国家文物局 State Administration of Cultural Heritage

国家中医药管理局 State Administration of Traditional Chinese Medicine

国家外汇管理局 State Administration of Foreign Exchange

国家档案局 State Archives Administration

(3) 美国政府行政部门翻译

Department of State (DOS) 美国国务院

Department of Treasury 美国财政部

Department of Defense (DOD) 美国国防部

Department of Justice (DOJ) 美国司法部

Department of Commerce (DOC) 美国商务部

Department of Agriculture (USDA) 美国农业部

Department of Education (ED) 美国教育部

Department of Transportation (DOT) 美国交通部

Department of Labor (DOL) 美国劳工部

Department of Health and Human services (HHS) 美国卫生部

Department of Veterans Affairs (VA) 退伍军人事务部

Department of Energy (DOE) 能源部

Department of Interior (DOI) 美国内政部

Department of Housing and Urban Development (HUD) 美国住房和城市发展部

Department of Homeland Security (DHS) 美国国土安全部

(4) 不同等级行政单位的翻译

×× Provincial Committee of CPC 某省委

Secretary of a provincial Party Committee 省委书记

Governor of Province 省长

××City Committee of CPC 某市委

××County Committee of CPC 某县委

××Town Committee of CPC 某镇委

Bureau 局长

Counselor 参赞

Attaché 专员

Chief Judge 审判长

Chief Procurator 检察长

Section Chief 科长

Village Head 村长

(5) 学段及学校类型的翻译

Elementary School 小学(美国)

Middle School 初中

High School 高中(美国)

College/University 大学

Institute/College of Science and Technology 理工学院

Normal University 师范大学

Institute of Art and Crafts 工艺美术学院

Correspondence School 函授大学

Radio and TV University 广播电视大学

Adult School 成人学校

Boarding School 寄宿学校

(6) 职称及职位的翻译

Elementary/Middle/High School Principle 小学/初中/高中校长

President 大学校长

Dean 院长

Department Head 系主任

Provost 教务长

Lecture 讲师

Assistant professor 助理教授

Adjunct professor 客座教授

Tenure 终身教授

Associate Professor 副教授

Professor 教授

Graduate assistant(G. A.)助教

Monitor 班长(中国)

Class Teacher 班主任(中国)

(7) 学位及学历的翻译

PhD(Doctor of Philosophy)哲学博士

Doctor 博士

Bachelor 学士

Master 硕士

Doctoral graduate 博士研究生

Graduate/postgraduate(美/英) 研究生

Junior college graduate 大专毕业生

Undergraduate 本科生

Director/President of Hospital(医院)院长

Doctor-in-Charge 主治医师

Senior Doctor 主任医师

Head Nurse 护士长

Nurse 护士

Librarian 图书管理员

Librarian Chief 图书馆馆长

Head Chef 厨师长

Curator 博物馆长

(8) 企业部门及职位的翻译

董事会	Board of Directors	人力资源部	Human Resources Dept.
董事长	Chairman	人事部	Personnel Dept.
名誉董事长	Honorary Chairman	人力资源总监	Director of Human Resources
执行董事	Executive Director	人事专员	HR Specialist
首席执行官	CEO	销售部	Sales Dept.
总裁	President	市场部	Marketing Dept.
副总裁	Vice-President	国际贸易部	International Trade Dept.
执行总裁	Managering Director	促销员	Sales Promoter
总经理	General Manager	客户经理	Customer Manager
厂长	Factory Director	推销员	Salesman
总经理办公室	General Manager Office	生产部	Production Dept.
总监	Chief Officer	首席运行官	COO
副总经理	Vice General Manager	产品研发部	R & D Dept.
秘书长	Secretary General	总设计师	Chief Designer
主任	Director	企划部	Planning Dept.
副主任	Deputy Director	质量控制部	Quality Control Dept.
财务部	Accounting/Financial Dept.	质量控制员	Quality Control
财务总监	CFO	安全控制员	Safety Control
财务经理	Accounting/Financial Manager	项目部	Project Dept.
主管会计	Chief Accountant	工程部	Engineering Dept.
注册会计师	CPA	总工程师	Chief Engineer
审计员	Auditor	发货部	Dispatch Dept.
统计员	Statistician	采购部	Purchasing Dept.
会计	Accountant	采购经理	Merchandising Manager
出纳	Cashier	材料部	Material Dept.
公关部	Public Relations Dept.	物流部	Logistics Dept.
培训部	Training Dept.	售后服务部	After-sales Dept.
培训专员	Training Specialist	技术部	Technology Dept.
广告部	Advertising Dept.	技术工程师	Technical Engineer